Reasoning from the Scriptures

with the

MORMONS

Ron Rhodes
& Marian Bodine

HARVEST HOUSE PUBLISHERS
Eugene, Oregon 97402

The Scripture quotations in this book are taken from the King James
Version of the Bible.

REASONING FROM THE SCRIPTURES WITH THE MORMONS

Copyright ©1995 by Harvest House Publishers
Eugene, Oregon 97402

Library of Congress Cataloging-in-Publication Data

Rhodes, Ron.
    Reasoning from the Scriptures with the Mormons / by Ron Rhodes
and Marian Bodine.
        p.   cm.
    Includes bibliographical references and indexes.
    ISBN 1-56507-328-2
    1. Church of Jesus Christ of Latter-Day Saints—Controversial
literature.   2. Mormon Church—Controversial literature.   3. Witness
bearing (Christianity)   4. Apologetics.   I. Bodine, Marian, 1930–.
II. Title.
BX8645.R48   1995
289.3—dc20   95-11785
                                                                  CIP

Printed in the United States of America.

95 96 97 98 99 00 01 / 10 9 8 7 6 5 4 3 2 1

To Jerry Bodine

Jerry, my friend and colleague, you are truly appreciated! Thanks for your many faithful years of service.

—Ron Rhodes

To my husband, Jerry, for all the years you spent in careful research and verification of documentary evidence in the field of Mormonism. Only eternity will reveal the fruit of your labors.

—Marian Bodine

Acknowledgments

We are truly appreciative for the pioneering work Walter Martin did in the field of Mormonism. Though he is no longer with us, he continues to bear fruit in his writings and tapes. We are also appreciative to the leadership and staff of the institute he founded—the CHRISTIAN RESEARCH INSTITUTE. God has blessed this ministry in a marvelous way.

A special thanks goes to Bob Hawkins, Jr., Eileen Mason, Steve Miller, and the entire staff of Harvest House Publishers for getting behind this project. Their commitment means a lot to us.

Last, but by no means least, we want to sincerely thank our families for their sacrificial support during the significant time it took to write this book.

Contents

Preface

When I wrote *Reasoning from the Scriptures with the Jehovah's Witnesses* in 1993, I did not anticipate the tremendous volume of mail the book would generate. Many of those who wrote asked for a similar book—with the same unique user-friendly format—dealing with the Mormons. That request is now fulfilled with the publication of this book.

I am joined by an able colleague, Marian Bodine, who has many years of experience in witnessing to Mormons. I am thankful for her participation.

It is our collective prayer that God would use this book for His glory and for the extension of His kingdom.

—*Ron Rhodes, Th.D.*

Introduction:
Mormonism Today

It used to be that the Mormon church was a small cult[1] on the fringes of society. Since its founding in 1830, however, the Mormon church (officially known as the Church of Jesus Christ of Latter-day Saints, or LDS church) has steadily moved away from the fringes and into the mainstream of American religion. This is largely due to a conscious effort by the church to present a strong image of respectability to the public.[2]

There are presently over four million Mormons in the United States. This represents impressive growth. Indeed, in 1950 there were only one million Mormons in America.[3] In terms of worldwide growth, it is estimated that the Mormon (LDS) church is growing at a rate of 1,500 new members per day.[4] (That works out to more than one new Mormon per minute, 24 hours each day.) Today there are close to nine million Mormons worldwide. Such growth is not surprising, since the Mormons now boast of over 50,000 full-time missionaries.

The Incredible Wealth of the Mormon Church

Without a doubt, the Mormon church is one of wealthiest religious bodies in the world. It takes in an estimated $4.7 billion per year, controls at least 100 companies or businesses (including a $300 million-a-year media conglomerate), and has an investment portfolio in excess of $1 billion.[5] That's a lot of money for a cult to control.

According to an eight-month investigation by *The Arizona Republic* newspaper, the Mormon church's annual income would place it about 110th on the Fortune 500 list of industrial corporations. It would rank among companies such as Gillette and Chiquita Brands International.[6]

The Arizona Republic also reports that the Mormon church's business subsidiaries "generate an additional $4 billion per year in sales, which, if counted in the total, would make [it] an $8 billion-a-year corporation, comparable with Union Carbide and Borden Products."[7] As well, the Mormon church is "one of the nation's largest private landowners, with holdings in all 50 states."[8]

Such wealth is a key factor in the steady growth of the church and its penetration of mainstream America. The Mormon church spends an estimated $550 million per year on its missionary efforts.[9] This breaks down to over $10 million spent each week on its missionary program. (And this is apart from the money individual Mormon missionaries must raise for their support from family and friends.) A lot of this money goes into media efforts, which reach over 350 million people each year. [10]

The Mormon Media Empire

The Mormon church makes as effective use of media as any religious group in the world. Researchers who have studied the Mormons' use of media say the church "responds to public relations problems as quickly as any image-conscious corporation. It commands a powerful public relations apparatus that smoothly markets Mormonism to the world."[11] Mormon media outlets include television, print ads, radio, and much more.

Television

The *New York Times* reports that the Mormon church "pays for an extensive campaign of television commercials that deal with everyday issues, like the demands of parenting, rather than heavy-handed religious appeals." [12] By focusing on family-related issues in a positive and uplifting way, the church has succeeded in drawing attention away from its cultic doctrine and onto its mainstream image. These commercials have run on such powerful platforms as Ted Turner's WTBS, TNT, CNN, and Headline News. [13]

What are these commercials like? "In one of the new Mormon commercials, an attractive female librarian is pictured saying that of all the great books written by great authors, she prefers to read about the Savior. She then explains that, besides the Bible, there's another testament of Jesus Christ—the Book of Mormon." [14]

Another major Mormon commercial "portrays Christ as a baby and then continues with His life until the crucifixion. It concludes that after Christ's resurrection His ministry continued and it didn't end with the Bible—it ended with the Book of Mormon." [15]

Still another series of Mormon television ads is called "Homefront." These commercials show poignant and humorous vignettes of domestic life. "Encouraging patience and understanding between parents and children, they end with: 'A thought from The Church of Jesus Christ of Latter-day Saints—The Mormons.' " [16]

Many Mormon commercials provide toll-free phone numbers that viewers can call to receive a free copy of the Book of Mormon, which is often hand-delivered by a pair of smiling Mormon missionaries. [17] Of course, people love to call in for free books!

The question is, How effective have these Mormon commercials been? The Mormon *Church News* reports that the results of the commercials are "impressive." [18] Mormon leaders say the commercials make it much easier for church missionaries to accomplish their task in local communities. People seem to be more receptive to the missionaries after having viewed the wholesome, positive commercials.

Ads in Publications

The Mormon church has also purchased advertisements in popular publications such as *Reader's Digest* and *TV Guide*. These ads typically portray the church as a wholesome, all-American institution—focusing on their apparently virtuous lifestyles instead of setting forth their cultic doctrines.

Mormon sources report that these ads are bringing significant increases in missionary work. Like their television commercials, Mormon ads in publications offer a free copy of the Book of Mormon. [19]

Radio

The Mormons also make effective use of radio. At any given moment during the day, virtually millions of adults across America are listening to Mormon-owned radio stations. [20] Major Mormon radio markets currently include New York City, Los Angeles, Dallas, Seattle, Chicago, Kansas City, San Francisco, Salt Lake City, and Phoenix. [21] Mormon leaders say that radio announcements about the Book of Mormon are bringing many responses. [22]

Media Muscle

In keeping with the above, an article in *The Salt Lake Tribune* reports that effective media use and advertising has contributed to a sharp upsurge in Mormon converts and missionary effectiveness. "Media activities have been instrumental in the growth experienced by the church's missionary program," said Elder Russell M. Ballard of the Quorum of the Twelve Apostles. "Each year, the number of people reached by the media increases." [23] Ballard estimated that a total audience of 357.4 million people is reached in a single year through public-service programs.

In short, the Mormons have media muscle, and they're not shy about flexing it. Effective use of the media is one of the primary means the Mormon church is using to penetrate mainstream America.

Mormons and the Interfaith Movement

In years past, the Mormon hierarchy boldly—even condescendingly—positioned their religion in opposition to "Christendom" (*see* chapter 3). Today, however, the Mormons are increasingly involved with the interfaith movement in America. That's because they are attempting to position themselves as being on the same level of legitimacy as Protestants, Catholics, and Jews. [24] In fact, in 1988 the Mormons joined with 22 groups—Protestant, Catholic, and Jewish—in the National Interfaith Cable Coalition, producing religious and values-oriented programs on America's VISN television network. [25]

An Associated Press article entitled "Mormons Forge Links with Other Faiths" demonstrates the Mormons' pursuit of interfaith ties in the past decade:

> In 1986, Mormons became part of the Religious Alliance Against Pornography, a wide ecumenical cross-section. In 1984, they affiliated with Religion in American Life involving most major U.S. denominations in seeking to stimulate weekly worship. Also in the mid-80s, Mormons entered into interreligious relief work, including aid to the homeless. They contributed about $5 million to relief efforts in famine-ravaged central Africa, much of it through Catholic Relief Services and the American Red Cross. [26]

Mormon Apostle Dallin H. Oaks said, "I think the outlook for our being involved with others is good. . . . I think other groups need us, and we need other groups." [27] The trend toward interfaith involvement contributes immeasurably to the Mormon church's goal of being perceived as a mainstream Christian denomination.

Are Mormons Christians?

In 1992 Stephen Robinson—chairman of the Department of Ancient Scripture at the church's Brigham Young University—

wrote a book entitled, *Are Mormons Christians?* Among a host of recent efforts by Mormons to gain respectability and acceptance for their church as Christian, this book is one of the most important and sophisticated. Robinson seeks to prove that "arguments used to exclude Latter-day Saints [Mormons] from the 'Christian' world are flawed."[28] After all, he says, Mormons believe in Christ, use His name in their official church title, and believe in the Bible.

In chapter one of the book, Robinson offers a generic definition of Christianity that is so inclusive that it appears Mormons indeed are Christians. Robinson's primary definition of a Christian is derived from *Webster's Third New International Dictionary:*

> One who believes or professes or is assumed to believe in Jesus Christ and the truth as taught by him; an adherent of Christianity; one who has accepted the Christian religious and moral principles of life; one who has faith in and has pledged allegiance to God thought of as revealed in Christ; one whose life is conformed to the doctrines of Christ.

But are Mormons Christians in the sense that the Bible defines Christians? Theologian Gordon Lewis is right when he says that Robinson's approach to legitimizing Mormonism "can only succeed if a Christian does not need to believe in one personal, transcendent God, one incarnate Christ, the completed atonement, and one gospel of grace through faith alone [Mormons do not believe these things, as we will demonstrate in this book]."[29]

Lewis notes that "historians may classify every group that calls itself Christian as Christian. Jesus Christ, however, did not do this. Jesus taught that 'the way' was narrow and that we should not assume that all who call Jesus 'Lord' are really Christians (Matthew 5:20; 7:13–23)."[30] We have written this book to help you introduce the Mormon to the *true* Lord of Scripture.

How to Use This Book

As you peruse the table of contents, you will notice that each chapter deals with a specific issue. Each chapter begins with a short summary of what the Mormons believe about a particular subject. Following this, you will find discussions of the major passages Mormons cite in supporting their deviant theology. Quotations from Mormon books and magazines are liberally sprinkled throughout.

In almost every chapter you will find suggested "leading questions" you can use in your witnessing encounters. For your convenience, these questions are set apart in the text. This makes it easy for you to quickly find the questions you need to make your point.

Keep in mind that the questions are only *representative* of the kinds of issues you might want to bring up regarding specific Bible passages. Be careful not to assume that just because you ask one or more of these questions, the Mormon will promptly repent of his faulty views and become a Christian. The questions *are not* presented as "scripts" which—if precisely followed—guarantee that the Mormon will see the light. (The Mormon may or may not respond on any given occasion.) These questions are simply examples of apologetic argumentation. If used consistently, they can help you effectively demonstrate to the Mormon that his or her views are unbiblical.

You must also realize that Mormons are well trained by their church in how to propagate their views. Hence, you should be ready for some debate. Don't let this intimidate you. The book you are holding in your hands will help you to "reason from the Scriptures" with the Mormons. But should the Mormon ask you a question that you don't know how to answer, simply follow Dr. Walter Martin's lead and say, "That's a good question. I don't know the answer. But I'm going to look into this matter and we'll talk about it the next time you come by." There is no shame in doing this.

Now, this book may be read straight through, in which case you will have a good grasp of Mormon theology and how to refute it. Or, you may consult individual chapters as needed. Each chapter is essentially self-contained. And since each chapter deals with a distinct area of doctrine with the major passages cited by Mormons, you will find this an easy-to-use reference tool that you can pull off the bookshelf to "bone up" in a matter of minutes on how to refute Mormon doctrine.

1

Where Did Mormonism Come From?

T he Mormon church is unquestionably among the largest and most influential pseudo-Christian cults in the world today. Contrary to biblical Christianity, Mormonism

- denies the scriptural doctrine of the Trinity and the true deity of Christ;
- teaches that there is more than one God (they believe there are *many*);
- teaches that God the Father is literally an exalted man with a physical body of flesh and bones;
- teaches that human beings can become gods themselves ("As man is, God once was; as God is, man may become"[1]);
- teaches that Jesus was born into this world through the physical, sexual union between God the Father and Mary;
- teaches that eternal life is attained by a person's works and not by grace alone.[2]

The Mormon church crosses the line of Christian orthodoxy in many ways, yet it continues to grow in strength and numbers at a fast pace throughout much of the free world. The question is, Where did Mormonism come from?

For the sake of simplicity, we will present highlights from early Mormon history as officially taught by the LDS church today. Corrections and clarifications will be added where needed.

Mormonism's founder, Joseph Smith, Jr., was born in Sharon, Vermont, on December 23, 1805. Eleven years later, Smith, along with his large family, moved to Palmyra, New York.

Beginning around 1819, there were revivals and an unusual amount of excitement on the subject of religion in the area where Smith lived. In 1820, at age 15, he was troubled by the conflict he saw among the people and clergy of the Methodist, Presbyterian, and Baptist churches. His mother, sister, and two brothers joined the Presbyterian church, while Joseph later claimed he felt drawn toward the Methodists.

Because of such "great confusion and strife among the different denominations and because he was so unacquainted with men and things, to come to any conclusion who was right and who was wrong,"[3] he did not know what to do about joining a church. But he was soon to receive divine direction on the issue.

Joseph Smith's First Vision

The Details

One day in the spring of 1820 as Joseph Smith was reading James 1:5—"If any of you lack wisdom, let him ask of God, that giveth to all men liberally, and upbraideth not; and it shall be given him"—that verse suddenly came alive to him. He determined he would ask God which church to join and went into the woods to pray aloud for the first time. After much oppression following his prayer, he was finally answered in a vision.

When the light rested upon me I saw two Personages, whose brightness and glory defy all description, standing above me in the air. One of them spake unto me, calling me by name and said, pointing to the other—*"This is My Beloved Son. Hear Him!"* . . .

I was answered that I must join none of them [churches] for they were all wrong; and the Personage who addressed me said that all their creeds were an abomination in his sight; that those professors were all corrupt; that: "they draw near to me with their lips, but their hearts are far from me, they teach for doctrines the commandments of men, having a form of godliness, but they deny the power thereof."[4]

The official account states that young Smith accordingly did not join any of the denominations. But neither did he attempt to "draw near" to his Lord and live a virtuous life. Instead, Smith later confessed, during the next three years he frequently "fell into many foolish errors, and displayed the weakness of youth, and the foibles of human nature."[5] (Some of Smith's contemporaries listed treasure hunting and other occultic practices as among the noteworthy "errors" of his youth.[6])

The Discrepancies

We must point out that there are significant and irreconcilable discrepancies in the existing accounts of what is known as Joseph Smith's "First Vision" (there are at least six of them). This should be of great concern to Mormons, for, as then-apostle (and later prophet) Ezra Taft Benson said, "This glorious appearing of God the Father and his Son Jesus Christ . . . is the greatest event that has transpired in this world since the resurrection of our Lord."[7] Moreover, in the words of another recent Mormon prophet, "the appearing of the Father and the Son to Joseph Smith is the *foundation* of the church."[8] Indeed, if the First Vision accounts are not true, then the foundation of Mormonism crumbles.

The chart below highlights just a few of the problems in two major First Vision accounts—the 1832 version from

Smith himself, and the church's 1838–39 version, which is the basis for the story as told officially by the church today.

First Vision Accounts

	1832 Version	*1838–39 Version*
Personage(s)	Smith claimed *only* a vision of Christ.	Smith claimed a vision of both the Father *and* the Son.
Seeking God	Bible reading stirred Smith to seek God.	A revival motivated Smith to seek God.
Churches Wrong	Smith already knew all the churches were wrong.	The "two personages" informed Smith the churches were wrong.[9]

These are just a few of the serious discrepancies we could point out.* (For example, Brigham Young and other early Mormon leaders directly contradicted the above accounts.) From the available evidence, it would appear that the First

---

* Possible Mormon comeback: Some Mormons may attempt to argue that the accounts were "rendered through different scribes, at different times, from a different perspective, for different purposes, and to different audiences. It is not surprising, therefore, that each of them emphasizes different aspects of the Prophet's experience" (see *A Sure Foundation: Answers to Difficult Gospel Questions* [Salt Lake City, UT: Deseret, 1988], p. 169). None of the accounts change the basic message of the First Vision, we are told. Besides, the differences in the accounts are not unlike those found in the four Gospels.

In response, you must point out that 1) these accounts do not just present different "aspects," but set forth *flatly contradictory assertions;* 2) the accounts most assuredly *do* change the basic message of the First Vision; and 3) differences in the Gospel accounts (which are easily explainable) do not lend support to the irreconcilable contradictions in the First Vision accounts. (You will want to consult *When Critics Ask,* by Norman Geisler and Thomas Howe [Wheaton, IL: Victor Books, 1992], for good information and argumentation in regard to the differences in the gospel accounts.)

Vision accounts are not grounded in reliable history, but are the invention of a highly imaginative mind. [10]

Moroni Appears to Joseph Smith

Smith claimed that on September 21, 1823, after he had gone to bed, "I betook myself to prayer and supplication to Almighty God for forgiveness of all my sins and follies, and also for a manifestation to me, that I might know of my state and standing before him; for I had full confidence in obtaining a divine manifestation, as I previously had one." [11]

This time, a "messenger sent from the presence of God" named Moroni appeared to Smith and said "there was a book deposited, written on gold plates, giving an account of the former inhabitants of this continent, and the source from whence they sprang. He also said that the fulness of the everlasting Gospel was contained in it, as delivered by the Savior to the ancient inhabitants." [12] Moroni further informed Smith that the "Urim and Thummin"—a translation device described as "two stones in silver bows"—were buried with the plates.

Moroni appeared again to Smith—three times in the same night, once the following day, and annually for the next four years. Smith was told that when permission to retrieve the plates was finally given, he would be forbidden to reveal them to anyone except select individuals, lest he be destroyed. [13]

Nine months after Smith married Emma Hale in 1827, Moroni allowed him to retrieve the plates with the charge to keep them safe until the angel "should call for them." According to the church, Smith translated the sacred records on the plates from "Reformed Egyptian" into English. [14] David Whitmer, one of three main witnesses who allegedly saw the plates, gave the following testimony about the translation process:

> I will now give you a description of the manner in which the Book of Mormon was translated. Joseph Smith would put the seer stone into a hat, and put his face in the hat,

drawing it closely around his face to exclude the light; and in the darkness the spiritual light would shine. A piece of something resembling parchment would appear, and on that appeared the writing. One character at a time would appear, and under it was the interpretation in English. Brother Joseph would read off the English to Oliver Cowdery, who was his principal scribe, and when it was written down and repeated to Brother Joseph to see if it was correct, then it would disappear, and another character with the interpretation would appear. Thus the Book of Mormon was translated by the gift and power of God, and not by any power of man.[15]

According to the church, sometime after the translation was complete, the golden plates were removed by Moroni and are hence unavailable for inspection. This means that there is no concrete evidence that the plates ever, in fact, existed. In any event, the original Book of Mormon was published in 1830.

Before the plates were taken from the earth, three witnesses— David Whitmer, Martin Harris, and Oliver Cowdery—prayed with Joseph Smith that they might see them. According to Mormon accounts, an unnamed angel appeared in June of 1829 and displayed the plates to them so that each could see the engravings himself.* (It is interesting to note that all three individuals eventually left the church. Martin Harris, however, returned to the Mormon church late in his life, even though in the interim he had said that several other churches were true.)**

---

*Later, eight more witnesses claimed to have seen and felt the gold plates with the engravings that had "the appearance of ancient work."

**Possible Mormon comeback: Some Mormons may attempt to argue that Oliver Cowdery never wavered in his belief in the Book of Mormon (see *A Sure Foundation: Answers to Difficult Gospel Questions* [Salt Lake City, UT: Deseret, 1988], p. 41). They believe that historical documents that seem to indicate otherwise are forged documents that are not true. You will want to consult *The Case Against Mormonism,* by Jerald and Sandra Tanner [Salt Lake City, UT: Utah Lighthouse Ministry, 1967], for a full treatment of this issue.

In May of that year, Smith and Cowdery journeyed into the woods to pray about baptism for the remission of sins. While they were praying, John the Baptist appeared and conferred the Aaronic Priesthood upon them and gave them instructions about how to baptize each other. Later, Peter, James, and John conferred the Melchizedek Priesthood upon them. [16]

The Birth of the "One True Church"

Since Joseph Smith had been told by Jesus that all other churches, creeds, and those who professed them were false and abominable, the "one true church" was organized on April 6, 1830, by Smith and five others in Fayette, New York. [17] At the founding meeting, Smith received a revelation from God that he was to be "a seer, a translator, a prophet, and an apostle." [18]

As the church grew, so did public opposition, forcing the Mormons to move on to other areas. Joseph Smith was instructed by the Lord to move the church to Ohio, "and this because of the enemy and for your sakes." [19] In February 1831, Smith arrived in Kirtland, Ohio, and established the church there.

Trouble Escalates

Within months of arriving in Kirtland, it became evident that the church would soon need to move on yet again. Wherever Smith and the "saints" were, trouble seemed to follow.

In the middle of July 1831, Smith and a few of his followers arrived in Independence, Missouri. At once he received a revelation indicating that "Zion" would be established at this place, [20] a temple would be built, and the "saints" should purchase much land in that vicinity and "in the regions round about." [21] Smith and some other individuals returned to Kirtland while leaving some of the followers in Missouri to buy land and establish the church there.

Smith continued to live in Kirtland, but the church printed many of his early revelations under the title "Book of Commandments" in Missouri in mid-1833. Public opposition to the teachings of Mormonism grew swiftly. The Mormons' rapid growth and unconventional beliefs caused great alarm among non-Mormons in Jackson County, who issued a manifesto in July of that year stating their charges against the Mormons and their intent to remove them.

When the Mormons refused, Missourians began a violent campaign against the church, its members, and property, destroying the church's printing office in the process. Smith, still in Kirtland, learned of the trouble and raised a large group of men to ride to Missouri to defend his followers. During this time he also received revelations from the Lord (who, ironically, did not seem to know what was going on[22]).

In the fall of 1835 Smith published the Doctrine and Covenants, a dramatic reworking of the now-suppressed Book of Commandments. Many changes were made—both deletions and additions—to those original "revelations." Earlier that same year Smith also acquired assorted Egyptian artifacts, including papyrus fragments taken from the cavities of some mummies. He attempted to translate portions of them and thus produced the Book of Abraham.[23] This book, along with "Joseph Smith—History," an extract of his own "translations" of Matthew and the Book of Moses (allegedly lost from the Old Testament and restored to Smith through revelation), and the Articles of Faith were combined to create a single volume entitled The Pearl of Great Price—the third book of Mormon scriptures.

Although the Mormons continued to move from one Missouri county to another in the attempt to find a place to live, Smith continued to give revelations that caused his church even more trouble. The Mormons and non-Mormons were virtually at war, with atrocities being committed by both sides.

Governor Boggs of the state of Missouri tried in many ways to quiet the problems connected with the Mormons, but the trouble continued to escalate. Finally, in October of 1838 he issued an order to the militia stating that because of "the attitude of open and avowed defiance of the laws, and of having made open war upon the people of this state . . . the Mormons must be treated as enemies and exterminated or driven from this state."[24]

The Mormons scattered. Some were killed and others were jailed, but many made it out of Missouri to Illinois, where they built an attractive city called Nauvoo (which, Joseph Smith asserted, was Hebrew for "beautiful place," and was briefly the second-largest city in Illinois). While there, Smith was the mayor of the city, the general of his own army, a candidate for president of the United States, and the Prophet, Seer, and Revelator of the Mormon church.

The Downfall of Joseph Smith

On June 7, 1844, a group of dissident Mormons published a newspaper detailing the grievances they had against Smith. It was the first and last issue of the *Nauvoo Expositor*. Smith knew that the charges of polygamy and of his mishandling of church funds (among others) would cause much trouble for him. Days later, his city council decided to destroy the printing office and the presses. This act resulted in Smith's arrest for treason, and he, his brother Hyrum, and two other Mormon leaders were jailed in Carthage, Illinois.

On June 27, a mob stormed the jail, killing Joseph and Hyrum Smith and wounding the other men. Before Smith died, however, he used a six-shooter to wound a few of the men in the mob during the blazing gun battle. Smith's role as God's "Prophet, Seer, and Revelator" came to an abrupt end in bloody violence.

Brigham Young Takes Over

Brigham Young, the senior Mormon apostle at the time of Smith's death, soon assumed leadership of the church. He led a company of the Latter-day Saints across the treacherous Great Plains, reaching the valley of the Great Salt Lake in Utah in July of 1847, and built their new Zion, Salt Lake City. He ruled the people with an iron hand and both practiced and encouraged polygamy throughout the remainder of his life.

The earthly practice of polygamy (now confined to the celestial realms) would "officially" end, however. On September 24, 1890, a "manifesto" was issued by Wilford Woodruff, fourth president of the Mormon church, declaring his advice that all Mormons give up the practice. Among the obvious reasons for this were that the church's top leaders were in jail or in hiding, the United States government threatened to confiscate its temple and other property, and Utah had no chance of gaining statehood otherwise.

The Mormon Church Today

When Joseph Smith and five friends formed the Mormon church in 1830, no one could have guessed it would reach the magnitude it has today. Indeed, today the Church of Jesus Christ of Latter-day Saints (the Mormon church) is a thriving religious body. It has a membership of nearly nine million, and a missionary force of about 50,000 that spreads its "gospel" throughout the world. Brigham Young University projects that by the year 2080 there will be more than 256 million Mormons worldwide, assuming that the present rate of the church's growth continues. [25]

2

Witnessing to Mormons

Witnessing to Mormons can be a trying experience. But you can greatly enhance your chances of success in reaching a Mormon for Christ by *deciding in advance* to handle your witnessing encounters in a certain way. This chapter is comprised of some helpful suggestions we've picked up over the years.

Understand the Mormon's Dilemma

For a Mormon to become a Christian entails a potentiaᴵ sacrifice of great magnitude. Indeed,

> Mormons who contemplate leaving the organization know that they risk losing their LDS spouse, their children, their parents, and any other relatives or close friends in the faith. A man who leaves the church faces the possibility that his Mormon wife will listen to encouragement from others in the sect to divorce him, since women are taught that achieving their heavenly goal in the afterlife depends on their being married in the temple to a Mormon man. From the point of view of these individuals, a religious organization is, in effect, holding their relatives hostage. [1]

In view of this, the Christian must be sensitive and understanding of the dilemma the Mormon is in. The Mormon is motivated to remain a Mormon because he or she might endanger a relationship with a loved one. This points to the need for you to . . .

Prepare by Prayer

Be sure to pray regularly about your witnessing opportunities. Remember, only God in His mighty power can lift the veil of cultic darkness from the human heart (2 Corinthians 4:4; cf. 3:17; John 8:32). Pray fervently for those you witness to and *pray often* (Matthew 7:7–12; Luke 18:1–8; James 5:16).

Prayer is especially important if you have a prearranged appointment with a Mormon. In such cases you can pray for the Mormon by name and ask for God's intervention in his or her life.

Also, once the Mormon arrives at your home, be sure to open your time together with a brief prayer—but make sure *you* do the praying. "Mormons will want to lead in prayer, but it is not proper for a Christian to bow his head while the Mormons pray since they are praying to a 'heavenly Father' who is an exalted man of flesh and bones with numerous wives. This is not the heavenly Father of the Bible or Christianity. The Mormons are usually agreeable to you praying, so do so in addition to your earlier praying."[2]

Get to Know Mormons on a Personal Level

It is important that you try to develop a personal relationship with the Mormon to whom you want to witness. Make every effort to be hospitable, inviting him (or her) to dinner or refreshments.

Remember, people like to know that you genuinely care for them—so show that you are interested and be a good listener.

(As the saying goes, "People don't care how much you know until they know how much you care.") Above all, do not be phony about your concern; sooner or later, the Mormon will perceive your true motivation and become disillusioned. Encourage the Mormon to tell you about him- or herself. If he or she has a need and you can reach out in a helpful way, by all means make that a priority. Many Mormons have been taught to believe that only other members of the "one true church" help those in need.

Don't move forward in a mad rush to discuss spiritual things, especially if you have the opportunity to work toward developing a personal relationship. When the Lord opens the door for witnessing, however, *be ready to walk through it.*

The exception to this rule, of course, is if you know for certain that you will never see that particular Mormon again. Then you will want to cover as much doctrinal ground as possible, biblically refuting the most blatant heresies in Mormon theology and giving a strong personal testimony of what Jesus has done in your life.

For Prearranged Meetings, Invite Another Christian

Mormon missionaries, whether full-time or local part-timers, often show up on your doorstep in twos. If you have a prearranged meeting set up with some Mormons, we think it's a good idea to have another Christian friend with you for the meeting. There is strength in numbers! (Remember, a rope of many strands is not easily broken.) Jesus Himself sent out His disciples "by two and two" (Mark 6:7).

By having another Christian present, you will not only feel more comfortable and bold in confronting the Mormons about their deviant doctrines, you'll also give your friend an opportunity to learn from you about witnessing techniques. As well, your friend can pray silently as you are witnessing—and perhaps may even share a doctrinal insight that you hadn't thought of.

Encourage an Examination of Beliefs

When a Mormon shows up on your doorstep, one of the first remarks you should make is to encourage him or her to thoroughly examine his or her beliefs. After all, the Bible encourages us to do this.

Second Corinthians 13:5, for example, tells us, "Examine yourselves, whether ye be in the faith." Tell the Mormon that you would like to examine the Scriptures and test both of your religious beliefs by those Scriptures. This will lay a foundation for all that follows.

You might mention that even Mormon leaders encourage such a scriptural examination. Mormon apostle Orson Pratt, for example, said:

> Convince us of our error of doctrine if we have any, by rea-
> son, by logical arguments, or by the word of God, and we
> will be ever grateful for the information, and you will ever
> have a pleasing reflection that you have been instruments
> in the hands of God of redeeming your fellow beings from
> the darkness which you may see enveloping their minds.[3]

Mormon prophet Joseph Fielding Smith (who later became the tenth president of the LDS church) said, "If Joseph Smith was a deceiver, who willfully attempted to mislead the people, then he should be exposed; his claims should be refuted, and his doctrines shown to be false, for the doctrines of an impostor cannot be made to harmonize in all particulars with divine truth."[4]

No less an authority than Brigham Young also made this powerful and valid challenge: "Take up the Bible, compare the religion of the Latter-day Saints with it, and see if it will stand the test."[5] Take the Mormon up on this offer, and test Mormonism by the Scriptures.

Be Kind and Gentle, Yet Firm

It is imperative that Christians not have a hostile attitude when Mormons show up on the doorstep. After all, we are called to share the good news of the gospel with them so that they might be saved from sure destruction (Matthew 28:19–20).

Look at it this way: If you came to find out that some pills in a local store had been laced with cyanide, you'd do everything you could to warn individuals about the danger so they wouldn't be poisoned and killed. What we must realize is that there is also *spiritual* cyanide being disseminated on a massive level by the Mormon church. Hence, the most loving action we can take when Mormons show up on our doorstep is to warn them of this poison and share the truth with them. To show hostility and turn them away is to short-circuit an opportunity for them to come to the truth and be saved.

While being kind and gentle, however, you must also take a firm stand in setting forth and defending the truth of the gospel. Remember, eternal souls are at stake. Just as the first-century Christians were bold in their witness for Christ, so also must we be bold witnesses (Acts 2:32; 3:15; 4:33; 13:30–31).

Don't Assume All Mormons Have the Same Beliefs

Do not assume all Mormons hold to the same beliefs, nor that all Mormons know exactly what their church teaches about various doctrinal issues. If you witness to Mormons long enough, you will soon discover the wisdom of this policy.

Why are many rank-and-file Mormons unaware of certain teachings officially espoused by their church?

In part this is due to the complex historical development of Mormon doctrine, with new publications and speeches by living prophets redefining and reinterpreting earlier thought. Also, the organization's hierarchical structure allows for beliefs to be embraced by the leadership without being communicated to the general membership or to the public. A prime example of this was the indulgence in plural marriage by Joseph Smith and his inner circle of associates while official church publications and public announcements condemned the practice. Still another reason for doctrinal ignorance on the part of many Mormons is the secretive (they call it sacred) nature of temple ceremonies. Church members who have not earned a "temple recommend" from their local leaders never get to learn the oaths, the key words, the covenants, and the secrets of the priesthood available only to temple Mormons.[6]

Don't Tell a Mormon What He or She Believes

In keeping with the above, do not *tell* Mormons what they believe. Instead, *ask* them about their beliefs. Say, "Do you believe . . . ?"

If they say no to a particular question about their doctrine, you might say, "I am glad *you* don't believe that, but do you know whether your *church* teaches it?" If they answer that their church does not teach such a thing, ask, "What would you do if you found out your church *does* teach that?" Of course, you should be prepared to back up your claims with documented evidence or photocopies from Mormon sources.[7]

Define Your Terms Clearly

Mormons use many Christian words—such as *God, Jesus Christ, atonement,* and *salvation*—but they pour their own cultic meanings into those words. The Christian must ever stand on guard regarding this semantic subterfuge. As Walter Martin said,

What the Mormons mean by theological terms and what the Bible and the true church mean by them are entirely different. The importance of destroying the "terminology block" cannot be overemphasized. No matter how good your presentation is, and no matter how much you have researched and studied, so that you can present the gospel in an orthodox manner, if you cannot communicate, you are wasting your time. Always define your terms when witnessing to a Mormon.[8]

It is especially important that you do not push for a decision for Christ until you have shown the Mormon the differences between the Mormon Jesus and the Jesus of the Bible. Some Christians have asked a Mormon to pray to receive Jesus, and the Mormon receives the Jesus of Mormonism, not the true Jesus who *alone* can save.

Take Your Time

When Mormons show up on the doorstep, the tendency of many Christians is to lambaste them with all the heresies in the Mormon belief system. This is what I call "the flame-thrower approach" to cult evangelism. The problem is, this approach rarely yields positive results in terms of leading a cultist to Christ.

A much better approach is to take your time and not force the Mormon to digest more than he or she can take during one sitting. Many cult experts have noted that it is better to focus on one or two issues during each meeting and deal with them thoroughly rather than "get it all out on the table" in a single sitting. (Remember, even Jesus told the disciples, "I have yet many things to say unto you, but ye cannot bear them now" [John 16:12]. Jesus was sensitive to how much His listeners could handle in a single sitting.[9])

If the Mormon is moving too fast, jumping around from doctrine to doctrine or verse to verse, slow him down. Suggest to him, "Instead of jumping around, let's make sure that we thoroughly discuss each doctrine (or Bible verse) before we go on to another one."

If you don't follow that policy, you will likely find yourself being taken down "rabbit trails" that rarely lead to anything productive. You will find that you cannot satisfactorily respond to one issue before another is brought up. Make every effort to avoid this pitfall, as the discussion can become meaningless if you don't stay on track long enough to make your point.

Not infrequently the Mormon may interrupt your presentation with a question prefaced with, "Well, what about . . . ?" Usually this leads to a change of subject. Kindly remind the Mormon that for clarity's sake it is important that he or she allow you to finish your point. Likewise, be courteous and allow him or her to respond without interruption.

If you engage in a thoughtful discussion during your initial encounter with a Mormon—and you remain kind and respectful in the process—he or she will not only be impressed with your manner but will likely make another appointment to come back to discuss other issues. *This is what you want to happen!*

The late Wesley Walters, an expert in Mormonism, was right when he said, "Seldom does one lead a Mormon, a member of the Church of Jesus Christ of Latter-day Saints, to Christ at the first encounter. One should be ready for some lengthy conversations over a considerable period of time before the Mormon will be ready to abandon his beliefs for a personal relationship with Christ."[10]

Disarm the Mormon's "Testimony"

Sometimes the Mormon will defensively interrupt you with his or her testimony, which is essentially, "I testify to you that Joseph Smith is a prophet of God, the Mormon church is true, Jesus is the Christ, the president of the Mormon church is a prophet on the earth today, and I say this in the name of Jesus Christ. Amen."

You might reply, "Your personal testimony is actually invalid because *I* testify to you that Joseph Smith was a false prophet, the Mormon church is not true, Jesus Christ is my Lord and Savior, the president of the Mormon church is not a prophet on the earth today, and I say this in the name of Jesus Christ. Amen." Your testimony is just as valid as the Mormon's. With the force of his or her testimony effectively neutralized, chances are that he or she will not interrupt you with that subjective tactic again. [11]

Stress the importance of basing religious truth not on someone's testimony but on the objective Word of God. Remind the Mormon of what Proverbs 14:12 says: "There is a way which *seemeth* right unto a man; but the end thereof are the ways of death" (emphasis added). On the other hand, Jesus has assured us that His Word will remain forever (Mark 13:31).

Use Only the King James Version of the Bible

Don't try using your New American Standard Bible or New International Version with a Mormon. You will need to use the King James Version because this is the version officially accepted and used by the Mormon church. (Throughout this book, all Scripture quotations are from the King James Version.)

Also, do not allow a Mormon to cite a Scripture verse off the top of his head. Mormons often misquote Bible verses. Say something like, "Let's turn to that passage and read it in context."

Read Bible Verses Aloud

One helpful technique for dealing with the "triggered responses" of the Mormons is to request that they read a particular verse aloud, and then ask, "What is being said here?"

If they spout off the typical Mormon interpretation, ask them to read it aloud again, *slowly and carefully*—and ask again what is being said. If you are persistent, you'll help the Mormons see for themselves that there are contradictions and problems with the Mormon view.

Ask Leading Questions

You will not be able to force your opinion of what a verse means on a Mormon. But if you can help the Mormon discover problems in Mormon theology *for himself,* then you've accomplished an important goal in your witnessing. Harry L. Ropp, a Christian author who served as a missionary to Mormons, said that creating doubt in a Mormon's mind is an effective way to overcome ingrained teachings that inhibit Mormons from accepting the true gospel. [12]

One great way to help a Mormon discover problems in Mormon theology is by asking strategic questions based on key verses, all the while remaining tactful and kind. Remember, Jesus often asked questions to make a point. David Reed rightly notes that "rather than shower his listeners with information, [Jesus] used questions to draw answers out of them. A person can close his ears to facts he doesn't want to hear, but if a pointed question causes him to form the answer in his own mind, he cannot escape the conclusion—because it's a conclusion that he reached himself." [13] We must use this same type of methodology with Mormons.

The right question, asked in a nondefensive, nonchallenging, unemotional way, may cause the Mormon to find him- or herself face to face with a doctrine (such as the absolute deity of Christ) that is completely contrary to what the Mormon church teaches. By considering such a question, the Mormon is forced to come to a conclusion in his or her own mind. In fact, if you and the Mormon mutually agree to meet every week or two to discuss different issues, you can be confident that the cumulative effect of such questions will slowly but surely erode his belief system so that he is more open to the true gospel.

In each chapter of this book, we will suggest sample questions you might ask the Mormon. But remember what we said in the introduction: Don't assume that just because you ask one or more of these questions the Mormon will promptly repent of his faulty views and become a Christian. The questions *are not* presented as "scripts" which—if precisely followed—guarantee that the Mormon will see the light. (The Mormon may or may not respond on any given occasion.) These questions are simply examples of apologetic argumentation. If used consistently, questions like these can help you effectively demonstrate to the Mormon that his or her views are unbiblical.

Also keep in mind that Mormons don't always use the exact same approach when dealing with a particular passage of Scripture. Sometimes they may present a sophisticated line of argumentation that you haven't heard before. If that happens, don't panic. Take one verse at a time. Examine the context. Compare Scripture with Scripture. And if they ask you a question that you don't know how to answer, simply say, "That's a good question. I don't know the answer. But I'm going to look into this matter and we'll talk about it the next time you come by."

Undermine the Mormon Church's Authority

Mormons read the Scriptures and interpret various doctrines through the lens of the LDS church. Therefore, in every doctrinally focused encounter you have with a Mormon, you will want to watch for opportunities to undermine the authority of the LDS church by demonstrating that its leaders—including founder Joseph Smith—were (and are) false prophets. By so doing, you help to remove this distorted "pair of glasses" so the Mormon can see more clearly.

If you can lovingly demonstrate that Mormon prophets have contradicted one another and have been wrong time and time again in their predictions, this will serve to call into question everything else the LDS church teaches. As you continue to chip away at the Mormon's confidence in the LDS church, you will find it easier to make doctrinal points with him or her (via leading questions like those in this book).

In the chapters to come we will expose some of the more important false prophecies. You will want to thoroughly familiarize yourself with them so they will be at your fingertips during the witnessing encounter.

Disarm the "Attack" Accusation

Mormons often object to Christian efforts to criticize Mormonism by saying something like, "Mormons don't attack you; why are you attacking us?"

If a Mormon says this to you, you should respond by pointing out that Joseph Smith, based on his alleged First Vision, said that all the existing churches were "all wrong" and "corrupt." It is therefore the Mormons who "attacked" first. Christians are simply defending the Christian faith against the attack of Mormonism.

Read Other Good Literature About the Mormons

The book you are holding in your hands will help you "reason from the Scriptures" with Mormons. But there are other good books that will help equip you for other important aspects of witnessing to Mormons. For example:

- A book that will help you understand why people leave the Mormon church is *Ex-Mormons: Why We Left,* edited by Latayne C. Scott (Grand Rapids, MI: Baker Book House, 1993).
- A book that will help you understand Mormon culture and the Mormon's relentless pursuit of "perfection" is *Speaking the Truth in Love to Mormons,* by Mark J. Cares (Milwaukee, WI: Northwestern Publishing House, 1993).
- A book that will help you understand the occultic elements in Mormonism is *Mormonism, Magic and*

Masonry, by Jerald and Sandra Tanner (Salt Lake City, UT: Utah Lighthouse Ministry, 1988).
* A general book that will help you see how Mormons and other cultists twist Scripture toward their own ends is *Scripture Twisting: 20 Ways the Cults Misread the Bible,* by James W. Sire (Downers Grove, IL: InterVarsity Press, 1980).

By exposing yourself to books that deal with different aspects of Mormonism, you will become an effective tool in the hands of God for bringing these lost souls into the kingdom of light.

3

The Mormon Church:
The Restored Church?

According to the official version of Joseph Smith's First Vision account, Joseph went out in the woods to pray and ask God which church he should join. He claimed that two personages appeared to him in dazzling light. One of the personages, the "Beloved Son," told him he shouldn't join any of the churches because they were all wrong, the Christian creeds were abominable, and all those who professed them were corrupt.[1]

Since all the churches were wrong, this meant that the "one true church"—with its priesthood authority (*see* chapter 12)—needed to be restored. Joseph Smith, Mormons say, was the one the Lord chose for this monumental restoration.

From Joseph Smith to the present, Mormons leaders have spoken of the total apostasy they say occurred sometime after the death of the apostles. And they believe there is a great deal of biblical evidence that foretells this apostasy.

Actually, according to Mormons, there have been seven apostasies. They believe the "gospel" and its "doctrines, ordinances, and priesthood"—called "dispensations"—were given to Adam, Enoch, Noah, Abraham, Moses, and the Nephites (a Book of Mormon people), only to completely fail repeatedly.[2] There were allegedly restorations after each period of apostasy. But Mormons view the Church of Jesus Christ of Latter-day Saints as "the last in the series of restorations that have occurred through the ages."[3]

The final apostasy occurred because "as the Apostles were killed, revelation to guide the Lord's church ceased, along with authority to operate it."[4] Not only did the church suffer a complete apostasy in biblical lands, but also on the American continent.

According to the Book of Mormon, Jesus visited the American continent after his resurrection and chose 12 more disciples (three of whom allegedly never died—*see* 3 Nephi 28:7). Even so, another great apostasy occurred. And within a few hundred years, there was not even a shred of Christianity left among the original inhabitants.

Thus, in the minds of Mormons, the final restoration of the one true church was established through Joseph Smith on April 6, 1830.[5] "The need of a restoration implies that something important was lost after the departure of the primitive Christian church."[6] That which was lost was restored through Joseph Smith.

What exactly was lost? It is claimed by Mormons that proper church organization with its respective offices (and the authority to perform ordinances) was lost, along with continual revelation through God's appointed representatives. The true gospel had also been lost in its completeness from the Bible due to "designing priests" removing its "plain and precious" truths, primarily before the end of the first century.

Throughout the history of the Mormon church, Mormon leaders have consistently argued that theirs is the only true church—the "restored" church—and that all other churches of Christendom are apostate. Consider this sampling:

- Brigham Young, the second president of the Church of Jesus Christ of Latter-day Saints, said, "The Christian world, so called, are heathens as to their knowledge of the salvation of God."[7]

- Orson Pratt, a leading Mormon apostle, said, "All other churches are entirely destitute of all authority from God: and any person who receives Baptism, or the Lord's Supper from their hands will highly offend God, for he looks upon them as the most corrupt of all people."[8]

- The late apostle Bruce McConkie, one of the church's foremost doctrinal authorities, said, "Mormons . . . have the only pure and perfect Christianity now on earth."[9] He also declared, "All other systems of religion are false,"[10] and that "if it had not been for Joseph Smith and the restoration, there would be no salvation. There is no salvation outside the Church of Jesus Christ of Latter-day Saints."[11]

- George Q. Cannon, a member of the LDS First Presidency, wrote, "The various organizations which are called churches throughout Christendom, though differing in their creeds and organizations, have one common origin. They all belong to Babylon. God is not the founder of them."[12]

As the official *History of the Church* puts it, "Nothing less than a complete apostasy from the Christian religion would warrant the establishment of the Church of Jesus Christ of Latter-day Saints. . . . There was no possible excuse for the introduction of a new Christian sect."[13] In an attempt to defend their position on a total apostasy, Mormons cite a number of scriptures from the New Testament. It is to these scriptures that we now turn our attention.

REASONING FROM THE SCRIPTURES

Acts 3:20–21—*A Promise of Restoration?*

The Mormon Teaching. In Acts 3:20–21 we read, "He shall send Jesus Christ, which before was preached unto you:

Whom the heaven must receive until the times of restitution of all things, which God hath spoken by the mouth of all his holy prophets since the world began." Mormons say this passage points to an apostasy and a subsequent time of "restoration." In his book *A Marvelous Work and a Wonder,* apostle LeGrand Richards tells us:

> When looking for the second coming of the Christ as herein promised, we must realize that he will not come before there is a "restitution of all things." It is obvious that there cannot be a restitution of that which has not been taken away. Therefore, this scripture is another very plain prediction of apostasy—the taking of the gospel from the earth—with a promise of a complete restoration of all things spoken by all the holy prophets since the world began. [14]

The "restitution of all things," Mormons say, is actually the restoration of the gospel, and it is that to which all the holy prophets looked forward. This restored gospel comes to us via the restoration of the one true church through Joseph Smith. [15]

The Biblical Teaching. Evangelical Christians have several interpretations for Acts 3:20–21. Many Bible expositors believe the reference deals with a restoration of Israel. After all, Peter *is* speaking specifically to the "men of Israel" in this sermon (*see* Acts 3:12), and he speaks of the fulfillment of all that the prophets had foretold (verse 18).

Craig S. Keener, in his helpful *Bible Background Commentary,* points out that "Jewish people expected Israel's restoration; this was a central message of the Old Testament prophets (e.g., Is. 40:9–11; Jer. 32:42–44; Ezek. 37:21–28; Hos. 11:9–11; 14:4–7; Amos 9:11–15), and Peter seems to have it in view here." [16]

Other scholars take the reference to "restoration" or "restitution" more generally. These individuals believe that "the restitution of all things is to be understood as the day of judgment and of the consummation of the age when the Lord will return." [17]

Regardless of which interpretation is correct, we can know with certainty what Acts 3:20-21 *does not say.* The text and surrounding context do not even remotely hint that there would be a total apostasy of the entire church. Mormons are simply reading something into the text that is not there. This is called *eisogesis* (reading a meaning *into* the text), as opposed to *exegesis* (drawing the meaning *out of* the text). By allowing the text to speak for itself, a person would never come to the conclusion that Acts 3:20-21 is referring to a complete apostasy of the church.

You will want to emphasize to the Mormon that a good interpretative principle to use in interpreting difficult passages is this: "Scripture interprets Scripture." (*See* chapter 10 for details on how to interpret the Bible.) By consulting other scriptures in the Bible and comparing them with one another, it becomes clear that there *never* would be a total apostasy of the entire church. For example:

Jesus said to Peter, "Thou art Peter, and upon this rock I will build my church; and *the gates of hell shall not prevail against it"* (Matthew 16:18, emphasis added). To say that the entire church went into apostasy is in direct conflict with this verse.

_____ *Ask* . . . _____

- Would you please read aloud from Matthew 16:18?

- How could Jesus' words be correct if the church would soon go into complete apostasy?

- Do you think Jesus was wrong in what He said? Or is, perhaps, the Mormon church wrong?

Jesus promised His followers, "Lo, I am with you alway, even unto the end of the world" (Matthew 28:20). Jesus could not possibly be with His followers "unto the end of the world" if the entire church went into apostasy. Jesus' words do not give even the slightest hint that there would come a complete apostasy. Rather, His words indicate that His sustaining power would endure with His followers until the end!

____ *Ask* . . . _____

- Would you please read aloud from Matthew 28:18–20?

- Does it sound like Jesus knew there would come a total apostasy?

- How long would Jesus remain with His followers after His ascension into heaven?

- How could Jesus' words be true if a complete apostasy of the entire church was to come soon?

- Was Jesus wrong in making this statement to His followers? Or is the Mormon church wrong?

In Ephesians 3:21 the apostle Paul says, "Unto him be glory *in the church by Christ Jesus throughout all ages, world without end*" (emphasis added). How could God be glorified in the church "throughout all ages" if the entire church fell into apostasy? Nothing would be more unglorifying to God than a totally apostate church!

____ *Ask* . . . _____

- Would you please read aloud from Ephesians 3:21?

- How could God be glorified in the church "throughout *all* ages" if the entire church fell into apostasy?

You will also want to emphasize that Ephesians 4:11–16 speaks of the Christian church growing to spiritual maturity, not spiritual degeneracy. The picture portrayed in Ephesians 4 is that of a church steadily growing toward spiritual maturity, not of a church becoming totally apostate.

_____ *Ask* . . . _____

- Would you please read aloud from Ephesians 4:11–16?

- Is it not clear that this passage speaks of the Christian church growing to spiritual maturity, not spiritual degeneracy?

You can further strengthen your argument by pointing out that the apostle Peter affirmed that "the word of the Lord *endureth for ever.* And this is the word which by the gospel is preached unto you" (1 Peter 1:25, emphasis added; cf. Matthew 24:35). Because the word of the Lord endures forever, it bears its fruit *in every age* among those who remain faithful to it. There is no indication in Scripture that there would be a time when the entire church would fall away from the word of the Lord that "endures forever."

Moreover, Jesus affirmed to His followers, "Where two or three are gathered together in my name, there am I in the midst of them" (Matthew 18:20). Even though there were many people throughout church history who became apostate, there were always *some* faithful believers who remained committed to God's Word, and these individuals knew of the reality of Jesus Christ in their midst.

Acts 20:29–31—*The Distortion of Truth*

The Mormon Teaching. In Acts 20:29–31 we read, "I know this, that after my departing shall grievous wolves enter in among you, not sparing the flock. Also of your own selves shall men arise, speaking perverse things, to draw away disciples after them. Therefore watch, and remember, that by the space of three years I ceased not to warn every one night and day with tears."

According to Mormon leaders, the apostle Paul prophesied that an apostasy would occur and had already begun. Paul allegedly foresaw that false teachers—"wolves"—would come in and there would not be a single sheep spared. In addition, supposedly trustworthy church members would arise and speak false and pernicious doctrines, and these doctrines would be followed. Therefore, in the above scripture, it is clear that Christ's church was to be totally abandoned to apostasy.

Commenting on this verse, apostle James E. Talmage writes in *The Articles of Faith:* "It is evident that the Church was literally driven from the earth. . . . But the Lord in His mercy provided for the re-establishment of His Church in the last days, and for the last time. . . . This restoration was effected by the Lord through the Prophet Joseph Smith."[18]

The Biblical Teaching. Mormons completely ignore the setting of this passage. If you consult the broader context of the book of Acts, it is clear that Paul is addressing a specific group of people in Acts 20:29–31. Going back to verse 17, we note that Paul is speaking to the elders of the church in Ephesus. He was warning the *Ephesian* elders of something that would soon be happening in *their own* church. Paul was not talking about the church in general (all over the world), but a *specific* local church in Asia Minor—that of the Ephesians.[19]

The renowned scholar F.F. Bruce explains the fulfillment of Paul's prophetic warning in early church history: "That this development did in fact take place at Ephesus is evident from the Pastoral Epistles (cf. 1 Tim. 1:19f.; 4:1ff.; 2 Tim. 1:15; 2:17f.; 3:1ff.) and from the letter to the Ephesian church in Rev. 2:1ff. The Pastoral Epistles tell of a general revolt against Paul's teaching throughout the province of Asia; and John is bidden to reproach the Christians of Ephesus for having abandoned their first love. Foreseeing these trends, then, Paul urges the Ephesian elders to be watchful."[20]

Certainly Paul's words cannot be twisted and distorted to mean that the entire Christian church would completely abandon the true gospel of Christ. If Paul meant that a universal apostasy would take place—with not one member of the church remaining faithful to the truth—why did he write to the church at Ephesus, "Unto Him be glory *in the church by Christ Jesus throughout all ages,* world without end" (Ephesians 3:21, emphasis added)?

_____ *Ask . . .* _____

- According to Acts 20:17, who is the apostle Paul speaking to?

- What local church, then, are Paul's words intended for in verses 29–31?

- Did you know that the event Paul warned the Ephesian church about in Acts 20:29–31 actually occurred, according to other passages in the Bible (1 Timothy 1:19f.; 4:1f.; 2 Timothy 1:15; 2:17f.; 3:1f.)?

- Would you please read aloud from Ephesians 3:21?

- How could the apostle Paul say, "Unto Him be glory *in the church by Christ Jesus throughout all ages,* world without end," if the entire church was soon to go into complete apostasy?

Galatians 1:8—*Another Gospel*

The Mormon Teaching. In Galatians 1:6–8 we read, "I marvel that ye are so soon removed from him that called you into the grace of Christ unto another gospel; which is not another; but there be some that trouble you, and would pervert the gospel of Christ. But though we, or an angel from heaven, preach any other gospel unto you than that which we have preached unto you, let him be accursed."

The Mormons often cite this verse in their attempt to prove that the early church became completely apostate (believing "another gospel") and was thus in need of restoration. [21] This restoration allegedly came through the Mormon prophet Joseph Smith.

The Biblical Teaching. First you will want to make clear what Galatians 1:8 *does not* say. The text does not even remotely hint that there would be a total apostasy of the entire church. Mormons are reading something into the text that is not there. By allowing Galatians 1 to speak for itself, a person would never come to the conclusion that it is referring to a complete apostasy of the entire church.

You will then want to clarify the nature of the false gospel the Galatians had bought into: It was a gospel of legalism, which added works to faith. This was not the same gospel Paul had preached and by which the Galatians had been saved. Apparently false teachers had been at work confusing the Galatians (*see* Acts 15:24; 20:29–30).

The *New Bible Commentary* explains the problem this way:

> What complicated matters for Paul . . . was that the error into which the Galatians were falling was not simply the result of a weakness among the believers. It had an external source. Certain Jewish Christians, unhappy with the way Paul freely invited Gentiles to come to God, had begun to visit the churches he had established. Their purpose was to "Judaize" these Gentile believers; to persuade them that, after believing in Christ, they must take an additional step and become Jews through circumcision. [22]

This, in effect, added law to the grace Paul had been preaching.

It is clear, then, that the "other gospel" being taught in Galatia had to do with salvation through works (*see* Galatians 3:1–2). There are numerous other so-called "gospels" that pervert the true gospel of Christ (Galatians 1:7). These include the "doctrine of Balaam," the "doctrine of the Nicolaitans," and the "doctrine" of "that woman Jezebel, which calleth herself a prophetess" (Revelation 2:14,15,20-24).[23]

No matter what kind of gospel it is and no matter who it comes from (even an angel), if it goes against the authoritative gospel already handed down, it is to be rejected and is accursed by God. Commentator G. Walter Hansen explains, "Even the authority of a messenger from heaven or the authority of Paul himself must be tested by loyalty to the gospel. It is important to note that Paul holds himself accountable to this ultimate measure of authority."[24]

Measuring the "gospel" of Mormonism against that expressed in Galatians and the rest of the New Testament (a gospel *of grace,* not works), it becomes abundantly clear that the LDS *works*-gospel is in fact "another" gospel that must be pronounced anathema—accursed by God, and deadly to people seeking to enter His kingdom.

_____ *Ask . . .* _____

- Did you know that in Galatians 1:8 the apostle Paul was talking about a specific historical situation in which Judaizers had infiltrated the church in Galatia and had convinced people that besides believing in Jesus Christ, they must also be circumcised to gain salvation?

- According to Galatians 1:6-9, what is Paul's response to this *works*-gospel?

- Do you see that if someone presents a gospel that goes against the authoritative gospel already handed down (in the New Testament), it is to be rejected and is accursed by God?

- Does the "gospel" of Mormonism agree with or go against the *grace*-gospel as defined in the New Testament?

(Be ready to respond, whether they say "agree with" or "go against." If they say "agree with," then you will want to point out the folly in their statement [*see* chapter 18 of this book]. If they say "go against," ask them what Galatians 1:8 says about their "gospel.")

At some point in your discussion about the alleged universal apostasy of the church, you will want to turn the Mormon's attention to Hebrews 12:28: "We receiving a kingdom *which cannot be moved,* let us have grace, whereby we may serve God acceptably with reverence and godly fear" (emphasis added). Since the kingdom these Christians received could never be moved, it is obvious that there couldn't have been a total apostasy of the church.

_____ *Ask* . . . _____

- Would you please read aloud from Hebrews 12:28?

- Does it seem to you as if the writer of Hebrews thought there could be a *total* apostasy?

- How could there be a total apostasy if Christians belong to a kingdom *which cannot be moved?*

---

2 Thessalonians 2:3—*A Great Rebellion*

The Mormon Teaching. In 2 Thessalonians 2:3 we read, "Let no man deceive you by any means: for that day shall not come, except there come a falling away first, and that man of sin be revealed, the son of perdition."

According to *The Great Apostasy* by Mormon apostle James E. Talmage, "In his second epistle to the 'church of the Thessalonians,' Paul declares that the spirit of iniquity was then already operative . . . predicting the rise of the apostate church, with its blasphemous assumptions of power, as a condition antecedent to the second coming of Christ."[25]

Therefore, Paul again foretells the apostasy—pointing to the need for a restored church (namely, the LDS church).[26]

The Biblical Teaching. Again, you will want to begin by emphasizing what 2 Thessalonians 2:3 *does not* say. The text does not tell us there would come a total apostasy of the entire church. Mormons are reading something into the text that is not there. By allowing the text to speak for itself, a person would never come to the conclusion that it is referring to a complete apostasy of the entire church.

When you talk to a Mormon about this verse, it is important to stress that Paul is focusing not on a wide-scale apostasy that has occurred throughout the ages, but a specific, distinguishable apostasy that is still to come (*see* 1 Timothy 4:1–3; 2 Timothy 3:1–5; 4:3–4; James 5:1–8; 2 Peter 2;3:3–6; Jude).[27] This is an *end-time* apostasy that occurs at some point before the second coming of Christ (*see* verse 1, which sets the context by making specific reference to the coming of the Lord Jesus Christ). Paul is speaking about a *distinguishable* apostasy headed by a *distinguishable* "man of sin" (Antichrist), and he says it will take place before the *distinguishable* second coming of Christ at a specific point in time.

The manifestation of this "man of sin" will be an actual historical event in the future. As Bible expositor Thomas Constable notes, in the original Greek text "Paul used a tense for the verb *is revealed* which indicates that this revelation will be a decisive act that will take place at a definite moment in history (cf. verses 6, 8). He will be fully associated with and characterized by 'lawlessness.' "[28]

Your point, of course, is that Mormons abuse this passage when they say that the entire church would be characterized by complete apostasy. This passage refers to an apostasy, *yes,* but not a total apostasy of the universal church.

You should explain to the Mormon that the apostasy spoken of in 2 Thessalonians 2:3 culminates in the second coming of Christ, not the formation of the Mormon church.

_____ *Ask* . . . _____

- Would you please read aloud from 2 Thessalonians 2:1–3?

- Does the apostasy spoken of in this passage culminate in the second coming of Christ, or the founding of the Mormon church?

In the course of your discussion, you will want to point out that even Mormon scriptures argue against the idea that there was a complete apostasy of the entire church. Third Nephi 28:1–8, for example, makes reference to three faithful Nephite disciples *who have never died.* As well, Doctrine and Covenants 7:1–8 teaches that the apostle John never died and will live up to the time that Jesus returns. If these believers are still among us, as Mormon scriptures teach (and extensive modern Mormon folklore would claim), then this means that a total apostasy of the entire church could not have occurred. Christianity could not have vanished from the face of the earth with these individuals still alive on earth.

_____ *Ask* . . . _____

- Did you know that 3 Nephi 28:1–8 makes reference to three faithful Nephite disciples who have never died?

- Did you know that Doctrine and Covenants 7:1–8 teaches that the apostle John never died?

- If these individuals are still alive, as Mormon scriptures teach, then how can anyone say that a *complete* apostasy came upon the *entire* church and Christianity vanished from the face of the earth?

1 Timothy 4:1–2—*Doctrines of Demons*

The Mormon Teaching. In 1 Timothy 4:1–2 we read, "Now the Spirit speaketh expressly, that in the latter times some shall depart from the faith, giving heed to seducing spirits, and doctrines of devils; speaking lies in hypocrisy; having their conscience seared with a hot iron."

According to Mormon leaders, this passage contains still another prophecy of the great apostasy—foretelling how the true gospel would be lost and doctrines of demons would be substituted for it. Thus a restoration of the church became necessary. [29]

The Biblical Teaching. This verse *does* teach that an apostasy of the church would occur, but that is not the issue. The issue is, How *extensive* will the apostasy be? The text itself gives us the answer. Notice that it does not say, "In the latter times *all* shall depart from the faith." Rather, it says, "In the latter times *some* shall depart from the faith." Hence, the verse is not teaching that there would come a complete falling away from the truth by the entire Christian church.

____ *Ask* . . . ____

- Would you please read aloud from 1 Timothy 4:1?

- According to the verse, how many will abandon the faith?

- Can we agree, then, that this verse does not teach there would be a complete apostasy of the entire Christian church?

We should also note that the apostasy mentioned in 1 Timothy 4:1–3 is a particular kind of apostasy. The context of this passage indicates that this variety of apostasy is related to Gnostic dualism, which draws a distinction between spirit and matter.[30] According to dualism, *spirit* is good and *matter* is evil.

The false teachers mentioned in 1 Timothy 4 (*see* especially verse 3) were the kind who "believed all appetites relating to the body are . . . evil and should be rooted out, including normal desires for sex and food."[31] These false teachers forbade people to get married and ordered them to abstain from certain foods.

Even though apostasy has indeed characterized many people in the church throughout the centuries, the evidence of history and Scripture indicate strongly that the apostasy in 1 Timothy is a *specific kind* with dualistic, matter-versus-spirit roots. That's why 1 Timothy 4:1–2 cannot be used to allege a complete apostasy of the entire Christian church.

After you have discussed all the above, remind the Mormon that in the introduction to the official LDS *History of the Church,* we are told in no uncertain terms that "nothing less than *a complete apostasy* of the Christian religion would warrant the establishment of the Church of Jesus Christ of Latter-day Saints" (emphasis added).[32] Since the passages we've examined predict not total apostasy but only partial apostasy, does this mean that the establishment of the Church of Jesus Christ of Latter-day Saints was not necessary after all?

____ *Ask* . . . _____

- Did you know that the introduction to the *History of the Church* says that "nothing less than a *complete apostasy* of the Christian religion would warrant the establishment of the Church of Jesus Christ of Latter-day Saints"?

- Since the passages we've looked at indicate not total apostasy but only *partial* apostasy, does this mean that the organization of the Church of Jesus Christ of Latter-day Saints was not necessary after all?

Revelation 14:6—*The Angel Moroni?*

The Mormon Teaching. In Revelation 14:6 we read, "I saw another angel fly in the midst of heaven, having the everlasting gospel to preach unto them that dwell on the earth, and to every nation, and kindred, and tongue, and people."

According to Mormons, when the angel Moroni appeared to Joseph Smith, it was in direct fulfillment of this prophecy.[33] The everlasting gospel was restored, and since that time it has been preached and will be preached until it has been proclaimed to all who dwell on the earth.[34]

The Biblical Teaching. The reference to "another angel" in Revelation 14:6 seems to indicate an angel *in addition to* the seven angels introduced in Revelation 8:2 and in contrast to the other angels mentioned in Revelation 8:3 and 10:1. We must ask the Mormon: If you are so sure the angel in Revelation 14:6 is Moroni, then who are all these other angels? If you are not sure who they are, then, to be consistent, shouldn't you admit that you don't know who the angel of Revelation 14:6 is?

____ *Ask . . .* _____

- Did you know there are seven angels mentioned in Revelation 8:2 and there is reference to "another angel" in both Revelation 8:3 and 10:1?

- If you're so sure the angel in Revelation 14:6 is Moroni, then who are all these other angels?

- If you are not sure who these other angels are, then, to be consistent, shouldn't you admit that you don't know who the angel of Revelation 14:6 is?

It appears that the actual *content* of the "gospel" proclaimed by the angel in Revelation 14:6 is found in the next verse. This seems to make sense when we read Revelation 14:6–7 as a single unit:

> I saw another angel fly in the midst of heaven, having the everlasting gospel to preach unto them that dwell on the earth, and to every nation, and kindred, and tongue, and people, *Saying with a loud voice,* Fear God, and give glory to him; for the hour of his judgment is come: and worship him that made heaven, and earth, and the sea, and the fountains of waters (emphasis added).

Contextually this interpretation fits quite well.[35] And, of course, the Mormon interpretation (that this refers to Moroni appearing to Joseph Smith) does not fit at all. The angel's message is one of "glory to God" and "judgment is coming," not a message related to the Mormon gospel of Joseph Smith.

_____ *Ask . . .* _____

- Would you please read aloud from Revelation 14:6–7?

- According to verse 7, what is the *content* of the angel's message?

- Since the primary role of angels in the book of Revelation is to announce or carry out various judgments, doesn't it make good sense to interpret Revelation 14:6 in the same way—that is, as an angel speaking about God's judgment?

- With that in mind, does this sound like the Mormon gospel to you?

History Debunks the Mormon Claim

When we trace the history of the Christian church, it becomes clear that the Mormon claim of a "restoration" is pure fiction. As David Reed and John Farkas correctly point out,

> With church history so well preserved, it is possible for us today to trace the development of doctrines and practices over the years. We can follow the course of the debates over Gnosticism, Arianism, Sabellianism and so on. Yet the mountains of manuscripts dating back nearly two thousand years, nowhere do we find evidence that the church originally thought anything resembling the "restored gospel" of Mormonism . . . . If it were true that the church fouded by Jesus Christ originally taught such LDS doctrines as the Plurality of Gods, men becoming Gods, celestial marriage, and God the Father having once been a man, and if it were true that those doctrines were later set aside in favor of what is now considered orthodoox Christainity there would certainly be some record of this . . . . But no such evidence is available.[36]

History, then, is not on the side of the Mormon church. By contrast, history has always been the friend of orthodox Christianity.

Downplaying the Exclusivist Doctrines

In the introduction we noted that in recent years the LDS church has become increasingly involved with the Interfaith movement.[37] Of course, Mormons recognize that as long as they aggressively claim that *theirs* is the only true church, it will be difficult for them to pursue working relationships with Protestants, Catholics, and others. In recent years, the Mormon church has softened its stance on this claim. Indeed, some Mormon leaders are now denying that Mormonism has the harsh view of orthodox Christianity for which it is known.[38]

In order to make this denial plausible, however, Mormon scholars have had to adopt strained interpretations of founder Joseph Smith's "only true church" statements.[39] For example, according to the canonized version of Joseph Smith's account of his First Vision (in which he allegedly beheld God the Father and Jesus Christ), Smith reports what he was told in response to his inquiry about which church he should join:

> I was answered that I must join none of them, for they were all wrong; and the Personage who addressed me said that all their creeds were an abomination in his sight, that those professors were all corrupt; that: "they draw near to me with their lips, but their hearts are far from me, they teach for doctrines the commandments of men, having a form of godliness, but they deny the power thereof."[40]

One conciliatory Mormon leader offered the following explanation of Joseph Smith's words: "By reading the passage carefully, we find that the Lord Jesus Christ was referring only to that particular group of ministers in the Prophet Joseph Smith's community who were quarreling about which church was true."[41]

Similarly, Brigham Young University professors Daniel Peterson and Stephen Ricks write:

> What the Lord told Joseph Smith in the grove was that the churches and creeds of 1820 were defective and distorted by error. He did not say that they were entirely and utterly wrong (since they preserve much truth), nor did he say that each and every Christian church would always be wrong. . . . He did not say that Christianity, as such, is false. There is nothing logically wrong with saying the churches of 1820 were incorrect on many important issues ("corrupt"), and then saying that the Church of Jesus Christ of Latter-day Saints (organized in 1830) is true.[42]

This revisionist line of reasoning fails because, if this were so, all Joseph Smith had to do was move to a neighboring community and seek out a minister who wasn't corrupt. It wouldn't have been necessary to completely "restore" the church of Jesus Christ on earth by founding the Mormon church.[43]

_____ *Ask . . .* _____

- Did Joseph Smith say that all churches were an abomination in God's sight and that God instructed him not to join any of them?

- Why, then, is the Mormon church becoming increasingly involved with the Interfaith movement, working with Protestants, Catholics, and others on joint ventures like the VISN Cable Network and disaster aid?

- Does this mean that Protestants and Catholics are less an abomination to God than before, or does it mean that the Mormon church was wrong about the Protestants and Catholics all along?

4

Mormon Leaders:
True Prophets of God?

M ormons claim that God has always used chosen prophets through whom He reveals His instructions, laws, ordinances, and gospel. Since the days of Adam, there have been prophets on the earth who had a testimony of Jesus Christ and were ordained to lead the church in righteousness. When sin became too rampant, Mormons say, the everlasting covenants given through the prophets were taken away or lost, only to leave the people of the earth to grope in spiritual darkness without any revelation from the Lord.

In the "meridian of time," the Savior—Jesus Christ—came and restored the gospel once again. "It was His will, of course, that it should remain among men as a means of eternal salvation. However, Jesus knew that this would not be the case, and that the time would come when darkness would take the place of gospel light, and the priesthood would be withdrawn from men and the church be driven into the wilderness."[1]

The great prophet Joseph Smith, however, came in the fullness of time to restore that which had been lost.

Latter-day Saints call him "the Prophet" because in the tradition of Old and New Testament prophets, he depended on REVELATION from God for his teachings, not on his own learning. They accept his revelations, many of them published as the DOCTRINE AND COVENANTS and as the PEARL OF GREAT PRICE, as scripture to accompany the Bible. As a young man, Joseph Smith also translated a sacred record from ancient America known as the BOOK OF MORMON. These revelations and records restored to the earth the pure gospel of Christ. Joseph Smith's role in history was to found the Church of Jesus Christ based on this restored gospel in preparation for the second coming of Christ.[2]

The official church magazine, *The Ensign,* explains the central role of Joseph Smith:

Joseph Smith, like Adam, Enoch, Noah, Abraham, Moses, and others, stands as a dispensation head. The dispensation head becomes the means by which the knowledge and power of God are channeled to men and women on earth. He becomes the means by which the gospel of Jesus Christ—the plan of salvation and exaltation—is revealed anew, the means by which divine transforming powers, including saving covenants and ordinances, are extended to people during an age of time called a dispensation.*
The dispensation head stands as the preeminent prophetic witness of Christ.[3]

In the book *This Generation Shall Have My Word Through You,* apostle Bruce McConkie spoke of the importance of Joseph Smith's role as God's prophet:

Every prophet is a witness of Christ; every dispensation head is a revealer of Christ; every dispensation head is a

---

*Note that references to "dispensation" here do not mean that Mormonism has connections with the orthodox Christian system of thought known as Dispensationalism. *See* Charles C. Ryrie, *Dispensationalism Today* (Chicago, IL: Moody Press, 1975).

revealer of Christ for his day; and every other prophet or apostle who comes is a reflection and an echo and an exponent of the dispensation head. All such come to echo to the world and to expound and unfold what God has revealed through the man who was appointed for that era to give his eternal word to the world.[4]

The mantle of "Prophet, Seer, and Revelator" thus fell on Joseph Smith (and continues to apply to his successors in the office of church president).[5] And through the restoration of the Aaronic and Melchizedek Priesthoods, all church ordinances could again be performed with the authority that is according to the will and commandments of God.[6]

After the death of Joseph Smith, Brigham Young—who was president of the Council of the Twelve Apostles—was sustained as church president. "The senior apostle is always chosen and set apart as the President of the Church, and through this system of apostolic succession, the Lord has made provision for the kingdom on earth."[7] Thus, in its president the Church of Jesus Christ of Latter-day Saints has a Prophet, Seer, and Revelator leading the church as the mouthpiece of God at virtually all times.

It is obvious that Mormonism "must *stand or fall on the story of Joseph Smith.* He was either a true prophet of God— divinely called, properly appointed and commissioned—or he was one of the biggest frauds this world has ever seen. *There is no middle ground.*"[8]

In the authoritative Mormon work *Doctrines of Salvation,* we read:

> If Joseph Smith was a deceiver, who willfully attempted to mislead the people, then he should be exposed; his claims should be refuted, and his doctrines shown to be false, for the doctrines of an impostor cannot be made to harmonize in all particulars with divine truth. If his claims and declarations were built upon fraud and deceit, there would appear many errors and contradictions which would be

easy to detect. The doctrines of false teachers will not stand the test when tried by the accepted standards of measurement, the scriptures.[9]

In what follows, then, we shall examine some of the scriptures cited by Mormons in their attempt to validate Joseph Smith and other Mormon leaders as prophets of God.

REASONING FROM THE SCRIPTURES

Amos 3:7—*God Reveals His Plans to Prophets*

The Mormon Teaching. Amos 3:7 tells us, "Surely the Lord GOD will do nothing, but he revealeth his secret unto his servants the prophets." This verse makes it clear, Mormons say, that a prophet is needed on the earth today. Without a prophet, who holds the authority of the priesthood, God will not communicate His will for the church, and the world will remain in spiritual darkness.

Human wisdom, they teach, can never lead to a full understanding of eternal truth. God is the only source of truth in regard to the plan of personal salvation. Mormons "testify" that in these last days, there is a prophet on the earth who receives revelation from God and leads the church. Who is this prophet?

Citing Amos 3:7 in support of the Mormon view, Bruce McConkie said, "Any new revelation for the Church would, of course, be presented to the people by the President of the Church, *he being the mouthpiece of God on earth*"[10] (emphasis added). Each Mormon president is viewed as God's mouthpiece or prophet on the earth.[11]

The Biblical Teaching. We cannot properly interpret Amos 3 to mean that God will always and perpetually have His prophet on earth, without which the church will remain in darkness. That is a complete distortion of the verse.

In context, God was about to bring judgment against His people because of their disobedience. The stage is set for us in Amos 3:1: "Hear this word that the LORD hath spoken against you, O children of Israel, against the whole family which I brought up from the land of Egypt." The words that follow through the rest of Amos 3 are words of judgment.

Amos 3:7 simply states that God had warned His people that judgment would follow disobedience, but the people had ignored the prophets. In fact, according to Amos 2:12, the people had told the prophets to keep quiet because they didn't like what they were hearing.

Bible expositor Donald R. Sunukjian explains Amos 3:7 this way:

> Just as one event does not take place unless another necessary event has already happened, so the sovereign Lord does nothing regarding the history of Israel without first revealing His plan to His servants the prophets. But once this revelation has occurred—once the "lion has roared and attacked" (cf. 1:2; Hosea 5:14; 11:10; 13:7), once the sovereign Lord has spoken—Israel's judgment is sure to follow. [12]

As we examine the history of Israel, one fact becomes abundantly clear: God often gave revelation to His prophets before a major change took place that related in some way to the Israelites. That's what is happening in Amos 3:7. God gave revelation to the prophets that *judgment was coming.* The Mormon church's use of Amos 3:7 to establish an immutable doctrine that there must be a prophet on the earth today is a gross twisting of Scripture; Amos 3:7 says nothing of the sort.

One point you will want to emphasize to the Mormon is that in Old Testament times the biblical test for a prophet was 100-percent accuracy. Anything less than 100 percent brought death by stoning (Deuteronomy 13:1–8). Do Mormon prophets pass the test? Hardly. You may want to challenge the Mormon about the issue of prophetic accuracy.

Ask . . .

- Did you know that Joseph Smith once prophesied that the United States government would be overthrown in the 1800s?

- Did you know that Joseph Smith once prophesied that the New Jerusalem would be built in Missouri _in his generation?_

- Did you know that Brigham Young once prophesied that the Civil War would fail to end black slavery?

- Did you know that Brigham Young said that both the moon and the sun were inhabited?

If the Mormon tries to argue that the above prophecies were not uttered by these Mormon prophets, then you can point him or her to the appropriate Mormon sources. For example, Joseph Smith's prophecy of the New Jerusalem being built in Missouri is found in the Doctrine and Covenants:

> [The] city shall be built, beginning at the temple lot, which is appointed by the finger of the Lord, in the western boundaries of the State of Missouri, and dedicated by the hand of Joseph Smith, Jun., and others with whom the Lord was well pleased.
>
> Verily this is the word of the Lord, that the city New Jerusalem shall be built by the gathering of the saints, beginning at this place, even the place of the temple, which temple shall be reared _in this generation._
>
> For verily _this generation shall not all pass away_ until an house shall be built unto the Lord[13] (emphasis added).

What about the overthrow of the United States government? Point the Mormon to Joseph Smith, who, in _History of the Church,_ said this:

> I prophesy in the name of the Lord God of Israel, unless the United States redress the wrongs committed upon the

Saints in the state of Missouri and punish the crimes committed by her officers that in a few years the government will be utterly overthrown and wasted, and there will not be so much as a potsherd left, for their wickedness in permitting the murder of men, women, and children. [14]

If the Mormon balks at the false prophecy about the Civil War, point him or her to Brigham Young's statement in the *Journal of Discourses:* "Will the present struggle free the slave? No; but they are now wasting away the black race by thousands." [15]

Regarding Brigham Young's affirmation that the moon and the sun were inhabited, point the Mormon to the *Journal of Discourses* (July 24, 1870):

Who can tell us of the inhabitants of this little planet that shines of an evening, called the moon? ... When you inquire about the inhabitants of that sphere you find that the most learned are as ignorant in regard to them as the most ignorant of their fellows. So it is with regard to the inhabitants of the sun. Do you think it is inhabited? I rather think it is. Do you think there is any life there? No question of it; it was not made in vain. [16]

In each of the above cases the Mormon "prophet" was clearly a false prophet. What they predicted simply did not come to pass (or was patently untrue). Do not let Mormons sidestep this important fact!

There are other occasions in which we would expect God to reveal certain things to Mormon "prophets"—if indeed they really were prophets in the first place. One example of this is the Mormon prophet's remarkable failure in the highly publicized Mark Hofmann case.

In 1980, Hofmann unveiled a manuscript that was supposed to link church founder Joseph Smith to the occult, but the manuscript turned out to be a forgery. Hofmann also ended up killing two innocent people—one was involved in purchasing forged documents for the church, the other was the wife of another person involved in purchasing the forged documents.

_____ *Ask . . .* _____

- Why didn't God reveal to the Mormon prophet in the early and mid-1980s that Mark Hofmann's documents were forgeries? The church paid hundreds of thousands of dollars for those forgeries and announced them as true documents.

- Why didn't God tell the Mormon prophet that Mark Hofmann was going to murder two innocent people, including one who was a Mormon bishop involved in purchasing the forged documents for the church?

There is another question worth asking about Mormon prophets. When an LDS prophet becomes mentally incapacitated, as was the case with the late Mormon church president (Ezra Taft Benson), how can he possibly know the secrets God is trying to reveal to (and through) him, much less make the day-to-day decisions needed for the well-being of a growing worldwide church? How can he function as "God's mouthpiece" on earth?

_____ *Ask . . .* _____

- When an LDS prophet becomes mentally incapacitated—as happened with Ezra Taft Benson—how can he possibly know the secrets God is trying to reveal to him?

- How can he function as "God's mouthpiece" on earth?

Mark Cares, a pastor in "Mormon country," makes an additional point worth noting in regard to Amos 3:7. Whereas in this and other Old Testament passages it is clear that the prophets always warned God's people prior to judgment, today we have the Bible to warn us. "Since we now have the

Bible, we no longer need a continual stream of prophets. The Bible is all we need."[17] As 2 Timothy 3:15–17 tells us,

> From a child thou hast known the holy scriptures, which are able to make thee wise unto salvation through faith which is in Christ Jesus. All scripture is given by inspiration of God, and is profitable for doctrine, for reproof, for correction, for instruction in righteousness: That the man of God may be perfect, thoroughly furnished unto all good works.

Back in the days of Amos, they didn't have the complete written Word of God. Today it is different. Because we have the Bible, and because it is *trustworthy* and *complete* (*see* chapters 8–9 of this book), we have all we need.

1 Corinthians 12:28—*God's Appointment of Prophets*

The Mormon Teaching. In 1 Corinthians 12:28 we read, "God hath set some in the church, first apostles, secondarily prophets, thirdly teachers, after that miracles, then gifts of healings, helps, governments, diversities of tongues."

According to Mormonism, the primitive church on earth was established by Jesus Christ in "the meridian of time." He appointed the necessary officers to carry out the Father's plan. But then the church—along with its priesthood authority, which included the divinely mandated church organization—was lost from the world by a universal apostasy. The mark of the only true church on earth today is that it will have the same church officers—*including prophets.*

Citing 1 Corinthians 12:28 for support, Bruce McConkie proclaimed, "Where there are no apostles and prophets there is no divine Church, but where these officers are found, there is the Church of Christ in all its glory, beauty, and perfection."[18] Since the LDS church is the only church with the proper authority structure, Mormons argue, theirs is the only true church.

The Biblical Teaching. It is true that God gave "the church" apostles, prophets, teachers, workers of miracles, those having gifts of healing, those with gifts of administration, and those who can speak in tongues. But two of these gifts—apostleship and prophecy—were strictly *foundational* gifts that are no longer extant today in the strict biblical sense.*

We must remember the important principle that *Scripture interprets Scripture*. When we turn to other passages of the Bible, it becomes clear that the church was built on the *foundation* of the apostles and prophets (Ephesians 2:20).

Of course, once a foundation is built, it never needs to be built again. Once the foundation of a building is laid, then the foundation is built *upon*. In like fashion, the "building" of the church rests on the foundation of the apostles and prophets, but we don't need to build any *new* foundations.

That's why in our day we do not have apostles and prophets who give new revelations on the same level of authority as the Bible. There is no need for such apostles and prophets, since they have already (long ago) served their God-ordained function of providing the foundation of the church.

_____ *Ask* . . . _____

- What do you think Ephesians 2:20 means when it says that God's household is built on the *foundation* of the prophets and the apostles?

- Once a foundation is built, does it have to be built again, and again, and again?

---

*Some people may have a gift of prophecy in the loose sense of "forth-telling"(or speaking forth) God's inscripturated Word, but there are no "fore-telling" prophets on the level of Isaiah, Ezekiel, and Daniel

Let's take a closer look at the real nature of apostleship as a foundational gift. According to Scripture, the apostles were the special recipients of God's self-revelation. They recognized that God was providing revelation through them (1 Corinthians 2:13; 1 Thessalonians 2:13; 1 John 1:1–3). The apostles recognized their divine authority (1 Corinthians 7:10; 11:23ff.). They were also hand-picked by the Lord or the Holy Spirit (Matthew 10:1–4; Acts 1:26).

We already noted that God's household was founded on the apostles (Ephesians 2:20), and that once a foundation is properly constructed, it never needs to be laid again. Well, Scripture is also clear that, in the true New Testament sense, *there can be no apostles today.*

An apostle had to be an *eyewitness* to the resurrected Christ. When Paul was proving his apostleship in 1 Corinthians 9:1, he said, "Am I not an apostle? . . . have I not seen Jesus Christ our Lord?" Later in the same book, Paul said that the resurrected Christ appeared to James, then to all of the apostles, and finally ("last of all") to Paul himself (1 Corinthians 15:7–8). Obviously, no one living today can *truly* claim to have witnessed the resurrected Christ, and hence there can be no apostles. Paul was "last."

Now, any religious group can *claim* to have apostles in their midst—and they can even claim that their "apostles" have witnessed the resurrected Christ. Predictably, the Mormons speak of their apostles as having had personal visitations of Christ (thereby making them "eyewitnesses" of the resurrected Christ). But there are certain distinctives that were true of the biblical apostles that forever set them apart from mere pretenders.

For example, according to the New Testament, the true biblical apostles were *all* authenticated by miraculous signs. In 2 Corinthians 12:12 Paul says, "Truly the signs of an apostle were wrought among you in all patience, in signs, and wonders, and mighty deeds." Pay special attention to the first appearance of the word "signs." The sign of true apostleship was the ability to do great miracles in God's power.

The apostle Peter raised a person from the dead in Acts 9:36–42. The apostle Paul did likewise in Acts 20:6–12. Our question, then, is this: Can so-called Mormon apostles do the kinds of miracles Peter and Paul did? Do they have the "sign" of true apostleship? When did Mormon apostle Bruce McConkie, for example, ever raise anyone from the dead?

We must also point out that the apostles are utterly unique in that they were granted an eternal place of honor. In the description of the New Jerusalem (God's eternal city) in Revelation 21, we read that "the wall of the city had twelve foundations, and in them the names of the twelve apostles of the Lamb" (Revelation 21:14).

When the uniqueness of the apostles is coupled with the fact that the primary test for a book's inclusion in the New Testament was *apostolicity* (which means that the book had to either be *written by* an apostle or *approved by* an apostle), it seems clear that the revelatory process is over and done with (cf. Ephesians 2:20; Hebrews 1:1; 2:3–4).[19] Hence, we can properly conclude that the Book of Mormon is not "new revelation," and that Mormon "apostles" are not apostles at all. They are false apostles (*see* 2 Corinthians 11:13–14).[20]

_____ *Ask* . . . _____

- Did you know that according to the Bible, an apostle had to be an eyewitness of the resurrected Jesus Christ (1 Corinthians 9:1; 15:7–8)?

- Since no one today can honestly claim to have personally witnessed the resurrected Christ in the flesh, doesn't this mean there can be no apostles today? (The Mormons may claim their apostles have had visitations from Jesus Christ. Keep going . . .)

- Did you know that the words of the biblical apostles were all confirmed by miraculous works (Acts 3:3–11; 5:15–16; 9:36–42; 20:6–12)?

- Second Corinthians 12:12 says, "Truly the *signs* of an apostle were wrought among you in all patience, in signs, and wonders, and mighty deeds" (emphasis added). What is the "sign" of an apostle?

- Can Mormon apostles do the kinds of miracles, signs, and wonders that the biblical apostles did?

- Did you know that the biblical apostles' names (twelve in all) will be engraved in the New Jerusalem, God's eternal city (Revelation 21:14)?

- Why aren't the Mormon apostles' names engraved—or anywhere to be found—in the New Jerusalem?

- In view of the Bible's clear teaching on apostles, is it right to claim that the Mormon church has living apostles who are on a par with the biblical apostles?

That there is no continuing revelation today by "apostles" and "prophets" is also confirmed by the injunction found in Jude 3: "Earnestly contend for the faith which was once [for all] delivered unto the saints" (insert based on the Greek text).

What is "the faith" referred to in Jude 3? In the Greek text, the definite article "the" preceding "faith" points to the *one and only* faith; there is no other. "The faith" refers to "the apostolic teaching and preaching which was regulative upon the Church" (*see* Acts 6:7; Galatians 1:23; 1 Timothy 4:1).[21] Walter Bauer, William Arndt, and Wilbur Gingrich—in their authoritative Greek lexicon—tell us that "faith" in this verse refers to "that which is believed, [a] body of faith or belief, [a] doctrine."[22]

Most significant is the fact that this body of truth was communicated "once for all." The word translated "once for all" (Greek: *apax*) refers to something that has been done for all time, something that *never* needs repeating. The revelatory process was finished after this "faith" had "once for all" been delivered.

It is also important to note that the word "delivered" in Jude 3 is an aorist passive participle. This indicates an act that was *completed in the past* with *no continuing element*. There would be no new "faith" or body of truth (such as the Book of Mormon or Pearl of Great Price)!

___ *Ask* . . . _____

- Would you please read aloud from Jude 3?

- What do you think "the faith" is referring to? (If they are not sure, explain.)

- Did you know that Greek scholars tell us that the original Greek of this text literally says this "faith"—or body of apostolic truth—was given *once for all,* never needing to be given again?

- Did you know that Greek scholars say the word for "delivered" is an aorist passive participle, which means the "delivering" was *completed in the past?*

Now, even if a person hypothetically granted that revelation *does* continue today (and we emphasize "hypothetically," since we don't believe revelation, in the scriptural sense, continues today), any present-day revelation would *have* to be consistent with the previous revelation because the same Holy Spirit would be its author.

Remember what the apostle Paul said about those who set forth a gospel that contradicts the true gospel: "But though we, or an angel from heaven, preach any other gospel unto you than that which we have preached unto you, let him be accursed" (Galatians 1:8). We are to reject and condemn any teaching that contradicts previous authoritative teaching from God.

Paul spoke of the importance of making sure that new claims to truth be measured against what we know to be true from Scripture. Paul commended the Berean Christians because they examined the Scriptures every day to see if what Paul said was true (Acts 17:11). The Bereans set an example for all to follow. Paul warned the Thessalonian Christians to test everything (1 Thessalonians 5:21). Paul taught that all Scripture is God-breathed and is useful for teaching, rebuking, correcting, and training in righteousness (2 Timothy 3:16). Scripture has a corrective nature.

Since "revelations" by Mormon "prophets" and "apostles" do not measure up to Scripture, their revelations are to be rejected. Mormon prophets and apostles are false prophets and apostles.

Now, at some point in your discussion, you will want to challenge the Mormon about the Mormon church's authority structure.

_____ *Ask* . . . _____

- Would you please show me in the Bible where the primitive church had the offices of "First Presidency," "Patriarch to the Church," and "High Priest," like the Mormon church presently has?

- How can the Mormon church claim it is restoring the original church structure and organization when such an organizational structure is nowhere to be found in the Bible?

- Is it correct to say that in the Mormon church *prophets* are first and *apostles* are second? (Mormonism teaches this.)

- Does not 1 Corinthians 12:28 indicate that the first-century pattern was *apostles* first and *prophets* second? How do you explain this?

Ephesians 4:11—*God's Prophets Serve the Body of Christ*

The Mormon Teaching. In Ephesians 4:11 we read, "He gave some, apostles; and some, prophets; and some, evangelists; and some, pastors and teachers." Mormons say their present church structure (with prophets) is the same as the early church, just as God intended. Their Sixth Article of Faith affirms, "We believe in the same organization that existed in the primitive church, namely, apostles, prophets, teachers, evangelists, etc."

In his book *Mormon Doctrine,* Bruce McConkie says, "Basically, church organization is the same in all ages; the same organization that existed in the primitive Church prevails now."[23] McConkie says that the offices of apostle and prophet "will remain in the Church 'till we all come in the unity of the faith, and of the knowledge of the Son of God, unto a perfect man, unto the measure of the stature of the fulness of Christ' (Eph. 4:13)."[24]

The Biblical Teaching. The office of apostle must meet the qualifications as required in the primitive church (*see* Acts 1:21–22). Therefore, as noted earlier, there can be no apostles on the earth today, for no one can meet those qualifications.

Further, we noted that the household of faith is "built upon the foundation of the apostles and prophets, Jesus Christ himself being the chief corner stone" (Ephesians 2:20). We repeat: Once the foundation is built (with the apostles and the prophets), it is never built *again.* It is built *upon.*

You will want to use the same basic arguments in addressing this passage as were used in answering the Mormon interpretation of 1 Corinthians 12:28. You will find it well worth your time to commit some of those arguments to memory.

At some point in your discussion with the Mormon, you will want to talk about how the Holy Spirit leads believers into truth. Recall that Mormons teach that without a prophet in the church today, the world remains in darkness. This cannot be true for the simple reason that *the Holy Spirit is our teacher.* Jesus Himself said:

> When he, the Spirit of truth, is come, he will guide you into all truth: for He shall not speak of himself; but whatsoever he shall hear, that shall he speak: and he will show you things to come. He shall glorify me: for he shall receive of mine, and shall show it unto you. All things that the Father hath are mine: therefore said I, that he shall take of mine, and shall show it unto you (John 16:13–15).

There is no need of a prophet to lead us into all truth when every Christian has personal access to the teaching and illuminating ministry of the Holy Spirit.

The apostle John affirmed this again when he wrote to believers generally: "The anointing which ye have received of him abideth in you, and *ye need not that any man teach you:* but as the same anointing teacheth you of all things, and is truth, and is no lie, and even as it hath taught you, ye shall abide in him" (1 John 2:27, emphasis added).

___ *Ask . . .* ___

- Would you please read aloud from John 16:13–15?

- Next, would you please read from 1 John 2:27?

- According to these verses, what is one of the ministries of the Holy Spirit in our lives today?

- With the Holy Spirit as our teacher, as promised in Scripture, how can anyone say that we remain in darkness (or apostasy) without a prophet of God on the earth?

- Would you say that the Holy Spirit is incapable of keeping us out of darkness?

A Key Consideration: True Today, But Not Tomorrow

Depending on who is leading the Mormon church as Prophet, Seer, and Revelator, that which is true today may literally not be true tomorrow. In fact, Joseph Smith changed theology and doctrine within his own lifetime as president of the church.

For example, Smith went from a clear teaching of only *one God* in the Book of Mormon[25] to an *unspecified number of gods* in Doctrine and Covenants[26] and "Gods" in the Book of Abraham.[27] He went from teaching that God is a *personage of Spirit* in the "Lectures on Faith" (lecture five)[28] to teaching that God has a *body of flesh and bones* in Doctrine and Covenants 130:22—and soon thereafter, to the teaching that *we* can become gods ourselves in Doctrine and Covenants 132!

Moreover, Joseph Smith first said David and Solomon's possession of many wives and concubines was *abominable* in the Book of Mormon.[29] Later he said they were *justified* in the very same behavior in Doctrine and Covenants.[30]

_____ *Ask* . . . _____

- Why is it that God's alleged prophet Joseph Smith went from belief in only *one God* in the Book of Mormon to an *unspecified number of gods* in Doctrine and Covenants and *Gods* in the Book of Abraham?

- Why is it that the prophet Joseph Smith went from teaching that God is a *personage of Spirit* in the "Lectures on Faith" (lecture five) to teaching that God has a *body of flesh and bones* in Doctrine and Covenants 130?

- Why is it that Joseph Smith first said David and Solomon's possession of many wives and concubines was *abominable* in the Book of Mormon, then later said they were *justified* in the very same behavior in Doctrine and Covenants?

Brigham Young officially taught the infamous Adam-God doctrine[31] while his successors have virtually refused to recognize its existence.* Some Mormons try to claim that it was only a "theory," or that President Young was misquoted, or that enemies of the church have taken ideas expressed by him on only one occasion out of context. For Mormons who believe that Young was *not* always speaking as a prophet when he delivered his sermons, they should consider just two of his claims to authority:

- "I have never yet preached a sermon and sent it out to the children of men, that they may not call Scripture."[32]
- "I say now, when they [my sermons] are copied and approved by me they are as good Scripture as is couched in this Bible, and if you want to read revelation read the sayings of him who knows the mind of God."[33]

____ *Ask* . . . _____

- Did you know that Brigham Young repeatedly and officially taught that Adam was literally God the Father?

- Did you know that Brigham Young claimed his sermons were on par with Scripture?

- Did you know Deuteronomy 13:1–5 says that any supposed prophet who seeks to lead God's people after false gods was to be put to death?

- What do you make of all this?

---

*This doctrine teaches that Adam (also known as Michael) is God the Father and is literally the father of our premortal spirits, and the literal father of Jesus Christ in the flesh. It was taught by Young on numerous occasions, as early LDS church publications and the private journals of Mormon leaders and eyewitnesses attest. For a fuller explanation and documentation, see Jerald and Sandra Tanner, *Major Problems of Mormonism* (Salt Lake City, UT: Utah Lighthouse Ministry, 1989), pp. 61–65.

Related to our present discussion, the prophet-leaders of the Mormon church have made it clear how they expect church members to respond to church leadership:

> Any Latter-day Saint who denounces or opposes, whether actively or otherwise, any plan or doctrine advocated by the "prophets, seers, and revelators" of the Church is cultivating the spirit of apostasy . . . Lucifer . . . wins a great victory when he can get members of the Church to speak against their leaders and to do their own thinking? . . .
>
> When our leaders speak, the thinking has been done. When they propose a plan—it is God's plan. When they point the way, there is no other which is safe. When they give direction, it should mark the end of controversy.[34]

So, when doctrines change, the Mormon people are not to express concern, for the thinking has been done. By trying to prevent church members from "thinking," Mormon leaders are essentially hoping to perform a spiritual lobotomy on them.

_____ *Ask* . . . _____

- Does it bother you when Mormon leaders like Joseph Smith and Brigham Young make major changes in doctrine?

- Does it bother you when certain Mormon church leaders tell you that you are not to express concern about this because the thinking has already been done for you?

It is especially interesting that Joseph Fielding Smith—a senior apostle and leading Mormon doctrinal authority who went on to become the tenth prophet and president of the LDS church—went against the idea of unquestioning obedience and taught that Mormons *should* check out what the prophets taught:

When prophets write and speak on the principle of the gospel, they should have the guidance of the Spirit. If they do, then all that they say will be in harmony with the revealed word. If they are in harmony then we know that they have not spoken presumptuously. Should a man speak or write, and what he says is in conflict with the standards which are accepted, with the revelations the Lord has given, then we may reject what he has said, no matter who he is. [35]

In 1980, as the senior apostle who was next in line for the Mormon presidency, Ezra Taft Benson—the prophet of the church from 1985 to 1994—gave a speech entitled "The Fourteen Fundamentals of a Prophet" to a Brigham Young University Devotional Assembly. He virtually contradicted the above-stated teaching of Joseph Fielding Smith by returning to the all-important high authority of the prophet. Among the "Fundamentals" he taught that day (which was later reprinted by the church) was that "the living prophet is more vital to us than the standard works [Mormon Scriptures]." [36]

This statement implies that if the "living prophet" disagrees with or overrides a doctrine found in the Book of Mormon, Doctrine and Covenants, the Pearl of Great Price, or the Bible ("as far as it is translated correctly"), he could set it aside and bring forth his "inspired" doctrine as a revelation. This statement encouraged Mormons to rely on what the current prophet says and *not* to depend on the "Scripture."

_____ *Ask* . . . _____

- Do you believe the proclamations of the Mormon church's president/prophet are more authoritative than Scripture?

- Which Mormon prophet do you think was right: Joseph Fielding Smith, who said the teachings of the prophet should be tested against Scripture, or Ezra Taft

Benson, who elevated the authority of the prophet over Scripture?

• Was one of these Mormon prophets—as "God's mouthpiece"—in error? Which one?

To emphasize his point, Benson's third "Fundamental" proclaimed that "the living prophet is more important to us than a dead prophet." At the time Benson made his proclamations, he was not the prophet of the church. When Spencer W. Kimball died in 1985, the elderly Benson stepped into this lofty position. A few years later, Benson became mentally incapacitated and—though he was still physically alive—he was genuinely incapable of performing his official duties. So until his physical death in 1994, he was a "living prophet" who was virtually nonfunctional.

Steve Benson, a nationally known political cartoonist and the grandson of Ezra Taft Benson, wrote these revealing words:

> In the name of maintaining faith, church leaders peddled the myth that the Mormon prophet [Ezra Taft Benson] was actively at the helm when, in fact, he was incapacitated. Propping him up for photo sessions as if he were some kind of storefront mannequin was a calculated, conspiring abuse of power, not to mention disrespectful and undignified for a man we love.
>
> Only later, through a press leak, did Mormons learn that total legal authority to run the church had been secretly transferred *years earlier* from President Benson to his counselors via his signature machine. Yet the church continued to deceptively preach that he was still in charge and only recently admitted he is, in fact, incapable of meaningful leadership[37] (emphasis added).

Howard W. Hunter, 86, became Prophet of the Mormon church after Benson died of heart failure on May 30, 1994. In a newspaper interview, Hunter was asked an important question: "As prophet and seer of the church, do you see yourself as speaking infallibly? And how would you define infallible?" Hunter responded:

That's an interesting question. I'll answer the first part. I would not presume to hold myself [personally] as infallible, except on matters that are clearly defined by Scripture and by revelations. When [infallible] things are defined, we feel that the answer is scriptural and scripturally placed. Then, we take a strong stand. As far as infallibility is concerned, the officers of the church and the Council of the Twelve will support the First Presidency [Hunter and his two counselors] without question or difference of opinion. There would be one opinion. . . . There's a powerful unity in the leadership of the church that is followed without deviation by the membership.[38] *

We see, then, that different presidents of the Mormon church have taught different things regarding *their* personal authority versus the authority of *written Scripture*. But if they were all prophets speaking as "mouthpieces" for the same God, then why wasn't there perfect unity among them, as there is among the genuine prophets of the Bible?

In this chapter we looked at many evidences that proved that Joseph Smith and other Mormon leaders were false prophets. We close with one final evidence. Even if Joseph Smith and other Mormon leaders had been flawless in the many predictions they made (which, as we have seen, was not the case), they would *still* be categorized as false prophets because they set forth a different god than the God of Christianity (Deuteronomy 13:1–3). They also set forth a different Jesus and a different "gospel." There is no doubt that they were, indeed, false prophets.

---

*Howard W. Hunter died on March 3, 1995, and was succeeded by Gordon B. Hinckley on April 1, 1995.

How ironic that Joseph Smith himself said:

The only way of ascertaining a true prophet is to compare his prophecies with the ancient Word of God, and see if they agree. . . . When, therefore, any man, no matter who, or how high his standing may be, utters, or publishes, anything that afterwards proves to be untrue, he is a false prophet. [39]

5

The Book of Mormon—Part 1: Is It "Another Testament" of Jesus Christ?

Joseph Smith said, "I told the brethren that the Book of Mormon was the most correct of any book on earth, and the keystone of our religion, and a man would get nearer to God by abiding by its precepts, than any other book."[1]

The Book of Mormon* is an abridged account of God's dealings with the original inhabitants of the American continent from about 2247 B.C. to A.D. 421. According to the Mormons, the book was originally engraved on gold plates by ancient prophets, deposited in a stone box, and buried in the Hill Cumorah. It is said to be God's uncorrupted revelation to humankind, the "fulness of the everlasting gospel,"[2] and "another Testament of Jesus Christ."

The record gives an account of two "great civilizations." One of these, under the leadership of a man named Lehi, came to America from Jerusalem in 600 B.C.

---

* The Book of Mormon is one of the Mormons' four "standard works" of Scripture. The other three are the Bible, the Pearl of Great Price, and Doctrine and Covenants. *See* Bruce McConkie, *Mormon Doctrine,* p. 764.

and afterward separated into two nations because of sin. Those who obeyed God were known as the Nephites, and those who had fallen into sinful rebellion were known as Lamanites. (Nephi and Laman were sons of Lehi; Nephi chose the righteous path, Laman did not.) Before the Lamanites' rebellion they were "white, and exceeding fair and delightsome." But "that they might not be enticing unto my people the Lord God did cause a skin of blackness to come upon them."[3] The Lamanites thus had darkened skin as a result of God's curse.

The other civilization, we are told in the introduction to the Book of Mormon, "came much earlier when the Lord confounded the tongues at the Tower of Babel. This group is known as the Jaredites. After thousands of years, all were destroyed except the Lamanites, and they are the principal ancestors of the American Indians."[4]

Lehi, a prophet in the Book of Mormon, first foretells the coming of the Messiah in clear and concise words in 600 B.C.[5] "The crowning event recorded in the Book of Mormon is the personal ministry of the Lord Jesus Christ among the Nephites soon after his resurrection."[6] The Book of Mormon also "puts forth the doctrines of the gospel, outlines the plan of salvation, and tells men what they must do to gain peace in this life and eternal salvation in the life to come."[7]

How did the Book of Mormon eventually come into the possession of Joseph Smith? The following account in its introduction tells us:

> After Mormon [a Nephite historian-prophet] completed his writings, he delivered the account to his son Moroni, who added a few words of his own and hid up the plates in the hill Cumorah. On September 21, 1823, the same Moroni, then a glorified, resurrected being, appeared to the Prophet Joseph Smith and instructed him relative to the ancient record and its destined translation into the English language.[8]

The ancient records engraved on the gold plates were allegedly written in the language of the prophet Lehi, "which consists of the learning of the Jews and language of the Egyptians."[9] It was later identified as Reformed Egyptian hieroglyphics, a lost language. Miraculously, deposited with the gold plates was (allegedly) the "Urim and Thummim,"* a divine translating device, so that Joseph Smith, who had very little education, could translate the record "by the gift and power of God."

How does the Book of Mormon measure up to the Bible? In the book *Mormon Doctrine* we read:

> Almost all of the doctrines of the gospel are taught in the Book of Mormon with much greater clarity and perfection than those same doctrines are revealed in the Bible. Anyone who will place in parallel columns the teachings of these two great books on such subjects as the atonement, plan of salvation, gathering of Israel, baptism, gifts of the Spirit, miracles, revelation, faith, charity, (or any of a hundred other subjects), will find conclusive proof of the superiority of Book of Mormon teachings.[10]

People who read the Book of Mormon can know that it is true by following the challenge of Moroni 10:4–5 (in the Book of Mormon):

> And when ye shall receive these things, I would exhort you that ye would ask God, the Eternal Father, in the name of Christ, if these things are not true; and if ye shall ask

---

* Joseph Smith's "Urim and Thummim" should not be confused with the Urim and Thummim mentioned in the Bible (Exodus 28:30). Though biblical scholars are unsure what they were, it seems likely that they were precious stones kept in a pouch that were used on occasion to determine God's will. They were *never* used as (nor were they designed to be) translation devices. See *The Zondervan Pictorial Encyclopedia of the Bible,* ed. Merrill C. Tenney, vol. 5 (Grand Rapids, MI: Zondervan Publishing House, 1978), pp. 850–52.

with a sincere heart, with real intent, having faith in Christ, he will manifest the truth of it unto you, by the power of the Holy Ghost. And by the power of the Holy Ghost ye may know the truth of all things.

_____ REASONING FROM THE SCRIPTURES _____

Deuteronomy 4:2—*Disarming a Christian Objection to the Book of Mormon?*

The Mormon Teaching. In Deuteronomy 4:2 we read, "Ye shall not add unto the word which I command you, neither shall ye diminish aught from it, that ye may keep the commandments of the LORD your God which I command you."

Christians often argue against the idea that God gives additional revelations, such as those found in the Book of Mormon. Often they cite Revelation 22:18 to reinforce their view: " I testify unto every man that heareth the words of the prophecy of this book, If any man shall add unto these things, God shall add unto him the plagues that are written in this book."

When Christians cite this verse, Mormons typically point to Deuteronomy 4:2, which contains essentially the same warning. Mormons argue that if Revelation 22:18 forbids the Book of Mormon as Scripture, then Deuteronomy 4:2 forbids the rest of the Old Testament as well as the New Testament— that is, "we would be compelled to reject all the books of the Bible from Deuteronomy on."[11] Hence, Revelation 22:18 can't be cited against the Book of Mormon.

The Biblical Teaching. We will examine Revelation 22:18 later in the chapter. As for Deuteronomy 4:2, the Mormons have clearly twisted the meaning of this verse in favor of the Book of Mormon. A careful reading of the text indicates that the verse is not forbidding further revelation from God. Rather, God was simply forbidding people from adding anything *on their own* to what God inspired.[12]

David Reed and John Farkas correctly point out that "when the command came from God to Jeremiah the prophet, saying, 'Thus speaketh the LORD God of Israel, saying, Write thee all the words that I have spoken unto thee in a book' (Jer. 30:2), it was proper for Jeremiah to comply. What would have been wrong would have been for Jeremiah to add on his own to what the LORD told him to write." [13]

We find this emphasis on not adulterating the Word of God with the words of finite man repeated elsewhere in Scripture. For example:

- Deuteronomy 12:32—"What thing soever I command you, observe to do it: thou shalt not add thereto, nor diminish from it."
- Deuteronomy 18:20—"The prophet, which shall presume to speak a word in my name, which I have not commanded him to speak, or that shall speak in the name of other gods, even that prophet shall die."
- Proverbs 30:6—"Add thou not unto his words, lest he reprove thee, and thou be found a liar."
- Jeremiah 26:2—"Thus saith the LORD; Stand in the court of the LORD's house, and speak unto all the cities of Judah, which come to worship in the LORD's house, all the words that I command thee to speak unto them; diminish not a word."

Again, then, Deuteronomy 4:2 is not forbidding further revelation from God. Rather, it pointedly forbids human beings from adding anything to it on their own.

_____ *Ask* . . . _____

- Does it make sense to you that God would not want His Word *added* to or *subtracted from* by finite and sinful human beings?

    (To set the context for the next question, read aloud from Deuteronomy 12:32; 18:20; and Jeremiah 26:2.)

- Interpreted in the larger context of the whole Old Testament, isn't it clear that Deuteronomy 4:2 was not forbidding further revelation from God, but was rather simply forbidding human beings from adding anything to it on their own?

- For the sake of argument, if the Book of Mormon is not a God-inspired book, but is, in fact, a manmade book, what implications would Deuteronomy 4:2 then have for the Book of Mormon?

(This question will help open the door for you to show the Mormon insurmountable problems in the Book of Mormon [see the next chapter]. You will want to prove to the Mormon that the Book of Mormon is not a God-inspired book but a man-made book.)

Isaiah 29:1–4—*A Reference to the Book of Mormon?*

The Mormon Teaching. In Isaiah 29:1–4 we read:

Woe to Ariel, to Ariel, the city where David dwelt! add ye year to year; let them kill sacrifices. Yet I will distress Ariel, and there shall be heaviness and sorrow: and it shall be unto me as Ariel. And I will camp against thee round about, and will lay siege against thee with a mount, and I will raise forts against thee. And *thou shalt be brought down, and shalt speak out of the ground, and thy speech shall be low out of the dust, and thy voice shall be, as of one that hath a familiar spirit, out of the ground, and thy speech shall whisper out of the dust* (emphasis added).

Mormons distort this passage to make it appear that it is speaking about the Book of Mormon. Though the biblical reference concerns only the Jews (in Jerusalem), Mormons say the passage looks beyond the Jews and refers to the so-called Nephites, who allegedly inhabited North America long ago.

Apostle James E. Talmage says, "These predictions of Isaiah could not refer to Ariel of Jerusalem, because their speech has not been 'out of the ground,' or 'low out of the dust'; but it refers to the remnant of Joseph who were destroyed in America upwards of fourteen hundred years ago. The Book of Mormon describes their downfall, and truly it was great and terrible. . . . This remnant of Joseph in their distress became *as* Ariel."[14]

Talmage concludes, "Isaiah's prediction that the nation thus brought down should 'speak out of the ground,' with speech 'low out of the dust' was literally fulfilled in the bringing forth of the Book of Mormon, the original of which was taken out of the ground, and the voice of the record is as that of one speaking from the dust."[15]

What is incredible is that the Mormons cite the reference to the "familiar spirit" as if this is a good thing. They think the Isaiah passage indicates that the Book of Mormon will have a "familiar spirit" in the sense that Bible readers will see things in the Book of Mormon he or she is already *familiar with*—that is, the Book of Mormon will have a familiar ring to it.

The ever-popular Mormon book *A Marvelous Work and a Wonder* by apostle LeGrand Richards draws the following conclusion from the Isaiah passage: "Now, obviously, the only way a dead people could speak 'out of the ground' or 'low out of the dust' would be by the written word, and this the people did through the Book of Mormon. Truly it has a familiar spirit, *for it contains the words of the prophets of the God of Israel*"[16] (emphasis added).

The Biblical Teaching. Isaiah called Jerusalem "Ariel." This name probably means "hearth of God." If so, it is appropriate, since Jerusalem was the location of the altar on which sacrifices were burned. The name Ariel fits the context of judgment as well, for in verse 2 Jerusalem is called "an altar hearth."

The prophet Isaiah was saying that the coming judgment by God would be so devastating that the bloodshed and flames would make Jerusalem comparable to an altar on which sacrifices were burned. As John A. Martin notes, "Though

Jerusalem is where *festivals* were celebrated before God (Isa. 29:1), the city would be besieged and fighting and bloodshed would turn it into a virtual *altar hearth*." [17]

Isaiah 29:1–4 indicates that just as the altar of burnt offerings in Jerusalem was surrounded daily by the victims that were offered, so the walls of the city would be surrounded by the dead bodies of those who had rebelled against the Lord. [18] This is a picture of gruesome judgment.

This judgment against Jerusalem was fulfilled during Sennacherib's siege of the city in 701 B.C. [19] God used Sennacherib (ruler of Assyria from 705–681 B.C.) to punish His own people. During this attack, the fire and bloodshed indeed made the city seem like an altar hearth. God's fire of judgment "burned" the city.

We can know with certainty that Isaiah meant Jerusalem when he addressed "Ariel" because he called it "the city where David dwelt" (Isaiah 29:1a). We know from Old Testament history that David settled in Jerusalem, which was originally called Jebus, after taking the city from the Jebusites (2 Samuel 5:6–9).

In essence, Isaiah said to Jerusalem's inhabitants, "Add year to year and let your cycle of festivals go on." Evidently the people of Jerusalem saw that life was continuing as usual and knew that they were maintaining the outward forms of religion, including the religious festivals. For this reason they did not expect judgment. But Isaiah's statement implies that a year was coming that would be different from previous years, and that the cycle of religious life would then be broken.

Notice that even though it was the Assyrians who would surround and besiege Jerusalem, the prophecy cites God as saying, "I will distress Ariel" (Isaiah 29:2), and "I will camp against thee round about, and will lay siege against thee with a mount, and I will raise forts against thee" (verse 3). God would work through Assyria to accomplish His purposes for Jerusalem.

As a result of the siege, Jerusalem would be (figuratively speaking) brought down to the ground, *as if buried* (Isaiah 29:4). From the ground, Jerusalem would mumble or whisper. The word translated "whisper" was often used in Old Testament times to speak of the communication between mediums and spiritists and those who were dead. This indicates that the people of Jerusalem would speak as if from the realm of the dead.[20]

Bible expositor Albert Barnes explains: "The sense here is that Jerusalem, that had been accustomed to pride itself on its strength, would be greatly humbled and subdued. Its loud and lofty tone would be changed. It would use the suppressed language of fear and alarm as if it spoke from the dust, or in a shrill small voice, like the pretended conversers with the dead."[21]

By His great judgment against the Israelites, God would make a mockery of their so-called "covenant of death." What is the "covenant of death"? Back in Isaiah 28:15 we read, "Because ye have said, We have made a *covenant with death,* and with hell are we at agreement; when the overflowing scourge shall pass through, it shall not come unto us: for we have made lies our refuge, and under falsehood have we hid ourselves" (emphasis added). The Israelites had apparently made a "covenant with death" in the sense that some of Judah's leaders had promised to serve the gods of the underworld if those gods would protect them. Apparently some people were involved in necromancy and some form of spiritism.

With misplaced confidence in their own plans and belief in necromancy, these leaders asserted that when an overwhelming scourge sweeps by, it cannot touch them (Isaiah 28:15). They thought they were safe from the Assyrians. But since their covenant with death was a lie, or falsehood, and could not be trusted, Judah was not as safe as its leaders thought. Their refuge, or hiding place, could not protect them, as we see in Isaiah 29:1–4.

Isaiah 29:1–4, then, is actually a pronouncement of horrific judgment against Jerusalem. The purpose of the judgment was to get the nation of Judah to repent and return to God.

Now, recall that apostle James E. Talmage said that "these predictions of Isaiah could not refer to Ariel of Jerusalem, because their speech has not been 'out of the ground,' or 'low out of the dust.' "[22] There are two points here on which to challenge the Mormon. First, you will want to emphasize that Ariel is clearly identified as "the city where David dwelt" (Isaiah 29:1a). We know from Old Testament history that David settled in Jerusalem, originally called Jebus, after taking the city from the Jebusites (2 Samuel 5:6–9). "Ariel" therefore cannot refer to a location somewhere in North America.

Second, you will want to mention that Talmage was wrong in saying Jerusalem hadn't been brought low. In fact, Jerusalem *had* been humbled such that their speech was "out of the ground," or "low out of the dust." This horrific judgment against Jerusalem was fulfilled during Sennacherib's siege of the city in 701 B.C.

_____ *Ask* . . . _____

- Would you please read aloud from Isaiah 29:1a?

- Ariel is here identified as "the city where David settled." Where was that city? (David certainly didn't live anywhere in North America.)

- May I turn to 2 Samuel 5:6–9 and read to you what the Bible says about the city where David settled? (Emphasize that it was Jerusalem, which was originally called Jebus.)

- In context, then, Ariel is referring to Jerusalem, right?

- Can you see that as a result of Sennacherib's siege of the city in 701 B.C., Jerusalem had been humbled such that their speech was "out of the ground," or "low out of the dust"?

When talking with a Mormon about this passage, you should focus not only on what the passage really means but also on what a "familiar spirit" is. There are at least 15 Old Testament references to "familiar spirits" and all of them deal with *witchcraft* or *spiritism* (*see* Leviticus 19:31; 20:6, 27; 1 Samuel 28:3–9; 2 Kings 21:6; 23:24; Isaiah 8:19; 19:3; 29:4). Therefore, when the Book of Mormon claims it has a familiar spirit, it is inadvertently claiming a relationship with the demonic.

The word "familiar" is actually from the Latin word *familiaris,* meaning a "household servant." The word was apparently intended to express the idea that sorcerers had spirits as their servants ready to obey their every command. "Familiar spirits" are clearly rooted in occultism, and that's why God condemns anything related to familiar spirits. As Deuteronomy 18:9–12 says,

> When thou art come into the land which the LORD thy God giveth thee, thou shalt not learn to do after the abominations of those nations. There shall not be found among you any one that maketh his son or his daughter to pass through the fire, or that useth divination, or an observer of times, or an enchanter, or a witch, or a charmer, or a consulter with *familiar spirits,* or a wizard, or a necromancer. For *all that do these things are an abomination unto the LORD:* and because of these abominations the LORD thy God doth drive them out from before thee (emphasis added).

___ *Ask . . .* ___

- Did you know that every single reference to a "familiar spirit" in the Old Testament relates to necromancy or spiritism?

- Did you know that in passages like Deuteronomy 18:9–12 God condemns anyone who relates in any way to a familiar spirit?

- In view of this, what do you make of the claim by Mormon leaders that the Book of Mormon has a "familiar spirit"?

Isaiah 29:11-12—*The Book of Mormon: A Book Sealed?*

The Mormon Teaching. In Isaiah 29:11–12 we read, "The vision of all is become unto you as the words of a book that is sealed, which men deliver to one that is learned, saying, Read this, I pray thee: and he saith, I cannot; for it is sealed: And the book is delivered to him that is not learned, saying, Read this, I pray thee: and he saith, I am not learned."

Mormons claim these verses refer to the Book of Mormon, or to the gold plates from which Joseph Smith translated the Book of Mormon. We find a reference to these sealed plates in the testimony of Martin Harris, one of the alleged three witnesses to the Book of Mormon and Joseph Smith's "first assistant."[23]

Harris took a copy of some of the characters which Joseph had drawn off the plates to a Professor Charles Anthon, a gentleman celebrated for his literary attainments. Here is Harris's account:

Professor Anthon stated that the translation was correct, more so than any he had before seen translated from the Egyptian. I then showed him those which were not yet translated, and he said that they were Egyptian, Chaldaic, Assyriac, and Arabic; and he said they were true characters. He gave me a certificate, certifying to the people of Palmyra that they were true characters, and that the translation was also correct. . . . He asked me how the young man found out that there were gold plates in the place where he found them. I answered that an angel of God had revealed it unto him. "He then said to me, 'Let me see that certificate'" . . . When he took it, he tore it to pieces, saying there was no such thing now as the ministering of angels, and that if I would bring the plates to him he would translate them. *I informed him that part of the plates were sealed, and that I was forbidden to bring them. He replied, "I cannot read a sealed book."* I left him and went to Dr. Mitchell, who sanctioned what Professor Anthon had said respecting the characters and translation[24] (emphasis added).

Isaiah 29:11–12 is cited, then, as a prediction that the Book of Mormon would be taken to Professor Anthon at Columbia College, who would refuse to read it (because he couldn't read a "sealed book"), and that the book would be given to the "unlettered youth," Joseph Smith.

The Biblical Teachng. The Mormon interpretation of Isaiah 29:11–12 has several problems. One is that the text shows the subject is a *vision* and not a *book*. The visions God gave to the prophets of that day had become as meaningless to the people as the words of a book that was sealed. Isaiah was referring to the condition of the people *at that time* and not of some future era:

The prophet refers not only to his own communications, but to those of his contemporaries, and of all who had gone before him. The sense is, that although they had the communications which God had made to them, yet they did not understand them. They were as ignorant of their true nature as a man who can read is of the contents of a letter that is sealed up, or as a man who cannot read is of the contents of a book that is handed to him.[25]

When speaking to a Mormon about this passage, you will want to show that there are multiple discrepancies between Isaiah's account and the Mormon scenario. For example:

• According to Martin Harris, the professor said the translation was correct. But Anthon could have said this *only if he read the plates*—not just some characters scribbled on a paper by Joseph Smith. Notice, however, that Isaiah said the learned man *could not read it* because it was sealed. The only way the professor knew the plates were "sealed" was because Harris told him they were.

- In Isaiah 29:11-12, the book went to the learned man first, *then* to the unlearned. But the Mormon story has the book of gold delivered first to the unlearned Smith, who copied some of the characters (allegedly from the golden plates) on a piece of paper which was *then* taken by Harris to the "learned" Anthon. In Isaiah the *same sealed book* was taken to both the learned man and the unlearned man. But Anthon did not receive any book, sealed or unsealed.
- In Isaiah the book was delivered to the unlearned and he simply said, "I am not learned." He made no effort to read or translate it. But Smith claimed he (Smith) *did* read the book, even though he was unlearned.

In view of such insurmountable discrepancies, how can Mormons say Isaiah 29:11-12 relates in any way to the Book of Mormon? This is a complete distortion of Scripture.

Amazingly, Mormon apostle LeGrand Richards concluded that "Professor Anthon did not realize that he was literally fulfilling the prophecy of Isaiah."[26] The professor, however, certainly didn't believe he was fulfilling Mormon prophecy. Indeed, in a letter to E.D. Howe, a Painsville, Ohio, newspaper editor, Anthon related the events as a hoax and a scheme to cheat Harris out of money. Instead of fulfilling prophecy, Anthon became somewhat of a prophet himself in that Harris actually did lose money—for Harris sold his farm and gave the money to Joseph Smith to help pay for the publishing costs of the Book of Mormon.

_____ *Ask* . . . _____

- How could professor Anthon say the translation was correct when all he could assess were some of the characters drawn on a piece of paper by Joseph Smith?

- In Isaiah, the book went to the learned man first and then to the unlearned. But the Mormon story has the book of gold delivered first to the unlearned Smith, and then a paper with characters copied from the plates delivered to the "learned" Anthon. How do you explain this discrepancy?

- In Isaiah, the book was delivered to the unlearned man, who simply said, "I am not learned." He made no effort to read or translate it. But Smith claimed he *did* read the book, even though he was unlearned. How do you explain this discrepancy?

Ezekiel 37:16–17—*Is the "Stick of Joseph" the Book of Mormon?*

The Mormon Teaching. In Ezekiel 37:16–17 we read, "Moreover, thou son of man, take thee one stick, and write upon it, For Judah, and for the children of Israel his companions: then take another stick, and write upon it, For Joseph, the stick of Ephraim, and for all the house of Israel his companions: And join them one to another into one stick; and they shall become one in thine hand."

Mormons argue that the ancient prophets wrote on papyrus, leather, or other writing material, and wound this material on a perpendicular piece of wood or stick. These sticks were allegedly also known as scrolls or books. The Mormons say Ezekiel 37:16–17 is hence speaking of the *Bible* (Judah) and the *Book of Mormon* (Joseph)—two "sticks."[27] LeGrand Richards says, "Could this promise be fulfilled in a simpler and more perfect manner than it was through the coming forth of the Book of Mormon? . . . The two records have now been joined together, constituting a complete fulfillment of another great prophecy."[28] They were to be joined together and *both* accepted as Scripture.

The Biblical Teaching. The idea that the two sticks in Ezekiel 37:16–17 refer to the Bible and the Book of Mormon is clearly made impossible by the verses that follow—verses 18 through 28. By reading these verses, and by following the principle that Scripture interprets Scripture, we can learn what the two "sticks" are by letting Scripture define them.

In fact, verse 22 alone clearly identifies the "sticks": "I will make *them* one nation in the land upon the mountains of Israel; and one king shall be king to *them* all: and *they* shall be no more *two nations,* neither shall they be divided into *two kingdoms* any more at all" (Ezekiel 37:22, emphasis added). Obviously the "sticks" are not the Bible and the Book of Mormon; they are *two nations,* or *two kingdoms.*

Bible expositor Charles H. Dyer explains the context of Ezekiel 37 this way:

> After Solomon died the nation of Israel split asunder, in 931 B.C. The Southern Kingdom was known as Judah because Judah was its larger tribe and because the country was ruled by a king from that tribe (cf. 1 Kings 12:22–24). The Northern Kingdom was called Israel, or sometimes Ephraim (e.g., Hosea 5:3,5,11–14) either because Ephraim was the strongest and most influential tribe or because the first king of Israel, Jeroboam I, was an Ephraimite (1 Kings 11:26). Israel was taken into captivity by Assyria in 722 B.C., and Judah was taken into exile by Babylon in 605, 597, and 586 B.C.[29]

Ezekiel 37:18–28 clearly shows that the uniting of the "sticks" pictures God's restoring and reuniting His people in the land as a single nation (*see* Hosea 1:11). They would be cleansed of their backsliding and God would "be their God" (cf. Ezekiel 11:20; 14:11; 36:28; 37:27).

_____ *Ask* . . . _____

- Wasn't the Book of Mormon written on golden plates and not on papyrus that could be wound around a stick?

- Doesn't it make sense that we should let Scripture interpret Scripture? That is, shouldn't we let Scripture define its own words for itself?

- Please read aloud from Ezekiel 37:22, and tell me what this verse says about the true identity of the two sticks.

- Will you admit that the Mormon church is reading something into this passage that is not there?

You will also want to explain to the Mormon that in ancient times, when parchments were wrapped around sticks, they were called *scrolls,* not *sticks.* The Hebrew word for "sticks" (*'es*) is typically used to refer simply to wood, tree, or timber, not scrolls (Numbers 15:32; *see also* 1 Kings 17:10; 2 Kings 6:6; Lamentations 4:8). If Ezekiel had meant to talk about two scrolls in Ezekiel 37, there was a perfectly good word he could have used (Hebrew: *saipher*). But he chose a different word, and for a reason: *He wasn't talking about scrolls or books.*

Emphasize that in verse 16 the Lord told Ezekiel precisely what to write on the two sticks, and it was not "the Bible" on one and the "Book of Mormon" on the other. Rather, he was told, "Take thee one stick, and write upon it, *For Judah,* and for the children of Israel his companions: then take another stick, and write upon it, *For Joseph,* the stick of Ephraim, and for all the house of Israel his companions" (emphasis added). Then point out that many times in Old Testament history, sticks, rods, and staffs were used by the children of Israel to write their tribes and genealogy upon.[30] That is certainly the case in Ezekiel 37.

2 Corinthians 13:1–2—*The Book of Mormon a Second "Witness" to the Bible?*

The Mormon Teaching. Second Corinthians 13:1 tells us, "This is the third time I am coming to you. In the mouth of two or three witnesses shall every word be established."

According to Mormons, the Bible is one witness of Jesus Christ and the Book of Mormon is another testament of Him.

Thus, as Mormon apostle LeGrand Richards affirms, "two witnesses" have been established in regard to the mission of Jesus Christ in the world.[31]

The Biblical Teaching. In this passage the apostle Paul is simply warning the Corinthian church—a *carnal* church—about the consequences of their continuing to remain in sin. As theologian Charles Ryrie points out, "Paul warned that, if necessary, trials were going to be held when he came, in which Jewish rules of evidence-giving would be applied (Deut. 19:15)."[32]

What do these "rules of evidence" entail? Deuteronomy 19:15 tells us one such rule: "At the mouth of two witnesses, or at the mouth of three witnesses, shall the matter be established." Jesus had drawn from this verse when He gave instructions to the disciples about church discipline (*see* Matthew 18:16; cf. John 8:17; 1Timothy 5:19; Hebrews 10:28; 1John 5:8)

You will want to mention to the Mormon that the Bible already contains multiple witnesses to Christ and His gospel. After all, the Bible is made up of 66 books written by some 40 authors. So even if we conceded that 2 Corinthians 13:1–2 demanded more than one written "witness" of Jesus Christ, there are plenty of such witnesses in the individual books of the Bible. These books were not compiled into a single volume (the Bible) until years later. Hence, their individual "testimonies" carry great weight.

_____ *Ask . . .* _____

- Did you know that the Bible is actually a collection of 66 different books written by dozens of writers?

- Can you see, then, that in terms of the gospel of Christ alone, we already have multiple witnesses—such as Matthew, Mark, Luke, and John?

After making this point, you will then want to emphasize that 2 Corinthians 13:1-2 has nothing to do with the Bible as a "witness" anyway. Explain the proper context: Paul was dealing with a problem in Corinth and warning certain church members that if they did not turn from their sin, they would face trials based upon Jewish rules of evidence.

James 1:5—*Praying About the Book of Mormon*

The Mormon Teaching. In James 1:5 we read, "If any of you lack wisdom, let him ask of God, that giveth to all men liberally, and upbraideth not; and it shall be given him." This is the verse Joseph Smith claims he was reading when he decided to go out in the woods to pray and ask God which church he should join.

Mormon missionaries frequently urge the non-Mormon to pray about the Book of Mormon and ask God if it is true. When the Christian refuses to do this, the missionaries can become insistent to the point of laying a "guilt trip" on those who are reluctant to agree to their challenge.

The Mormons will inevitably appeal to Moroni 10:4 (in the Book of Mormon) to support the idea of praying about the Book of Mormon:

> And when ye shall receive these things, I would exhort you that ye would ask God, the Eternal Father, in the name of Christ, if these things are not true; and if ye shall ask with a sincere heart, with real intent, having faith in Christ, he will manifest the truth of it unto you, by the power of the Holy Ghost.

The Biblical Teaching. In a moment we will talk about the contextual meaning of James 1:5 in a "mock dialogue." But for now you might begin your discussion with the Mormon by asking him, Does a person have to pray whether to commit murder? Commit adultery? Commit incest?

Terrorize a playground? Use cocaine?[33] Obviously, a person does not need to pray about whether to carry out such actions because Scripture has *already* given us biblical commands and principles that tell us God's thoughts about them.

So it is with the Book of Mormon. We don't need to pray about whether to accept it because God has already made clear His feelings on the matter. Where so? you might ask. In Galatians 1:6–8 we read, "I marvel that ye are so soon removed from him that called you into the grace of Christ unto *another gospel:* Which is not another; but there be some that trouble you, and would *pervert the gospel of Christ.* But though we, or an angel from heaven, preach *any other gospel* unto you than that which we have preached unto you, let him be accursed" (emphasis added).

What are some of the doctrinal perversions in the Book of Mormon? One of the more significant ones is the heresy known as modalism—the view that the Father, Son, and Holy Spirit are simply *three modes of manifestation* (as opposed to three Persons in the one Godhead). Ether 3:14a (in the Book of Mormon) tells us, "Behold, I am he who was prepared from the foundation of the world to redeem my people. Behold, I am Jesus Christ. I am the Father and the Son" (*see also* Mosiah 15:1–5). Trinitarianism, in contrast, holds that the Father and the Son are *eternally distinct.*

The Book of Mormon also teaches *baptismal regeneration*— the idea that baptism is an absolute necessity for salvation. Second Nephi 9:23–24 tells us, "He commandeth all men that they must repent, and be baptized in his name, having perfect faith in the Holy One of Israel, or they cannot be saved in the kingdom of God. And if they will not repent and believe in his name, and be baptized in his name, and endure to the end, they must be damned; for the Lord God, the Holy One of Israel, has spoken it" (cf. Ether 4:18; 3 Nephi 3:37–38; 18:16; 21:20–22; Mormon 3:2; Moroni 7:34).

In view of the above, the gospel of the Book of Mormon clearly constitutes *"another* gospel" as defined in the book of

Galatians (that is, the Book of Mormon teaches *another God* and imposes *conditions* on salvation). We therefore need not pray about whether the Book of Mormon is true.

____ *Ask . . .* ____

- Does a person have to pray about whether to commit murder? Commit adultery? Commit incest? Terrorize a playground? Use cocaine? (They'll say no.)

- Why not?

- And so it is with the Book of Mormon. We don't have to pray about it because God has already given us His wisdom on the matter in Galatians 1:6–8. (Explain the verse.)

Pastor Mark Cares suggests a strategy similar to the above:

You might pose the question: If a Muslim asked them to pray about the truthfulness of the Koran, would they do so? Most whom I have asked that said they shouldn't because they already knew it couldn't be true. You could then tell them that neither do you have to pray about the Book of Mormon because God has already revealed to us that it isn't true. If they say how has God revealed that, point to Galatians 1:8,9 and get the discussion back on how to live eternally with the Heavenly Father. [34]

____ *Ask . . .* ____

- If a Muslim asked you to pray about the truthfulness of the Koran, would you do so? (The Mormon will say no.)

- Why not?

- Neither do we have to pray about the Book of Mormon, because God has already revealed that it isn't true (Galatians 1:6–8).

(You could also ask: If a "Moonie" asked you to pray about the truthfulness of Reverend Moon's book *The Divine Principle,* would you do so? If a Satanist asked you to pray about the truthfulness of *The Satanic Bible,* would you do so?)

Supplement your comments on Galatians 1:6–8 with some other key verses. For example, 1 Thessalonians 5:21 instructs us to *test* all things (not "*pray* to see if something is true").* Acts 17:11–12 encourages us to follow the example of the Bereans by testing religious claims against the Bible. The Bereans were certainly believers in prayer, but that was not the measuring stick for truth. They knew that the Bible alone was the measuring stick for truth, and hence it was the sole standard for testing religious claims. Also, we are instructed in 1 John 4:1 to test the spirits. As Bill McKeever puts it, "As Christians we are to test the spirits, not pray over them."[35]

Here's another strategy: When asked to pray about the Book of Mormon, you might respond, Which Book of Mormon do you want me to pray about? The 1830 edition? The 1921 edition? Or today's edition, which has over 4,000 changes from the original 1830 edition? Then use this as a launch pad to point out some of the specific changes that have been made in the Book of Mormon over the years.[36]

_____ *Ask* . . . _____

• Which Book of Mormon do you want me to pray about? The 1830 edition? The 1921 edition? Or today's edition, which has over 4,000 changes from the original 1830 edition?

---

* If the Mormon should try to argue that praying *is* a test, go straight to Acts 17, where the Bereans are shown utilizing the proper test—the Word of God. Mention that the Bereans were specifically commended (in contrast with the Thessalonians, who were told to test all things).

Furthermore, even if you did pray about the Book of Mormon and receive confirmation that it is true, then which church would you join? Virtually dozens (over 100) of different churches have been founded which use the Book of Mormon and claim Joseph Smith as a prophet of God.

Besides all the above reasons for not praying about the Book of Mormon, we also need to emphasize that it can actually be dangerous for a naive Christian to accept the Mormon's challenge to pray "with a sincere heart, with real intent, having faith in Christ." Satan—the great counterfeiter, father of lies, and god of confusion—will do all he can to confirm in a person's heart that the Book of Mormon is true. Christian beware!

A Mock Dialogue

Following is a mock dialogue that illustrates one way you might deal with a Mormon who asks you to pray about the Book of Mormon. This approach focuses on the context of James 1.[37]

Mormon: I'd like you to read and pray about the Book of Mormon, asking God if it's true.

Christian: Can you show me in the Bible where we are told to pray about a book or a prophet to find out the truth?

Mormon: James 1:5 says, "If any of you lack wisdom, let him ask of God, that giveth to all men liberally and upbraideth not; and it shall be given him."

Christian: That passage is not speaking about praying about a book or a prophet. The context deals with testings and trials and temptations (verses 2,3,12).

Mormon: That is your interpretation!

Christian: That is what the passage says in context. There seems to be a clear connection between this verse and the preceding ones. James had been talking about the purpose of trials (verses 2–4). He anticipates that some of his readers will say they cannot discover any divine purpose in their trials. In that case, he says, they are to ask God for wisdom.

Thus, *it is up to you* to demonstrate that this verse applies to praying about a book in order to discover whether it is true or not. Show me from the context how such an interpretation is possible.

Mormon: I *know* the Book of Mormon is true because I prayed about it.

Christian: Acts 17:11–12 gives us an example of how to test a teaching or a doctrine, which would include a religious book. Paul and Silas went to the synagogue of the Jews in Berea and preached the gospel of Jesus Christ. The passage states that the Bereans received the word with all readiness of mind, which means that they were open to accept the word which was preached to them. But first they searched the Scriptures daily to determine if what they were being told was scriptural and therefore true. The Scripture calls them noble for responding in this way. You will notice that they didn't test Paul's teaching through prayer, but by putting it to the test of Scripture. When they saw that the teaching accorded with Scripture, then many of them believed.

Mormon: But I prayed, and I have a burning in my bosom that confirms my belief in the Book of Mormon. Don't you believe in prayer? Do you think our Heavenly Father would allow me to be deceived when I prayed to Him?

Christian: Have you considered the possibility that the "burning" in your bosom might have occurred because you were hit by a fiery dart of the wicked one (Ephesians 6:16)?

Mormon: Do you mean Satan?

Christian: Yes!

Mormon: No, I haven't considered that.

Christian: Let me ask you a question: Where did you get the idea to pray about the Book of Mormon?

Mormon: Well, we are exhorted to pray with a sincere heart and receive a testimony from the Holy Ghost in Moroni 10:4–5.

Christian: So the idea to pray about the Book of Mormon came from the Book of Mormon itself, right? Suppose for a moment that the Book of Mormon is not true. Now, I know that you believe that it is, but just for the sake of argument suppose that it is not a historical document, but rather a counterfeit not inspired by the God who inspired the Bible. Who, then, would be the real inspiration behind a counterfeit book that claims to be from God?

Mormon: Satan?

Christian: Right! Now, since the admonition to read and pray about the Book of Mormon comes from the Book of Mormon itself, if its author is in reality Satan, who do you think would give the answer that the Book of Mormon is true?

Mormon: Well, if Satan *were* the author, which he isn't, he would have to be the one who gives the answer that the Book of Mormon is true.

Christian: That is correct, and that is why it is spiritually dangerous to pray about whether the Book of Mormon is true. The Bible makes it clear that the Book of Mormon is false (take a look at Galatians 1:6–8). To pray for an answer about it is to ignore what God *has already said,* which is to dishonor Him. We have only ourselves to blame, then, if Satan comes and answers such an irresponsible prayer. You must rely on the authority of the Bible itself to prove all things.

Revelation 22:18—*Disarming a Christian Objection to the Book of Mormon?*

The Mormon Teaching. In Revelation 22:18 we read, "I testify unto every man that heareth the words of the prophecy of this book, If any man shall add unto these things, God shall add unto him the plagues that are written in this book."

Mormons say they have not added either to the book of Revelation or to the Bible. God knew there would be lost books and corrupted text in the Bible. Therefore, He preserved the true doctrine in the Book of Mormon and continues to give revelation today through His prophet as He did in former times. LeGrand Richards says that Revelation 22:18 *does not* "prevent the Lord from adding to what he had revealed."[38]

The Biblical Teaching. The warning in Revelation 22:18 is against the willful distortion of the message of the book of Revelation itself. In some ways it is similar (at least in tone and spirit) to Paul's stern words about false gospels in Galatians 1:6–8.[39]

We suggest you point out three key facts to Mormons in regard to this verse:

1. *The contents of the book of Revelation are from God.* In Revelation 1:1, for example, we read, "The Revelation of Jesus Christ, *which God gave unto him,* to show unto his servants things which must shortly come to pass" (emphasis added).

2. *God's words are faithful and true.* In Revelation 19:9 we read, "And he saith unto me, These are the true sayings of God." In Revelation 21:5 John said, "And he said unto me, Write: for these words are true and faithful." And in Revelation 22:6 we read, "He said unto me, These sayings are faithful and true."

3. *Therefore, we cannot tamper with the book of Revelation.* The injunction in Revelation 22:18 specifically addresses *adding to* or *subtracting from* the book of Revelation. Other biblical books are not included in the picture here. But Revelation 22:18 definitely has implications for Joseph Smith, for he added to and subtracted from the Bible—*including the book of Revelation* —to produce the *Inspired Version* of the Bible. *Joseph Smith violated the injunction in Revelation 22:18.* And modern LDS authorities are Smith's accomplices—and are therefore subject to the curse themselves—by actively publishing and propagating Smith's corruptions in the book of Revelation. (Smith's material is included in the official LDS edition of the Bible.)

We are not talking about minor changes. For example, Revelation 19:15 in the King James Version says, "And out of his mouth goeth a sharp sword, that with it he should smite the nations: and he shall rule them with a rod of iron. . . ." But Joseph Smith changed this to say, "And out of his mouth proceedeth the word of God, and with it he will smite the nations; and he will rule them with the word of his mouth. . . ."

Revelation 5:6 in the King James Version says, "And I beheld, and, lo, in the midst of the throne and of the four beasts, and in the midst of the elders, stood a Lamb as it had been slain, having seven horns and seven eyes, which are the seven Spirits of God sent forth into all the earth." But Joseph Smith changed this to read, ". . . having twelve horns and twelve eyes, which are the twelve servants of God, sent forth into all the earth." These are clearly substantive changes that significantly alter the meaning of the text.

_____ *Ask* . . . _____

- Since Revelation 22:18 commands against adding to or subtracting from the book of Revelation—and since Joseph Smith, in fact, did add to and subtract from the book of Revelation to produce his so-called *Inspired Version*—then hasn't Joseph Smith violated this stern injunction?

- Do you really want to place your eternal destiny in the hands of a man who so blatantly violated this injunction?

6

The Book of Mormon—Part 2: Insurmountable Problems

I n this chapter we will focus our attention on some of the major problems with the Book of Mormon. We will take a look at . . .

- how thousands of changes have been made in it over the years;
- how it is permeated with plagiarisms;
- how there is no archaeological support for its people and places;
- how current Mormon doctrine directly contradicts the Book of Mormon.

Taken together, the cumulative weight of these problems is utterly damning.

We urge you to keep in mind that this chapter contains *only summaries* of these important issues. Since the primary thrust of this book is limited to helping you reason with Mormons from the Bible, you may want to consult some of the excellent books that specialize in the insurmountable problems in the Book of Mormon. [1] Then you will be thoroughly equipped when a Mormon shows up on your doorstep.

Changes in the Book of Mormon

There were more than 3,913 changes between the original edition of the Book of Mormon published in 1830 and the ones printed and issued through the mid-1970s. The 1981 edition introduced between one and two hundred additional word changes.[2]

The Ensign (an official LDS church magazine) defends the many changes this way: "Most changes correct typographical errors, misspellings, matters of grammar or style—such as changing singular to plural—and incorporate corrections made by the Prophet Joseph Smith."[3] In fact, many of the changes *are* related to spelling and grammar, though some are quite substantial (as we will see in a moment). But that doesn't solve the Mormon dilemma.

The problem is, the Mormon account of how Joseph Smith went about translating the Book of Mormon would seem to disallow *any possibility* of *any errors* or the need for changes—even relating to misspellings and grammar mistakes. David Whitmer, one of the three witnesses to the Book of Mormon, gives the following details on the translation process:

> I will now give you a description of the manner in which the Book of Mormon was translated. Joseph Smith would put the seer stone into a hat, and put his face in the hat, drawing it closely around his face to exclude the light; and in the darkness the spiritual light would shine. A piece of something resembling parchment would appear, and on that appeared the writing. One character at a time would appear, and under it was the interpretation in English. Brother Joseph would read off the English to Oliver Cowdery, who was his principal scribe, and when it was written down and repeated to Brother Joseph to see if it was correct, then it would disappear, and another character with the interpretation would appear. Thus the Book of Mormon was translated by the gift and power of God and not by any power of man.[4]

According to the *History of the Church of Jesus Christ of Latter-day Saints,* following the translation of the Book of Mormon, Joseph Smith said he heard a voice from out of a bright light above him that said, "These plates have been *revealed by the power of God,* and they *have been translated by the power of God. The translation of them which you have seen is correct,* and I command you to bear record of what you now see and hear" (emphasis added).[5]

Oliver B. Huntington recorded in his journal that in 1881, Joseph F. Smith, who later became the sixth president of the Mormon church, taught that the Lord gave Joseph Smith the *exact English wording and spelling* that should be used in the Book of Mormon:

> Saturday Feb. 25, 1881 . . . Heard Joseph F. Smith describe the manner of translating the Book of Mormon . . . Joseph did not render the writing on the gold plates into the English language in his own style of language as many people believe, but every word and every letter was given to him by the gift and power of God. . . . The Lord caused each word spelled as it is in the book to appear on the stones in short sentences or words, and when Joseph had uttered the sentence or word before him and the scribe had written it properly, that sentence would disappear and another appear. And if there was a word wrongly written or even a letter incorrect the writing on the stones would remain there. . . . and when corrected the sentence would disappear as usual.[6]

In view of this precise process—a process that involved *individual characters* and *specific words*—it would seem there is room for no human error. (Joseph Smith went on to boast that the Book of Mormon is the "most correct of any book on earth."[7]) But the 4,000-plus changes that have been made in the Book of Mormon since 1830 are clearly impossible to reconcile with the Mormon account of how the Book of Mormon was translated.

_____ *Ask . . .* _____

- Did you know that following the translation of the Book of Mormon, Joseph Smith said: "We heard a voice from out of the bright light above us, saying, 'These plates have been *revealed by the power of God,* and they *have been translated by the power of God. The translation of them which you have seen is correct*' "?[8] (emphasis added).

- Did you know that over 4,000 changes have been made in the Book of Mormon since its original publication in 1830? Even articles in your own *Ensign* magazine concede that changes have been made.

- How do you reconcile these many changes with the testimony that the heavenly messenger speaking to Joseph Smith said the original translation was done by the power of God and was "correct"?

- How do you reconcile these many changes with the testimony that the translation process—utilizing a "seer stone"—involved *individual characters* and *specific words?*

We must conclude that Mormon leaders are not being honest. How can they claim that the Book of Mormon is the "most correct book on earth,"[9] knowing full well that many thousands of changes have been made in it through the years?[10]

Steve Benson, the grandson of the late Mormon church president and propet Ezra Taft Benson,[11] wrote the following indictment in a newspaper article: "Troubling to us was the pathological unwillingness of the Mormon Church to deal forthrightly with its doctrine and history. Our personal study revealed that church canon, history, and scripture had been surreptitiously altered, skewed, rewritten, contradicted, and deleted."[12]

Lest some people think that only minor grammatical and punctuation changes have been made in the Book of Mormon, consider the following chart:

CHANGES IN THE BOOK OF MORMON

Verse	The 1830 Version	Today's Version
1 Nephi 11:21	"And the angel said unto me, Behold the Lamb of God, yea, even *the eternal Father"* (emphasis added).	"And the angel said unto me: Behold the Lamb of God, yea even *the son of the eternal Father"* (emphasis added).
1 Nephi 11:32	"And it came to pass that the angel spake unto me again, saying: Look! And I looked and beheld the Lamb of God, that he was taken by the people; yea, *the everlasting God* was judged of the world; and I saw and bear record" (emphasis added).	"And it came to pass that the angel spake unto me again, saying: Look! And I looked and beheld the Lamb of God, that he was taken by the people; yea, *the Son of the everlasting God* was judged of the world; and I saw and bear record" (emphasis added).
1 Nephi 13:40	"These last records . . . shall make known to all kindreds, tongues, and people, that the Lamb of God is *the Eternal Father* and Savior of the world . . ." (emphasis added).	"These last records . . . shall make known to all kindreds, tongues, and people, that the Lamb of God is *the Son of the Eternal Father* and the Savior of the world . . ." (emphasis added).
Mosiah 21:28	". . . *King Benjamin* had a gift from God, whereby he could interpret such engravings" (emphasis added).	". . . *King Mosiah* had a gift from God, whereby he could interpret such engravings" (emphasis added).*

---

*Jerald and Sandra Tanner write, "From chronology found in the Book of Mormon (*see* Mosiah 6:3–7 and 7:1), it would appear that king Benjamin should have been dead at this time. The name, therefore, was changed to Mosiah." (*See* Jerald and Sandra Tanner, *Major Problems of Mormonism* (Salt Lake City, UT: Utah Lighthouse Ministry, 1989), p. 160.

You will find it beneficial to obtain photocopies of these passages from the 1830 edition of the Book of Mormon. Then you can prove to the Mormon that substantial changes have, in fact, been made. It is not difficult to obtain photocopies of these passages and other important documents that are useful for witnessing to Mormons.*

_____ *Ask* . . . _____

- Did you know that the 1830 edition of the Book of Mormon had the following words at 1 Nephi 11:21: "And the angel said unto me, Behold the Lamb of God, yea, even *the eternal Father*"? (emphasis added).

- Yet later editions of the book read, "And the angel said unto me: Behold the Lamb of God, yea even *the son of the eternal Father*" (emphasis added).

- Did you know that the 1830 edition of the Book of Mormon had the following words at Mosiah 21:28: ". . . *King Benjamin* had a gift from God, whereby he could interpret such engravings"? (emphasis added).

- Yet later editions of the book read, ". . . *King Mosiah* had a gift from God, whereby he could interpret such engravings" (emphasis added).

- How do you explain these major changes in the Book of Mormon?

Emphasize that these are not mere grammatical or punctuation changes, but are changes of substance that affect doctrine. *Do not let the Mormon avoid or sidestep the damaging implications of this.* [13]

---

*For photocopies of these verses in the original 1830 version of the Book of Mormon, contact Utah Lighthouse Ministry, Box 1884, Salt Lake City, UT, 84110.

Plagiarisms in the Book of Mormon

The Book of Mormon has not only seen thousands of changes over the years, the book is also undermined by the many plagiarisms it contains from the King James Version of the Bible. In fact, there are whole chapters that have been lifted from the book of Isaiah.

Now, here is a thorny problem for Mormons: The Book of Mormon has some 27,000 words that were taken directly from the King James Version of the Bible. There are whole verses lifted right out of the King James Version.* The problem, then, is this: If the Book of Mormon was first penned between 600 B.C. and A.D. 421, as claimed, how could it contain such extensive quotations from the A.D. 1611 King James Version, which was not written for another 1200 to 2000 years?[14] This is not a subject most Mormons like to talk about.

You will want to show the Mormon some specific examples of plagiarisms in the Book of Mormon. Place a King James Version of the Bible and the Book of Mormon right next to each other and look up a few of the following passages. This may seem like a tedious process, but the point you make by going through it is one the Mormon will not soon forget.

King James Version	Book of Mormon
the Holy Ghost descended in a bodily shape like a dove upon him (Luke 3:22)	the Holy Ghost come down out of heaven and abide upon him in the form of a dove (1 Nephi 11:27)
bare record that this is the Son of God (John 1:34)	bear record that it is the Son of God (1 Nephi 11:7)

---

*An excellent resource you may want to consult is *The Use of the Bible in the Book of Mormon* by H. Michael Marquardt. Contact Utah Lighthouse Ministry, Box 1884, Salt Lake City, UT, 84110.

through the power of the Holy Ghost (Romans 15:13)	by the power of the Holy Ghost (1 Nephi 10:17)
the same yesterday, and today, and for ever (Hebrews 13:8)	the same yesterday, to-day, and forever (1 Nephi 10:18)
the earth did quake, and the rocks rent (Matthew 27:51)	the earth and the rocks, that they rent (1 Nephi 12:4)
first shall be last; and the last shall be first (Matthew 19:30)	last shall be first, and the first shall be last (1 Nephi 13:42)
all sick people that were taken with divers diseases . . . and those which were possessed with devils (Matthew 4:24)	who were sick, and who were afflicted with all manner of diseases, and with devils (1 Nephi 11:31)
pervert the right ways of the Lord (Acts 13:10)	pervert the right ways of the Lord (1 Nephi 13:27)
endureth to the end shall be saved (Matthew 10:22)	endure unto the end . . . shall be saved (1 Nephi 13:37)
made them white in the blood of the Lamb (Revelation 7:14)	made white in the blood of the Lamb (1 Nephi 12:11)
that old serpent, which is the Devil (Revelation 20:2)	that old serpent, who is the devil (2 Nephi 2:18)
blood, and fire, and vapor of smoke (Acts 2:19)	blood, and fire, and vapor of smoke (1 Nephi 22:18)
death and hell delivered up the dead (Revelation 20:13)	death and hell must deliver up their dead (2 Nephi 9:12)
he which is filthy, let him be filthy still: and he that is righteous, let him be righteous still (Revelation 22:11)	they who are righteous shall be righteous still, and they who are filthy shall be filthy still (2 Nephi 9:16)
shall be saved; yet so as by fire (1 Corinthians 3:15)	shall be saved, even if it so be as by fire (1 Nephi 22:17)
and there shall be one fold, and one shepherd (John 10:16)	and there shall be one fold and one shepherd (1 Nephi 22:25)
by the works of the law shall no flesh be justified (Galatians 2:16)	by the law no flesh is justified (2 Nephi 2:5)

I know whom I have believed (2 Timothy 1:12)	I know in whom I have trusted (2 Nephi 4:19)
endured the cross, despising the shame (Hebrews 12:2)	endured the crosses of the world, and despised the shame (2 Nephi 9:18)
shalt be thrust down to hell (Luke 10:15)	shall be thrust down to hell (2 Nephi 9:34)
He that is not with me is against me (Luke 11:23)	they who are not for me are against me, saith our God (2 Nephi 10:16)
by grace are ye saved (Ephesians 2:8)	through the grace of God that ye are saved (2 Nephi 10:24)
grind him to powder (Matthew 21:44)	grind them to powder (2 Nephi 26:5)
for there is nothing covered, that shall not be revealed (Matthew 10:26)	There is nothing which is secret save it shall be revealed (2 Nephi 30:17)
the Lamb of God, which taketh away the sin of the world (John 1:29)	the Lamb of God, which should take away the sins of the world (2 Nephi 31:4)
darkness rather than light (John 3:19)	darkness rather than light (2 Nephi 26:10)
withered; and men gather them, and cast them into the fire, and they are burned (John 15:6)	wither away, and we will cast them into the fire that they may be burned (Jacob 5:7)
the lake of fire (Revelation 20:14)	a lake of fire (2 Nephi 28:23)
one faith, one baptism (Ephesians 4:5)	one faith and one baptism (Mosiah 18:21)
he which is filthy, let him be filthy still (Revelation 22:11)	he who is filthy shall remain in his filthiness (Alma 7:21)
this Melchizedek . . . to whom also Abraham gave a tenth part of all (Hebrews 7:1–2)	this same Melchizedek to whom Abraham paid . . . of one-tenth part of all (Alma 13:15)

the elements shall melt with fervent heat, the earth (2 Peter 3:10)	the elements should melt with fervent heat, and the earth (3 Nephi 26:3)
an anchor of the soul, both sure and steadfast (Hebrews 6:19)	an anchor to the souls of men, which would make them sure and steadfast (Ether 12:4)
old things are passed away; behold, all things are become new (2 Corinthians 5:17)	Old things are done away, and all things have become new (3 Nephi 12:47)
partakers of the heavenly calling (Hebrews 3:1)	partakers of the heavenly gift (Ether 12:8)
and heard unspeakable words, which it is not lawful for a man to utter (2 Corinthians 12:4)	and heard unspeakable things, which are not lawful to be written (3 Nephi 26:18)
the name of thy holy child Jesus (Acts 4:30)	the name of his Holy Child, Jesus (Moroni 8:3)
all these worketh that one and the selfsame Spirit, dividing to every man severally as he will (1 Corinthians 12:11)	all these gifts come by the Spirit of Christ; and they come unto every man severally, according as he will (Moroni 10:17)
Charity suffereth long, and is kind; charity envieth not . . . is not puffed up . . . seeketh not her own, is not easily provoked, thinketh no evil; Rejoiceth not in iniquity, but rejoiceth in the truth; Beareth all things . . . hopeth all things, endureth all things (1 Corinthians 13:4–7)	charity suffereth long, and is kind, and envieth not . . . is not puffed up, seeketh not her own, is not easily provoked, thinketh no evil, and rejoiceth not in iniquity, but rejoiceth in the truth, beareth all things . . . hopeth all things, endureth all things (Moroni 7:45)
the Judge of quick and dead (Acts 10:42)	the Eternal Judge of both quick and dead (Moroni 10:34)[15]

After going through some of the above . . .

_____ *Ask . . .* _____

- The Book of Mormon was written sometime between 600 B.C. and A.D. 421, right?

- The King James Version was first published in A.D. 1611, right?

- If the Book of Mormon was written between 600 B.C. and A.D. 421, how could it contain such extensive quotations from the A.D. 1611 King James Version, which was not to come for another 1200 to 2000 years?

It is highly significant that in the many King James plagiarisms in the Book of Mormon, *even the italicized words* from the King James Version were plagiarized. This is relevant because, as noted in the preface of the King James Version, the italicized words were not in the original languages but were *added* by the King James translators to provide clarity. How could the Book of Mormon, which was written long before the King James Version, happen to include "inserted clarifying words" from the King James translators?

Archaeology and the Book of Mormon

Down through the years, Mormons have claimed that archaeological finds have proven the veracity and reliability of the Book of Mormon. But is there support for such claims?

We must keep in mind that according to the Mormon Scriptures, the Nephite and Lamanite nations had *huge* populations that lived in *large,* fortified cities. They allegedly waged *large-scale* wars with each other for hundreds of years, culminating in a conflict in which hundreds of thousands of people were killed in A.D. 385 near Hill Cumorah in present-day New York State (*see* Mormon 6:9–15).

If all this really happened, you would think we'd find archaeological evidence to support it. But no evidence has ever surfaced. While there is massive archaeological evidence to support the people and places mentioned in the Bible, such evidence is completely missing in regard to the Book of Mormon and other Mormon Scriptures. [16]

_____ *Ask . . .* _____

• If there were large-scale wars, culminating in a conflict in which hundreds of thousands of people were killed in A.D. 385 near Hill Cumorah in present-day New York State, wouldn't we find some archaeological evidence— *from non-Mormon archaeologists* —that such a conflict occurred?

You must emphasize to the Mormon that Mesoamerica has been studied so thoroughly by non-Mormon archeologists that one of them certainly would have come forward by now with evidence in support of the Book of Mormon *if what is in the Book of Mormon is really true*. But that has not happened. The evidence is completely lacking from non-Mormon archaeologists.

Let us consider a case in point: Prestigious non-Mormon archaeological institutions deny any evidence of a "Reformed Egyptian" language. For many years the National Museum of Natural History, Smithsonian Institute, in Washington, D.C. has sent this response to inquiries about the Book of Mormon:

Reports of findings of ancient Egyptian, Hebrew, and other Old World writings in the New World in pre-Columbian contexts have frequently appeared in newspapers, magazines, and sensational books. *None have been shown to have occurred* in any part of the Americas before 1492 except for a few Norse rune stones which have been found in Greenland[17] (emphasis added).

So, one of the most prestigious of all archaeological institutions does not agree that any writings such as those Joseph Smith claimed was written on the plates have been found on American soil. There is virtually no evidence that a "Reformed Egyptian" language ever existed on the American continent.

The Institute also affirmed, "Smithsonian archaeologists see no direct connection between the archaeology of the New World and the subject matter of the book [of Mormon]."[18] Similarly, the Bureau of American Ethnology asserts, "There is no evidence whatever of any migration from Israel to America, and likewise no evidence that pre-Colombian Indians had any knowledge of Christianity or the Bible."[19]

_____ *Ask . . .* _____

- Do you find it curious that archaeologists at one of the most respected institutions in the world—the Smithsonian Institution—see no archeological support for the Book of Mormon, or for a migration from Israel to America?

During 1987, Ray Matheny, a professor of anthropology at Brigham Young University, wrote an article about his dig in El Mirador. His article was published in *National Geographic* magazine. After reading the article, Mormonism researcher Jerry Bodine (at Christian Research Institute) wrote a letter to Dr. Matheny in December 1987 and asked him if he had found any evidence in El Mirador supporting the Book of Mormon. Dr. Matheny replied:

At present we have no proof identification of any important site by name except the ancient city Teotihuacan in the Valley of Mexico. We know this particular identification only because the Aztecs of the 16th century told the Spaniards its name. There are other similar cases of the 16th century but these only identify a handful of minor sites.

I would not dare make a claim for anything about ancient cultures unless there was ample evidence to back it up. To do otherwise would be to deceive and be intellectually dishonest, misusing my position as an investigative scientist. While some people choose to make claims for the Book of Mormon through archaeological evidences, to me they are made prematurely, and without sufficient knowledge.

I do not support the books written on this subject . . . I believe that the authors are making cases out of too little evidence and do not adequately address the problems that archaeology and the Book of Mormon present. I would feel terribly embarrassed if anyone sent a copy of any book written on this subject to the National Museum of Natural History—Smithsonian Institute, or other authority, making claims that can not as yet be substantiated.

This may sound very negative to you, but my intent is to let you know that there are very severe problems in this field in trying to make correlations with the scriptures. Simply put, there is not enough of a science base to make a case. Speculation, such as practiced so far by Mormon authors, has not given church members credibility. Much more research, both in the field and in laboratories, must be carried out before such correlations can ever be attempted.[20]

_____ *Ask . . .* _____

- Did you know that even a Mormon scholar at Brigham Young University—Dr. Ray Matheny—said there is a great lack of archaeological evidence for historical accounts in the Book of Mormon?

In a letter dated February 4, 1982, the National Geographic Society denied that archaeologists placed any weight on the Book of Mormon: "Neither the Society nor any other institution of equal prestige has ever used the Book of Mormon in locating archaeological sites. Although many Mormon sources claim that the Book of Mormon has been substantiated by archaeological findings, this claim has not been verified scientifically."[21]

In another letter, Dr. Chris Moser—of the Mesoamerican Archaeology Study Unit—answered a reply to questions about the Book of Mormon. One of the points he made was that "while I have several Mormon friends, some of them are archaeologists, and as I admire their moral code and way of life, *I am afraid that the Book of Mormon has no basis in fact*"[22] (emphasis added).

In an article published in *Dialogue: A Journal of Mormon Thought,* Dee Green, Assistant Professor of Anthropology at Weber State College, said,

> The first myth we need to eliminate is that Book of Mormon archaeology exists. . . . If one is to study Book of Mormon archaeology, then one must have a corpus of data with which to deal. We do not. . . . No Book of Mormon location is known with reference to modern topography. Biblical archaeology can be studied because we do know where Jerusalem and Jericho were and are, but we do not know where Zarahemla and Bountiful (nor any other location for that matter) were or are.[23]

In view of the above, if some Mormon missionaries show up on your doorstep and claim that the Book of Mormon has archaeological support, put the burden of proof on them. Ask for hard documentation *from non-Mormon sources* that you can examine. If they have no such documentation, the case is closed. Unsubstantiated claims cannot be accepted!

_____ *Ask* . . . _____

- You say the Book of Mormon has archaeological support. Prove it. I would like to see hard evidence *from non-Mormon* archaeologists. (You must insist on non-Mormon archaeological evidence.)

- While we're at it, can we also look at the hard evidence in support of the Bible? (See chapters 8 and 9 of this book for a summary of evidence.)

Over the years, many Mormon scholars have tried hard to find Book of Mormon lands somewhere in Central America. These scholars, however, disagree amongst themselves about *where* in Central America the Book of Mormon lands may be (some say the Costa Rica area, others say the Yucatan peninsula, and still others say the Tehuantepec area). While the Tehuantepec theory is currently favored by most Mormon scholars, even these scholars disagree about how the Book of Mormon fits the Tehuantepec area. There is so much conjecture among Mormon scholars! But the hard facts remain:

No one had ever heard of Zarahemla, Nephi, Manti, Cumorah, or Mormon until 1830, and still none of the Book of Mormon place names can be positively identified. None of the persons described in the Book of Mormon is known from *other* sources to have actually existed, except certain figures in the Bible (Isaiah, Malachi, Christ). In every way the evidence for the basic authenticity of the Bible is direct, tangible, and undisputed even by knowledgeable unbelievers. By contrast, the alleged "evidence" for the Book of Mormon is all indirect, hypothetical, and convincing only to Mormons. [24]

Current Mormon Doctrine and the Book of Mormon

The Book of Mormon, the keystone of the Mormon religion, contains very little in terms of the "Mormonism" as taught by the Mormon church today. Among other things, the Book of Mormon says nothing about . . .

- Mormon church organization
- the Aaronic priesthood
- the "plurality of Gods" doctrine
- the "God is an exalted man" doctrine
- the doctrine that men may become gods
- the doctrine of three degrees of glory, or three kingdoms
- the "plurality of wives" doctrine
- the "celestial marriage" doctrine with all the elaborate temple ceremonies and oaths
- baptism for the dead
- the "word of wisdom" doctrine
- the doctrine of preexistence
- the doctrine of eternal progression

Some of these Mormon doctrines may be unfamiliar to you. Don't be concerned; we will address them later in the book. Suffice it to say at this point that these doctrines—all of them central to Mormon theology—are nowhere to be found within the pages of the Book of Mormon.

_____ Ask . . . _____

- How can the Mormon church claim that the Book of Mormon is the "fullness of the everlasting gospel" when so much important Mormon doctrine is missing from it?*

---

*Possible Mormon comeback: Some Mormons may attempt to argue that the Book of Mormon only seeks to lead people to belief in Christ. The writers of the Book of Mormon—including Nephi, Jacob, Mormon, and Moroni— allegedly did not intend to communicate all the teachings and ordinances of the gospel (see *A Sure Foundation: Answers to Difficult Gospel Questions* [Salt Lake City, UT: Deseret, 1988], p. 13). But if this is the case, why is the Book of Mormon said to contain the "fullness" of the everlasting gospel? The fact remains, many key elements in the Mormon system of salvation are missing from the Book of Mormon.

It is also interesting that some of the teachings found in the Book of Mormon are not followed in present-day Mormonism. These are documented in the following chart:

Doctrine	Book of Mormon Reference
There is only one God	Mosiah 15:1–5; Alma 11:28,29; 2 Nephi 31:21
God is unchanging	Mormon 9:9,19; Moroni 8:18; Alma 41:8; 3 Nephi 24:6
God is a spirit	Alma 18:24–28; 22:9–11
The Holy Spirit . . .	*Dwells in man*—Alma 18:35; *Is God*—Alma 18:28; *Created all*—Alma 22:9–11
Jesus Christ . . .	*Is God*—2 Nephi 10:3; Mosiah 13:34–35; 15:1–5; *Was virgin born*—Alma 7:10; *Created all*—3 Nephi 9:15
God the Father . . .	*Redeemed man*—Mosiah 13:32; *Created all*—Jacob 4:9
Polygamy condemned	Jacob 1:15; 2:23,24,27,31; 3:5; Mosiah 11:2,4; Ether 10:5,7

Of course, Mormons do not like to talk about this. But the reality is that the Book of Mormon has many ideas in it that directly contradict present-day Mormon beliefs. We recommend that you go through the chart above and ask these questions:

Ask . . .

- Why do so many present-day Mormon beliefs contradict the Book of Mormon?

- Are we to conclude that the Book of Mormon is wrong? Or is present-day Mormon leadership in error? Which is it?

By bringing up the issues we've discussed in chapters 5 and 6 on the Book of Mormon, you may succeed in undermining the Mormon's faith in it. But don't stop there. You will also want to show the Mormon why he or she should trust the Bible. The next four chapters will help you accomplish this.

7

What Mormons Say About the Bible

T he Mormons' eighth "Article of Faith" affirms, "We believe the Bible to be the word of God, as far as it is translated correctly."[1] Ask a Mormon what is meant by this, however, and he or she will typically launch into the Mormon belief that because of *poor transmission,** large portions of the Bible have been lost down through the centuries. They also feel that the portions of the Bible that have survived have become *corrupted* because of faulty transmission.[2]

Hence, while Mormons acknowledge that the original manuscripts penned by the biblical authors were the Word of God, what passes as "the Bible" today is corrupt. It can only be trusted insofar as "it is translated correctly."

Mormons find support for their view in the Book of Mormon. According to 1 Nephi 13:38, the Bible is incomplete: "Wherefore thou seest that after the book hath gone forth through the hands of the great and abominable

---

* The word *transmission,* as used here, refers to the process by which the biblical manuscripts have been copied and recopied down through the ages.

church, that *there are many plain and precious things taken away from the book,* which is the book of the Lamb of God" (emphasis added). Since Mormons believe the Book of Mormon is the Word of God, personally translated by the prophet Joseph Smith, the implication is given that the Book of Mormon is more reliable than the Bible.

When were these "plain and precious things" taken out of the Bible? Brigham Young University professor Robert J. Matthews tells us the corruption took place before the end of the first century.

> Soon after the New Testament was written there were persons among the Gentiles who systematically, with wicked motives and evil intent, removed portions of the sacred word, and took from the Bible much very important doctrinal information. . . . In order to do this effectively two things were necessary: (1) It had to be done early, before there were multiple copies of the various books; and (2) It had to be an inside job by someone near the source, who had access to the original or earliest copies. . . . In other words, the process began early, by the end of the first century, and continued in the second and third centuries A.D.[3]

How Was the Bible Corrupted?

What kinds of corruptions has the Bible suffered? Mormon apostle Mark E. Petersen tells us: "Many insertions were made, some of them 'slanted' for selfish purposes, while at times deliberate falsifications and fabrications were perpetrated."[4] Petersen claims that "the Bible as we know it is a different volume from what it was—and would have been—had it not been changed so much by those with selfish interests."[5] Mormon apostle Orson Pratt once went so far as to ask, "Who, in his right mind, could, for one moment, suppose the Bible in its present form to be a perfect guide? Who knows that even one verse of the Bible has escaped pollution?"[6]

Pratt also said:

> The Hebrew and Greek manuscripts of the Bible from which translations have been made, are evidently very much corrupted. . . . The learned are under the necessity of translating from such mutilated, imperfect, and, in very many instances, contradictory copies as still exist. This uncertainty, combined with the imperfections of un-inspired translators, renders the Bibles of all languages, at the present day, emphatically the words of men, instead of the pure word of God.[7]

This is one of the main reasons why modern revelation—and the Book of Mormon in particular—is so necessary. Robert J. Matthews stated, "Many important concepts once in the Bible but now missing from it have been restored through the Book of Mormon and other Latter-day revelations."[8]

Can't Rely on a Single Verse?

The above statements by Mormon leaders contain a fatal flaw, and you can use this to your advantage when witnessing to a Mormon. As Jerald and Sandra Tanner cogently point out,

> Pratt's statement that the Bible may have been changed so much that we can't even rely upon one verse sounds very strange in light of the fact that the Book of Mormon quotes hundreds of verses from the Bible. In almost all cases these verses carry the same meaning as they do in the Bible. . . . The Bible cannot be discredited without casting doubt on the Book of Mormon also. If the Bible is all wrong, then the Book of Mormon is also.[9]

Ask . . .

- Do you read the Bible? Why?

- Mormon apostle Orson Pratt said, "Who, in his right mind, could, for one moment, suppose the Bible in its present form to be a perfect guide? Who knows that even one verse of the Bible has escaped pollution?" [10] Do you agree with Pratt that the Bible has been changed so much that we may not be able to rely upon a single verse?

(If he or she says yes, ask:)

- How can the Mormon church in good conscience publish its own version of the Bible—the King James Version—for use by church members?

(If he or she disagrees with Orson Pratt, say:)

- So you as a Mormon have the freedom and prerogative to disagree with your own general authorities?

(The Mormon will probably hedge here. If he or she says they can disagree with the teachings of a Mormon general authority, say:)

- Based on Doctrine and Covenants, Bruce McConkie concluded that "men are saved by giving heed to the words of the prophets and apostles sent among them and are damned for failure to heed the inspired testimony." [11] Do you agree with that statement?

(The above questions will cause conflict in the mind of the Mormon. These questions will likely unsettle him or her. At this point, you might bring up the Book of Mormon in the following way:)

- Since the Book of Mormon quotes virtually hundreds of verses directly from the King James Version of the Bible, what does Orson Pratt's statement about not being able to rely upon a single verse of the Bible say about the Book of Mormon? Do you see any conflict here?

- Is it possible to say what Pratt said about the Bible without saying something negative about the Book of Mormon? Please explain.

Wesley P. Walters, who had many years of experience in witnessing to Mormons, tells us about a great strategy he picked up from missionary Ira Ransom:

> Pastor Ira Ransom, a longtime missionary to the Mormons . . . hit on the idea of beginning any discussion by asking the Mormon, "How reliable is the Bible?" He had them tell him where they thought the Bible text was unreliable, and he promised to avoid those passages. Usually the Mormon was unable to cite a single reference, but if he or she could think of one or two, he simply noted them down and agreed to avoid them. This enabled him to get directly to the Bible without a lengthy argument. [12]

Ask . . .

• How reliable is the Bible?

(After he or she mentions any specific verses that "aren't reliable," say:)

• Can we just avoid those verses then, and continue our discussion from the rest of the Bible?

By using this approach, you can effectively eliminate a key Mormon argument from his or her apologetic arsenal. We recommend that you do this as close to the beginning of your witnessing encounter as possible.

Lost Books of the Bible?

Some Mormons try to make much of the fact that the Bible mentions specific books that are not contained in the Bible as Scripture. Luke 1:1, for example, says that _"many_ have taken in hand to set forth in order a declaration of those things which are most surely believed among us" (emphasis added). There is also a reference to the book of Jasher (Joshua 10:13; 2 Samuel 1:18) and the "book of the wars of the LORD" (Numbers 21:14). Mormons thus conclude that these are lost books of the Bible, when, in fact, there is no evidence that these books were ever intended to become a part of the canon of Scripture.

Simply because a book is *cited* in the Bible does not mean that the book belongs *in* the Bible. If the Mormon brings up this argument, you might point out that if these books belonged in the Bible, then God could have restored them when Joseph Smith—under "divine inspiration"—corrected the King James Version of the Bible.[13] But Smith did not "restore" these lost books.

_____ *Ask* . . . _____

- If these books cited in Scripture represent lost books of the Bible, as the Mormon church claims, then why weren't they restored to the Bible when Joseph Smith— under "divine inspiration"—corrected the King James Version of the Bible?

- If Joseph Smith did not restore these books to the Bible, does that mean Mormon authors are wrong in saying that they are lost books of the Bible?

- Where are the lost books of the Bible found in the Book of Mormon, the "most correct of any book on earth"?

Joseph Smith's "Inspired Version" of the Bible

Mormon founder Joseph Smith is credited with the "translation" of the *Inspired Version* of the Bible. Actually, Smith did not come up with a new translation at all. Rather, he took

the King James Version of the Bible and added to and subtracted from it—not by examining Bible manuscripts, but
allegedly by "divine inspiration."

Bruce McConkie says that "at the command of the Lord
and while acting under the spirit of revelation, the Prophet
[Joseph Smith] corrected, revised, altered, added to, and
deleted from the King James Version of the Bible to form
what is now commonly referred to as the *Inspired Version* of
the Bible."[14] Virtually thousands of changes were introduced
into the King James Version by Joseph Smith.[15]

We must emphasize that Smith didn't do *any* manuscript
study whatsoever. Rather he simply rewrote certain Bible
passages in the light of supposed new revelations from
God.[16] This means that we cannot verify Smith's "translation" by any objective means.

It is also worth noting that while it took a large group of
the world's greatest Bible scholars (who knew Hebrew and
Greek) years to finish their work on the King James Version,
it took Joseph Smith a mere three years to complete his
work—despite the fact that he had virtually no knowledge of
the biblical languages. You might ask the Mormon about this.

_____ *Ask* . . . _____

- Does it strike you as odd that while it took a large
  group of the world's greatest Bible scholars years to
  finish their work on the King James Version, it took
  Joseph Smith a mere three years to complete his
  work—despite the fact that he had no knowledge of the
  biblical languages?

A significant passage that was added by Joseph Smith in
Genesis 50 predicts Smith's own coming: "And that seer
will I bless . . . and his name shall be called Joseph, and it
shall be after the name of his father . . . for the thing which

the Lord shall bring forth by his hand shall bring my people unto salvation."[17]

_____ *Ask*... _____

- Does it strike you as being even slightly suspect that Joseph Smith inserted a passage into the King James Version of the Bible that predicted his own coming?

The Mormon Dilemma

David A. Reed and John R. Farkas, authors of several Christian books on Mormonism, note that the Joseph Smith translation has apparently put the Mormon church in somewhat of a dilemma:

> Some of Smith's revisions to the King James text fail to agree with the same passages as quoted in the Book of Mormon. Other portions contradict current Mormon doctrine. Therefore, fully endorsing it could prove embarrassing, but flatly rejecting it as erroneous would discredit Smith as a prophet. Instead, LDS leaders have sidestepped the issue by alleging that the work Smith began in 1831 was left unfinished at his untimely death in 1844; numerous errors remain in the uncorrected portions of the King James text, and therefore publication would be inappropriate. However, in a letter Smith wrote dated July 2, 1833 at Kirtland, Ohio, he states that he "this day finished the translating of the Scriptures" (*History of the Church*, vol. 1, p. 368).[18]

_____ *Ask*... _____

- Since in your own *History of the Church* it says that Joseph Smith claimed in July 1833 to have *completed* "the translating of the Scriptures," why hasn't the Mormon church ever published the *Inspired Version*?

While the Mormon church has never officially canonized the *Inspired Version,* it has bestowed a "high status" on it by including excerpts from it in the notes of their version of the King James Bible.[19] This was a "compromise" solution no doubt designed to avoid or at least minimize embarrassment to the church.[20]

The Authority of Scripture

When speaking to a Mormon about the changes Joseph Smith made to the King James Version, you might point out that Smith claimed an authority that was not even claimed by Jesus Christ Himself—namely, the authority to alter the text of Scripture.[21]

Remind the Mormon of what Jesus said in Matthew 5:18: "Verily I say unto you, Till heaven and earth pass, one jot [the smallest letter] or one tittle [the least stroke of a pen] shall in no wise pass from the law, till all be fulfilled" (inserts added). Jesus considered the Word of God as absolutely authoritative. He dared not change it. How, then, could Joseph Smith claim to have an authority to do something that even Christ could not do?

You will want to point out that when Jesus was tempted by the devil during His 40 days in the wilderness, the devil misquoted Scripture in an attempt to thwart Christ. Christ responded, however, by affirming the *absolute authority* of Scripture by saying, "It is written . . ." (Matthew 4:4,7,10).

_____ *Ask* . . . _____

- How could Joseph Smith claim the authority to do something that Christ could not—namely, the authority to change the text of Scripture?

- Why was it necessary for Joseph Smith to make changes in the Bible when Jesus said, "Verily I say unto you, Till heaven and earth pass, one jot or one tittle shall in no wise pass from the law, till all be fulfilled" (Matthew 5:18)?

You will want to emphasize that some of the changes Joseph Smith made to the Bible were in the book of Revelation. Revelation 19:15 in the King James Version says, "And out of his mouth goeth a sharp sword, that with it he should smite the nations: and he shall rule them with a rod of iron. . . ." But Joseph Smith changed this to say, "And out of his mouth proceedeth the word of God, and with it he will smite the nations; and he will rule them with the word of his mouth. . . ."

Revelation 5:6 in the King James Version says, "And I beheld, and, lo, in the midst of the throne and of the four beasts, and in the midst of the elders, stood a Lamb as it had been slain, having seven horns and seven eyes, which are the seven Spirits of God sent forth into all the earth." But Joseph Smith changed this to read, ". . . having twelve horns and twelve eyes, which are the twelve servants of God, sent forth into all the earth." These are substantive changes that significantly alter the meaning of the text.

Joseph Smith's work, then, brings him under the judgment described in Revelation 22:18–19: "I testify unto every man that heareth the words of the prophecy of this book, If any man shall add unto these things, God shall add unto him the plagues that are written in this book: And if any man shall take away from the words of the book of this prophecy, God shall take away his part out of the book of life, and out of the holy city, and from the things which are written in this book."

___ *Ask . . .* ___

- What do you think Revelation 22:18–19 tells us in regard to Joseph Smith adding to and subtracting from the book of Revelation?

You will also want to emphasize to the Mormon how Scripture attests to its enduring nature. For example, Isaiah

40:8 tells us, "The grass withereth, the flower fadeth: but the word of our God shall stand for ever." Matthew 24:35 quotes the words of Jesus: "Heaven and earth shall pass away, but my words shall not pass away."

____ *Ask* . . . ____

- How do you reconcile Jesus' statement in Matthew 24:35—"Heaven and earth shall pass away, but my words shall not pass away"—with Joseph Smith's work on the *Inspired Version*?

8

The Inspiration, Inerrancy, and Authority of the Bible

When you engage in discussions with Mormons, it is critical that you be prepared to affirm the inspiration, inerrancy, and authority of the Bible. This is important because, as we have seen earlier, the Mormons place faith in their own latter-day "Scriptures"—the Book of Mormon, for example—and trust the Bible only insofar as it is "translated correctly."

In this chapter you will find a brief defense of the Bible's inspiration, inerrancy, and authority. We recommend that you memorize some of the Bible references in this chapter so that when God brings a Mormon to your doorstep, you will be prepared to defend the Bible as His Word to humankind.

What Is Inspiration?

We can define biblical inspiration as God's superintending of the human authors so that, using their own individual personalities (and even their writing styles), they composed and recorded *without error* His revelation to man in the words of the original autographs. Inspiration means that "the Holy Spirit of God superintended the human writers in the production of Scripture so that what they wrote was precisely what God wanted written."[1]

Another way to define inspiration is suggested by Norman Geisler and William Nix: "Inspiration is that mysterious process by which the divine causality worked through the human prophets without destroying their individual personalities and styles, to produce divinely authoritative writings."[2]

When you break the doctrine of inspiration down to its essential elements, there are seven key factors:

1. Divine origin and causality;
2. Human agency;
3. Written verbally (in words);
4. Plenary (*all* of Scripture is inspired, not just parts of it);
5. Only the "autographs" (the original documents penned by the biblical authors) are inspired;
6. Because Scripture is inspired, it is inerrant; and
7. Because Scripture is inspired and inerrant, it alone has final authority.

The word *inspiration* literally means "God-breathed" in the Greek text. And because Scripture is breathed out by God, it is *true* and *inerrant*. Consider the following syllogism*:

Major Premise:	God is true (Romans 3:4).
Minor Premise:	God *breathed out* the Scriptures (2 Timothy 3:16).
Conclusion:	Therefore, the Scriptures are true (John 17:17).[3]

As illustrated above, the inerrancy of Scripture can be inferred by premises that are themselves taught by Scripture. We

---

* A *syllogism* is a form of deductive reasoning consisting of a major premise, a minor premise, and a conclusion.

read in Scripture that truth is an attribute of God (Jeremiah 10:10; John 1:14; 14:6; 17:3), and that God speaks truthfully—that is, He does not lie (Numbers 23:19; 1 Samuel 15:29; Romans 3:3–4; Titus 1:2). We also are told that Scripture is "breathed out" by God (2 Timothy 3:16). The Word of God, then, is true (John 17:14,17; cf. Psalm 119:142,151,160; Revelation 21:5; 22:6).

The Holy Spirit Is the Agent of Inspiration

Second Peter 1:21 tells us that "prophecy came not in old time by the will of man: but holy men of God spake as they were moved by the Holy Ghost." The word "moved" in this verse means to be "borne along" or "carried along."

Even though human beings were used in the process of writing down God's Word, they were all literally "borne along" by the Holy Spirit. Commenting on this verse, theologian Charles Ryrie says "the human wills of the authors were not the originators or the carriers of God's message. . . . God did not permit the will of sinful man to divert, misdirect, or erroneously record His message."[4] Geisler and Nix explain that "God *moved* and the prophet *mouthed* these truths; God *revealed* and man *recorded* His word."[5]

Interestingly, the Greek word for "moved" in 2 Peter 1:21 is the same word found in Acts 27:15–17. There, we read that a group of experienced sailors could not navigate their ship because the wind was so strong. The ship was being driven, directed, and carried about by the wind. This is similar to the Spirit's driving, directing, and carrying the human authors of the Bible as He wished. The word "moved," then, is a strong one, indicating the Spirit's complete superintendence of the human authors. Yet, just as the sailors were active on the ship (though the wind, not the sailors, controlled the ship's movement), so also were the human authors active in writing as the Spirit directed.

Hence, as theologian Robert Lightner concludes, "the Holy Spirit of God was the divine author of Scripture. Though he used erring humans as penmen, he supernaturally (miraculously) superintended them as they wrote, keeping them from all error and omission."[6]

Edward J. Young, in his book *Thy Word is Truth,* explains inerrancy this way: "The Scriptures possess the quality of freedom from error. They are exempt from the liability to mistake, incapable of error. In all their teachings they are in perfect accord with the truth."[7] And this "quality of freedom from error" is a direct result of the Holy Spirit's superintendence of the human authors of Scripture.

In *Explaining Inerrancy: A Commentary,* produced by the International Council of Biblical Inerrancy, we read that inspiration

> involves a divine superintendence which preserved the writers in their word choices from using words that would falsify or distort the message of Scripture. . . . Evangelical Christians have wanted to avoid the notion that biblical writers were passive instruments like pens in the hands of God, yet at the same time they affirm that the net result of the process of inspiration would be the same. Calvin, for example, says that we should treat the Bible as if we have heard God audibly speaking its message. That is, it carries the same weight of authority as if God himself were heard to be giving utterance to the words of Scripture. . . . That does not mean that Calvin believed or taught that God did in fact utter the words audibly. . . . But we are saying that inspiration, however God brought it about, results in the net effect that every word of Scripture carries with it the weight of God's authority.[8]

Inspiration in the Old Testament

The Old Testament recognized that it was the Holy Spirit who spoke through its writers (2 Samuel 23:2–3). Indeed, many Old Testament passages quoted in the New Testament are said to have the Holy Spirit as their author, even though a human prophet actually spoke the words in the Old Testament (*see* Mark 12:36; Acts 1:16; 28:25; Hebrews 3:7; 10:15–16).

OLD TESTAMENT CITATIONS IN THE NEW TESTAMENT

Old Testament Designation	New Testament Designation
The psalmist said (Psalm 95:7)	The Holy Spirit said (Hebrews 3:7)
The psalmist said (Psalm 45:6)	God said (Hebrews 1:8)
The psalmist said (Psalm 102:25,27)	God said (Hebrews 1:10–12)
Isaiah said (Isaiah 7:14)	The Lord spoke by the prophet (Matthew 1:22–23)
Hosea said (Hosea 11:1)	The Lord spoke by the prophet (Matthew 2:15)
Eliphaz's words (Job 5:13)	God's Word (1 Corinthians 3:19)

Acts 1:16 is an excellent example. There we read, "Men and brethren, this scripture must needs have been fulfilled, which *the Holy Ghost by the mouth of David spake* before concerning Judas, which was guide to them that took Jesus" (emphasis added). Likewise, we read in Acts 4:2–25: "When they heard that, they lifted up their voice to God with one accord, and said, *Lord, thou art God,* which hast made heaven, and earth, and the sea, and all that in them is: *Who by the mouth of thy servant David hast said,* Why did the heathen rage, and the people imagine vain things?" (emphasis added). And again, we read in Acts 28:25: "When they agreed not among themselves, they departed, after that Paul had spoken one word, *Well spake the Holy Ghost by Isaiah the prophet unto our fathers"* (emphasis added).

God's Words in the Mouths of the Prophets

In 2 Samuel 23:2 we read the following words from the mouth of David: "The Spirit of the LORD spake by me, and his word was in my tongue." Here is a clear reference to a human being used as a mouthpiece for the spirit of God. Similarly, we read in Isaiah 59:21, "As for me, this is my covenant with them, saith the LORD; *My spirit that is upon thee, and my words which I have put in thy mouth . . ."* (emphasis added). Though God used people in the process of communicating His words, it is clear that the Holy Spirit was in charge of the process so that no human error or opinion entered into the picture.

Turning to Jeremiah 1:9 we read, "The LORD put forth his hand, and touched my mouth. And the LORD said unto me, Behold, I have put my words in thy mouth." Again, we see that God is in control of the process of communicating His word to man.

Speaking of the Old Testament prophets in general, Zechariah 7:12 tells us, "Yea, they made their hearts as an adamant stone, lest they should hear the law, and *the words which the LORD of hosts hath sent in his spirit by the former prophets:* therefore came a great wrath from the LORD of hosts" (emphasis added).

Inspiration in the New Testament

Jesus promised His followers that the Holy Spirit would work through them to provide an accurate recounting of the events of His life (John 14:26). And because of this, you and I can trust the Bible as the Word of God. The Holy Spirit superintended the process from beginning to end. Let's look at more details of this doctrine in the New Testament.

The New Testament Books Are "Scripture"

2 Timothy 3:16. Here we read that "all scripture is given by inspiration of God, and is profitable for doctrine, for reproof, for correction, for instruction in righteousness."

When Paul said that "all scripture" is inspired, did he have in mind just the Old Testament (which is a common New Testament usage of the word "scripture"), or did he have a larger grouping in mind—a grouping that included some New Testament books?* This is an important question, and we think the latter option is the case for at least two reasons:

1. The apostle Paul had already described a specific New Testament book as "scripture" in his first letter to Timothy (*see* 1 Timothy 5:18, where the Gospel of Luke is called Scripture). It therefore makes sense that when Paul used the term "scripture" in his second letter to Timothy, he was thinking not just of Old Testament books but also of New Testament books that had been written up to that time.

2. The apostle Peter uses the same Greek word for "scripture" to describe the writings of the apostle Paul (2 Peter 3:16).

These observations help us to realize that by the time 2 Timothy 3:16 was written, all of the New Testament books had already been written except for 2 Peter, Hebrews, Jude, and the apostle John's writings. In view of this, Paul was surely including these books in the phrase "*all Scripture* is given by inspiration" in 2 Timothy 3:16 (emphasis added). And since the remaining books were later acknowledged as belonging to the canon of Scripture, we may safely say that 2 Timothy 3:16 speaks about all 66 books of the Bible.

Now, the word "inspiration" in 2 Timothy 3:16 comes from a Greek word meaning "God-breathed." The Greek form is *passive*. This means the Bible is the *result* of the "breath of God." If the word form were *active,* then the verse would be saying that all the Bible breathes or exudes God.

---

*For explanations as to why the Book of Mormon is not true revelation and is not Scripture, see chapters 4–6 of this book.

But here we are told that God *breathed out* something—namely, the Scripture. The Bible, then, originated from God.

1 Timothy 5:18. Here, the apostle Paul joins an Old Testament verse and a New Testament verse and calls them *both* (collectively) Scripture (Deuteronomy 25:4 and Luke 10:7). It is not unusual that—in the context of first-century Judaism—an Old Testament passage was called Scripture in the New Testament. But it is highly significant that a New Testament verse was called Scripture so soon after it was written.[9]

Only three to six years had elapsed between the time Luke was written and 1 Timothy was written (Luke is dated around A.D. 60; 1 Timothy is dated around A.D. 63). Yet, despite this, Paul does not hesitate to place Luke on the same level as the Old Testament (the book of Deuteronomy).

We must also note that Jesus Christ consistently emphasized His very high view of Scripture. You'll find it worthwhile to look up the passages in the following chart and even commit some of them to memory.

JESUS' VIEW OF THE BIBLE

Divine Inspiration	Matthew 22:43
Indestructibility	Matthew 5:17–18
Infallibility	John 10:35
Final Authority	Matthew 4:4,7,10
Historicity	Matthew 12:40; 24:37
Scientific Accuracy	Matthew 19:2–5
Factual Inerrancy	John 17:17
Christ-Centered Unity	Luke 24:27; John 5:39
Spiritual Clarity	Luke 24:25
Faith and Life Sufficiency	Luke 16:31 [10]

New Testament Claims About Scripture's Origin

1 Corinthians 2:13. The apostle Paul said he spoke "not in the words which man's wisdom teacheth, but which the Holy Ghost teacheth; comparing spiritual things with spiritual."

In this passage Paul (who wrote a large portion of the New Testament) affirms that his words were authoritative because they were rooted not in fallible man but infallible God (the Holy Spirit). The words were *taught* by the Holy Spirit. The Spirit here is the Spirit of *truth,* who was promised to the apostles to teach and guide them into all the *truth* (*see* John 16:13).

1 Corinthians 14:37. In this verse Paul says, "If any man think himself to be a prophet, or spiritual, let him acknowledge that the things that I write unto you are the commandments of the Lord." Paul's writings have divine authority because they are "commandments of the Lord," not the words of fallen man.

1 Thessalonians 2:13. Paul says, "For this cause also thank we God without ceasing, because, when ye received the word of God which ye heard of us, ye received it not as the word of men, but as it is in truth, the word of God, which effectually worketh also in you that believe."

Again, the reason that Paul's words were authoritative is that they were rooted in God, not in man. God used Paul as His instrument to communicate *His* word to man. Regarding this, note the following summary formulated by the Synod of the Christian Reformed Church in 1961:

> It is significant that Paul, while holding to the view of a canon of God-breathed writings which constitute "the oracles of God," claims for his own teaching, either oral or written, equal status. The word that he preached was not "the word of men" but "the word of God" (1 Thess. 2:13). That which he wrote was "the commandment of the Lord" (1 Cor. 14:37). He that does not obey the writing of the apostle is to be disciplined (2 Thess. 3:14). If any man preach or teach any other gospel than that which Paul

proclaimed, he is to be accursed (Gal. 1:8-9). When Paul speaks as an apostle of Jesus Christ to the churches it is "Christ that speaketh" in him (2 Cor. 13:3). Paul did not learn his gospel at the feet of men but rather received it "through revelations of Jesus Christ," Gal. 1:12, some of which were "exceeding great" (2 Cor. 12:7).[11]

Fulfilled Prophecy: A Proof of Divine Inspiration

From the book of Genesis to the book of Malachi, the Old Testament abounds with anticipations of the coming Messiah. Numerous predictions—fulfilled to the "crossing of the t" and the "dotting of the i" in the New Testament—relate to His birth, life, ministry, death, resurrection, and glory. These fulfilled prophecies constitute a powerful apologetic for the inspiration of Scripture.*

The New Testament writers often pointed to how Christ was the specific fulfillment of a messianic prophecy in the Old Testament. Below is a sampling of these prophecies.

MESSIANIC PROPHECIES FULFILLED BY JESUS CHRIST

Topic	Old Testament (Prophecy)	New Testament (Fulfillment in Christ)
Seed of woman	Genesis 3:15	Galatians 4:4
Line of Abraham	Genesis 12:2	Matthew 1:1
Line of Jacob	Numbers 24:17	Luke 3:23,34
Line of Judah	Genesis 49:10	Matthew 1:2
Line of Jesse	Isaiah 11:1	Luke 3:23,32

---

* Of course, Mormons will try to argue that the Book of Mormon is a fulfillment of Bible prophecy. *See* chapter 5 of this book for information on how to respond to this claim.

Line of David	2 Samuel 7:12–16	Matthew 1:1
Virgin birth	Isaiah 7:14	Matthew 1:23
Birthplace: Bethlehem	Micah 5:2	Matthew 2:6
Forerunner: John	Isaiah 40:3; Malachi 3:1	Matthew 3:3
Escape into Egypt	Hosea 11:1	Matthew 2:14
Herod kills children	Jeremiah 31:15	Matthew 2:16
King	Psalm 2:6	Matthew 21:5
Prophet	Deuteronomy 18:15–18	Acts 3:22–23
Priest	Psalm 110:4	Hebrews 5:6–10
Judge	Isaiah 33:22	John 5:30
Called "Lord"	Psalm 110:1	Luke 2:11
Called "Immanuel"	Isaiah 7:14	Matthew 1:23
Anointed by Holy Spirit	Isaiah 11:2	Matthew 3:16–17
Zeal for God	Psalm 69:9	John 2:15–17
Ministry in Galilee	Isaiah 9:1–2	Matthew 4:12–16
Ministry of miracles	Isaiah 35:5–6	Matthew 9:35
Bore world's sins	Psalm 22:1	Matthew 27:46
Ridiculed	Psalm 22:7–8	Matthew 27:39,43
Stumbling stone to Jew	Psalm 118:22	1 Peter 2:7
Rejected by own people	Isaiah 53:3	John 7:5,48
Light to Gentiles	Isaiah 60:3	Acts 13:47–48
Taught parables	Psalm 78:2	Matthew 13:34
Cleansed the Temple	Malachi 3:1	Matthew 21:12

Sold for 30 shekels	Zechariah 11:12	Matthew 26:15
Forsaken by disciples	Zechariah 13:7	Mark 14:50
Silent before accusers	Isaiah 53:7	Matthew 27:12–19
Hands and feet pierced	Psalm 22:16	John 20:25
Heart broken	Psalm 22:14	John 19:34
Crucified with thieves	Isaiah 53:12	Matthew 27:38
No bones broken	Psalm 22:17	John 19:33–36
Soldiers gambled	Psalm 22:18	John 19:24
Suffered thirst on cross	Psalm 69:21	John 19:28
Vinegar offered	Psalm 69:21	Matthew 27:34
Christ's prayer	Psalm 22:24	Matthew 26:39
Disfigured	Isaiah 52:14	John 19:1
Scourging and death	Isaiah 53:5	John 19:1,18
His "forsaken" cry	Psalm 22:1	Matthew 27:46
Committed self to God	Psalm 31:5	Luke 23:46
Rich man's tomb	Isaiah 53:9	Matthew 27:57–60
Resurrection	Psalm 16:10; 22:22	Matthew 28:6
Ascension	Psalm 68:18	Luke 24:50–53
Right hand of God	Psalm 110:1	Hebrews 1:3

It is only logical to conclude that if these prophecies were written many hundreds of years before they were fulfilled—and if they could never have been foreseen and depended upon factors outside human control for their fulfillment—and if *all* of these prophecies were, in fact, fulfilled correctly—then clearly the Scriptures are divine in origin and not manmade.

Archaeological Support for the Bible

Unlike the Book of Mormon, the Bible's accuracy and reliability has been proved and verified over and over again by archaeological finds produced by both believing *and* nonbelieving scholars and scientists. This includes verification for numerous customs, places, names, and events mentioned in the Bible. [12] Nelson Glueck, a specialist in ancient literature, said, "It can be stated categorically that no archaeological discovery has ever controverted a biblical reference." [13]

As noted in an earlier chapter, the Book of Mormon makes reference to numerous places, cities, and sites, and not a single one has ever—we repeat, *ever*—been located. This is completely unlike the situation with the Bible. Indeed, Bible scholar Donald J. Wiseman said, "The geography of Bible lands and visible remains of antiquity were gradually recorded until today more than 25,000 sites within this region and dating to Old Testament times, in their broadest sense, have been located. . . ." [14] Twenty-five thousand sites is a lot! Well-known Bible scholar William F. Albright said, "Discovery after discovery has established the accuracy of innumerable details, and has brought increased recognition of the value of the Bible as a source of history." [15] Archaeological studies have been a true friend to the Christian Bible, but are a total nightmare to the Book of Mormon (*see* chapter 6).

Early Literary Evidence in Support of the Bible

Support for the authenticity and reliability of the New Testament Gospels is found in many, many quotations from both Christian *and* secular sources that date close to the time of Christ.

Christian Sources

Christian leaders who lived between A.D. 95 and 170 consistently pointed to the reliability of the New Testament Gospels. For example:

1. *Clement* was a leading elder in the church at Rome. In his epistle to the Corinthians (c. A.D. 95), he cites portions of Matthew, Mark, and Luke, and introduces them as the actual words of Jesus. He speaks of these citations as a unit, using the singular *Gospel* to refer to their combined testimony.[16]

2. *Papias,* the bishop of Hierapolis in Phrygia and author of *Exposition of Oracles of the Lord* (c. A.D. 130), cites the Gospels of Matthew, Mark, Luke, and John, presumably as canonical. He specifically refers to John's Gospel as containing the words of Jesus.[17]

3. *Justin Martyr,* the foremost apologist of the second century (A.D. 140), considered all four Gospels to be Scripture.[18]

4. *The Didache,* an ancient manual of Christianity that dates between the end of the first century and the beginning of the second century, cites portions of the three synoptic Gospels and refers to them as the words of Jesus. This manual quotes extensively from Matthew's Gospel.[19]

5. *Polycarp,* a disciple of the apostle John, quotes portions of Matthew, Mark, and Luke, and refers to them as the words of Jesus (c. A.D. 150).[20]

6. *Irenaeus,* a disciple of Polycarp (c. A.D. 170), quoted from 23 of the 27 New Testament books, omitting only Philemon, James, 2 Peter, and 3 John.[21]

Clearly, not only were Matthew, Mark, Luke, and John accepted as Scripture as they were written (*see* 1 Timothy 5:18; 2 Peter 3:16), there are also many early sources dating between A.D. 95 and 150 that refer to these Gospels as containing the actual words of Christ. History, then, is on the side of the New Testament Gospels.

Non-Christian Sources

Besides Christian witnesses in the early centuries of Christianity, there were also non-Christian sources who were alive near the time of Christ and who corroborate Christ as a historical figure. For example, Jewish historian Flavius Josephus (born A.D. 37) made reference to "Jesus, the so-called Christ." Roman historian Cornelius Tacitus (born A.D. 52) wrote of "Christus," who was "put to death by Pontius Pilate." Pliny the Younger (A.D. 112) spoke of the "trouble-some sect of Christians." Suetonius (A.D. 120) spoke of disturbances over "Chrestus" (Christ).[22] All in all, the "external evidence" for the reliability of the Bible is overwhelming.

The Divine Authority of the Bible

The authority of the Bible is a natural outgrowth of the Bible as *inspired revelation from God*. As Robert Lightner says,

> When the questions of revelation and inspiration with regard to the Bible have been answered, the issue of authority will have been settled. In other words, how one views revelation and inspiration will determine how he views the Bible's authority. . . . Since the written revelation from God has been recorded under the Spirit's superintendence and is "the very breath of God," it is therefore authoritative—just as authoritative as the One who gave it.[23]

According to the International Council on Biblical Inerrancy, "the authority of Scripture cannot be separated from the authority of God. Whatever the Bible affirms, God affirms. And what the Bible affirms (or denies), it affirms (or denies) with the very authority of God."[24] Theologian Rene Pache agrees, noting that "if God entirely inspired Scripture (as we have seen that He did), then Scripture is vested with His authority."[25]

The Mormon must come to see that the Bible is, in fact, the Word of God and therefore carries the authority *of God* over his or her feelings, any other purported scripture, and indeed, his or her very life. For the Mormon (or anyone else) to disdain the Bible is equivalent to disdaining God Himself.

9

Manuscript Support for the Bible's Reliability

O ne of the most significant contrasts between the Book of Mormon and the Bible is that the Book of Mormon lacks any manuscript evidence whatsoever, and the Bible is supported by virtually thousands upon thousands of reliable manuscripts. It is therefore the height of folly for Mormons to suggest that the Book of Mormon is more reliable than the Bible.

It is beyond the scope of this chapter to present a full treatise on the manuscript support for the Bible's reliability. Other good sources are available for this.[1] However, what follows in this chapter will help you show the Mormon that the Bible has solid objective evidence on its side, whereas the Book of Mormon does not.

Manuscript Evidence for the New Testament

Unlike the Book of Mormon's complete lack of manuscript evidence, there are more than 24,000 partial and complete manuscript copies of the New Testament. These manuscript copies are very ancient and they are available for inspection *now.* There are also some 86,000 quotations of the New

Testement from the early church fathers* and several thousand lectionaries (church-service books containing Scripture quotations used in the early centuries of Christianity).[2] The bottom line is this: *The New Testament has an overwhelming amount of evidence supporting its reliability.*

____ *Ask* . . . _____

- There are 24,000 partial and complete manuscript copies of the New Testament. Is there even a single extant plate supporting the Book of Mormon?

- What do you think this says about the Bible as opposed to the Book of Mormon?

The Variants in the Manuscripts Are Minimal

In the many thousands of manuscript copies we possess of the New Testament, scholars have discovered that there are some 150,000 "variants."[3] This may seem like a staggering figure to the uninformed mind. Mormons like to cite such numbers to make it appear that the Bible is untrustworthy.[4] But to those who study the issue, the numbers are not as serious as they may initially appear. Indeed, a look at the hard evidence shows that the New Testament manuscripts are amazingly accurate and trustworthy.

When we assess these 150,000 variants, we discover that 99 percent hold virtually no significance whatsoever.[5] Many of them simply involve a missing letter in a word; some involve reversing the order of two words (such as "Christ Jesus" instead of "Jesus Christ"); some may involve the absence of one or more insignificant words. Ultimately, only about 50 of the variants have any real significance—and even then, *no*

*Men in the early centuries of Christianity who were the orthodox champions of the church and exponents of its faith.

doctrine of the Christian faith or any moral commandment is affected by them.[6]

In *Explaining Inerrancy: A Commentary,* published by the International Council on Biblical Inerrancy, we read the following words about the reliability of the New Testament text:

> For more than ninety-nine percent of the cases the original text can be reconstructed to a practical certainty. Even in the few cases where some perplexity remains, this does not impinge on the meaning of Scripture to the point of clouding a tenet of the faith or a mandate of life. Thus, in the Bible as we have it (and as it is conveyed to us through faithful translations) we do have for practical purposes the very Word of God, inasmuch as the manuscripts do convey to us the complete vital truth of the originals.[7]

By practicing the science of textual criticism—comparing all the available manuscripts with each other—we can determine what the original document said. Perhaps an illustration will help here.

Let us suppose we have five manuscript copies of an original document that no longer exists. Each manuscript copy is different. Our goal is to compare the copies and ascertain what the original said. Here are the five copies:

Manuscript #1:	Jesus Christ is the Savior of the whole world.
Manuscript #2:	Christ Jesus is the Savior of the whole world.
Manuscript #3:	Jesus Christ s the Savior of the whole world.
Manuscript #4:	Jesus Christ is th Savior of the whole world.
Manuscript #5:	Jesus Christ is the Savor of the whole world.

Could you, by comparing the manuscript copies, determine what the original document said . . . with a high degree of certainty that you are correct? Of course you could.

This illustration may be overly simplistic, but a great majority of the 150,000 variants are solved by using this methodology. By comparing the various manuscripts, all of which contain *very minor* differences like the above, it becomes fairly clear what the original must have said. As Anthony Hoekema has pointed out, "most of the manuscript variations concern matters of spelling, word order, tenses, and the like; no single doctrine is affected by them in any way."[8]

We must also emphasize that the enormous number of manuscripts we possess greatly narrows the margin of doubt regarding what the original biblical document said. As New Testament scholar F.F. Bruce says, "If the number of [manuscripts] increases the number of scribal errors, it increases proportionately the means of correcting such errors, so that the margin of doubt left in the process of recovering the exact original wording is not so large as might be feared; it is in truth remarkably small."[9]

Ask . . .

- Would it surprise you to learn that—according to Bible scholars—out of the 150,000 variations that exist in the thousands of New Testament manuscripts, only about 50 have any real significance, and even those don't affect a single doctrine?

- Would you mind if I gave you an illustration to demonstrate the insignificance of most of the variations?

  (If the Mormon agrees, then go over the illustration mentioned above: "Jesus Christ is the Savior of the whole world." Then ask:)

- Since scholars tell us that 99 percent of the variations are just like this, do you think it's possible that Mormon leaders have overexaggerated their claims about the unreliability of the New Testament?

The New Testament Versus Other Ancient Books

By comparing the manuscript support for the Bible with manuscript support for other ancient documents and books, it becomes overwhelmingly clear that no other ancient piece of literature can stand up to the Bible. Manuscript support for the Bible is unparalleled!

Norman Geisler tells us, "There are more [New Testament] manuscripts copied with greater accuracy and earlier dating than for any secular classic from antiquity."[10] Rene Pache adds, "The historical books of antiquity have a documentation infinitely less solid."[11] Dr. Benjamin Warfield concludes, "If we compare the present state of the text of the New Testament with that of no matter what other ancient work, we must . . . declare it marvelously exact."[12]

COMPARISON OF ANCIENT TEXTS [13]

Ancient Author	Date Written	Earliest Copy	Number of Copies	Accuracy of Copies
Caesar	1st cent. B.C.	A.D. 900	10	———
Livy	1st cent. B.C.	———	20	———
Tacitus	c. A.D. 100	A.D. 1100	20	———
Thucydides	5th cent. B.C.	A.D. 900	8	———
Herodotus	5th cent. B.C.	A.D. 900	8	———
Demosthenes	4th cent. B.C.	A.D. 1100	200	———
Mahabharata	———	———	———	90%
Homer	9th cent. B.C.	———	643	95%
New Testament	1st cent. A.D. (A.D. 50–100)	2nd cent. A.D. (c. A.D. 130)	5,000	99+%

In regard to the chart on the previous page, Norman Geisler makes three key observations for our consideration:

(1) No other book is even a close second to the Bible on either the *number* or early dating of the copies. The average secular work from antiquity survives on only a handful of manuscripts; the New Testament boasts thousands. (2) The average *gap* between the original composition and the earliest copy is over 1,000 years for other books. The New Testament, however, has a fragment within one generation from its original composition, whole books within about 100 years from the time of the autograph [original manuscript], most of the New Testament in less than 200 years, and the entire New Testament within 250 years from the date of its completion. (3) The degree of *accuracy* of the copies is greater for the New Testament than for other books that can be compared. Most books do not survive with enough manuscripts that make comparison possible. [14]

From this documentary evidence, then, we can see that the New Testament writings are superior to comparable ancient writings. "The records for the New Testament are vastly more abundant, clearly more ancient, and considerably more accurate in their text." [15]

_____ *Ask . . .* _____

- The Bible has more manuscript support than any other ancient document. What does this say to you?

- Is it not clear that the Bible is the best-attested ancient piece of literature in existence anywhere?

- Did you know that—according to scholars—the time span between the writing of the original biblical documents and the manuscript copies was very short? What does this say to you?

The Church Fathers and the New Testament

As noted at the beginning of this chapter, in addition to the many thousands of New Testament manuscripts, there are over 86,000 quotations of the New Testament in the works of the early church fathers. There are also New Testament quotations in thousands of early church lectionaries (worship books).

Dan Story, in his excellent book *Defending Your Faith,* is right when he says that "there are enough quotations from the early church fathers that even if we did not have a single copy of the Bible, scholars could still reconstruct all but 11 verses of the entire New Testament from material written within 150 to 200 years from the time of Christ." [16] Consider the following chart, which includes just a sampling of the early church fathers.

EARLY PATRISTIC QUOTATIONS OF THE NEW TESTAMENT [17]

Writer	Gospels	Acts	Pauline Epistles	General Epistles	Revelation	Totals
Justin Martyr	268	10	43	6	3	330
Irenaeus	1,038	194	499	23	65	1,819
Clement Alexandria	1,017	44	1,127	207	11	2,406
Origen	9,231	349	7,778	399	165	17,922
Tertullian	3,822	502	2,609	120	205	7,258
Hippolytus	734	42	387	27	188	1,378
Eusebius	3,258	211	1,592	88	27	5,176
Grand Totals	19,368	1,352	14,035	870	664	36,289

As this chart indicates, we have over 36,000 quotations from a mere seven church fathers alone. Can any other ancient document boast of such widespread and reliable support?

___ *Ask* . . . ___

- Did you know that there are enough quotations from the early church fathers that even if we did not have a single manuscript copy of the Bible, scholars could reconstruct all but 11 verses of the entire New Testament?

Manuscript Evidence for the Old Testament

The Dead Sea Scrolls prove the accuracy of the transmission of the Bible. In fact, in these scrolls discovered at Qumran in 1947, we have Old Testament manuscripts that were written about 1,000 years earlier (150 B.C.) than the previous manuscripts we possessed (which dated to A.D. 900).[18] What's amazing is that when we compare the two sets of manuscripts, it is clear that they are essentially the same, with very few changes. The fact that manuscripts separated by 1,000 years are essentially the same indicates the incredible accuracy of the Old Testament's manuscript transmission.

One example of how the Dead Sea Scrolls compare to other manuscripts is the book of Isaiah. Dr. Gleason Archer said, "Even though the two copies of Isaiah discovered in Qumran Cave 1 near the Dead Sea in 1947 were a thousand years earlier than the oldest dated manuscript previously known (A.D. 980), they proved to be *word for word identical* with our standard Hebrew Bible in more than 95 percent of the text. The 5 percent of variation consisted chiefly of obvious slips of the pen and variations in spelling"[19] (emphasis added).

Apologist Dan Story concludes, "From manuscript discoveries like the Dead Sea Scrolls, Christians have undeniable evidence that today's Old Testament Scripture, for all practical purposes, is exactly the same as it was when originally inspired by God and recorded in the Bible."[20] Combine this with the massive amount of manuscript evidence we have for the New Testament, and it is clear that the Christian Bible—unlike the Book of Mormon—is a trustworthy and reliable book.

It is ironic to note that some Mormons had thought they would find support for the Book of Mormon in the Dead Sea Scrolls. However, not only did the Dead Sea Scrolls *not* restore the allegedly lost "plain and precious things" to the Bible (as they were hoping), the scrolls also added weighty support for the reliability and authenticity of the Bible.[21]

Jerald and Sandra Tanner make this observation:

The Dead Sea Scrolls . . . should provide a great deal of evidence for the Book of Mormon if it is really an ancient record. The Isaiah scroll found at Qumran Cave 1 should have caused a great deal of joy among Mormon scholars, for here is a manuscript of Isaiah which is hundreds of years older than any manuscript previously known. Surely, if the Book of Mormon were true, this manuscript would be filled with evidence to support the text of Isaiah in the Book of Mormon and thus prove that Joseph Smith was a prophet of God. Instead of proving the Book of Mormon, however, it has turned out to be a great disappointment to Mormon scholars.[22]

The Dead Sea Scrolls prove that the copyists of biblical manuscripts took great care in going about their work. "These copyists knew they were duplicating God's Word, so they went to incredible lengths to prevent error from creeping into their work . . . the scribes carefully counted every line, word, syllable, and letter to ensure accuracy."[23]

____ *Ask . . .* ____

- Did you know that the Dead Sea Scrolls, discovered in 1947 at Qumran, contained a copy of almost every Old Testament book?

- Did you know that the Old Testament manuscripts discovered at Qumran date 1,000 years earlier than the previous manuscripts we possessed?

- Did you know that when scholars compared the two sets of manuscripts—one set dating around A.D. 900, the other around 150 B.C.—they found almost no differences?

- What does this tell you about the reliability of how the biblical manuscripts were transmitted?

God's Preservation of the Bible

The Westminster Confession declares, "The Old Testament in Hebrew and the New Testament in Greek, being immediately inspired by God and, by His singular care and providence *kept pure in all ages,* are therefore authentical; so in all controversies of religion, the Church is finally to appeal unto them"[24] (emphasis added).

The Westminster Confession* makes an important point here: The God who had the power and sovereign control to *inspire* the Scriptures is surely going to continue to exercise His power and sovereign control in the *preservation* of Scripture.

One vivid example of how God has preserved the Scriptures appears in the text of the New Testament. Christ Himself had full confidence that the Old Testament passages He

---

* A systematic exposition of Calvinist orthodoxy formulated in A.D. 1646.

quoted had been faithfully preserved through the centuries. Greg L. Bahnsen comments on this:

> Because Christ raised no doubts about the adequacy of the Scripture as His contemporaries knew them, we can safely assume that the first-century text of the Old Testament was a wholly adequate representation of the divine word originally given. Jesus regarded the extant copies of His day as so approximate to the originals in their message that He appealed to those copies as authoritative. The respect that Jesus and His apostles held for the extant Old Testament text is, at base, an expression of the confidence in God's providential preservation of the copies and translations as substantially identical with the inspired originals. [25]

Hence, Bahnsen concludes, "the Bible itself indicates that copies can *faithfully reflect the original text* and therefore function authoritatively" [26] (emphasis added).

_____ *Ask* . . . _____

- Christ Himself used manuscript copies of the Old Testament—copies that were far removed from the original biblical documents. Yet He clearly trusted their reliability. What does this tell you about Christ's attitude toward manuscript copies?

- Does this not indicate that manuscript copies can faithfully reflect the original text and therefore function authoritatively?

10

Rightly Interpreting the Bible

In your discussions with Mormons, you will want to demonstrate 1) the inspiration, inerrancy, and authority of the Bible, 2) the reliable transmission of the Bible through biblical manuscripts, 3) problems with the Book of Mormon, *and* 4) how to rightly interpret the Bible. In this chapter, we will briefly look at the proper method for interpreting the Bible.*

The word *method* comes from the Greek word *methodos,* which means "a way or path of transit." Methodology in Bible study is therefore concerned with "the proper path to be taken in order to arrive at Scriptural truth."[1] This clearly implies that people can take *improper* paths. The errant Bible interpretations offered by the Mormon church are an illustration of that.

---

* For a more detailed treatment on interpreting the Bible, see Robert A. Traina, *Methodical Bible Study* (Wilmore, KY: Asbury Theological Seminary, 1952); Norman L. Geisler, *Explaining Hermeneutics: A Commentary,* with Exposition by J.I. Packer (Oakland, CA: International Council on Biblical Inerrancy, 1983); and Bernard Ramm, *Protestant Bible Interpretation* (Grand Rapids, MI: Baker Book House, 1978).

Of course, proper methodology is essential to many fields of endeavor. A heart surgeon does not perform open heart-surgery without following proper, objective methodology. (Would you trust a heart surgeon to operate on you if he said he intended to discard objective methodology and instead opt for the subjective approach of cutting you where he *feels* like cutting you?)

Improper methodology in interpreting Scripture is nothing new. Even in New Testament times, the apostle Peter warned that there were teachings in the inspired writings of Paul "which they that are unlearned and unstable wrest [distort], as they do also the other scriptures, unto their own destruction" (2 Peter 3:16, insert added). This verse tells us that mishandling the Word of God is dangerous. Indeed, mishandling the Bible is a path to destruction. Such is the case with the Mormon church: If a person follows its biblical interpretations, he is on the road to destruction—*eternal* destruction.

Contrary to the practices of some false teachers in Corinth, the apostle Paul handled the Word of God faithfully (2 Corinthians 4:2). Paul admonished young Timothy to follow his example: "Study to show thyself approved unto God, a workman that needeth not to be ashamed, *rightly dividing the word of truth*" (2 Timothy 2:15, emphasis added).

God Created Language for a Purpose

A plain reading of Genesis indicates that when God created Adam in His own rational image (Genesis 1:26), He gave Adam the gift of intelligible speech. This enabled Adam to communicate objectively with his creator (and with other human beings) via sharable linguistic symbols called words. Indeed, God sovereignly chose to use human language as a medium of revelational communication.[2]

If the primary purpose of God's gift of language was to make it possible for Him to communicate with human beings, then we can conclude that He would reveal Himself via language and expect man to accept His words in a literal, normal, and plain sense. This view of language is a prerequisite to understanding not only God's spoken word but His written Word (Scripture) as well.

The Bible as a body of literature exists because human beings need to know certain spiritual truths that they cannot attain by themselves. Thus these truths must come to them from without—that is, via objective, special revelation from God (Deuteronomy 29:29). And the only way to understand these revelations is if we interpret the words of Scripture according to God's original design for language—that is, according to the ordinary, plain, literal sense of each word.

The Keys to Interpreting Scripture

Seeking the Author's Intended Meaning

Instead of superimposing a meaning on the biblical text, the objective interpreter seeks to discover the author's intended meaning (the only *true* meaning). We must recognize that the meaning of a passage is fixed by the author and is not subject to alteration by readers. Meaning is *determined* by the author; it is *discovered* by readers.[3]

Our goal must be *exegesis* (drawing the meaning out of the text) and not *eisogesis* (superimposing a meaning onto the text). By using eisogesis instead of exegesis, a Marxist interpreter could, for example, so skew the meaning of the U.S. Constitution that it ends up reading like a socialistic document. Mormon teachers have done the same type of thing with the Holy Scripture. They so skew the meaning of the biblical text that it comes out saying something entirely different than what was intended by the author. (The book you are holding in your hands is filled with examples!)

Only by objective methodology can we bridge the gap between our minds and the minds of the biblical writers. Indeed, our method of interpreting Scripture is valid or invalid to the extent that it really unfolds the meaning a statement had for the author and the first hearers or readers.

> *For a good illustration of how important it is to seek the author's intended meaning, see the discussion on Revelation 14:6 in chapter 3.*

Examining the Full Context

> A woman entered the Democratic primary for governor of the state of Texas. She was convinced that the Bible had told her she would win the nomination. When she received the official list of names from the primary she saw her name printed last. Then she read in her Bible, "Many that are first will be last, and the last first" (Matthew 19:30). On the basis of that verse she thought God was telling her she would win. But she lost.[4]

This amusing story, told by theologian Paul Enns, illustrates the need for interpreting Scripture in its proper context. Taken out of context, the Scriptures can be twisted to say just about anything.

Seeking the biblical author's intended meaning necessitates interpreting Bible verses *in context*. Every word in the Bible is part of a verse, and every verse is part of a paragraph, and every paragraph is part of a book, and every book is part of the whole of Scripture.[5]

No verse of Scripture can be divorced from the verses around it. Interpreting a verse apart from its context is like trying to analyze a Rembrandt painting by looking at only a single square inch of the canvas, or trying to analyze Handel's "Messiah" by listening to a few short notes. The context is absolutely critical to properly interpreting Bible verses. (You will notice in this book that most Mormon misinterpretations of Scripture are corrected by consulting the context.)

In interpreting Scripture, there is both an immediate context and a broader context. The immediate context of a verse is the paragraph (or paragraphs) of the biblical book in question. The immediate context should *always* be consulted when interpreting Bible verses.

The broader context is the whole of Scripture. As Bernard Ramm has noted, "the entire Holy Scripture is the context and guide for understanding the particular passages of Scripture."[6] We must keep in mind that the interpretation of a specific passage must not contradict the total teaching of Scripture. Individual verses do not exist as isolated fragments, but as parts of a whole. The exposition of these verses, therefore, must involve exhibiting them in right relation both to the whole and to each other. *Scripture interprets Scripture.* As J.I. Packer says, "if we would understand the parts, our wisest course is to get to know the whole."[7]

The Westminster Confession likewise affirms, "The infallible rule of interpretation of Scripture is *the Scripture itself;* therefore, when there is a question about the true and full sense of any Scripture, it must be searched and known by other places that speak more clearly"[8] (emphasis added).

The International Council on Biblical Inerrancy explains it this way: "One passage sheds light on another. Hence the first commentary the interpreter should consult on a passage is what the rest of Scripture may say on that text."[9] Indeed, "we should look to Scripture to interpret Scripture and deny as a matter of method that particular texts, all of which have the one Holy Spirit as their source, can be genuinely discrepant with each other."[10]

For an illustration of how important it is to consult the context, see the discussion on Isaiah 29:1–4 in chapter 5.

Taking into Account Historical Considerations

Historical considerations are especially important in properly interpreting the Word of God. The Christian faith is based on historical fact. Indeed, Christianity rests on the foundation of the historical Jesus whose earthly life represents God's full and objective self-communication to humankind (John 1:18).

Jesus was *seen* and *heard* by human beings as God's ultimate revelation (1 John 1:1–3). This is why He could forcefully claim, "If ye had known me, ye should have known my Father also" (John 14:7).

When the apostle Paul spoke with the religious men of Athens, he affirmed that the reality of the future judgment of all humanity rests on the objective, historical evidence for the resurrection of Jesus (Acts 17:16f.). This evidence is recorded for us in the New Testament Gospels—documents that are based on eyewitness testimony and written very close in time to the events that they report. Based on how people respond to God's objective, historical revelation contained in Scripture, they will spend eternity in a real heaven or a real hell.

For an illustration of the importance of historical considerations, see the discussion on Acts 20:29–31 in chapter 3.

Making Correct Genre Judgments

A literal approach to Scripture recognizes that the Bible contains a variety of literary genres, each of which has certain characteristics we must recognize before we can interpret the text properly. Biblical genres include the historical (for example, Acts), the dramatic epic (Job), poetry (Psalms), wise sayings (Proverbs), and apocalyptic writings (Revelation).

Making an incorrect genre judgment will lead a person far astray when interpreting Scripture. A parable should not be treated as history, nor should poetry or apocalyptic literature (both of which contain many symbols) be treated as straightforward narrative. The wise interpreter allows his knowledge of genres to control how he approaches each individual biblical text. In this way, he can accurately determine what the biblical author intended to communicate to the reader.[11]

Now, even though the Bible contains a variety of literary genres and many figures of speech, the biblical authors *most often* employed literal statements to convey their ideas. And where they used a literal means to express their ideas, the Bible expositor must employ a corresponding means to explain those ideas—namely, a literal approach. A literal method of interpreting Scripture gives to each word in the text the same basic meaning it would have in normal, ordinary, customary usage—whether employed in writing, speaking, or thinking. Without such a method, communication between God and man is impossible.

> *For an illustration showing the importance of making a correct genre judgment, see the discussion of Psalm 82:1,6 in chapter 14. (The Psalms often use metaphors. In this passage, the word "god" is used metaphorically.)*

Interpreting the Old Testament in Light of the New Testament

God gave revelation to humankind *progressively* throughout Old and New Testament times. He didn't just give His entire revelation for all time to our first parents, Adam and Eve, or to Moses, the Lawgiver. Rather, as time went on—as the centuries slowly passed—God progressively gave more and more revelation so that by the time the New Testament was complete, He had told us everything He wanted us to know.*

In view of this, a key interpretive principle is that we should always interpret the Old Testament according to the

---

*You must be careful here. The Mormon may try to turn the tables on you and attempt to use the argument for "progressive revelation" to support the idea of "continuing revelations" from God. See chapter 4 for arguments that refute continuing revelations.

greater light of the New Testament. Theologian Benjamin Warfield illustrates this principle:

> The Old Testament may be likened to a chamber richly furnished but dimly lighted; the introduction of light brings into it nothing which was not in it before; but it brings out into clearer view much of what is in it but was only dimly or even not at all perceived before.... The Old Testament revelation of God is not corrected by the fuller revelation which follows it, but only perfected, extended and enlarged. [12]

The Old Testament, then, is much clearer when approached through the lens of the New Testament.

For an illustration demonstrating the importance of interpreting the Old Testament according to the greater light of the New Testament, see the discussion of Genesis 14:18 in chapter 12.

Depending on the Holy Spirit

Scripture tells us that we are to rely on the Holy Spirit's illumination to gain insights into the meaning and application of Scripture (John 16:12–15; 1 Corinthians 2:9–11). It is the Holy Spirit's work to throw light upon the Word of God so that the believer can assent to the meaning intended and act on it. [13]

The Holy Spirit, as the "Spirit of truth" (John 16:13), guides us so that "we might know the things that are freely given to us of God" (1 Corinthians 2:12). This is quite logical: Full comprehension of the *Word of God* is impossible without prayerful dependence on the *Spirit of God,* for He who *inspired* the Word (2 Peter 1:21) is also its supreme *interpreter.*

	Interpretation	Illumination
Effort	Work of man	Work of God
Preparation	Academic	Spiritual
Precondition	Open mind	Open heart
Motivation	Curiosity	Obedience
Object	Meaning (What?)	Significance (So what?)
Insight	Intellectual	Spiritual
Errors	Correctable	Not correctable
Results	Knowledge (apprehension of truth)	Wisdom (application of truth) [14]

Illumination is necessary because man's mind has been darkened through sin (Romans 1:21), preventing him from properly understanding God's Word. Human beings cannot understand God's Word apart from God's divine enablement (Ephesians 4:18). [15]

It is beyond the scope of this chapter to provide a full discussion of the Holy Spirit's ministry of illumination. Other good sources are available for this. [16] However, we do want to emphasize that this aspect of the Holy Spirit's ministry operates within the sphere of man's rational capacity, which God Himself gave man (*see* Genesis 2–3). James Sire comments that "illumination comes to the 'minds' of God's people—not to some nonrational faculty like our 'emotions' or our 'feelings' [like a 'burning in the bosom']. To know God's revelation means to use our minds. This makes knowledge something we can share with others, something we can talk about. God's Word is in words with ordinary rational content" [17] (insert added).

Related to this, theologian Roy Zuck reminds us that the Holy Spirit's role in interpretation does not mean interpreters can ignore common sense and logic. Since the Holy Spirit is "the Spirit of truth" (John 14:17; 15:26; 16:13), He does not teach concepts that fail to meet the tests of truth. In other words, "the Holy Spirit does not guide into interpretations that contradict each other or fail to have logical, internal consistency."[18]

We must also keep in mind that the Holy Spirit will never communicate to us any doctrine or meaning of Scripture that is not *contained already in Scripture itself.* The Holy Spirit makes men "wise *up to* what is written, not beyond it."[19] Indeed, "the function of the Spirit is not to communicate *new* truth or to instruct in *matters unknown,* but to illuminate what is revealed *in* Scripture."[20]

Following the Example of Jesus Christ

Jesus consistently interpreted the Old Testament literally, and this includes the Creation account of Adam and Eve (Mark 10:6), Noah's Ark and the flood (Matthew 24:38–39; Luke 17:26–27), Jonah and the great fish (Matthew 12:39–41), Sodom and Gomorrah (Matthew 10:15), and the account of Lot and his wife (Luke 17:28–29). In his book *The Saviour and the Scriptures,* theologian Robert P. Lightner notes—following an exhaustive study—that Jesus' interpretation of Scripture "was always in accord with the grammatical and historical meaning. He understood and appreciated the meaning intended by the writers according to the laws of grammar and rhetoric."[21]

Jesus affirmed the Bible's divine inspiration (Matthew 22:43), its indestructibility (Matthew 5:17–18), its infallibility (John 10:35), its final authority (Matthew 4:4,7,10), its historicity (Matthew 12:40; 24:37), its factual inerrancy (Matthew 22:29–32), and its spiritual clarity (Luke 24:25). Moreover, He emphasized the importance of each word of Scripture (Luke 16:17). Indeed, He sometimes based His argumentation on a single expression of the biblical text (Matthew 22:32,43–45; John 10:34).

Is the Bible Alone Sufficient?

That the average person can understand Scripture without having to rely upon a church (like the Mormon church[22]) for the "authoritative teaching" is evident in the fact that Jesus taught *openly* and *with clarity,* and expected His followers to *understand His meaning.*[23] Recall that following His arrest, Jesus was questioned by the High Priest about His disciples and His teaching. Jesus responded:

> *I spake openly to the world;* I ever taught in the synagogue, and in the temple, whither the Jews always resort; and in secret have I said nothing. Why askest thou me? ask them which heard me, what I have said unto them: behold, *they know what I said* (John 18:20–21, emphasis added).

According to Jesus, those who heard Him could clearly enunciate what He had openly communicated. There were no confusing or obscure meanings in His words that required an "authoritative interpretation" by a (Mormon) church.

Notice what the apostle Paul said about the Scriptures to young Timothy: "From a child thou hast known the holy scriptures, which are able to make thee wise unto salvation through faith which is in Christ Jesus" (2 Timothy 3:15). This verse points to the complete sufficiency of Scripture in the life of a believer.

In Timothy's day, Jewish boys formally began studying the Old Testament Scriptures when they were five years of age. Timothy had been taught the Scriptures by his mother and grandmother beginning at that age. Clearly, 2 Timothy 3:15 indicates that the *Scriptures alone* are sufficient to provide the necessary wisdom that leads to salvation through faith in Christ. The *Scriptures alone* (not the authoritative teaching of the Mormon church) are the source of spiritual knowledge.

Then, 2 Timothy 3:16–17 tells us that *all Scripture* is "profitable for doctrine, for reproof, for correction, for instruction in righteousness: That the man of God may be perfect, throughly furnished unto all good works."* This verse does not say that Scripture *as seen through the lens of the Mormon church* is "profitable for doctrine, for reproof," and so on. It is *Scripture* that does these things. And the reason Scripture can do these things is because all Scripture is inspired by God (verse 16a). The word *inspiration* means "God-breathed." Scripture is sufficient because its source is God.

It is noteworthy that the phrase "throughly furnished" in verse 17 means "complete, capable, fully furnished, proficient in the sense of being able to meet all demands."[24] *Scripture alone* makes a person complete, capable, and proficient. God's Word furnishes all that we must know to become saved and to grow in grace. Dependence on the Mormon church (or any other church) is out of the question.

Correctly Handling the Word of Truth

Jesus said His words lead to eternal life (John 6:63). But for us to receive eternal life through His words, they must be taken as He intended them to be taken. A cultic (Mormon) reinterpretation of Scripture that yields another Jesus and another gospel (2 Corinthians 11:3–4; Galatians 1:6–9) will yield only eternal death (Revelation 20:11–15). Our prayer is that through this chapter and the rest of this book you will become equipped to help the Mormon understand the true Gospel and meet the true Jesus of Scripture.

---

*The Mormon may try to tell you that "all Scripture" includes Mormon latter-day revelations. This is not the case; *see* chapters 5–9 for evidences against the Book of Mormon and evidences for the Bible.

11

The Alleged Migration to Ancient America

Mormons tell us that when God confounded the language of the people at the Tower of Babel, there was a particular group of people—Jared and his brother, with their family and friends—who sought refuge. Jared's brother was "a large and mighty man, and a man highly favored of the Lord." Jared said to his brother: "Cry unto the Lord, that he will not confound us that we may not understand our words."[1] So, the Lord had compassion on them and did not confound their words, but instead led them to cross the great ocean to a promised land that was more choice than any other in all the world. This took place around 2250 B.C.

Following the Lord's instructions, they prepared eight vessels and took with them birds, animals, fish, and bees. Their vessels were blown across the ocean by a fierce wind, and in 344 days they arrived at the promised land—the American continent. God promised that here, He would make them the greatest nation on earth.

After this relatively small group of people arrived, they multiplied exceedingly over all the face of the land. However, disputes—and eventually wars—broke out among the people, and they divided into two nations. Things continued to worsen until eventually *everyone* was killed, down to the last two generals—Coriantumr and Shiz. According to Mormon records, Shiz was killed by Coriantumr, who also died on that very day, "destroyed by the hand of the Lord."[2]

According to the Book of Mormon, there was another great (and more important) migration to America under the leadership of a Jewish prophet named Lehi. Here's how it allegedly came about:

Sometime around 600 B.C., just before the children of Israel were taken captive into Babylon, the Lord gave the prophet Lehi a vision of what was going to happen as a result of the sins of Israel. Lehi went out and preached to the Jews, but they mocked him and sought to take his life. The Lord then spoke to Lehi in a dream and told him to take his family and depart into the wilderness.

Lehi did as he was commanded and left Jerusalem with his family, taking none of his gold, silver, or precious things, but only provisions and tents. He traveled along the river that emptied into the mouth of the Red Sea. However, the Lord then spoke to Nephi, the youngest son of Lehi and Sariah, and told him to go back to Jerusalem and get the brass plates from Laban that contained the record of the Jews and the genealogy of their forefathers.

Nephi and his brothers—Laman, Lemuel, and Sam—went back to Jerusalem, and Nephi was constrained by the hand of the Lord to slay Laban to get the plates because the record needed to be preserved in their hands. Zoram, the servant of the deceased Laban, decided to join Nephi and the others.

When they arrived back at the tent of their father Lehi, he took the plates, searched them, and discovered that they contained the five books of Moses and a record of the Jews from the beginning—down to the reign of Zedekiah, King of Judah, and the prophecies of Jeremiah. He also found his genealogy on the plates and discovered that his family had descended from Joseph of old through Manasseh.

The Lord spoke again to Lehi and told him that his sons needed wives so they could "raise up seed unto him" in the land of promise. So Nephi and his brothers went back to the house of Ishmael. Ishmael's wife, unmarried daughters, married sons, and their families went with Nephi and his brothers. They finally arrived back at the tent of their father, Lehi.

After about seven years in the wilderness, God commanded Nephi to build a ship. Now, over the years Laman and Lemuel had grown to hate Nephi, but the Lord changed their hearts and together they built the ship.

Lehi's family, friends, and children loaded the ship with heavy provisions, entered the craft, departed, and were driven forth by a strong wind. They finally arrived at the promised land—the American continent—in about 589 B.C.

They multiplied rapidly, and ended up splitting into two main nations. The righteous people were called the Nephites, which included Nephi and most likely Sam, Jacob, and Joseph, and they remained an "exceedingly fair and delightsome people" (4 Nephi 1:10).

In contrast, Laman and Lemuel and their families—known as the Lamanites—rebelled against the Lord, and God punished them by giving them dark skin.[3] They warred continually over hundreds of years, and the Nephites eventually became more unrighteous than the Lamanites. Finally, the Lamanites killed off all the Nephites. And, according to Mormon history, the Lamanites—the only survivors of this ancient migration to America—are the ancestors of the American Indians.

The above history was allegedly written on plates by a prophet named Mormon. This "history" chronicled his people from around 600 B.C. to A.D. 385, the time of the final battles that wiped out the Nephites. When Mormon finished his work, he is said to have entrusted the plates to his son Moroni, who supposedly finished the history and then hid the plates in the

Hill Cumorah around A.D. 421. Fourteen hundred years later, the prophet Joseph Smith was led to the hill by the "angel" Moroni to retrieve the plates. (This is the *same* Moroni, only now he is said to be an angel.)

REASONING FROM THE SCRIPTURES

Genesis 11:8–9—*A Migration to America?*

The Mormon Teaching. According to Genesis 11, God had to judge humankind because of their prideful rebellion against Him. Genesis 11:8–9 tells us, "The LORD scattered them abroad from thence upon the face of all the earth: and they left off to build the city. Therefore is the name of it called Babel; because the LORD did there confound the language of all the earth: and from thence did the LORD scatter them abroad upon the face of all the earth."

According to Mormons, Genesis 11:8–9 tells of the scattering of mankind all across the earth—and among those who were scattered (allegedly) were the Jaredites, who were blown by a mighty wind during their voyage to the American continent. As explained by James E. Talmage,

> Amidst the confusion of Babel, Jared and his brother importuned the Lord that they and their associates be spared from the impending disruption. Their prayer was heard, and the Lord led them with a considerable company, who, like themselves, were free from the taint of idolatry, away from their homes, promising to conduct them to a land choice above all other lands.... They reached the ocean and there constructed eight vessels, called barges, in which they set out upon the waters.... After a passage of three hundred and forty-four days, the colony landed on the American shores.[4]

The Biblical Teaching. Answering the Mormon view is rather simple—at least from a biblical perspective. Read the text carefully: "The LORD scattered them abroad from thence upon the face of all the earth: and they left off to build the city. Therefore is the name of it called Babel; because the LORD did there confound *the language of all the earth:* and from thence did the LORD scatter them abroad upon the face *of all the earth*" (emphasis added).

There were *no exceptions* to God's work of "confounding languages." *All the earth* was affected. The Mormon interpretation of this passage is thus impossible; it flatly contradicts what Scripture says in Genesis 11:9.

_____ *Ask* . . . _____

- Would you please read aloud from Genesis 11:8–9?

- Does this passage say the language of *most* of the people was confounded, or does it say the language of *all the people of the earth* was confounded?

- Did you know that Joseph Smith's *Inspired Version* says "all" the people were confounded in Genesis 11:8?

- If the language of *all* the people was confounded, how can the Book of Mormon claim that God made an exception with Jared and his brother? Please explain.

The Hebrew word for "all the earth" (*'erets*) is one which, in the present context, points to *all* the inhabitants of the earth.[5] It is the exact same word that is used in Genesis 6:11–12: "*The earth* also was corrupt before God, and *the earth* was filled with violence. And God looked upon *the earth,* and, behold, it was corrupt; for all flesh had corrupted his way upon the earth" (emphasis added). Clearly the phrase "the earth" is pointing not to the physical planet but to *all the inhabitants* of the planet. Notice also that in this verse "the earth" is parallel to "all flesh." This is the sense of the phrase in Genesis 11:8–9.

Matthew 15:24—*The Lost Sheep of Israel*

The Mormon Teaching. Jesus said in Matthew 15:24, "I am not sent but unto the lost sheep of the house of Israel." In *Doctrines of Salvation*, by Joseph Fielding Smith, we read, "He [Jesus] must have referred to Israelites who were not in Palestine, and the visitation must have been one after his resurrection."[6]

In other words, Mormons relate the "lost sheep of the house of Israel" to Israel's scattering, and they believe Jesus was speaking of a visit to those representatives of Joseph's tribe who had migrated to America. These "lost sheep" are supposedly displaced Israelites on the American continent to whom Jesus appeared.

The Biblical Teaching. Mormons are again practicing eisegesis (reading a meaning into the text) as opposed to exegesis (drawing the meaning out of the text). Jesus isn't talking in Matthew 15:24 about "lost sheep" in America; rather, He was simply referring to "the Israelites to whom he was preaching in Judah and in Galilee who were in a 'lost' condition in God's eyes."[7] This is the plain and simple meaning of the text.

Craig S. Keener provides a helpful insight for understanding the backdrop to Jesus' statement in Matthew 15:24 by pointing back to Jesus' role as the prophesied "servant" in the book of Isaiah: "Jesus' statement in verse 24 does not preclude a later mission to Gentiles. The servant of Isaiah 53:6–8 suffers on behalf of the lost sheep of Israel (cf. 40:11; 56:11), but the servant's mission was ultimately to reconcile all nations to God (42:6; 49:6–7)."[8] This view is consistent with the Abrahamic covenant in Genesis 12, which says that because of the Messiah, "all families of the earth" would be blessed (verse 3).

Now, earlier in the book of Matthew, Jesus gives His disciples instructions regarding this *very same group* of "lost sheep of the house of Israel": "These twelve Jesus sent forth, and commanded them, saying, Go not into the way of the Gentiles, and into any city of the Samaritans enter ye not: But go rather to the lost sheep of the house of Israel" (Matthew 10:5–6). Here we see a clear contrast between "Gentiles" and the "lost sheep of the house of Israel" (that is, Gentiles and Jews). The disciples were sent forth to minister *to Jews.*

Now, the disciples fulfilled Christ's instructions *not* by traveling to America to share with any alleged "lost sheep of the house of Israel" there, but rather the "lost sheep" were *in cities in the immediate proximity of the disciples.* The disciples proclaimed the good news of Jesus Christ with "the lost sheep of the house of Israel" (unsaved Jews) *throughout Palestine.* This is the only possible meaning that fits the context. And this is the *same group* Jesus speaks of in Matthew 15:24.

In the outworking of God's plan of salvation, then, the good news of the kingdom of God was apparently to be preached first to the Jews—God's covenant people. But the Gentiles would not be excluded. God's offer was ultimately for all humankind, as we see in Christ's "Great Commission" to share the good news with all people everywhere (Matthew 28:19–20).

_____ *Ask . . .* _____

- Would you please read aloud from Matthew 10:5–6?

- Who were the disciples to proclaim the good news to?

- Is it not clear from the context that the disciples fulfilled Christ's instructions not by traveling to America to preach to "lost sheep" there, but rather to the "lost sheep of the house of Israel" (lost Jews) *in Palestine?*

- Can you see that these "lost sheep of the house of Israel" are the same "lost sheep" Jesus mentions in Matthew 15:24?

John 10:16—*The Migration of the "Other Sheep" to Israel*

The Mormon Teaching. In John 10:16 Jesus said, "And other sheep I have, which are not of this fold: them also I must bring, and they shall hear my voice; and there shall be one fold, and one shepherd."

Mormons tell us that the "other sheep" mentioned in this verse are the Nephites (displaced Israelites) in America. In their three-volume set *Doctrines of Salvation*, we read, "When the Savior visited the Nephites, he told them plainly that this reference to other sheep was a reference to them; but because of the hardness of the hearts of the disciples in Jerusalem, his Father commanded him to make no further reference to the nation of Nephites while instructing the Jews."[9]

The Biblical Teaching. It is clear from the context of John 10:16 that the phrase "other sheep" is referring to *Gentile* believers, not Jewish believers. In our endeavor to understand this passage, it is critical to recognize that in the Gospels the Jews were called "the lost sheep of the house of Israel" (Matthew 10:6; 15:24), and those Jews who followed Christ were called His "sheep" (John 10).

Jesus often referred to His Jewish disciples as sheep in His flock. For example, when Jesus was giving the twelve instructions for their future service, He said, "Behold, I send you forth *as sheep* in the midst of wolves: be ye therefore wise as serpents, and harmless as doves" (Matthew 10:16, emphasis added). Later, Jesus told the disciples that at His crucifixion they would scatter: "All ye shall be offended because of me this night: for it is written, I will smite the shepherd, and *the sheep of the flock* shall be scattered abroad" (Matthew 26:31, emphasis added).

Now, when Jesus said "*other* sheep I have, which are not of *this fold*," He was clearly referring to non-Jewish, Gentile believers.[10] When Jesus said these other sheep were "not of this fold," He was saying they were *outside of Judaism*. But because of what Christ accomplished, the Gentile believers, along with the Jewish believers, "shall be *one fold*," under *"one shepherd"* (John 10:16, emphasis added).

This is in perfect accord with Ephesians 2:1–22, where we are told that in Christ, Jews and Gentiles are reconciled in o*ne body.* Galatians 3:28 tells us that "there is neither Jew nor Greek [Gentile], there is neither bond nor free, there is neither male nor female: for *ye are all one* in Christ Jesus" (emphasis added). Likewise, Colossians 3:11 speaks of a renewal in which there is no distinction between Gentiles and Jews, circumcised and uncircumcised, slave and freeman, but Christ is all, and in all.

When Jesus said He had "other sheep" in John 10:16, then, He was indicating that salvation was not for the Jews only but for all people—including the Gentiles. We find this supported in a number of Scripture passages. In addition to the passages we've already looked at, Isaiah 49:6 makes specific reference to a "light to the Gentiles," and Luke 2:32 applies this verse to the person and work of Jesus Christ (cf. Acts 13:47; 26:23). These verses alone shows that Christ's mission extended even to the Gentiles and was not limited to just the Jews (*see* John 11:51–52; Acts 13:26; 28:28; and Romans 11:11,25).

_____ *Ask . . .* _____

- Would you please read aloud from John 10:16?

- Since Jesus' words in John 10:16 were addressed *specifically to Jews,* does it not make sense that when He referred to "other sheep" who were "not of *this fold*," He was talking about non-Jews who were not of the "fold" of Judaism?

- Please demonstrate from the context of John 10 that the reference in verse 16 deals with "sheep" in America.

The Lack of Archaeological Support

We noted in chapter 6 that there is no archaeological proof to support the Mormon claim of one or more migrations from Israel to America. We do not want to repeat all that we said in that chapter; however, here are the pertinent facts:

- According to the Book of Mormon, the Nephite and Lamanite nations had *huge* populations that lived in *large,* fortified cities.
- They allegedly waged *large-scale* wars with each other for hundreds of years, culminating in a conflict in which hundreds of thousands of people were killed in A.D. 385 in a restricted area near Hill Cumorah in present-day New York State (*see* Mormon 6:9–15).
- Yet there is no evidence that any of this ever happened.

___ *Ask* . . . ___

- If the Nephite and Lamanite nations really had huge populations that lived in large, fortified cities, don't you think there would be substantial archaeological evidence for their existence? Can you show me such evidence from *non-Mormon* archaeologists?

- If there were large-scale wars, culminating in a conflict in which hundreds of thousands of people were killed in A.D. 385 near Hill Cumorah in present-day New York State, wouldn't we find some archaeological evidence— heaps of skeletons, human remains, ancient weapons— that such a conflict occurred?

It is noteworthy that the Smithsonian Institution emphatically states, "There is no evidence whatever of any migration from Israel to America, and likewise no evidence that pre-Columbian Indians had any knowledge of Christianity or the

Bible."[11] Likewise, Mesoamerican archaeologist Michael Coe wrote in *Biblical Archaeology Review*, "It would be difficult to find a trained archaeologist who is not a Mormon who believes that the Mesoamerican Indians are descendants of the Israelites."[12] This, of course, is not welcome news to Mormons.

_____ *Ask . . .* _____

- Do you find it curious that archaeologists at one of the most respected institutions in the world—the Smithsonian Institution—see no archaeological support for the Book of Mormon or for a migration from Israel to America?

12

The "Restoration" of the Aaronic and Melchizedek Priesthoods

The Aaronic priesthood was originally conferred on Aaron and his sons. God said, "Take thou unto thee Aaron thy brother, and his sons with him, from among the children of Israel, that he may minister unto me in the priest's office, even Aaron, Nadab and Abihu, Eleazar and Ithamar, Aaron's sons" (Exodus 28:1). Later on, the tribe of Levi was chosen to assist Aaron in the priestly functions. Therefore, the Aaronic priesthood is synonymous with the Levitical priesthood.[1]

According to Mormon history, in May 1829 Joseph Smith and Oliver Cowdery were in the midst of working on the translation of the alleged gold plates of the Book of Mormon into English. They decided to go into the woods to pray about baptism for the remission of sins, which they found mentioned on the gold plates. As they were praying, "a messenger from heaven descended in a cloud of light."[2] The messenger laid his hands upon them and said:

> Unto you my fellow servants in the name of Messiah, I confer the Priesthood of Aaron, which holds the keys of the ministering of angels, and of the gospel of repentance,

and of baptism by immersion for the remission of sins; and this shall never be taken again from the earth until the sons of Levi do offer again an offering unto the Lord in righteousness.

He said this Aaronic Priesthood had not the power of the laying on hands for the gift of the Holy Ghost, but this should be conferred on us hereafter; and he commanded us to go and be baptized, and gave us directions that I should baptize Oliver Cowdery, and that afterwards he should baptize me.[3]

Thus, Joseph Smith baptized Oliver Cowdery, and afterward, Cowdery baptized Smith—and they *ordained each other* to the priesthood of Aaron. This is what the heavenly messenger—who, we are told, was John the Baptist[4]—commanded them to do.

John the Baptist also informed them that he was acting under the direction of Peter, James, and John, who held the keys of the Melchizedek priesthood. That higher priesthood would soon be conferred on Joseph Smith and Oliver Cowdery.

According to Mormon authorities, the Melchizedek priesthood—with all the authority and keys of the kingdom of God—was lost from the earth. "After the apostles ceased to minister among mortals, there was no one left holding the keys to authorize a person to be ordained to any priestly office, and in this manner the Lord took the priesthood from the earth"[5] after the death of the last apostle.

A darkness persisted as a result of the great apostasy that soon came upon the church. But Joseph Smith had been promised that the Lord would restore the priestly authority through him in the near future. After all, the priesthood is *eternal* in nature:

The Priesthood is everlasting. The Savior, Moses, and Elias, gave the keys to Peter, James, and John, on the mount, when they were transfigured before him. The priesthood is everlasting—without beginning of days or end of years; without father, mother, etc. If there is no change of ordinances, there is no change of Priesthood. Wherever the ordinances of the Gospel are administered, there is the Priesthood.[6]

Sometime between May 15 and June 30, 1829, Peter, James, and John allegedly came down from heaven and restored the Melchizedek priesthood to Joseph Smith. And by divine revelation, the Lord said this to Joseph Smith:

And this greater priesthood administereth the gospel and holdeth the key of the mysteries of the kingdom, even the key of the knowledge of God. Therefore, in the ordinances thereof, the power of godliness is manifest. And without the ordinances thereof, and the authority of the priesthood, the power of godliness is not manifest unto men in the flesh; for without this no man can see the face of God, even the Father, and live.[7]

Mormons say there is only one true church that has been given the priesthood authority to baptize, lay hands on for the reception of the Holy Spirit, and to administer the sacraments. "Thus," Bruce McConkie states, "as far as all religious organizations now existing are concerned, the presence or the absence of this priesthood establishes the divinity or falsity of a professing church."[8] Indeed, "if there is no Melchizedek priesthood on earth, the true Church is not here and the gospel of Christ is not available to men. But where the Melchizedek priesthood is, there is the kingdom, the Church, and the fulness of the gospel."[9]

Of course, we are told that the Mormon church does have this priesthood: and consequently, it is the only true church. James E. Talmage says, "The Latter-day Saints declare their high claim to the true Church organization, similar in all essentials to the organization effected by Christ among the Jews."[10] Bruce McConkie, in *Mormon Doctrine,* thus declares: "This priesthood—with all its powers, parts, keys, orders, and ramifications—is now fully operative among men. Again there is a kingdom of priests on earth, and the divine promise is that this situation will continue, the priesthood never again being lost."[11]

What Mormons presently teach is that male members of the church may first progress up a ladder through the Aaronic priesthood—which includes 1) deacon, 2) teacher, and 3) priest.[12] Then they can become ordained in the Melchizedek priesthood and move up to 4) elder, 5) seventies, 6) high priest, 7) patriarch, and 8) apostle.[13] These various offices in the priesthood include nearly every male member over the age of twelve.[14]

REASONING FROM THE SCRIPTURES

There is a big problem in the above-stated Mormon account that you should point out to the Mormon missionary on your doorstep. It has to do with being baptized by a person who has the authority to do so.

According to Mormon theology, unless a person is properly baptized by someone who has the authority to baptize, that person is improperly baptized and that baptism is of no effect. The person who is improperly baptized, we are told, remains unsaved.[15]

So, Joseph Smith—who had *not yet been baptized by someone who had the proper authority*—had no authority himself to baptize Oliver Cowdery. And Cowdery—thus improperly baptized—subsequently went on to improperly baptize Joseph Smith.

Ask . . .

- Is it true that, according to Mormon theology, unless a person is properly baptized by someone who has the authority to baptize, then that baptism is of no effect?

- Since Joseph Smith had not yet been baptized, how could he have had the authority to baptize Oliver Cowdery?

- Since Oliver Cowdery was improperly baptized, how then could he have had the authority to baptize Joseph Smith?

- If the priesthood in modern times came down to us through two improperly baptized men, then how can any Mormon claim to have the restored priesthood?

Genesis 14:18—*The Melchizedek Priesthood*

The Mormon Teaching. In Genesis 14:18 we read that "Melchizedek king of Salem brought forth bread and wine: and he was the priest of the most high God."

According to Mormons, Melchizedek had the honor of having his name used to identify "the Holy Priesthood, after the Order of the Son of God"—thus enabling men "to avoid the too frequent repetition" of the name of Deity.[16] In other words, "out of respect or reverence to the name of the Supreme Being, to avoid the too frequent repetition of his name, they, the Church, in ancient days, called that priesthood after Melchizedek."[17]

Of all God's ancient high priests, Mormons say, "none were greater" than Melchizedek (Alma 13:19). His position in the priestly hierarchy of God's earthly kingdom was like that of Abraham (Hebrews 7:4–10), whom he blessed (Genesis 14:18–20) and upon whom he allegedly conferred the priesthood.[18] This priesthood is supposedly eternal. And even though it was lost from the earth from the time of the last apostle, it has been restored through Joseph Smith.

The Biblical Teaching. So that we can better understanding Melchizedek and his significance, let us first point out that Bible scholars have long recognized that some Old Testament persons or things foreshadow the person or work of Christ in the New Testament. That is, in the revelatory process, God in His sovereignty so arranged the outworking of history so that certain individuals, things, events, ceremonies, and institutions served as *types* that foreshadowed Christ in His person or ministry.

According to Webster, a *type* is "a figure or representation of something to come."[19] Theologian Donald K. Campbell defines a type as "an Old Testament institution, event, person, object, or ceremony which has reality and purpose in biblical history, but which also by divine design foreshadows something yet to be revealed."[20] Types are therefore prophetic in nature, and many of the types we find in the Old Testament speak prophetically of Christ in some way.[21]

Of course, it is important to distinguish types and prophecies in their respective forms. Paul Lee Tan explains that "a *type* prefigures coming reality; a *prophecy* verbally delineates the future. One is expressed in events, persons, and acts; the other is couched in words and statements. One is passive in form, the other active."[22]

Types in the Old Testament are types not because man has said so but because God is sovereign in the revelatory process. The reason some Old Testament persons or things foreshadow Christ in the New Testament is that God planned it that way. As Bible scholar A. Berkeley Mickelsen says, "The correspondence is present because God controls history, and this control of God over history is axiomatic with the New Testament writers. It is God who causes earlier individuals, groups, experiences, institutions, etc., to embody characteristics which later he will cause to reappear."[23]

Now, all of this is simply to say that the reference to Melchizedek in Genesis 14 is a *type of Christ.* Melchizedek foreshadows or points forward to the person of Christ in some way.

We find affirmation of this in Hebrews 7:3, which tells us this about Melchizedek: "Without father, without mother, without descent, having neither beginning of days, nor end of life; but made like unto the Son of God; abideth a priest continually."

How, you may wonder, does this relate to Melchizedek being a "type" of Christ? Hebrews 7:3 is not telling us that the historical Melchizedek had no mother or father, or no beginning of days, but simply saying that the Old Testament Scriptures have no *record* of these events—and the record of these events is missing *by design*. Renowned Bible scholar F.F. Bruce provides us with some helpful insights here:

> When Melchizedek is described as being "without father, without mother, without genealogy, having neither beginning of days nor end of life," it is not suggested that he was a biological anomaly, or an angel in human guise. . . . If this point had been put to our author [that is, the author of Hebrews], he would have agreed at once, no doubt; but this consideration was foreign to his purpose. The important consideration was the account given of Melchizedek in holy writ; to him the silences of [Old Testament] Scripture were as much due to divine inspiration as were its statements. In the only record which Scripture provides of Melchizedek—Gen. 14:18–20—nothing is said of his parentage, nothing is said of his ancestry or progeny, nothing is said of his birth, nothing is said of his death. He appears as a living man, king of Salem and priest of God Most High; and as such he disappears. In all this—in the silences as well as in the statements—he is a fitting type of Christ[24] (inserts added).

Old Testament scholar Gleason Archer agrees with Bruce, noting that "the context makes clear that Melchizedek was brought on the scene as a type of the Messiah, the Lord Jesus. In order to bring out this typical character of Melchizedek, the biblical record purposely omits all mention of his birth, parentage, or ancestors."[25] As noted earlier, this is not to say that Melchizedek had no father or mother. Rather, "this verse simply means that none of those items of information was included in the Genesis 14 account and that they were purposely omitted in order to lay the stress on the divine nature and imperishability of the Messiah, the Antitype."[26]

It's also significant that Melchizedek's name is made up of two Hebrew words meaning "king" and "righteous." In addition, Melchizedek was a priest. Thus, Melchizedek foreshadows Christ as a righteous King/Priest.

We are also told that Melchizedek was the king of "Salem"—which, in Hebrew, means "peace." Bringing all this together, then, Melchizedek points forward to Jesus Christ as the righteous King/Priest of peace. Of course, these things were true of Melchizedek only in a *finite* sense (remember, he was a human being), whereas for Christ they are true in an *infinite* sense. Nevertheless, we can say that in a finite way, Melchizedek foreshadows Christ.

After explaining all this to the Mormon, you will want to challenge him or her on a key teaching of the Mormon church. Mormons claim that Melchizedek conferred his priesthood on Abraham when Abraham paid a tithe to him. However, this idea finds no support in the Bible. As Walter Martin said, "Mormons should be pressed at this juncture for the biblical evidence, the absence of which affords further opportunity to undercut their already weakened position."[27]

_____ *Ask . . .* _____

- Where in the Bible do we find that Melchizedek conferred the priesthood on Abraham?

- If that is not in the Bible, then doesn't that mean the Mormon church's position is unbiblical?

- Since the name "Melchizedek" indicates an individual who is a *righteous King/Priest of peace,* we must conclude that anyone who claims to be in the Melchizedek priesthood is in fact a righteous King/Priest of peace— just like Jesus Christ is described in Hebrews 7. Tell me, do you think you are a righteous King/Priest of peace?

Psalm 110:4; Hebrews 5:6—*The Mormons: Successors to Melchizedek's Priesthood?*

The Mormon Teaching. In Psalm 110:4 we read, "The LORD hath sworn, and will not repent, Thou art a priest for ever after the order of Melchizedek." We find these same words repeated in Hebrews 5:6.

According to the Mormons, the Melchizedek priesthood is an eternal priesthood that existed before creation. Bruce McConkie says, "Its institution was prior to 'the foundation of this earth, or the morning stars sang together, or the sons of God shouted for joy,' and is the highest and holiest priesthood, and is after the order of the Son of God."[28] Indeed, "the priesthood is an everlasting principle, and existed with God from eternity, and will to eternity, without beginning of days or end of years."[29] This priesthood was first given to Adam in mortality (Moses 6:67–68).

The Melchizedek priesthood was an *order*, Mormons say, and many worthy men held it down to the time of Moses, but then God had to take it from men. "Israel rebelled, rejected the higher law, and the Lord took Moses and the fulness of the priesthood from them."[30] From that time until the personal ministry of our Lord among men, the Aaronic priesthood was the most prevalent authority of God on earth.[31]

The Biblical Teaching. Psalm 110 is a messianic psalm that prophetically points forward to the person and work of Jesus Christ. Hebrews 5–8 and other New Testament passages apply Psalm 110 *to Christ alone,* not to human pretenders to the divine priesthood. (Remember, Jesus Himself quoted Psalm 110 when demonstrating that He—*as the Messiah*—was David's Lord [Mark 12:36].) As a messianic psalm, it points to Jesus Christ as a *King* (verses 1–3), *Priest* (verse 4), and *victorious Warrior* (verses 5–7).

When Psalm 110:4 says that Christ is a "priest for ever, after the order of Melchizedek," all it is saying is that—*like*

Melchizedek—Christ combines the offices of priest and king (see our earlier discussion of Genesis 14:18). The word "for ever" simply indicates that Christ's priesthood is permanent and irrevocable.

Commenting on this verse, Hebrew authority and Bible scholar Allan P. Ross said, "As a Priest Jesus sacrificed Himself by His death on the cross (Heb. 7:27–28; 10:10). Not in Aaron's line (cf. Heb. 7:11–18), He is the eternal High Priest (cf. Heb. 7:21–26, 28) of the New Covenant (cf. Heb. 8:13; 9:15). Because He is also the promised Davidic King, both offices are united in one Person."[32]

Now, by citing Psalm 110:4 and other passages out of context, the Mormon church hopes to build a case that the Melchizedek priesthood is for today because it is an "eternal" or "everlasting" priesthood. As demonstrated above, however, the Mormons are reading something into the text that is not there.

The fact is, there is not a single example anywhere in the New Testament of a believer ever being ordained to the Melchizedek priesthood—other than the single exception of the God-man, Jesus Christ. None of the disciples or apostles were ever ordained to this priesthood. Nor is there a single command or injunction anywhere in the New Testament instructing believers to seek ordination in this priesthood.

_____ Ask . . . _____

- Where does the New Testament say that Peter, James, and John held the Melchizedek priesthood?

- Where does the Bible say that any of the disciples or apostles ever held the Melchizedek priesthood?

- Where does the Bible say that anyone but Melchizedek and Jesus ever held the Melchizedek priesthood?

During your discussion, you may want to raise the point that women are not permitted to be ordained in the priesthood in the Mormon church. What this ultimately means is that a woman who has faithfully served the Mormon church throughout her life can suddenly be surpassed in authority *by her own 12-year-old son* (and her son's playmates!). [33]

There's another sensitive issue you may want to bring up. Before 1978, Mormon males of African descent were denied the priesthood. They were considered "cursed" by God because of their dark skin. This is clearly a racist doctrine. Bruce McConkie, in the 1958 edition of his book *Mormon Doctrine,* said, "Negroes in this life are denied the priesthood; under no circumstances can they hold this delegation of authority from the Almighty. The gospel message of salvation is not carried affirmatively to them. . . . Negroes are not equal with other races where the receipt of certain spiritual blessings are concerned . . ." [34]

Over the years, people both inside and outside the LDS church—including those involved in the civil rights movement—put a lot of pressure on the Mormon leadership for their racist position. Finally, on June 9, 1978, the church announced that its leaders had received a revelation from God permitting "all worthy males" to participate in its priesthood. [35]

_____ *Ask* . . . _____

• Why were Mormon males of African descent not allowed in the priesthood up until 1978?

(Don't let the Mormon sidestep this issue. Force him or her to admit that Mormon leaders once taught that black skin was an evidence of God's curse.)

• Does it make you at all uncomfortable being part of a church that taught this horrendous and hurtful doctrine for so long?

At some point you'll want to take the Mormon to Hebrews 7:23–24, which tells us, "And they truly were many priests, because they were not suffered to continue by reason of death: But this man [Jesus Christ], *because he continueth ever, hath an unchangeable priesthood*" (insert and emphasis added).

You'll want to emphasize that Christ's priesthood is eternal because Christ Himself is an eternal being. Unlike humans who perish and die, Christ exists eternally, and therefore His priesthood by its very nature is different than anything a man could offer. He is our eternal High Priest who lives forever.

Hebrews 7:24 tells us that Christ's priesthood is "unchangeable." This is an important word. New Testament scholar Edgar J. Goodspeed translates the verse as saying that Christ's priesthood is "untransferable."[36] The Greek word, *aparabatos,* indicates finality. Joseph Thayer's widely respected *Greek Lexicon* defines it this way: "Priesthood unchangeable and therefore not liable to pass to a successor."[37]

The *Theological Dictionary of the New Testament,* edited by Gerhard Kittel, tells us, "In the New Testament Hebrews 7:24 says that Christ has an eternal and imperishable priesthood, not just in the sense that it cannot be transferred to anyone else, but in the sense of 'unchangeable.'"[38] *The Complete Word Study Dictionary* likewise says this Greek word means that "Christ's priesthood cannot be transferred to another; it is final."[39]

Don't allow the Mormon to escape the importance of Hebrews 7:24. It clearly teaches us that Christ's priesthood is "unchangeable" in the sense that it is "without successors," "intransmissible," and "untransferable."*

---

*Possible Mormon comeback: Some Mormons may attempt to argue that the Greek word *aparabaton* has no genuine scholarly support for the meaning, "cannot pass from one to another" (see *A Sure Foundation: Answers to Difficult Gospel Questions* [Salt Lake City, UT: Deseret, 1988], p. 218). Of course, the citations in this chapter show *there is* scholarly support for defining *aparabaton* in this way. You will also want to point out that Bauer, Arndt, and Gingrich's authoritative *Greek-English Lexicon of the New Testament and Other Early Christian Literature* gives the meaning "without a successor" for *aparabaton* in Hebrews 7:24 (p. 80).

____ *Ask* . . . ____

- Would you please read aloud from Hebrews 7:23–24?

- Did you know that the Greek word for "unchangeable" in Hebrews 7:24 literally means "without successors," "intransmissible," and "untransferable"?

- What is Hebrews 7:24 telling us when it says that Christ's Melchizedek priesthood is "without successors," "intransmissible," and "untransferable"?

- Isn't it clear from Hebrews 7:24 that Christ's Melchizedek priesthood is "unchangeable"—and therefore unattainable by you and me—because "he continueth [for]ever"?

- How do you explain the absolute lack of Old or New Testament references to any *ordination to, offices in,* or *duties* of the Melchizedek priesthood (or to anyone else's holding it but Melchizedek and Jesus)?

You will also want to quote Hebrews 7:11–12 to the Mormon to prove the "passing away" of the Aaronic priesthood:

If therefore perfection were by the Levitical priesthood, (for under it the people received the law,) what further need was there that another priest should rise after the order of Melchizedek, and not be called after the order of Aaron? For the priesthood *being changed,* there is made of necessity a change also of the law (emphasis added).

Here is a crystal-clear statement from Scripture that there was a *change* in the priesthood. The Aaronic priesthood was *done away with* and *replaced* with something better—the priesthood of Jesus Christ, our *eternal* priest. This passing away of the Aaronic or Levitical priesthood was symbolized by the tearing of the veil leading to the Holy of Holies in the temple at the crucifixion (*see* Matthew 27:51).

Ask . . .

- In Hebrews 7:11–12, what does the text mean when it says the priesthood was "changed"?

- Doesn't a plain reading of the text indicate that the Aaronic priesthood was superseded by something better—the eternal priesthood of Jesus Christ?

Acts 3:20–21—_The Restoration of the Priesthoods_

The Mormon Teaching. In Acts 3:20–21 we read, "He shall send Jesus Christ, which before was preached unto you: Whom the heaven must receive until the times of restitution of all things, which God hath spoken by the mouth of all his holy prophets since the world began."

We've already discussed Acts 3:20–21 in response to the Mormon church's claim that it is God's _restored_ church (_see_ chapter 3). But we need to look at the passage again while we are on the subject of the Aaronic and Melchizedek priesthoods.

According to Mormons, the so-called "restitution" or "restoration" of all things could not have happened if the priesthoods had not also been restored to the earth. The true church, complete with the authority of the Melchizedek priesthood, is allegedly a fulfillment of the prophecy given in Acts 3:20–21.

As LeGrand Richards says in his book _A Marvelous Work and a Wonder,_ "In order that there might be a 'restitution of all things, which God hath spoken by the mouth of all his holy prophets since the world began' (see Acts 3:21), it was necessary that these two priesthoods be restored again to men upon this earth."[40]

The Biblical Teaching. It is amazing that the Mormon church claims to have "restored" the priesthoods because their so-called priesthoods _bear no resemblance_ to the priesthoods found in Scripture. Let us consider the Aaronic priesthood as a case in point.

First, Mormons are not descendants of Aaron (a key requirement—*see* Numbers 3:6–12). Moreover, the duties in the Mormon version of the Aaronic priesthood bear no resemblance to the duties of the priesthood as outlined in Exodus, Leviticus, Numbers, and Deuteronomy (such as offering sacrifices—*see* Exodus 29:38–44).

In addition, the Aaronic priests of the Bible served the one true God of the Bible. They were *monotheists,* not *polytheists* (like the Mormons). Clearly, the Mormon version of the Aaronic priesthood is entirely different than that of the Bible.[41]

It is ironic that a church that spends so much time doing genealogical work claims to have a restored Aaronic priesthood. The Aaronic priesthood was reserved *solely* for Aaron and his physical descendants—*no exceptions!* Not even Christ could be in the Aaronic priesthood: "For it is evident that our Lord sprang out of Judah; of which tribe Moses spake nothing concerning priesthood" (Hebrews 7:14).

___ *Ask . . .* ___

- Did you know that, according to the Bible, all those who were ordained to the Aaronic priesthood had to be physical descendants of Aaron (Numbers 3:6–12)?

- Since Mormons are not physical descendants of Aaron, how can they possibly be ordained to the Aaronic priesthood?

- Allow me to read to you from Numbers 3:10: "Thou shalt appoint *Aaron and his sons,* and *they* shall wait on their priest's office: and the stranger that cometh nigh shall be put to death" (emphasis added). Does this divine rule permit *anyone* else to enter this exclusive priesthood—then or now? Does this verse concern you?

There is another important point to make. Bill McKeever and Eric Johnson tells us,

> Leviticus chapter 8 gives elaborate details as to how the priest was to be consecrated for service. This complex rite included ceremonial washings, corporate prayer over the head of the sacrificial bullock, the slaying of the bullock, the sprinkling of its blood, and the burning of the sacrifice. This was followed by the sacrifice of two rams and the offering of bread. The initiates were then separated from the people for seven days in which they would perform numerous animal sacrifices. On the eighth day, they would again emerge to offer sacrifices and bless the people. If the Mormon priesthood is a restoration of the ancient priesthood, why are their priests not set apart in a similar fashion?[42]

_____ *Ask* . . . _____

- Did you know that according to the Bible, those who became Levitical priests were all required by explicit divine command to submit to ceremonial washings, the slaying of a bullock, the sprinkling of its blood, the burning of a sacrifice, separation from people for seven days, and other ceremonial rites?

- If the LDS church has "restored" the Aaronic (Levitical) priesthood—meaning that it claims to have the *exact same* priesthood—why are their priests not "set apart" in a similar fashion?

- Does this sound like a real "restoration" to you? Please explain.

Hebrews 5:1,4—*Priests Among Men*

The Mormon Teaching. In Hebrews 5:1,4 we read, "Every high priest taken from among men is ordained for men in things pertaining to God, that he may offer both gifts and sacrifices for sins. . . . And no man taketh this honor unto himself, but he that is called of God, as was Aaron."

According to Mormons, Hebrews 5:1,4 tells us that no man can arbitrarily assume that he has the authority to act for God. He must be properly appointed and ordained by someone who already has the authority of the priesthood. That is the way God has chosen to "call" men to specific areas of service.

Because Mormons believe they have a living "prophet" and "apostles" at the head of their church—and because they have the restored priesthoods—Mormons often challenge Christians with the question, "Where do you get your authority?"

Mormons believe that authority is a serious matter. They think the priesthood "is *the authority of God* given to men to act in all things for the salvation of mankind"[43] (emphasis added). Indeed, "the priesthood is the greatest power on earth. It is not only the *power of God* given to men on the earth to do his work, but it is the same power by which our Heavenly Father and Jesus Christ perform their work"[44] (emphasis added).

This emphasis on authority has tremendous ramifications in the Mormon church. Mormons believe that because their church has the *only* legitimate priesthood, then only baptisms (and other religious rites) performed in a Mormon church are valid. The question of authority, then, is very important.

The Biblical Teaching. In Hebrews 5:1–4, the writer of Hebrews is setting forth the qualifications for being a Levitical priest. The first qualification required the ability to sympathize with the weakness of people. The second, more important qualification was that the priest had to be chosen by God. F.F. Bruce elaborates:

If one qualification in a high priest is his ability to sympathize, another is his being called by God to this honorable service. No man can of his own accord set himself up as high priest, nor can he hold office validly by the gift of any earthly authority. . . . Aaron, the first of Israel's high priests, occupied his office by divine appointment (Ex. 28:1ff.; Lev. 8:1ff.; Num. 16:5; 17:5; 18:1ff.; Ps. 105:26), and so did his heirs and successors (Num. 20:23ff.; 25:10ff.). . . . If our author is to sustain his thesis that Jesus is His peoples' great high priest, he must produce comparable evidence of a divine call in His case.[45]

And that is exactly what the writer of Hebrews does in the next six verses (*see* Hebrews 5:5–10). So, in context, the whole point of Hebrews 5 is that *Christ is qualified* as our High Priest—our *sole, lone, unique* High Priest. This passage provides no support for the idea that other people can become priests (as Mormons would like to have it). Rather, it provides strong argumentation that *Christ alone* is our High Priest.

Going back to the question, "Where do you get your authority?" you will want to make several points to the Mormon. First, you will want to share the scriptural doctrine that all who personally place their faith in the Lord Jesus Christ are "priests" unto God. There are New Testament passages that make this clear beyond dispute. For example:

- Revelation 1:5–6 tells us, "Unto him that loved us, and washed us from our sins in his own blood, and *hath made us kings and priests unto God and his Father;* to him be glory and dominion for ever and ever. Amen" (emphasis added).
- 1 Peter 2:5 tells us, "Ye also, as lively stones, are built up a spiritual house, *a holy priesthood,* to offer up spiritual sacrifices, acceptable to God by Jesus Christ" (emphasis added).

Citing such passages will help to nullify the Mormons' view that their church holds all authority because it is in sole possession of the so-called restored priesthood. You—as a "priest" of God—have authority to speak the things of God.

Moreover, John 1:12 tells us that "as many as received him [Jesus Christ], to them gave he *power* to become the sons of God, even to them that believe on his name" (emphasis added). Believers have authority as God's sons—that is, as *members of God's family.*

Romans 8:14–17 tells us likewise:

> For as many as are led by the Spirit of God, they are the sons of God. For ye have not received the spirit of bondage again to fear; but ye have received the Spirit of adoption, whereby we cry, Abba, Father. The Spirit itself beareth witness with our spirit, that we are the children of God: And if children, then heirs; heirs of God, and joint-heirs with Christ; if so be that we suffer with him, that we may be also glorified together.

To help you see how you can respond to a Mormon in a discussion about authority, we've provided the following mock dialogue between a Mormon and a Christian. This dialogue brings up a number of the points we've emphasized in this chapter as well as a few new ones.

Mormon: By what authority do you (or, your pastor) preach, baptize, and, in general, act for God?

Christian: By the authority of Jesus Christ through the power of the Holy Spirit (John 1:12–13; Acts 1:8).

Mormon: But the authority to act for God comes through the Melchizedek priesthood. This was given to me by the laying on of hands by someone who has this authority.

Christian: Can you show me from the Bible where it states that the authority to preach the gospel, to baptize, and to offer the sacraments comes from being a member of the Melchizedek priesthood? In fact, can you show me in the New Testament where anyone but Jesus Christ ever held the Melchizedek priesthood?

Mormon: In Hebrews 5:4 it tells us that no one takes this honor unto himself, but he that is called of God, as was Aaron.

Christian: The very next verses in the book of Hebrews tell us that God called Jesus, *and no one else,* to the honor of holding the Melchizedek priesthood (Hebrews 5:5–10). Once again I must ask: Where does the New Testament state that the apostles or anyone else but Jesus ever held the Melchizedek priesthood, which Mormonism teaches is the authority to act for God?

Mormon: John 15:16 tells us that Jesus laid hands on His disciples and ordained them. This is where He gave them the Melchizedek priesthood.

Christian: The word "ordained" in John 15:16 means "to appoint." The verse tells us that Jesus appointed His disciples to go and bring forth fruit. John 15:16 does not mention the Melchizedek priesthood, nor does it say that Jesus laid hands upon them. *Nowhere* do the Gospels have Jesus laying hands on anyone to ordain them! In the book of Acts there are several scriptures that mention the laying on of hands for a person's ordination to service, but *none* speak of an ordination to the Melchizedek priesthood.

Mormon: By modern-day revelation we know that Peter, James, and John came down from heaven and ordained Joseph Smith to the Melchizedek priesthood, thereby once again restoring the church and the true authority to the earth.

Christian: In order to bestow the Melchizedek priesthood, Peter, James, and John would have to *possess* it. Where does the New Testament state that they or anyone but Jesus ever held the Melchizedek priesthood?

Mormon: We know this by modern-day revelation. And besides, the Bible does not state that the disciples *did not* hold the Melchizedek priesthood.

Christian: Please turn in your Bible to Hebrews 7:1–3. This passage tells us the qualifications for a priest in the order of Melchizedek. Let's determine whether you or anyone in your church meets these qualifications. The name

"Melchizedek" means "king of righteousness." Who is the King of Righteousness?

Mormon: Jesus, the Christ.

Christian: Correct! Now, Hebrews 7:26 gives us a key qualification for a Melchizedek priest: "For such a high priest became us, who is holy, harmless, undefiled, separate from sinners, and made higher than the heavens." Are you holy, harmless, undefiled, separate from sinners, and made higher than the heavens?

Mormon: No.

Christian: Therefore, you do not possess the Melchizedek priesthood nor the authority you presume to hold. However, when you have believed and received the *genuine* Jesus Christ *of the Bible* you will have the authority (John 1:12) and the correct priesthood (1 Peter 2:9–10).[46]

A Problem with Lineage

There is one final problem we want to make you aware of. In the Mormon Book of Abraham,[47] we are told that all Egyptians were cursed and could not hold the priesthood. Now, here's the problem this poses for Mormonism: Joseph Smith claimed he was from the tribe of Ephraim,[48] and the Book of Mormon people were from the tribe of Manasseh.[49]

Who were Ephraim and Manasseh? Well, the Egyptian Pharaoh gave Asenath—daughter of Potiphera, Priest of On—to Joseph of old as a wife. She bore him two sons: Ephraim and Manasseh.[50] They were half-Egyptian! Hence, descendants from Ephraim and Manasseh are *automatically disqualified from the priesthood.*

Occasionally, Mormons try to get around this by saying that the Hyksos people who were of Semitic origin were in power when Joseph of old was in Egypt. They claim that Asenath was not Egyptian, but was of Hyksos lineage.

However the name Asenath is an Egyptian name,[51] and her father Potiphera's name is an Egyptian derivative of Potiphar, who was an Egyptian.[52] Clearly they were Egyptians. Hence according to the Morman's own Book of Abraham, Joseph Smith could not possibly hold the priesthood.

____ *Ask* . . . ____

- Were you aware that the Book of Abraham said all Egyptians were cursed and could not possibly hold the priesthood (1:21,22,27)?

- Since Joseph Smith claimed he was a descendant of Ephraim—and since Ephraim was half-Egyptian—doesn't that disquality Joseph Smith from the priesthood?

- Since the Book of Mormon people were from the tribe of Manasseh (Alma 10:3), doesn't that mean they could not possibly hold the priesthood either?

13

The Mormon Doctrine of God— Part 1: Does God Have a Humanlike Body?

Mormons teach that God the Father was once a mortal man just like us (Doctrine and Covenants 130). They say He continually progressed to become a God—and that the rest of us, too, can become gods like Him by adopting and faithfully adhering to Mormonism.

Joseph Smith said that "if you were to see him [the Father] today, you would see him like a man in form. . . . He was once a man like us; yea . . . God himself, the Father of us all, dwelt on an earth, the same as Jesus Christ himself did"[1] (insert added). *The Journal of Discourses* says, "God himself was once as we are now and is an exalted man."[2]

How did the Father become an exalted man? Mormon general authority Milton R. Hunter provides the answer: "God the Eternal Father was once a mortal man who passed through a school of earth life similar to that through which we are now passing. He became God—an exalted being—through obedience to the same eternal Gospel truths that we are given opportunity today to obey."[3]

In the *Journal of Discourses* we read that "God our Heavenly Father was perhaps once a child and mortal like we are and rose step by step in the scale of progress, in the school of advancement; He has moved forward and overcome until He has arrived at the point where He is now."[4]

Today, then, "God the Eternal Father, our Father in Heaven, is an exalted, perfected, and glorified Personage having a tangible body of flesh and bones."[5] Joseph Smith exults, "God . . . is an exalted man, and sits enthroned in yonder heavens!"[6]

James E. Talmage recognizes that major creeds in Christian history—the Nicene Creed and the Athanasian Creed, for example—speak of God having an immaterial nature. In response to this idea, Talmage rebuts,

> The immateriality of God as asserted in these declarations of sectarian faith is entirely at variance with the scriptures, and absolutely contradicted by the revelations of God's person and attributes. . . . We affirm that to deny the materiality of God's person is to deny God; for a thing without parts has no whole, and an immaterial body cannot exist. The Church of Jesus Christ of Latter-day Saints proclaims against the incomprehensible God, devoid of "body, parts, or passions," as a thing impossible of existence, and asserts its belief in and allegiance to the true and living God of scripture and revelation.[7]

Bruce McConkie, in his book *Mormon Doctrine,* agrees with Talmage and says:

> False creeds teach that God is a spirit essence that fills the immensity of space and is everywhere and nowhere in particular present. In a vain attempt to support this doctrine, formulated by councils in the early days of the great apostasy, it is common for apologists to point to the statement in the King James Bible which says, "God is a Spirit" (John 4:22–24). The fact is that this passage is mistranslated; instead, the correct statement, quoted in context reads: "The hour cometh, and now is, when the true worshipers shall worship the Father in spirit and in truth; for the Father seeketh such to worship him. For unto such hath God promised his Spirit. And they who worship

him, must worship in spirit and in truth" (*Inspired Version,* John 4:25–26).[8]

What evangelical Christians believe regarding the immateriality and spirituality of God is thus categorized by Mormons as an apostate doctrine. But what do the Scriptures say?

As we will see in a moment, the Mormons have distorted and twisted a number of key Bible passages to support their heretical idea that God the Father has a physical body. The sampling of passages we share over the next few pages is representative of the kinds of verses Mormons bring up to support their viewpoint.[9]

REASONING FROM THE SCRIPTURES

Genesis 1:26–27—*The Image of God*

The Mormon Teaching. In Genesis 1:26–27 we read, "God said, Let us make man in our image, after our likeness: and let them have dominion over the fish of the sea, and over the fowl of the air, and over the cattle, and over all the earth, and over every creeping thing that creepeth upon the earth. So God created man in his own image, in the image of God created he him; male and female created he them."

Since man was created with a body of flesh and bones, Mormons claim Genesis 1:26–27 supports their view that God the Father has a physical body. The logic goes like this: If man has a physical body, and if man is in the image of God, then God too must have a physical body.

Joseph Fielding Smith, in the three-volume set *Doctrines of Salvation,* stated, "Joseph Smith beheld the Father and the Son; therefore he could testify with personal knowledge that the scriptures were true wherein we read: 'So God created man in his own image, in the image of God created he him; male and female created he them.' This was to be understood literally, and not in some mystical or figurative sense."[10]

The Biblical Teaching. Genesis 1:26–27 is not referring to man being created in the physical image of God. Bible expositor Donald Grey Barnhouse is right when he says, "It was not a physical image, for God is Spirit (John 4:24), and a spirit hath not flesh and bones (Luke 24:39)."[11]

_____ *Ask . . .* _____

- Did you know that John 4:24 says that God is spirit?

- Did you know that in Luke 24:39, Jesus said a spirit does not have flesh and bones?

- If God is spirit, and if a spirit does not have flesh and bones, then doesn't this mean that God is not flesh and bones?

- Can you see that if God is spirit and does not have flesh and bones, then clearly a physical image is not being referred to in Genesis 1:26–27?

(If the Mormon says John 4:24 is mistranslated and tries to cite Joseph Smith's *Inspired Version,* see chapter 7 on how to undermine this version.)*

If man was not created in God's physical likeness, then how exactly *was* he made in God's image? Bible scholar

---

*Possible Mormon comeback: Some Mormons argue that what is affirmed in John 4:24 is true—that God *is* spirit, but *this isn't the whole picture,* they say. God is a spirit, just as humans are a spirit, "in the combination of spirit and body that makes of you a living being. . . . Each of us is a dual being of spiritual entity and physical entity" (see *A Sure Foundation: Answers to Difficult Gospel Questions* [Salt Lake City, UT: Deseret, 1988], p. 97). If the Mormon argues this way, you will need to focus on the context of John 4. The whole reason Jesus argued for the *spiritual* nature of God was to emphasize that God can't be physically confined to this temple (Jerusalem) or that temple (Mount Gerazim). God is *spirit,* and hence can be found in both of these temples (and elsewhere—since He is omnipresent).

Allen P. Ross tells us that "being created in God's image means that humans share, though imperfectly and finitely, in God's nature, that is, in His communicable attributes (life, personality, truth, wisdom, love, holiness, justice), and so have the capacity for spiritual fellowship with Him."[12] This seems to fit the context of Genesis well, for throughout the rest of the book we find God engaged in fellowship with different human beings.

When discussing the "image of God" with a Mormon, you'll want to emphasize that God is not an exalted or glorified man. Point him or her to some of the many verses in the Bible that draw a clear distinction between God and human beings. For example:

- In Hosea 11:9 we find God Himself affirming, "I am God, and not man."
- Numbers 23:19 tells us that "God is not a man that he should lie; neither the son of man, that He should repent."
- In Romans 1:22–23 Paul draws a clear distinction between God and men when he says, "Professing themselves to be wise, they became fools, and changed the glory of the incorruptible God into an image made like to corruptible man."
- Isaiah 45:12 quotes God as saying, "I have made the earth, and created man upon it."

Ask . . .

- Would you please read aloud from Hosea 11:9 and tell me what you think it means?

- Would you please read aloud from Numbers 23:19 and tell me what you think it means?

- Don't these verses draw a clear distinction between God and man?

Next, you will want to point out that even the Book of Mormon denies that God is a glorified man. If your Mormon friend has a Book of Mormon with him or her, sit down and look up the following verses, which refer to the spiritual (nonphysical) nature of God:

- Alma 22:10—"And Aaron said unto him: Yea, he is that Great Spirit, and he created all things both in heaven and in earth. Believest thou this?"
- Alma 31:15—"Holy, holy God; we believe that thou art God, and we believe that thou art holy, and that thou wast a spirit, and that thou art a spirit, and that thou wilt be a spirit forever."*

___ Ask . . . ___

- Would you open your Book of Mormon and read aloud from Alma 31:15?

- How do you interpret the words, "that thou wast a spirit, and that thou art a spirit, and that thou wilt be a spirit forever"?

- This verse says God is a spirit and not a glorified man, correct?

- So, like the Bible, the Book of Mormon doesn't agree with the Mormon view of God, does it?

(Of course, the Book of Mormon is not truly Scripture like the Bible is. But these questions will help you show the Mormon that even their "scriptures" say God is a spirit.)

---

*Possible Mormon comeback: Some Mormons may attempt to argue that references to God as a "Great Spirit" do not conflict with the idea that God has a physical, material body. Some will argue that the "Great Spirit" is actually Jesus, or, as He is called in his premortal existence, *Jehovah*. This Great Spirit was the creator of all things. Some time *later*, he took on a physical, material body. Such an argument is not convincing. Reading the Book of Mormon references *at face value* seems to indicate that God is *perpetually* a "Great Spirit." As Alma 31:15 says, "Thou wilt be a spirit forever."

Another way you can affirm that God does not have a physical body is to show that, according to the Bible, *God the Father is invisible.* He can't be seen. With your King James Version of the Bible in hand, look up the following verses and ask the Mormon to read aloud from them:

- 1 Timothy 1:17—"Now unto the King eternal, immortal, invisible, the only wise God, be honor and glory for ever and ever. Amen."
- Colossians 1:15—"Who is the image of the invisible God, the first-born of every creature."
- John 1:18—"No man hath seen God at any time; the only begotten Son, which is in the bosom of the Father, he hath declared him."

_____ *Ask . . .* _____

- Would you please read aloud from 1 Timothy 1:17 and tell me what you think it says about God? Colossians 1:15? John 1:18?

- Don't all these verses indicate that God the Father is invisible?

Exodus 33:11—*The Face of God*

The Mormon Teaching. In Exodus 33:11 we read, "The LORD spake unto Moses face to face, as a man speaketh unto his friend. And he turned again into the camp: but his servant Joshua, the son of Nun, a young man, departed not out of the tabernacle." Mormons reason that since Moses saw the LORD *face to face,* then God must, in fact, have a real face. And if He has a real face, then He must have a whole physical body as well. [13]

The Biblical Teaching. The description of Moses speaking to God "face to face" cannot be taken to mean that God actually has a physical face that Moses saw with his physical eyes. Rather, "face to face" is simply a Hebrew way of indicating "personally," "directly," or "intimately."[14] Moses was in the direct presence of God and interacted with Him on a personal and intimate basis.

Vine's Expository Dictionary of Biblical Words informs us that the word *face* is used "anthropomorphically of God."* Though the Bible speaks of God *as if* He had a face, the Bible "clearly teaches that God is a spiritual being and ought not to be depicted by an image or any likeness whatever (Exod. 20:4)."[15]

Bible scholar John D. Hannah says that "God would speak to Moses face to face, as a man speaks with his friend (v. 11), that is, clearly and openly. Moses' speaking 'face to face' with God does not contradict the fact that he was not allowed to see God's face (v. 20) as 'face to face' is a figurative expression suggesting openness and friendship (cf. Num. 12:8; Deut. 34:10)."[16]

There are other examples of metaphorical language used of God in the Bible. For example, Psalm 91:4 says, "He shall cover thee with his feathers, and under his wings shalt thou trust: his truth shall be thy shield and buckler." Are we to take this literally and envision God as a giant bird with wings and feathers? Of course not. The psalmist is simply using metaphorical language to communicate spiritual truth.

_____ *Ask* . . . _____

- Does the fact that God is said to have feathers and wings in Psalm 91 mean that God literally has feathers and wings? Why not?

- This is clearly figurative language, isn't it?

- In the same way, can you see that the term *face* is used figuratively of God, especially since the Bible says God is a spirit (John 4:24) and is invisible (Colossians 1:15)?

---

*Anthropomorphic language metaphorically attributes human characteristics to God (face, hands, eyes, arm, and so on). It is not to be taken literally.

Examining the broader context of Exodus 33 helps us to see that God does not have a physical face that we can see with earthly eyes. Dropping down to verse 18, humble and meek Moses made one of the boldest requests ever made of God: "Show me thy glory." But God warned Moses, "Thou canst not see my face: for there shall no man see me, and live" (verse 20).

Then the Lord said to Moses, "There is a place by me, and thou shalt stand upon a rock: And it shall come to pass, while my glory passeth by, that I will put thee in a clift of the rock, and will cover thee with my hand while I pass by: And I will take away mine hand, and thou shalt see my back parts: but my face shall not be seen" (Exodus 33:21–23).

This statement that no human can see God and live is consistent with what we know about God from elsewhere in Scripture. We know from 1 Timothy 6:16 that God dwells in "light which no man can approach." And the apostle John said that "no one has ever seen God [the Father], but God the only Son [Jesus Christ], who is at the Father's side, has made him known" (John 1:18 NIV).

Since no human can see God in His full glory and live, what Moses requested of God was more than the Lord would grant for Moses's own good. Nevertheless, God did place Moses in a cleft in a rock—apparently a cavelike crevice—and He then let His glory pass by. "The glory of God refers first and foremost to the sheer weight or the reality of his presence. The presence of God would come near Moses in spatial terms."[17] But God's glory would also include indescribable illumination that was too brilliant for humans to witness.

So, what actually occurred during this encounter Moses had with God? Old Testament scholar Walter Kaiser explains that

Moses would not be able to endure the spectacular purity, luminosity, and reality of staring at the raw glory of God himself. Instead, God would protect Moses from accidental (and apparently, fatal) sight of that glory. Therefore, in a striking anthropomorphism (a description of the reality of God in terms or analogies understandable to mortals), God would protect Moses from the full effects of looking directly at the glory of God by placing his hand over Moses' face until all God's glory had passed by.[18]

It was only after God's glory had passed by Moses that He removed His gracious, protecting "hand" (another anthropomorphic term). Then Moses would view what God had permitted—God's "back." But what does this mean?

We know from other Bible passages that God is spirit and He is formless (*see* Isaiah 31:3; John 4:24). Just as the use of "hand" is an anthropomorphism, so also is the word "back" an anthropomorphism. And what does the word "back" indicate? Kaiser notes that the Hebrew word for "back" (*'achowr*) can easily be rendered the "aftereffects" of the glory that had passed by.[19] "This would fit the context as well as the range of meanings for the Hebrew word used. Moses did not see the glory of God directly, but once it had gone past, God did allow him to view the results, the afterglow, that His presence had produced."[20]

One interesting fact you will want to mention to the Mormon is that Joseph Fielding Smith, in *Doctrines of Salvation,* said that Christ is the Jehovah of the Old Testament:

> All revelation since the fall has come through Jesus Christ, who is the Jehovah of the Old Testament. In all of the scriptures, where God is mentioned and where he has appeared, it was Jehovah who talked with Abraham, with Noah, Enoch, Moses, and all the prophets. He is the God of Israel, the Holy One of Israel; the one who led that nation out of Egyptian bondage, and who gave and fulfilled the Law of Moses. The Father has never dealt with man directly and personally since the fall, and he has never appeared except to introduce and bear record of the Son. Thus the *Inspired Version* records that "no man hath seen God at any time, except he hath borne record of the son."[21]

This means that *even in Mormon theology* Exodus 33:11 should not be cited to support the idea that *God the Father* has a physical body. According to Mormon expositors, the verse is dealing with Jesus Christ, not the Father. So when Mormons tell you that Exodus 33:11 teaches that God has a physical body, their argument is faulty. They are trying to cite a verse about Jehovah (Jesus) in order to prove a point about Elohim (the Father).

_____ *Ask . . .* _____

- Did you know that Joseph Fielding Smith said that all revelatory appearances to Old Testament persons like Moses were appearances of *Jehovah* (or Jesus) and not *Elohim* (the Father)?

- Did you know Mormon expositors say that in Exodus 33 Moses is dealing with Jehovah, and not Elohim?

- Isn't it faulty, then, for you to cite a passage dealing with Jehovah (Jesus) in order to prove a point about Elohim (the Father)?

- And, by the way, did you know that the Mormon view that *Elohim* is the Father and *Jehovah* is Jesus is flawed as well?

(You will want to explain that the names "Elohim" and "Jehovah" are *both* used of the Father, and *both* are used of Jesus. A verse in which both terms are used of Jesus, for example, is Isaiah 40:3: "The voice of him that crieth in the wilderness, Prepare ye the way of the LORD [Jehovah], make straight in the desert a highway for our God [Elohim]." This entire verse is written in reference to Jesus Christ (*see* John 1:23).)

At some point in your discussion you will want to mention that Joseph Smith taught that a person could see God the Father *only* if he held the Mormon priesthood. Smith credits

God Himself with telling him through revelation that "without the ordinances thereof, and the authority of the priesthood, the power of godliness is not manifest unto men in the flesh; For without this no man can see the face of God, even the Father, and live."[22] The reason this statement is so significant is that *Joseph Smith had not been ordained to the priesthood when he claimed to have seen God in 1820.*

_____ *Ask . . .* _____

- Did you know that Joseph Smith said that a person could see God *only* if he held the Mormon priesthood?

- Did you know that Joseph Smith was not yet ordained in the priesthood at the time he claimed to have seen God in 1820?

- How do you explain this?

It is likely that when Mormons talk to you about God's alleged physical body, they will argue that God is an exalted man—that at one time He was just like you and me but He progressed to the point of exaltation and godhood. If they bring this up, you'll want to share with them some Bible verses that affirm God's unchanging nature. For example:

- Malachi 3:6 quotes God Himself: "I am the LORD, I change not."
- James 1:17 tells us, "Every good gift and every perfect gift is from above, and cometh down from the Father of lights, with whom is no variableness, neither shadow of turning."
- Psalm 102:26–27 says, "They shall perish, but thou shalt endure: yea, all of them shall wax old like a garment; as a vesture shalt thou change them, and they shall be changed: But thou art the same, and thy years shall have no end."

- Psalm 90:2 says, "Before the mountains were brought forth, or ever thou hadst formed the earth and the world, even from everlasting to everlasting, thou art God."
- Even the Book of Mormon says God does not change: "I know that God is . . . neither a changeable being; but he is unchangeable from all eternity to all eternity" (Moroni 8:18).

_____ *Ask . . .* _____

- Would you open your Bible and read aloud from Malachi 3:6 and tell me what God says about Himself?

- Please read aloud from Psalm 102:26–27. What does it say about God?

- Would you open up your Book of Mormon to Moroni 8:18 and see if it agrees with Malachi 3:6 and Psalm 102:26–27—that God is unchangeable? (Your goal is to demonstrate that even the Mormon "scriptures" do not agree with current Mormon theology. In reality, the Book of Mormon is not Scripture.)

- How do you reconcile these passages with the Mormon idea that God was a man who progressed to exaltation and godhood?

John 14:9—*The Father Has a Body Like the Son Does*

The Mormon Teaching. In John 14:9 we read, "Jesus saith unto him, Have I been so long time with you, and yet hast thou not known me, Philip? he that hath seen me hath seen the Father; and how sayest thou then, show us the Father?"

James E. Talmage comments, "Even in bodily appearance the Father and the Son are alike; therefore said Christ when importuned by Philip to show to him and others the Father: 'Have I been so long time with you, and yet hast thou not known me, Philip? He that hath seen me hath seen the Father."[23] Talmage concludes, "It is clear that the Father is a personal being, possessing a definite form, with bodily parts and spiritual passions."[24]

The Biblical Teaching. Mormons are reading an idea into John 14:9 that simply is not there. In context, this verse clearly tells us that Jesus' mission, His words, and His works centered on the Father. And in this way Jesus was the ultimate revelation of the Father. A cursory scan through John's Gospel confirms that.

The Bible tells us that Jesus' mission—the purpose of His coming—was to reveal the Father to humankind: "No man hath seen God at any time; the only begotten Son, which is in the bosom of the Father, he hath declared him" (John 1:18). That's why Jesus could say, "He that seeth me seeth him that sent me" (John 12:45) and, "He that receiveth me receiveth him that sent me" (John 13:20).

What are some of the ways Jesus revealed the Father? One is that Jesus revealed the Father's *message* to humankind: "I have not spoken of myself; but the Father which sent me, he gave me a commandment, what I should say, and what I should speak" (John 12:49). Jesus boldly affirmed, "I do nothing of myself; but as my Father hath taught me, I speak these things" (John 8:28).

Jesus' *works* also served to reveal the Father: "Then answered Jesus and said unto them, Verily, verily, I say unto you, The Son can do nothing of himself, but what he seeth the Father do: for what things soever he doeth, these also doeth the Son likewise" (John 5:19).

It is against this backdrop that Jesus said, "He that hath seen me hath seen the Father" in John 14:9. Jesus came as the ultimate revelation of the Father. But there is nothing at all in the context that supports the Mormon claim that God the Father has a physical body. This is especially apparent in the verses that immediately follow John 14:9: "The Father that *dwelleth in me,* he doeth the works. Believe me that I am in the Father, and the *Father in me*" (verses 10–11, emphasis added). If the Father has a physical body of flesh and bones, as Mormons claim, then how is it possible for the Father to dwell within Jesus?

_____ *Ask . . .* _____

- Would you please read aloud from John 14:10–11?

- If the Father has a physical body of flesh and bones, as the Mormon church claims, then how is it possible for the Father to dwell within Jesus?

Hebrews 1:3—*The "Exact Representation" of God*

The Mormon Teaching. In Hebrews 1:3 we read this testimony about Jesus: "Who being the brightness of his glory, and the express image of his person, and upholding all things by the word of his power, when he had by himself purged our sins, sat down on the right hand of the Majesty on high."

Addressing this verse, James E. Talmage says, "We are assured that Christ was in the express image of His Father, after which image man also has been created. Therefore we know that both the Father and the Son are in form and stature perfect men; each of them possesses a tangible body, infinitely pure and perfect and attended by transcendent glory, nevertheless a body of flesh and bones."[25]

Moreover, Mormons point out, if the Father did not have a physical body of flesh and bones, then how could Jesus Christ have possibly sat down at the "right hand" of the Father? If the Father has a right hand, then He must have a body of flesh and bones.

The Biblical Teaching. Again, the Mormons are reading an idea into the text that is not there. The phrase "right hand" does not in any way suggest that the Father has a body of flesh and bones. In the Jewish mind, the right hand referred to the place of honor.[26] Bible expositor Ray C. Stedman notes, "The phrase *sat down at the right hand* is meant symbolically, not literally, for God has no right hand. It denotes the supreme honor accorded to the triumphant Lord, who is risen from the dead."[27]

David Reed and John Farkas provide an illustration to help us understand the metaphorical meaning of the phrase: "We use a somewhat similar expression today when we speak of someone's right-hand man. If a historical account refers to Robert F. Kennedy as President John F. Kennedy's right-hand man, we do not therefore conclude that Bobby actually stood at Jack's right side."[28] In the same way, the statement that Christ sat down at the Father's "right hand" is simply a metaphorical expression affirming that Christ was in a position of authority.

_____ *Ask . . .* _____

- When we say that Robert F. Kennedy was President John F. Kennedy's right-hand man, does that mean he was always at the right side of President Kennedy?

- The phrase "right-hand man" is a metaphorical term, isn't it?

- In the same way, can you see that to say Christ sat down at the right hand of the Father is simply a metaphorical expression stating that Christ is now in a position of authority?

In Hebrews 1:3, Jesus is called the "brightness of his [the Father's] glory, and the express image of his person." The word "brightness" is literally "radiance," "effulgence," or "shining forth." The word indicates not a reflection but an outshining of resplendent light—a shining forth to the world of the very character, attributes, and essence of God in Jesus Christ (*see* John 1:14).

Christ is the radiating effulgence of the divine essence. He radiates the divine glory of God because He *is* God. Jesus is not just a reflection of the Father's glory; Jesus' glory radiates from within His very being. The term "brightness" ("radiance") in Hebrews 1:3, then, is speaking of Christ's *deity* (Exodus 33:20; John 1:18; 4:24; 5:37; Colossians 1:15; 1 Timothy 1:17; 6:16; 1 John 4:12).

The phrase "express image" was used among the ancients to speak of an engraving tool or a stamp—often in reference to the minting of coins. In common usage, however, it came to refer to the actual mark engraved or the impression made by the tool itself. The word thus indicates an "exact expression."

In the present context, Jesus is portrayed as the absolute authentic representation of God's being *in terms of the divine nature* (*see* John 14:9). The writer of Hebrews could not have affirmed Christ's deity in any stronger terms. Christ is "the 'exact representation of God's real being,' and all the essential characteristics of God are brought into clear focus in Him."[29] Indeed, "all that God is—not merely in His ways, but in His being—is expressed absolutely by the Son."[30]

Related to this, we read in Colossians 1:15 that Jesus is the "image of the invisible God." Norman Geisler notes that in this verse the Greek word *eikon* ("image") literally means "the very substance" of God.[31] As Jesus Himself said, "He that hath seen me hath seen the Father" (John 14:9). Christ is the image of the invisible God "in the sense that the nature and being of God are perfectly revealed in him."[32] Clearly, then, the term "image" in Colossians 1:15 has nothing to do with a *physical* image—especially since the Father is called "invisible."

_____ *Ask . . .* _____

- Is it possible to make a literal image of something that is invisible?

- Would you please read aloud from Colossians 1:15?

- What do you think Colossians 1:15 means when it says that Jesus is the "image of the invisible God"? (Stress the words "image" and "invisible.")

- Read in its proper context, doesn't it seem like "image" is referring to Christ's deity and not to any alleged physical body?

John 1:18—*Those Quickened by the Spirit Can See God*

The Mormon Teaching. In John 1:18 we read, "No man hath seen God at any time; the only begotten Son, which is in the bosom of the Father, he hath declared him."

This passage poses a problem to the Mormon view that people in Bible times saw God's physical body. That, no doubt, is the reason Joseph Smith retranslated the passage as saying, "No man hath seen God at any time, *except he hath borne record of the Son;* for except it is through him no man can be saved"[33] (emphasis added).

The Biblical Teaching. When you talk to Mormons about John 1:18, you need to put the burden of proof on them. Ask them for manuscript support for such a rendering. (It doesn't exist.) Ask them to show from the Greek text how such a translation is possible. (It isn't possible.) They will no doubt tell you that Joseph Smith made this critical change in the text of John 1:18 under "divine inspiration."

If this happens, we recommend that you talk with them about the inspiration, inerrancy, and authority of the Bible (*see* chapters 8–10). You can also go to chapter 7 and discuss the problems with Joseph Smith's *Inspired Version* of the

Bible. You might even mention a few of Joseph Smith's false prophecies and doctrinal reversals (*see* chapter 6). Try to undermine the Mormon's confidence in Joseph Smith and gain his or her trust that the Bible is indeed reliable. This will help you convince the Mormon that the biblical rendering of John 1:18 may be right after all.

Beyond that, you will want to make clear what John 1:18 is really teaching. This verse tells us that Jesus became flesh in order to act as *Revealer.* In the empirical world of ordinary sense perceptions, Jesus was *seen* and *heard* by human beings as God's ultimate revelation to humankind.

Theologian Robert Lightner explains the various ways Jesus Christ was a revelation of the Father:

> Christ revealed the Person of God as He had never been made known before. He declared the Father to man (cf. John 1:18; 14:8, 9; 1 Tim. 3:16). The glory of God was made known by Christ (John 1:14; 2 Cor. 4:6; Isa. 40:5). God's power was revealed by God's Son. He did this many times and in many different ways (John 3:2; 1 Cor. 1:24). The wisdom of God was made known in the Person of Christ (John 7:46; 1 Cor. 1:24). The life of God was also declared by Him (1 John 1:1–3). To be sure, God's boundless love was revealed and demonstrated by the Saviour (John 3:16; Rom. 5:8; 1 John 3:16). The grace of God, the undeserved favor which He bestowed upon mankind, was also revealed by the Lord Jesus (Luke 2:40; John 1:17; 2 Thess. 1:12).[34]

The statement in John 1:18 that "no man hath seen God at any time" simply means that no one has ever beheld God in His essential nature and full, unveiled glory. Certainly there were *theophanies* (temporary appearances of God) in Old Testament times. These brief appearances generally took place to give revelation to Old Testament patriarchs. But these were simply temporary visible manifestations of the invisible spiritual God (John 4:24). (See *Christ Before the Manger: The Life and Times of the Preincarnate Christ,* by Ron Rhodes, for more on this subject.[35])

The apostle Paul tells us that God the Father is by nature "invisible" (1 Timothy 1:17), and that God is one "who lives in unapproachable light, whom no one has seen or can see" (6:16 NIV). It is *only* in the person of Jesus Christ that the inner essence or nature of God is fully disclosed to humankind (John 1:18).[36] No human being can give such a revelation of God because no one—including Joseph Smith—has ever seen God in His full glory and majesty.

_____ *Ask . . .* _____

- Can we really trust the "prophet" Joseph Smith's rendering of John 1:18 in view of his many false prophecies? (*See* chapter 6.)

- Can we take Joseph Smith's rendering of John 1:18 seriously when there's no evidence for it in the Greek manuscripts, and especially when he proved with the so-called Book of Abraham that he dishonestly "translated" ancient records when he *did* have the supposed manuscripts? (*See* chapter 14 for information on the Book of Abraham.)

We suggest that when you close your discussion about the alleged flesh-and-bones body of God the Father, you should recap your main points to the Mormon. Briefly:

- *God is a spirit* (John 4:24), and *a spirit does not have flesh and bones* (Luke 24:39).
- The Bible says that *God is not a man* (Hosea 11:9).
- The Book of Mormon *denies that God is a glorified man* (Alma 22:10, 31:15; Mormon 9:9–11; Moroni 7:22, and 8:18).
- God the Father *is invisible* (Colossians 1:15).
- *Anthropomorphisms* (figures of speech)—such as "face" and "hands"—are often used of God in Scripture.

- God is *unchangeable* and does not "progress" to exaltation. Malachi 3:6 quotes the words of God this way: "I am the LORD, I change not."
- Even the Book of Mormon says *God does not change:* "I know that God is . . . neither a changeable being; but he is unchangeable from all eternity to all eternity."[37]

14

The Mormon Doctrine of God— Part 2: The Plurality of Gods

As is typical with many cults, the Mormons utilize Christian terminology but they pour their own cultic meanings into those words. The word *Trinity* is an example. Though some Mormons may use the word in describing their own view of God, they do not define it as orthodox Christians do.

Mormonism teaches that the Persons of the Trinity are not three Persons *in one being,* as historic Christianity has always taught (from the Bible); rather, Mormons say the Father, Son, and Holy Spirit are *three separate beings*—they are three separate, distinct Gods.[1]

In what way, then, are the three Persons of the Trinity *one?* Some Mormons say the three Persons are united in their common purpose. Others say they are "united as one in the attributes of perfection."[2] Either way, the Father, Son, and Holy Spirit are not viewed as one being.

Bruce McConkie reasons that "as each of these persons is a God, it is evident, from this standpoint alone, that a plurality of Gods exists. To us, speaking in the proper finite sense, these three are the only Gods we worship. But in addition there is an infinite number of holy personages, drawn from worlds without number, who have passed on to exaltation and are thus gods."[3]

Did Joseph Smith teach the doctrine of the plurality of Gods? Though references in the Book of Mormon (published early in his prophetic career) attest to the existence of only one God, Smith eventually went on to teach the plurality of Gods not only in his writings but also in his public speaking. In one message Smith said this:

> I will preach on the plurality of Gods. . . . I wish to declare I have always and in all congregations when I preached on the subject of the Deity, it has been the plurality of Gods. It has been preached by the Elders for fifteen years. I have always declared God to be a distinct personage, Jesus Christ a separate and distinct personage from God the Father, and that the Holy Ghost was a distinct personage and a Spirit: and these three constitute three distinct personages and three Gods. If this is in accordance with the New Testament, lo and behold! We have three Gods, anyhow, and they are plural; and who can contradict it?[4]

Joseph Fielding Smith adds that "Joseph Smith taught a plurality of gods, and that man by obeying the commandments of God and keeping the whole law will eventually reach the power and exaltation by which *he also* will become a god"[5] (emphasis added).

Spencer W. Kimball, a former president of the church, made the following remarks to a group about how they can become gods: "Brethren 225,000 of you are here tonight. I suppose 225,000 of you may become gods. There seems to be plenty of space out there in the universe. And the Lord has proved that he knows how to do it. I think he could make, or probably have us help make, worlds for all of us, for every one of us 225,000."[6]

Brigham Young said, "How many Gods there are, I do not know. But there never was a time when there were not Gods and worlds, and when men were not passing through the same ordeals that we are now passing through. That course has been from all eternity, and it is and will be to all eternity."[7]

Mormon apostle Orson Pratt said, "If we should take a million of worlds like this and number their particles, we should find that there are more Gods than there are particles of matter in those worlds."[8]

It is critical to recognize that in Mormon theology, just as Jesus has a Father, so the Father allegedly has a Father, and the Father of Jesus' Father has a Father. This endless succession of Fathers goes on and on, up the hierarchy of exalted beings in the universe.[9]

Joseph Fielding Smith expresses the Mormon logic behind the concept: "If Jesus Christ was the Son of God, and John discovered that God the Father of Jesus Christ had a Father, you may suppose that he had a Father also. Where was there ever a son without a Father? . . . Hence if Jesus had a Father, can we not believe that he had a Father also?"[10] Smith ponders, "Is this not a reasonable thought, especially when we remember that the promises are made to us that we may become like him?"[11] Hence, there is a Father of the Father of the Father of the Father of the Father, *ad infinitum.*

Not only are there numerous Father-gods, there is also a "Heavenly Mother." Even though the Mormon doctrine of a Heavenly Mother, who begets spirit-children in heaven, is not found in any Mormon scripture, it is definitely a teaching proclaimed by the General Authorities of the Mormon church, including the Prophet, Seer, and Revelator.

In *A Study of the Articles of Faith,* James E. Talmage says, "We are expressly told that God is the Father of our Spirits, and to apprehend the literalness of this solemn truth we must know that a Mother of Spirits is an existent personality."[12] In the book *Man: His Origin and Destiny,* we are told that "all men and women are in the similitude of the Universal Father and Mother, and are literally the sons and daughters of deity."[13]

Milton R. Hunter, who served in the First Council of the Seventy, said, "The stupendous truth of the existence of a

Heavenly Mother, as well as a Heavenly Father, became established facts in Mormon theology."[14] What do the "Heavenly Father" and "Heavenly Mother" do? In 1853, Orson Pratt explained:

> In the Heaven where our spirits were born, there are many Gods, each one of whom has his own wife or wives which were given to him previous to his redemption, while yet in his mortal state. Each God, through his wife or wives, raises up a numerous family of sons and daughters. . . . As soon as each God has begotten many millions of male and female spirits . . . he, in connection with his sons, organizes a new world, after a similar order to the one which we now inhabit, where he sends both the male and female spirits to inhabit tabernacles of flesh and bones. . . . The inhabitants of each world are required to reverence, adore, and worship their own personal father who dwells in the Heaven which they formerly inhabited.[15]

All of this is part and parcel of the polytheistic world of Mormonism. Mormons believe in numerous gods. Even though they believe the Father, Son, and Holy Spirit are the principal gods with whom we have to do, they also believe there are innumerable gods besides these. And they believe that *they, too,* will one day become gods.

REASONING FROM THE SCRIPTURES

Genesis 1:26–27—*A Plurality of Gods?*

The Mormon Teaching. In Genesis 1:26–27 we read, "God said, Let us make man in our image, after our likeness: and let them have dominion over the fish of the sea, and over the fowl of the air, and over the cattle, and over all the earth, and over every creeping thing that creepeth upon the earth. So God created man in his own image, in the image of God created he him; male and female created he them."

In the Book of Abraham (purportedly authored by Abraham himself and supernaturally translated by Joseph Smith from Egyptian papyri fragments and later included in the volume of Mormon scripture known as The Pearl of Great Price), a dramatically different version of the Genesis 1 account of creation is given—and the plural form, "Gods," is found throughout. The "Gods" created the universe, the Mormon scriptures teach.

Joseph Smith tried to justify this polytheistic rendering by stating that the Hebrew word usually translated God, *Elohim,* has a plural ending.[16] Smith said that "the doctrine of a plurality of gods is as prominent in the Bible as any other doctrine. It is all over the face of the Bible. It stands beyond the power of controversy. A wayfaring man, though a fool, need not err therein."[17] Smith was sure that "in the beginning, the head of the Gods called a council of the Gods; and they came together and concocted a plan to create the world and people it."[18]

The Book of Abraham 4:1–2 tells us that the "Gods organized and formed the heavens and the earth. . . . and the Spirit of the Gods was brooding upon the face of the waters."[19] In verses 26 and 27 we are told, "the Gods took counsel among themselves and said: let us go down and form man in our image, after our likeness. . . . So the Gods went down to organize man in their own image, in the image of the Gods to form they him, male and female to form they them."[20]

The Biblical Teaching. We must begin by pointing out that the collection of Egyptian writings that the LDS church now calls the Book of Abraham has no credibility whatsoever and is actually irrefutable proof that Joseph Smith had no divine ability to translate. In fact, some of the original papyri actually used by Smith to prepare the book were rediscovered in 1966 and translated by professional Egyptologists, who unanimously identified them as a collection of typical pagan funerary texts and confirmed that they had nothing to do with the ideas and events portrayed in the Book of Abraham.*

_____ *Ask . . .* _____

- Did you know that the actual ancient Egyptian writings that Joseph Smith called the Book of Abraham were rediscovered in 1966 and have been translated by top modern Egyptologists?

- Did you know that these Egyptologists identified the materials as coming from ancient pagan funerary texts like the *Book of the Dead,* and that not one of Joseph's "translations" comes even close to being right?

It is true that in Genesis 1:26–27 the Hebrew word for God, *Elohim,* has a plural ending. Yet you will want to emphasize two facts to the Mormon: 1) the plural ending on *Elohim* does not support the Mormon view that there are three distinct and separate personages in the Godhead; and 2) the plural ending does not contradict or conflict with the orthodox doctrine of the Trinity.

Christian scholars believe the plural form, *Elohim,* is actually a "plural of majesty"—pointing to the majesty, dignity, and greatness of God. Norman Geisler and Thomas Howe suggest that "the plural nature of the Hebrew word [*Elohim*] is designed to give a fuller, more majestic sense to God's name."[21] (Queen Victoria used a "plural of majesty" when—referring *only to herself*—she commented, "*We* are not amused.")

---

*An excellent resource on this subject is Charles M. Larson, ". . . *By His Own Hand Upon Papyrus*" (Grand Rapids, MI: Institute of Religious Research, 1992).

What about the plural pronouns ("Let *us* make man in *our* image")? Biblical grammarians tell us that the plural pronouns are a *grammatical necessity*. These grammarians point out that "the plural pronoun 'us' is simply required by the plural Hebrew noun *elohim* which is translated 'God' (Then God [*elohim,* plural] said, 'Let Us [plural] make man in Our [plural] image')."[22] In other words, the plural pronoun "us" corresponds grammatically with the plural form of the Hebrew word *Elohim.* One demands the other.

Of course, we need to emphasize to Mormons that the plural form of *Elohim* does not indicate that there is more than one God. That is an utter abuse of linguistics, and not a single scholar well-versed in the original languages of the Bible would ever go along with such an interpretation.[23] Why? Because Elohim is consistently portrayed as the *one true God* of Israel throughout the Old Testament. For example, Deuteronomy 6:4 says, "Hear, O Israel: The LORD [Jehovah] our God [Elohim] is one LORD [Jehovah]" (inserts added).

After explaining all this to the Mormon, open your Bible and read aloud from Genesis 1:26–27, this time emphasizing the italicized words: "God said, Let us make man in *our image*, after *our likeness:* and let them have dominion over the fish of the sea, and over the fowl of the air, and over the cattle, and over all the earth, and over every creeping thing that creepeth upon the earth. So God created man in *his own* image, in the *image of God* created *he* him; male and female created *he* them."

Point out how the phrases "*our* image" and "*our* likeness" in verse 26 are explained in verse 27 as "the image *of God*" and "in *his own* image." This supports the idea that even though plural pronouns were used in reference to God, *only one God was meant.* Then reiterate that Hebrew scholars say this is a "plural of majesty," pointing to the one true God's majesty, dignity, and greatness.

___ *Ask . . .* ___

- Would you allow me to read aloud from Genesis 1:26–27? Please listen especially to the words I emphasize. (Invite the Mormon to look on as you read.)

- Did you notice how the phrases "*our* image" and "*our* likeness" in verse 26 are explained in verse 27 as "the image *of God*" and "in *his own* image"?

- Do you think it's possible that Hebrew scholars are correct to call the plural form of *Elohim* a "plural of majesty"?

Even the Book of Mormon itself states plainly that there is only one God. If the Mormon happens to have a Book of Mormon with him or her, look up the following verses. You will find that the Book of Mormon actually disagrees with Mormon polytheism.

- In Alma 11:22–31, we find a strong affirmation that there is only one God. A man named Amulek opens a dialogue with Zeezrom by stating that he cannot say anything contrary to God's spirit. Hence, the words of Amulek are on par with the words of God himself. Zeezrom asks Amulek, "Is there more than one God?" Amulek answers, "No." Zeezrom then asks, "How knowest thou these things?" Amulek replies, "An angel hath made them known to me."*

---

*Possible Mormon comeback:** Some Mormons may attempt to argue that because the Father, Son, and Holy Spirit are "one in purpose, mission, and glory," the "three Gods" indeed are "one Eternal God," as Amulek said (see *A Sure Foundation: Answers to Difficult Gospel Questions* [Salt Lake City, UT: Deseret, 1988], p. 7). This is semantic double-talk. You can't say the Father, Son, and Holy Spirit are *distinct Gods* and at the same time say that they are "*one* Eternal God."

- Alma 11:44 tells us, "Be arraigned before the bar of Christ the Son, and God the Father, and the Holy Spirit, which is one Eternal God."
- In Mormon 7:7 we read the words, ". . . unto the Father, and unto the Son, and unto the Holy Ghost, which are one God."

Now, remember, Joseph Smith declared that the Book of Mormon was the most correct book on earth. After reading these verses aloud . . .

___ *Ask* . . . _____

- What do you think about all these verses in the Book of Mormon that say there is "only one true God" (as Alma says)?

- Tell me, is the Book of Mormon wrong, or is current Mormon doctrine (which teaches the plurality of Gods) wrong?

- Didn't Joseph Smith say the Book of Mormon was the most correct book on earth?

- If it's the most correct book on earth, how could it be wrong in saying that there is only one true God?

Psalm 82:1,6; John 10:34—*"Ye Are Gods"*

The Mormon Teaching. In Psalm 82:1,6 we read, "God standeth in the congregation of the mighty; he judgeth among the gods. . . . I have said, Ye are gods; and all of you are children of the most High." Jesus quotes from this very psalm in John 10:34 when speaking to a group of Jews: "Is it not written in your law, I said, Ye are gods?"

Mormons are sure that Psalm 82 supports the doctrine of the plurality of Gods.[24] If the psalmist said it, and if it was confirmed by no less than Jesus Himself, surely it is clear that there is a plurality of Gods in the universe.

The Biblical Teaching. When we read Psalm 82 carefully we find that God is pronouncing judgment against the evil judges of Israel. These judges were, of course, supposed to act righteously and be God's representatives on earth. As Old Testament scholar Walter C. Kaiser says, "Our Lord depended on these administrators, functioning as magistrates in the divinely ordained state, to bring a measure of immediate relief from the injustices and brutalities of life."[25] These were people "who had been especially chosen by God to be bearers of His saving truth and administrators of His holy law."[26]

But these judges became corrupt and were unjust in their dealings with men. God's charge against them was that they administered justice unjustly, showing favor to the wicked instead of upholding the rights of the helpless and oppressed.[27] And in verses 6–7, we find the psalmist Asaph addressing these unjust human judges: "I have said, Ye are gods; and all of you are children of the most High. But ye shall die like men, and fall like one of the princes."[28]

Hebrew scholars tell us that the Hebrew word *Elohim* can sometimes refer to human beings.* The judges were called "gods" *not* because they were actual deity but because they pronounced life-and-death judgments against people.

Looking at the context of Psalm 82, it is clear that the Lord, through Asaph, is speaking *in irony* in this verse. He is saying in effect, "I have called you 'gods,' but in fact you will die like the men that you really are."

This psalm helps us to understand what Jesus was saying in John 10:34. When Jesus quoted from this psalm, He was saying that what the Israelite judges were called in irony and

---

*See Francis Brown, S.R. Driver, and Charles A. Briggs, *A Hebrew and English Lexicon of the Old Testament* (Oxford: Clarendon Press, 1980), p. 41.

in judgment, *He is in reality.* "He does what they could not do, and is what they could never be."[29]

Notice also that in John 10:34 Jesus spoke in the present tense, "Ye *are* gods" (emphasis added). This is important, because not even Mormon leaders claim that they are gods at the present moment. Rather, they believe in a future exaltation. So John 10:34 doesn't properly fit the context of Mormon theology.

_____ *Ask . . .* _____

- Did you notice that Jesus spoke in the present tense in John 10:34—"Ye *are* gods"?

- Do you believe *you* are a God at the present moment?

(They'll say no. Keep going.)

- But Jesus said "Ye *are* gods"—as in the *present moment.* So Jesus couldn't have intended to communicate that His listeners were actually gods, right?

- Doesn't it make more sense to look at the context in Psalm 82, where we discover that the unjust judges were called "gods" only in irony and judgment? (Remind the Mormon that the judges *died* in judgment. Does that sound like a god?)

- Is it not clear from the context that what the Israelite judges were called in irony and in judgment, *Jesus is in reality?*

At this point you may want to pull out the "heavy guns" in your biblical arsenal. Open your Bible and read from Isaiah 44:8, where God Himself asks, "Is there a God beside me? yea, there is no God; I know not any."

If that verse it true, then God could not have had a Father and a Grandfather who were gods in their own rights (as Mormons teach). Otherwise, we'd have to say that the God speaking in Isaiah 44:8 was either lying or forgot His own Father.

Similarly, in Isaiah 43:10 God says, "*Before me* there was no God formed, neither shall there be *after me*" (emphasis added). Since there were no gods *before* the God of the Bible, this means that God had no Father-gods or Grandfather-gods *before* him. Since no gods will come *after* God, this means that none of His children will *become* Gods.

_____ *Ask* . . . _____

- Would you please read aloud from Isaiah 44:8?

- How do you reconcile this verse with the Mormon claim that God has a Father, and the Father has a Father, and so on? Did the God of Isaiah 44:8 forget His own Father?

- Doctrine and Covenants 96:30 says "the glory of God is *intelligence*" (emphasis added). So the God of Isaiah 44:8 couldn't have forgotten there were other gods, could He?

- Would you please read aloud from Isaiah 43:10?

- Since there were no gods *before* the God of the Bible, doesn't this mean that our Father had no Father-gods or Grandfather-gods *before* Him?

- Since no gods will come *after* God, doesn't this mean that none of His children will *become* Gods?

Matthew 3:16–17—*Separate Gods in Separate Places?*

The Mormon Teaching. In Matthew 3:16–17 we read, "Jesus, when he was baptized, went up straightway out of the water: and, lo, the heavens were opened unto him, and he saw the Spirit of God descending like a dove, and lighting upon him: And lo a voice from heaven, saying, This is my beloved Son, in whom I am well pleased."

James E. Talmage says:

> That these three are separate individuals, physically distinct from each other, is demonstrated by the accepted records of divine dealings with man. On the occasion of the Savior's baptism, John recognized the sign of the Holy Ghost; he saw before him in a tabernacle of flesh the Christ, unto whom he had administered the holy ordinance; and he heard the voice of the Father. The three personages of the Godhead were present, manifesting themselves each in a different way, and each distinct from the others.[30]

Thus, the Father, Son, and Holy Spirit cannot be "one person," as Trinitarians believe.

The Biblical Teaching. In Matthew 3:16–17 the doctrine of the Trinity is plainly evident: The *Son* is baptized, the *Father* speaks of His Son, and the *Holy Spirit* descends on the Son like a dove. You need to understand, however, that Mormons typically misdefine the Trinity as being "three in one Person." Mormon missionaries often think that if they can show you that the Father, Son, and Holy Spirit are distinct (as is evident in Matthew 3:16–17), then they've proven the Trinitarian "three-in-one-Person" doctrine wrong. They desperately want to prove that there are three distinct and separate *personages* evident in this passage.

Of course, Trinitarians do not believe in "three in one Person." Trinitarians believe that there is *one God,* but that within the unity of the Godhead there are three co-equal, co-eternal *Persons.* So the Trinity is not "three in one Person" but "three Persons in the one Godhead." You will want to clarify this carefully for the Mormon.

_____ *Ask . . .* _____

• Would you please define the Trinity for me?

(Listen carefully for something that sounds like "three in one Person." Then proceed to explain what the Trinity really is.)

If you can explain the basic points of the doctrine of the Trinity in a clear and concise way, you will give the Mormon a lot to think about after he or she leaves. We suggest that you familiarize yourself with the following points:

Definition of the Trinity. A theological definition of the Trinity is based on three lines of biblical evidence: 1) evidence that there is only one true God; 2) evidence that there are three Persons who are recognized as God; and 3) evidence for three-in-oneness within the Godhead.

Before we examine these three lines of evidence, it is important that we clarify what we *do not* mean by the word *Trinity.* In our attempt to understand God's triune nature, two errors must be avoided:

First, we must not conclude that the Godhead is composed of three separate and distinct individuals such as Peter, James, and Paul, each with their own unique characteristics or attributes. Such a concept leads to either *tritheism* (the belief that there are three Gods rather than three Persons within the Godhead), or, as is the case with the Mormons, *polytheism* (belief in many gods).

Second, we must not conclude that the Godhead is *one Person only* and that the triune aspect of His being is no more than three fields of interest, activities, or modes of manifestation—a view known as *modalism.* The fallacy of these errors will become clearer as we examine the biblical evidence for the Trinity.

Evidence for One God. The fact that there is only one true God is the consistent testimony of Scripture from Genesis to

Revelation. It is like a thread that runs through every page of the Bible. An early Hebrew confession of faith—the *Shema*—portrays this consistent emphasis: "Hear, O Israel: The LORD our God is one LORD" (Deuteronomy 6:4). In a culture saturated with false gods and idols, the *Shema* was particularly meaningful for the Israelites.

In the "Song of Moses," which Moses recited to the whole assembly of Israel following the exodus from Egypt, we find God's own words worshipfully repeated: "See now that I, even I, am he, and there is no god with me: I kill, and I make alive; I wound, and I heal: neither is there any that can deliver out of my hand" (Deuteronomy 32:39). The God of the Bible is without rival.

After God had made some astonishing promises to David (*see* the Davidic Covenant in 2 Samuel 7:12–16), David responded by offering praise to God: "Wherefore thou art great, O LORD God: for there is none like thee, neither is there any God beside thee, according to all that we have heard with our ears" (2 Samuel 7:22). Later, in the form of a psalm, David again praised God with the words, "Thou art great, and doest wondrous things: thou art God alone" (Psalm 86:10).

God Himself affirmed through Isaiah the prophet, "I am the first, and I am the last; and beside me there is no God" (Isaiah 44:6; *see* also 37:20; 43:10; 45:5,14,21–22). God later said, "I am God, and there is none else; I am God, and there is none like me" (46:9). The Book of Isaiah shows us that God often demonstrated that He alone is God by foretelling the future—something that false gods could never do (46:8–10).

The oneness of God is also often emphasized in the New Testament. In 1 Corinthians 8:4, for example, the apostle Paul asserted that "an idol is nothing in the world, and that there is none other God but one." James 2:19 likewise says, "Thou believest that there is one God; thou doest well: the devils also believe, and tremble." These and a multitude of other verses (for example, John 5:44; 17:3; Romans 3:29–30; 16:27; Galatians 3:20; Ephesians 4:6; 1 Thessalonians 1:9; 1 Timothy 1:17; 2:5; 1 John 5:20–21; Jude 25) make it absolutely clear that there is one and only one God.

Evidence for Three Persons Who Are Called God. Though Scripture clearly tells us there is *only one God,* in the unfolding of God's revelation to humankind we also see that there are *three distinct Persons*—the Father, the Son, and the Holy Spirit—who are called God.

- Peter refers to the "elect according to the foreknowledge of God the *Father*" (1 Peter 1:2, emphasis added).
- When *Jesus* made a post-resurrection appearance to doubting Thomas, Thomas said to Him, "My Lord and my God" (John 20:28). As well, the Father said of the Son, "Thy throne, O God, is for ever and ever" (Hebrews 1:8).
- In Acts 5:3–4, we are told that lying to the Holy Spirit is equivalent to lying to God. Peter said, "Ananias, why hath Satan filled thine heart to *lie to the Holy Ghost,* and to keep back part of the price of the land? While it remained, was it not thine own? and after it was sold, was it not in thine own power? why hast thou conceived this thing in thine heart? *thou hast not lied unto men, but unto God*" (emphasis added).

Besides being called God, each of the three Persons on different occasions are seen to possess the attributes of deity. For example:

- All three Persons possess the attribute of *omnipresence* (that is, all three are everywhere-present): the Father (Matthew 19:26), the Son (Matthew 28:18), and the Holy Spirit (Psalm 139:7).
- All three have the attribute of *omniscience* (all-knowingness): the Father (Romans 11:33), the Son (Matthew 9:4), and the Holy Spirit (1 Corinthians 2:10).

- All three have the attribute of *omnipotence* (that is, all three are all-powerful): the Father (Jeremiah 32:27), the Son (Matthew 28:18), and the Holy Spirit (Romans 15:19).
- *Holiness* is ascribed to each of the three Persons: the Father (Revelation 15:4), the Son (Acts 3:14), and the Holy Spirit (John 16:7–14).
- *Eternity* is ascribed to all three Persons: the Father (Psalm 90:2), the Son (Micah 5:2; John 1:2; Revelation 1:8,17), and the Holy Spirit (Hebrews 9:14).
- Each of the three Persons is individually described as *the truth:* the Father (John 7:28), the Son (Revelation 3:7), and the Holy Spirit (1 John 5:6).
- As well, each of the three is called *Lord* (Romans 10:12; Luke 2:11; 2 Corinthians 3:17), *everlasting* (Romans 16:26; Revelation 22:13; Hebrews 9:14), *almighty* (Genesis 17:1; Revelation 1:8; Romans 15:19), and *powerful* (Jeremiah 32:17; Hebrews 1:3; Luke 1:35).[31]

In addition to having the attributes of deity, each of the three Persons can do the *works* of deity. For example, all three were involved in the creation of the world: the Father (Genesis 2:7; Psalm 102:25), the Son (John 1:3; Colossians 1:16; Hebrews 1:2), and the Holy Spirit (Genesis 1:2; Job 33:4; Psalm 104:30).

Evidence for Three-in-Oneness. The evidence for three-in-oneness in the Godhead is immense. Let's look at two examples.

After Jesus had risen from the dead, He referred to all three Persons in the Trinity. He instructed the disciples, "Go ye therefore, and teach all nations, baptizing them in the name of *the Father,* and of *the Son,* and of *the Holy Ghost*" (Matthew 28:19, emphasis added). It is significant that the word "name" is singular in the Greek text, indicating that there is one God, but three distinct Persons within the Godhead—the Father, the Son, and the Holy Spirit.[32] Theologian Robert Reymond draws our attention to the importance of this verse for the doctrine of the Trinity:

Jesus does not say, (1) "into the names [plural] of the Father and of the Son and of the Holy Spirit," or what is its virtual equivalent, (2) "into the name of the Father, and into the name of the Son, and into the name of the Holy Spirit," as if we had to deal with three separate Beings. Nor does He say, (3) "into the name of the Father, Son, and Holy Spirit," (omitting the three recurring articles), as if "the Father, Son, and Holy Ghost" might be taken as merely three designations of a single person. What He does say is this: (4) "into the name [singular] of *the* Father, and of *the* Son, and of *the* Holy Spirit," first asserting the unity of the three by combining them all within the bounds of the single Name, and then [throwing] into emphasis the distinctness of each by introducing them in turn with the repeated article. [33]

Additional evidence for God's three-in-oneness is found in Paul's benediction in his second epistle to the Corinthians: "The grace of the Lord Jesus Christ, and the love of God [the Father], and the communion of the Holy Ghost, be with you all" (2 Corinthians 13:14, insert added). This verse shows the intimacy that each of the three Persons has with the believer.

Conclusion: We have seen that the doctrine of the Trinity is firmly grounded in three lines of biblical evidence: 1) evidence that there is only one true God; 2) evidence that there are three Persons who are God; and 3) evidence for three-in-oneness within the Godhead. You should familiarize yourself with these three lines of evidence so you can help Mormons to correct their misconceptions about the Trinity.

Acts 7:55–56—*Different Personages Called "God"*

The Mormon Teaching. In Acts 7:55–56 we read this about Stephen: "He, being full of the Holy Ghost, looked up steadfastly into heaven, and saw the glory of God, and Jesus standing on the right hand of God, And said, Behold, I see the heavens opened, and the Son of man standing on the right hand of God."

Mormons reason that since Stephen saw two distinct personages, then they must be distinct, separate Gods. James E. Talmage explains that "Stephen, at the time of his martyrdom, was blessed with the power of heavenly vision, and he saw Jesus standing on the right hand of God." He then attempts to draw a direct comparison with the First Vision of Joseph Smith, who, "while calling upon the Lord in fervent prayer, saw the Father and the Son, standing in the midst of light that shamed the brightness of the sun."[34]

The Biblical Teaching. First you will want to point out that the text does not say Stephen saw the physical, material body of God the Father. Rather, Stephen saw the *glory of God* and saw Jesus *standing on the right hand of God.*

That Stephen beheld the "glory of God" simply means that during his vision he saw the brilliant luminosity that often accompanies divine manifestations. This is illustrated for us in the book of Isaiah. According to Isaiah 6:1–5, Isaiah saw the incredible glory of "the LORD of hosts." The light was virtually blinding. When we get to the New Testament—in John 12:41—we are told that what Isaiah actually saw was the glory of Jesus Christ. The glory of God and the glory of Jesus Christ are clearly equated here. So, when Acts 7:55 says that Stephen saw the "glory of God," this does not mean that he saw the physical, material Father.

As we learned earlier, the phrase "right hand" does not in any way suggest that the Father has a body of flesh and bones. In the Jewish mind, the right hand simply referred to the place of honor.[35] Bible expositor Ray C. Stedman notes, "The phrase *sat down at the right hand* is meant symbolically, not literally, for God has no right hand. It denotes the supreme honor accorded to the triumphant Lord, who is risen from the dead."[36]

When Stephen saw Christ at the right hand of the Father, he witnessed Christ in His rightful place of authority—a position of prominence. Any suggestion that Stephen saw two distinct, physical personages is unwarranted and is simply reading an idea into the text that is not there.

You might find it beneficial to remind the Mormon of what other Bible verses say about the Father.

- John 1:18, for example, says, "No man hath seen God at any time; the only begotten Son, which is in the bosom of the Father, he hath declared him."
- First Timothy 1:17 tells us that the Father is the "King eternal, immortal, invisible."
- Colossians 1:15 refers to the Father as "the invisible God."

_____ *Ask* . . . _____

- Where in the text of Acts 7:55–56 do we read that Stephen saw the physical, material body of God the Father?

- If no man has seen God the Father at any time, as John 1:18 clearly tells us, then how could Stephen have seen the Father?

- If God the Father is invisible, as Colossians 1:15 clearly says, then how could Stephen have seen Him?

---

1 Corinthians 8:5—*"Gods" in Heaven and on Earth*

The Mormon Teaching. In 1 Corinthians 8:5 we read, "For though there be that are called gods, whether in heaven or in earth, (as there be gods many, and lords many)."

Addressing this verse, Joseph Smith once said that "Paul had no allusion to the heathen gods. I have it from God, and get over it if you can. I have a witness of the Holy Ghost, and a testimony that Paul had no allusion to the heathen Gods in the text."[37] Smith said, "Paul says there are Gods many and Lords many. I want to set it forth in a plain and simple manner."[38]

Bruce McConkie misleadingly assures us that this is not polytheism: "It should be remembered that polytheism has reference to pagan deities to whom reverence, devotion, and worship are given. It is not to be confused with the gospel truth that there are 'gods many, and lords many.' ... The saints are not polytheists."[39]

The Biblical Teaching. The "saints" *are* polytheists,* and they are basing their polytheism on distorted interpretations of biblical texts. You need to emphasize to the Mormon that when interpreting a Bible verse, a person must look at the surrounding context. And the context of 1 Corinthians 8 is clearly *monotheistic.*

To demonstrate this, ask the Mormon to read aloud from the verse immediately preceding 1 Corinthians 8:5: "We know that an idol is nothing in the world, and that *there is none other God but one*" (verse 4, emphasis added).[40] Then ask the Mormon to read aloud from the verse immediately following 1 Corinthians 8:5: "To us there is but *one God,* the Father, of whom are all things, and we in him; and one Lord Jesus Christ, by whom are all things, and we by him" (verse 6, emphasis added). The context, then, is *mono*theistic, not *poly*theistic.

_____ *Ask* . . . _____

- Do you believe it's important to consult the surrounding context when interpreting individual Bible verses?

- Would you please read aloud from 1 Corinthians 8:4?

- Does this verse support *mono*theism (belief in only one God) or *poly*theism (belief in many gods)?

- Would you please read aloud from 1 Corinthians 8:6?

- Does this verse support *mono*theism (belief in one god) or *poly*theism (belief in many gods)?

Polytheism is properly defined as "belief in more than one God." Mormons believe in more than one God and are thus polytheists.

Now, after demonstrating this, you will want to help the Mormon understand what the apostle Paul is talking about in 1 Corinthians 8:5. Note that Paul does not say there *are* many true gods and lords; rather, he refers to false, pagan entities who are *called* gods and lords. There is a world of difference between being *called* a god and actually *being* God. Shirley MacLaine says, "I am God," but that doesn't mean she *is* God. Similarly, just because Paul acknowledges that there are entities called gods doesn't mean they actually *are* gods.

_____ *Ask* . . . _____

- Can you see that there is a big difference between *being* God and simply being *called* a god?

- What does 1 Corinthians 8:5 focus on—*being* God or being *called* a god?

- Now that we have established the monotheistic context of 1 Corinthians 8:5—which is proven in the preceding and following verses (verses 4 and 6)—don't you think you may be reading an idea into this passage that isn't there?

In the context of 1 Corinthians 8, it is clear that the many gods are *false* gods because the discussion focuses on idols (*see* verse 4).[41] Apparently, these gods are the idols of Greek and Roman mythology. Paul, then, is simply acknowledging that in New Testament days many false gods were worshiped—though, in fact, such gods do not really exist. Paul, as a Hebrew of Hebrews, was monotheistic to the core and believed in only one God (1 Timothy 2:5; cf. Deuteronomy 6:4).

As a Jew, much of Paul's theology about God rested upon the book of Isaiah. You might want to share with the Mormon some of the statements God makes about Himself in that book:

THE ONE TRUE GOD IN THE BOOK OF ISAIAH

"Ye are my witnesses, saith the LORD, and my servant whom I have chosen: that ye may know and believe me, and understand that I am he: before me there was no God formed, neither shall there be after me" (Isaiah 43:10).

"Thus saith the LORD the King of Israel, and his redeemer the LORD of hosts; I am the first, and I am the last; and beside me there is no God" (Isaiah 44:6).

"Who hath formed a god, or molten a graven image that is profitable for nothing?" (Isaiah 44:10).

"Fear ye not, neither be afraid: have not I told thee from that time, and have declared it? ye are even my witnesses. Is there a God beside me? yea, there is no God; I know not any" (Isaiah 44:8).

"I am the LORD, and there is none else, there is no God beside me: I girded thee, though thou hast not known me" (Isaiah 45:5).

"Remember the former things of old: for I am God, and there is none else; I am God, and there is none like me" (Isaiah 46:9).

15

The Person of Jesus Christ in Mormonism

Mormon apologist Gilbert W. Scharffs wrote that "Latter-day Saints are Christians because they emphatically believe in Christ, use His name in their official church title, and believe in the Bible and the Book of Mormon, which testify repeatedly of the reality of Christ and the truth of His teachings. . . . Mormons are Christians. Christians are those who accept Christ as their Savior."[1]

But do Mormons believe in the Jesus of the *Bible?* According to official Mormon teaching, Jesus Christ was "begotten" as the first spirit-child of the Father (Elohim) and one of his unnamed wives (often referred to as "Heavenly Mother"). Jesus, as a spirit-son, then progressed in the spirit world until He became a God.[2] Christ, "by obedience and devotion to the truth . . . attained that pinnacle of intelligence which ranked Him as a God."[3]

In *The Life and Teaching of Jesus and His Apostles,* we read this about Jesus:

> He was the birthright son, and he retained that birthright by his strict obedience. Through the aeons and ages of premortality, he advanced and progressed

until, as Abraham described it, he stood as one "like unto God" [Abr. 3:24]. "Our Savior was a God before he was born into this world," wrote President Joseph Fielding Smith, "and he brought with him that same status when he came here. He was as much a God when he was born into the world as he was before."[4]

Prior to his incarnation, Jesus was the Jehovah of the Old Testament.[5] The Mormons' *Bible Dictionary* says that "Jehovah . . . is generally denoted by LORD or GOD, printed in small capitals [in the King James Version]. Jehovah is the premortal Jesus Christ and came to earth being born of Mary."[6]

How was Jesus conceived in Mary's womb? Mormon doctrine actually teaches that Jesus, in His mortal state, was begotten through sexual relations between a flesh-and-bone Heavenly Father and Mary—the only earthly offspring so conceived. Mormon authorities argue that Jesus as the "Son" of God was "begotten" of the Father, and these terms are to be taken *literally.* As Bruce McConkie says, "Christ was begotten by an Immortal Father in the same way that mortal men are begotten by mortal fathers."[7]

God the Father is a perfected, glorified, holy man, an immortal Personage. And Christ was born into the world as the literal Son of this Holy Being; he was born in the same personal real, and literal sense that any mortal son is born to a mortal father. There is nothing figurative about his paternity; he was begotten, conceived, and born in the normal and natural course of events, for he is the Son of God, and that designation means what it says.[8]

In case you wonder if this is the speculative viewpoint of only a few Mormon leaders, consider the following:

- Apostle Orson Pratt said that "the fleshly body of Jesus required a Mother as well as a Father. Therefore, the Father and Mother of Jesus, according to the flesh, must have been associated together in the capacity of Husband and Wife: hence the Virgin Mary must have been, for the time being, the lawful wife of God the Father."[9]

- Apostle James E. Talmage likewise stated that "Jesus Christ is the Son of Elohim both as spiritual and bodily offspring; that is to say, Elohim is literally the Father of the spirit of Jesus Christ and also of the body in which Jesus Christ performed His mission in the flesh."[10]

- President Ezra Taft Benson agreed:

[There is] no question as to the paternity of Jesus Christ. God was the Father of Jesus' mortal tabernacle, and Mary, a mortal woman, was His mother. . . . The Church of Jesus Christ of Latter-day Saints proclaims that Jesus Christ is the Son of God in the most literal sense. The body in which He performed His mission in the flesh was sired by that same Holy Being we worship as God, our Eternal Father. Jesus was not the son of Joseph, nor was He begotten by him. . . . He was the Only Begotten Son of our Heavenly Father in the flesh — the only child whose mortal body was begotten by our Heavenly Father.[11]

According to Mormon doctrine, then, Jesus was begotten not by the Holy Spirit but by the Father (Elohim). *Doctrines of Salvation* affirms that "Christ is not the Son of the Holy Ghost, but of the Father."[12]

Such a doctrine, of course, raises questions about the virginity of Mary. Mormon prophet Brigham Young claimed that Mary had more than one husband: "The man Joseph, the husband of Mary, did not, that we know of, have more than one wife, but Mary, the wife of Joseph, had another husband—that is, God the Father."[13] Such a viewpoint would seem to have negative implications about Mary's virginity.

Surprisingly, Mormon theologians maintain that even though the Father had sexual relations with Mary, she *remained* a virgin. Against every conventional understanding of the term, Bruce McConkie fancifully argues that a "virgin" is a woman who has had no sexual relations with a *mortal* man. Because God the Father was an *immortal* man, Mary remained a virgin after having relations with Him. He says, "Our Lord is the only mortal person ever born to a virgin, because he is the only person who ever had an immortal Father."[14]

Mormon doctrine also teaches that the Heavenly Father (Elohim) and the Heavenly Mother had *many* spirit children.[15] But Jesus was allegedly the first and highest of their spirit children. The church's official *Gospel Principles* manual tells us, "The first spirit born to our heavenly parents was Jesus Christ."[16] Doctrine and Covenants affirms that "Christ, the Firstborn, was the mightiest of all the spirit children of the Father."[17] James E. Talmage adds that "among the spirit-children of Elohim the firstborn was and is Jehovah or Jesus Christ to whom all others are juniors."[18] Mormons commonly refer to Jesus as "our elder brother."

Of course, this ultimately means that Jesus Christ is not unique. The only difference between Jesus and us is that Jesus was the *firstborn* of Elohim's children, whereas we, in our alleged pre-existence, were "born" later. It appears, then, that the important distinction between Jesus (Jehovah) and God's other premortal offspring is merely one of *degree,* not of *kind.*[19]

Related to this is the fact that, in Mormon theology, Lucifer is the spirit-brother of Jesus. "As for the Devil and his fellow spirits, they are brothers to man and also to Jesus and sons and daughters of God in the same sense that we are."[20]

Lucifer, Jesus' spirit-brother, allegedly did not like it when Jesus was appointed to be the Savior of the world. "The appointment of Jesus to be the Savior of the world was contested by one of the other sons of God. He was called Lucifer, son of the morning. Haughty, ambitious, and covetous of power and glory, this spirit-brother of Jesus desperately tried to become the Savior of mankind."[21] *Sibling rivalry?*

Mormons say that during His earthly years, Jesus, having taken on mortal existence, got married. In fact, we are told, Jesus was married to both Mary and Martha; He was a *polygamist*. Early apostle Orson Hyde explains it this way:

> It will be borne in mind that once on a time, there was a marriage in Cana of Galilee; and on a careful reading of that transaction, it will be discovered that no less a person than Jesus Christ was married on that occasion. If he was never married, his intimacy with Mary and Martha, and the other Mary also whom Jesus loved, must have been highly unbecoming and improper to say the best of it. [22]

This is most certainly related to the requirement for exaltation (i.e., attaining the goal of godhood) outlined in Doctrine and Covenants section 132—that is, no one can attain exaltation to the fullness of the blessings of the celestial kingdom outside of the marriage relationship. [23] Apparently this must have applied even to Jesus.

As we consider how we might respond to Mormon teachings about Jesus, it's important to know that Mormons do not worship Him. Not wanting to be branded polytheists, Mormons say that we cannot worship Jesus in the same way that we worship the Father. Only the Father (Elohim) can be truly worshiped. Yet we can confront Mormons by showing that there are numerous Old Testament passages that indicate we are to direct worship to Jehovah. And because Mormon theology teaches that Jesus is the Jehovah of the Old Testament, even Mormons have to acknowledge that we should worship Jesus.

Bruce McConkie responds to this argument by saying, "I know perfectly well what the Scriptures say about worshiping Christ and Jehovah, but they are speaking in an entirely different sense—the sense of standing *in awe* and being *reverentially grateful* to him who redeemed us" [24] (emphasis added).

Mormons also try to avoid polytheism by saying we should not pray to Jesus. [25] They say we should pray only to the Father (Elohim). Amazingly, Mormons seem to think that even though they believe in innumerable gods, they can avoid the label of polytheism if they affirm that they worship and pray to only one.

_____REASONING FROM THE SCRIPTURES_____

Jesus—A Mormon God Before He Was a Human?

It is generally understood among Mormons that a person cannot progress to godhood (i.e., exaltation) without passing through mortality and acquiring a physical body. In fact, Abraham 3:25 says that taking on a physical body is a *prerequisite* to eternal progression. According to Mormon theology, however, Jesus became a God *before* assuming a physical body.[26] You will want to ask the Mormon to explain this contradiction. (No Mormon we've met has adequately answered this.)

_____ *Ask . . .* _____

- According to Abraham 3:25, isn't taking on a physical body a *prerequisite* to eternal progression?

- Doesn't Mormonism teach that Jesus became a God before assuming a physical body?

- How do you explain this contradiction?

The Worship of Jesus Christ

You will want to debunk the Mormon claim that Jesus is not to be worshiped in the same way that the Father is. Begin by pointing out that Christ *was* worshiped (Greek: *proskuneo*) as God many times according to the Gospel accounts—and

He always accepted such worship as perfectly appropriate.
(Note that *proskuneo* is the exact same word used to talk
about worshiping the Father in the New Testament.)

Jesus accepted worship from Thomas (John 20:28); all the
angels are told to worship Jesus (Hebrews 1:6); wise men
worshiped Jesus (Matthew 2:11); a leper worshiped Him
(Matthew 8:2); a ruler bowed before Him in worship
(Matthew 9:18); a blind man worshiped Him (John 9:38); a
woman worshiped Him (Matthew 15:25); Mary Magdalene
worshiped Him (Matthew 28:9); and the disciples worshiped Him (Matthew 28:17). All these verses contain the
word *proskuneo,* the same word used in reference to worshiping the Father. And in every instance, Jesus accepted the
worship.

In contrast, consider Paul and Barnabas's reaction to worship when they miraculously healed a man by God's mighty
power. The people who witnessed the healing shouted, "The
gods are come down to us in the likeness of men" (Acts
14:11). When Paul and Barnabas perceived that the crowd
was preparing to worship them, "they rent their clothes, and
ran in among the people, crying out, And saying, Sirs, why
do ye these things? We also are men of like passions with
you" (verses 14–15). As soon as Paul and Barnabas saw what
was happening, they immediately corrected the gross mis-
conception that they were gods.

Yet Jesus never sought to correct His followers when they
bowed down and worshiped Him. Indeed, Jesus considered
such worship as perfectly appropriate. Of course, we wouldn't
expect Jesus to try to correct people in worshiping Him if He
truly was God in the flesh, as He claimed to be.

In your encounters with Mormons, you may want to mention that in the book of Revelation, God the Father and Jesus
Christ are clearly seen as receiving *the exact same worship.*
Point them to Revelation 4:10, which speaks of worshiping
the Father, and Revelation 5:11–14, which talks about worshiping the Lamb of God, Jesus Christ.

_____ *Ask* . . . _____

- In the book of Revelation, Jesus receives the *exact same worship* that is given to the Father. What does that tell us about Jesus' true identity?

- What implications does this have in regard to polytheism in the Mormon church?

The fact that Jesus willingly receives (and clearly condones) worship on various occasions says a lot about His true identity, for it is the consistent testimony of Scripture that *only God* can be worshiped. Exodus 34:14 tells us, "Thou shalt worship no other god: for the LORD, whose name is Jealous, is a jealous God" (cf. Deuteronomy 6:13; Matthew 4:10). The fact that Jesus *is* worshiped on numerous occasions, then, shows that He is in fact God.

Prayer to Jesus Christ

Mormons say that Jesus Christ is the Jehovah of the Old Testament. This creates a problem for Mormons because many verses in the Old Testament command us to pray to Jehovah (Deuteronomy 4:7; 2 Chronicles 7:14; Psalm 5:2; 32:6; Jeremiah 29:7,12).

If Jesus is Jehovah (as Mormons concede), and if we are to offer prayers to Jehovah, then why shouldn't we offer prayers to Jesus? Moreover, what about the New Testament verses where prayer is made directly to Jesus Christ (Acts 7:59; Romans 10:12)?

_____ *Ask* . . . _____

- Is Jesus the Jehovah of the Old Testament?

- Did you know there are many verses in the Old Testament that instruct people to pray directly to Jehovah? (Mention a few, like Deuteronomy 4:7 and Psalm 5:2.)

- If we should not pray to Jesus, then how do you explain Acts 7:59 and Romans 10:12, where prayer to Jesus is spoken of approvingly?

- Who do you think is right about prayer to Jesus—the Bible or the Mormon church?

Jesus Was Not the Spirit Brother of Lucifer

The Bible does *not* teach that Jesus Christ was the spirit-brother of Lucifer. Though we could cite many passages that refute this hideous doctrine, we will limit our attention to Colossians 1:16, where we are told that the entire angelic realm—including the angel Lucifer—was personally created by Jesus Christ: "By him were all things created, that are in heaven, and that are in earth, visible and invisible, whether they be thrones, or dominions, or principalities, or powers: all things were created by him, and for him."

The little phrase "all things" means that Christ created the whole universe of things. "Every form of matter and life owes its origin to the Son of God, no matter in what sphere it may be found, or with what qualities it may be invested. . . . Christ's creative work was no local or limited operation; it was not bounded by this little orb [earth]."[27] Everything—whether it is simple or complex, visible or invisible, heavenly or earthly, immanent or transcendent—is the product of Christ.

Now, it is noteworthy that Paul says that Christ created "thrones," "powers," "rulers," and "authorities." In the rabbinical (Jewish) thought of the first century, these words were used to describe different orders of *angels* (*see* Romans 8:38; Ephesians 1:21; 3:10; 6:12; Colossians 2:10,15; Titus 3:1). Apparently there was a heresy flourishing in Colossae (the city in which the Colossian Christians lived) that involved the worship of angels. In the process of worshiping angels, Christ had been degraded. So, to correct this grave error,

Paul emphasizes in Colossians 1:16 that Christ is the one who created all things—including all the angels—and hence, He is supreme and is alone worthy of worship.[28]

We know from Scripture that Lucifer is a created angelic being—a "cherub" (Ezekiel 28:13–19; cf. Isaiah 14:12–15). Since Lucifer was an angel, and since Christ created all the angels, it is clear that Christ is not a spirit-brother of Lucifer. Christ is not of the created realm; rather, He is the Creator. Lucifer and Christ are of *two entirely different classes*—the *created* and the *Creator.* You will want to carefully point this out to Mormons, especially when discussing verses they cite to support their deviant view that Jesus was procreated by the Father.

Exodus 6:3—*Jesus Is "Jehovah," the Father Is "Elohim"*

The Mormon Teaching. In Exodus 6:3 we read, "I appeared unto Abraham, unto Isaac, and unto Jacob, by the name of God Almighty, but by my name JEHOVAH was I not known to them."

References to Jehovah in the Bible, Mormons say, are actually references to Jesus Christ in His premortal state: "When one speaks of God, it is generally the Father who is referred to; that is, *Elohim.* All mankind are his children. The personage known as *Jehovah* in Old Testament times, and who is usually identified in the Old Testament as Lord (in capital letters), is the Son, known as Jesus Christ, and who is also a God . . . he being the eldest of the spirit children of Elohim."[29]

The Biblical Teaching. In your endeavor to refute the idea that Elohim and Jehovah are two separate gods—the Father being Elohim and Jesus being Jehovah—you will want to begin by showing the Mormon verses in the Bible which demonstrate that Elohim and Jehovah are one and the same God.

For example, in Genesis 27:20 we read, "Isaac said unto his son, How is it that thou hast found it so quickly, my son?

And he said, Because the LORD [Jehovah] thy God [Elohim] brought it to me" (inserts added). In this verse, Isaac refers to "Jehovah thy Elohim," clearly showing that Jehovah and Elohim are one and the same.

Likewise, the Almighty Himself declares in Exodus 3:6–7, "Moreover he said, I am the God [Elohim] of thy father, the God of Abraham, the God of Isaac, and the God of Jacob. And Moses hid his face; for he was afraid to look upon God. And the LORD [Jehovah] said, I have surely seen the affliction of my people which are in Egypt, and have heard their cry by reason of their taskmasters; for I know their sorrows" (inserts added). Again, Elohim and Jehovah are seen to be the same God.

_____ *Ask* . . . _____

- Would you please open your Bible and read aloud from Genesis 27:20?

- Did you know that the Hebrew word for "LORD" in this verse is *Jehovah,* and the Hebrew word for "God" is *Elohim?* (We recommend that you keep a copy of *Strong's Concordance* handy so you can prove to the Mormon that the words *Elohim* and *Jehovah* are, in fact, used in the verses we cite.)

- Doesn't this indicate that Jehovah and Elohim are one and the same God? Please explain.

- Would you please open your Bible and read from Exodus 3:6–7?

- Did you know that the Hebrew word for "LORD" in this passage is *Jehovah,* and the Hebrew word for "God" is *Elohim?*

- Does this not indicate that Jehovah and Elohim are one and the same God? Please explain.

You might also cite Jeremiah 32:18: "Thou shewest loving-kindness unto thousands, and recompensest the iniquity of the fathers into the bosom of their children after them: the Great, the Mighty God [Elohim], the LORD [Jehovah] of hosts, is his name (inserts added).

_____ *Ask* . . . _____

- Would you please open your Bible and read aloud from Jeremiah 32:18?

- Did you know that the Hebrew word for "Mighty God" in this verse is *Elohim,* and the Hebrew word for "God" is *Jehovah*?

- Does this not indicate that Jehovah and Elohim are one and the same God? How does that square with Mormon teaching?

Next, you will want to demonstrate to the Mormon that there are passages in the Bible where Jesus *alone* is clearly identified as Elohim, thereby disproving their claim that only the Father is Elohim and only Jesus is Jehovah.

A good place to begin is Isaiah 40:3: "The voice of him that crieth in the wilderness, Prepare ye the way of the LORD [Jehovah]; make straight in the desert a highway for our God [Elohim]." This entire verse was written in reference to the future ministry of Christ, according to John 1:23, and represents one of the strongest affirmations of Christ's deity in the Old Testament. Within the confines of a single verse Christ is called both Jehovah *and* Elohim.

Christ is also called Elohim in Isaiah 9:6: "Unto us a child is born, unto us a son is given: and the government shall be upon his shoulder: and his name shall be called Wonderful, Counselor, The mighty God [Elohim], The everlasting Father, The Prince of Peace."

_____ *Ask . . .* _____

- Would you please read aloud from Isaiah 40:3?

- Did you know that the Hebrew word for "LORD" in this verse is *Jehovah,* and the Hebrew word for "God" is *Elohim?*

- Did you know that according to John 1:23, this entire verse refers to the future ministry of Jesus Christ?

- Doesn't Isaiah 40:3 indicate that Jesus is not only Jehovah but is also Elohim?

- Would you please read aloud from Isaiah 9:6?

- Did you know that the Hebrew word for "mighty God" in this verse is *Elohim?*

- Doesn't this verse indicate that Jesus is Elohim?

You might also want to point out that Elohim—a common name for God in the Old Testament (used about 2,570 times)—literally means "Strong One." Its plural ending (*im* in Hebrew) is a "plural of majesty," pointing to the majesty and dignity of God.

Elohim is portrayed in the Old Testament as the powerful and sovereign Governor of the universe, ruling over the affairs of mankind. As related to God's sovereignty, the word *Elohim* is used "to describe Him as the 'God of all the earth' (Isa. 54:5), the 'God of all flesh' (Jer. 32:27), the 'God of heaven' (Neh. 2:4), and the 'God of gods and Lord of lords' (Deut. 10:17)."[30] It is therefore highly significant that this name is used in reference to Jesus Christ (Isaiah 9:6; 40:3).

Related to this, in Hebrews 1:8 the Father gives His own testimony regarding Christ's identity. Here, the Father is seen addressing the Son, and says, "Thy throne, *O God* [Greek, *Theos*], is for ever and ever: a scepter of righteousness is the scepter of thy kingdom." This is a direct quote from Psalm 45:6–7, where "God" is seen addressing "God" (using the Hebrew word *Elohim*). Though the concept of the Trinity is inscrutable to finite minds, this and other passages show us that the Father and the Son are *co-equal* and *co-eternal*—as Elohim. Neither is greater or lesser than the other in their divinity. Neither has existed longer than the other. They are equal yet distinct. And, of course, the same is true of the Holy Spirit.

The fact that Christ is called both Jehovah and Elohim in the Bible gives added significance to these words recorded for us in Matthew's Gospel: "Behold, a virgin shall be with child, and shall bring forth a son, and they shall call his name Immanuel, which being interpreted is, God with us" (Matthew 1:23).

Deuteronomy 6:4—*Jehovah Is Elohim*

The Mormon Teaching. In Deuteronomy 6:4 we read, "Hear, O Israel: The LORD our God is one LORD." This was a Jewish affirmation of faith in ancient days. It was and is known by its Hebrew name, the *Shema.*

As we noted earlier, Mormons believe that in the Bible, references to Elohim are the Father and references to Jehovah are Jesus: "When one speaks of God, it is generally the Father who is referred to; that is, *Elohim.* . . . The personage known as *Jehovah* in Old Testament times . . . is the Son, known as Jesus Christ . . . he being the eldest of the spirit children of Elohim."[31] Whenever Mormons say that, Deuteronomy 6:4 is an excellent passage to share because it so easily refutes their distorted teaching.

The Biblical Teaching. Notice how Jehovah and Elohim are equated in Deuteronomy 6:4: "Hear, O Israel: The LORD [Jehovah] our God [Elohim] is one LORD [Jehovah]" (inserts added). Clearly there is no way to make this verse fit with the Mormon idea that Elohim is the Father and Jehovah is Jesus.

Deuteronomy 6:4 emphasizes that there is one and *only one* true God. This is the consistent testimony of Scripture from Genesis to Revelation. It is like a thread that runs through every page of the Bible.

The *Shema* was particularly meaningful for the Israelites because they were surrounded by people who worshiped false gods and idols. The Jews made a habit of reciting this affirmation twice a day—once in the morning and once in the evening. The importance of the *Shema* is reflected in the Hebrew practice of requiring children to memorize it at an early age.

It is interesting to observe that the early Christians—who had a solidly Jewish background—did not hesitate to refer to Jesus as "Lord" and "God" despite their unbending monotheism (Romans 10:13; 1 Thessalonians 5:2; 1 Peter 2:3; 3:15).[32] Indeed, despite their commitment to the *Shema* in Deuteronomy 6:4, they had no scruple about applying to Jesus many Old Testament texts that were written in reference to the Lord God.

_____ *Ask* . . . _____

- Did you know that the word for "LORD" in Deuteronomy 6:4 is *Jehovah,* and the word for "God" is *Elohim?*

- Doesn't Deuteronomy 6:4 indicate that Elohim and Jehovah are *one and the same* God?

- The early Jewish Christians—who were clearly committed to the *Shema* in Deuteronomy 6:4—had no scruple about applying to Jesus many Old Testament texts that were written in reference to the one true God. How do you explain that?

Psalm 2:7—*Jesus: The Offspring of Heavenly Parents?*

The Mormon Teaching. In Psalm 2:7 we read, "I will declare the decree: the LORD hath said unto me, Thou art my Son; this day have I begotten thee."

Mormons typically interpret the word "begotten" in the sense of *procreation*. They think Psalm 2:7 is evidence that Jesus Christ was born as a spirit, the offspring of heavenly parents. "The first spirit born to our heavenly parents was Jesus Christ (see D&C 93:21). He is thus our elder brother. . . ."[33]

The Biblical Teaching. We suggest that you open your Bible and have the Mormon read aloud from Acts 13:33–34: "God hath fulfilled the same unto us their children, in that he hath *raised up Jesus again;* as it is also written in the second psalm, Thou art my Son, this day have I begotten thee. And as concerning that he *raised him up from the dead,* now no more to return to corruption, he said on this wise, I will give you the sure mercies of David" (emphasis added).

Explain to the Mormon that Acts 13:33–34—which speaks of the Father's resurrection of Jesus from the dead—is a fulfillment of the statement in Psalm 2:7, "Thou art my Son, this day have I begotten thee."[34] Point out that a basic interpretive principle is that *Scripture interprets Scripture.* The best way to find out what Psalm 2:7 means is to let Scripture tell us what it means. And according to Acts 13:33–34, the verse deals not with the Father's alleged procreation of Jesus but rather with Jesus' resurrection from the dead.

_____ *Ask* . . . _____

- Would you please read aloud from Acts 13:33–34?

- Isn't it clear that Scripture itself is interpreting the phrase in Psalm 2:7, "Thou art my Son, this day have I begotten thee"? Isn't it clear that Psalm 2:7 refers not to the Father's procreation of Jesus but rather the Father's resurrection of Jesus from the dead? Please explain.

You may also want to show the Mormon a few passages that affirm the eternality of Christ. Perhaps John 1:1 is a good verse to begin with: "In the beginning was the Word, and the Word was with God, and the Word was God." Why is Jesus called "the Word"? Simply because He is the Revealer of God (*see* John 1:18). Jesus is the full expression of all that God is.

"In the beginning" is a translation of the Greek words *en arche.* It is significant that these are the same two words that begin the book of Genesis in the Septuagint (which is the Greek translation of the Hebrew Old Testament). The obvious conclusion we must draw is that John's "beginning" is identical to the Genesis "beginning."[35]

Church father and philosopher Augustine believed that the universe was not created in time, but that time itself was created along with the universe.[36] Reformed theologian Louis Berkhof agrees and concludes, "It would not be correct to assume that time was already in existence when God created the world, and that He at some point in that existing time, called 'the beginning,' brought forth the universe. The world was created *with* time rather than *in* time. Back of the beginning mentioned in Genesis 1:1 lied a beginningless eternity."[37]

We can conclude, then, that when John said, "In the beginning was the Word, and the Word was with God, and the Word was God" (John 1:1), the phrase "in the beginning" refers to the beginning of time when the universe was created. When the time-space universe came into being, Christ the divine Word *was already existing* in a loving, intimate relationship with the Father and the Holy Spirit.

In view of this, we can say that the phrase "in the beginning" refers to a point in eternity past beyond which it is impossible for us to go. It is important to grasp this, because John tells us that "in the beginning [when time began] *was* the Word." The verb "was" in John 1:1 is an imperfect tense in the Greek, which indicates continued existence. The imperfect tense "reaches back indefinitely beyond the instant of the beginning."[38] Bible scholar Leon Morris notes that "the verb 'was' is most naturally understood of the eternal existence of the Word: 'the Word continually was.' "[39]

Thus, the *Word* (Jesus) did not come into being at a specific point in eternity past, but at that point at which all else began to be, He already was. No matter how far back we go in eternity past, we will never come to a point at which we could say of Christ the *Word* that "there was a time when He was not."

Because Christ is the eternal Word, all that can be said of God can also be said of Jesus Christ. As Leon Morris tells us, "John is not merely saying that there is something divine about Jesus. He is affirming that He is God, and doing so emphatically."[40]

The Mormon Jesus	The Biblical Jesus
A created being; the brother of Lucifer and of all mortals and angels.	Uncreated God.
Earned his own salvation.	As God, Christ required no salvation.
One of many savior-gods throughout the universe.	Unique (the Second Person of the one Godhead) and of supreme importance throughout eternity and in all creation.
Conceived by the physical sex act of the Father (Elohim) and Mary.	Conceived by the Holy Spirit, who overshadowed Mary, a true virgin.
A married polygamist.	An unmarried monogamist.

Even the Book of Mormon affirms the eternal nature of Jesus Christ. For example:

- Second Nephi attributes to Jesus this declaration: "Behold, I am God. . . . I am the same yesterday, today, and forever. . . . I, the Lord your God, have created all men. . . .

I am the same yesterday, today, and forever" (27:23; 29:7,9).

• Mosiah 3:5,8 says this:

For behold, the time cometh, and is not far distant, that with power, the Lord Omnipotent who reigneth, *who was, and is from all eternity to all eternity,* shall come down from heaven among the children of men, and shall dwell in a tabernacle of clay, and shall go forth amongst men, working mighty miracles, such as healing the sick, raising the dead, causing the lame to walk, the blind to receive their sight, and the deaf to hear, and curing all manner of diseases. . . . *And he shall be called Jesus Christ,* the Son of God, the Father of heaven and earth, the Creator of all things from the beginning; and his mother shall be called Mary (emphasis added).

_____ *Ask* . . . _____

• Would you please open your Book of Mormon and read aloud from 2 Nephi 27:23?

• Now turn to Mosiah 3:5,8 and read it aloud.

• What do these verses say about the eternal nature of Jesus Christ?

• Doesn't this contradict the current Mormon doctrine that Jesus came into being at a point in time, procreated by the Heavenly Father?

Matthew 1:18,20—*Jesus: Begotten of the Father?*

The Mormon Teaching. In Matthew 1:18,20 we read,

Now the birth of Jesus Christ was on this wise: When as his mother Mary was espoused to Joseph, before they came together, she was found with child of the Holy Ghost. Then Joseph her husband, being a just man, and not willing to make her a public example, was minded to put her away privily. But while he thought on these things, behold, the angel of the Lord appeared unto him in a dream, saying, Joseph, thou son of David, fear not to take unto thee Mary thy wife: for *that which is conceived in her is of the Holy Ghost* (emphasis added).

This is an extremely important passage in regard to Mormon doctrine simply because it goes against their idea that Jesus was begotten by the Father, not the Holy Spirit. Orson Pratt emphatically stated, "If He were begotten by the Holy Ghost, then He would have called *him* His Father."[41] In the *Journal of Discourses,* Brigham Young said, "When the Virgin Mary conceived the child Jesus, the Father had begotten him in his own likeness. He was not begotten by the Holy Ghost."[42]

The Biblical Teaching. Matthew 1:20 clearly says that Jesus was conceived by the Holy Spirit, and nowhere—in the Bible, the Book of Mormon, or any other Mormon scripture—do we find any claim or evidence that the Father had relations with Mary. There is no way for the Mormon to get around this.

_____ *Ask . . .* _____

- Would you please read aloud from Matthew 1:18–20?

- What does verse 18 say about the conception of Jesus?

- How do you reconcile this with the statement in the *Journal of Discourses* that Jesus "was not begotten by the Holy Ghost"?

You will want to point out that even the Book of Mormon says Jesus Christ was conceived by the Holy Ghost. Alma 7:10 says, "Behold, he shall be born of Mary, at Jerusalem which is the land of our forefathers, she being a virgin, a precious and chosen vessel, who shall be overshadowed and conceive by the power of the Holy Ghost, and bring forth a son, yea, even the Son of God."

_____ *Ask* . . . _____

- Would you open your Book of Mormon and read aloud from Alma 7:10?

- What does this verse say about the conception of Jesus?

- How do you reconcile this with the statement in the *Journal of Discourses* (and *Doctrines of Salvation* vol. 1:18) that Jesus "was not begotten by the Holy Ghost"?

Luke 1:34–35—*Jesus: "Fathered" by the Father?*

The Mormon Teaching. As noted above, Mormons say that Jesus Christ was begotten by the Father, not the Holy Ghost. When they bring this up, you'll want to show them Luke 1:34–35.

The Biblical Teaching. In Luke 1:34–35 we read, "Then said Mary unto the angel, How shall this be, seeing I know not a man? And the angel answered and said unto her, The Holy Ghost shall come upon thee, and the power of the Highest shall overshadow thee: therefore also that holy thing which shall be born of thee shall be called the Son of God."

_____ *Ask* . . . _____

- Would you please read aloud from Luke 1:34–35?

- What does this passage say about the conception of Jesus?

- How do you reconcile this with the statement in the *Journal of Discourses* (and *Doctrines of Salvation* vol. 1:18) that Jesus "was not begotten by the Holy Ghost"?

Jesus Christ: Eternal God

Mormons accept the idea that Jesus is Jehovah (or, more properly, *Yahweh*). But they do not understand the full implications of this name. You will want to help them understand that the name Yahweh (Jehovah) affirms that Jesus never came into being (by procreation, for example) but has existed for all eternity as God.

The name Yahweh, which occurs some 5,300 times in the Old Testament, is connected with the Hebrew verb "to be." We first learn of this name in Exodus 3, where Moses asked God what name He should be called by. God replied, "I AM THAT I AM: and he said, Thus shalt thou say unto the children of Israel, I AM hath sent me unto you" (verse 14).

The phrase "I AM" is not the word *Yahweh.* However, "I AM" (in verse 14) and Yahweh (in verse 15) are both derivatives of the same verb, "to be." The name "I AM THAT I AM," which God revealed to Moses in verse 14, is intended as a full expression of His eternal nature, and is then shortened to Yahweh in verse 15. The names have the same root meaning and can be considered interchangeable.

Most important, the name Yahweh conveys the idea of eternal self-existence. Yahweh never came into being at a point in time, for He has always existed. He was never born; He will never die. He does not grow older, for He is beyond the realm of time. To know Yahweh is to know the eternal one.[43]

David F. Wells, in his book *The Person of Christ*, points us to some important parallels between Christ and Yahweh and demonstrates that Christ is not someone who came into being at a point in time (procreated by the Father), but is, in fact, eternal God Himself.

> If Yahweh is our sanctifier (Exod. 31:13), is omnipresent (Ps. 139:7–10), is our peace (Judg. 6:24), is our righteousness (Jer. 23:6), is our victory (Exod. 17:8–16), and is our healer (Exod. 15:26), then so is Christ all of these

things (1 Cor. 1:30; Col. 1:27; Eph. 2:14). If the gospel is God's (1 Thess. 2:2, 6–9; Gal. 3:8), then that same gospel is also Christ's (1 Thess. 3:2; Gal. 1:7). If the church is God's (Gal. 1:13; 1 Cor. 15:9), then that same church is also Christ's (Rom. 16:16). God's Kingdom (1 Thess. 2:12) is Christ's (Eph. 5:5); God's love (Eph. 1:3–5) is Christ's (Rom. 8:35); God's Word (Col. 1:25; 1 Thess. 2:13) is Christ's (1 Thess. 1:8; 4:15); God's Spirit (1 Thess. 4:8) is Christ's (Phil. 1:19); God's peace (Gal. 5:22; Phil. 4:9) is Christ's (Col. 3:15; cf. Col. 1:2; Phil. 1:2; 4:7); God's "Day" of judgment (Isa. 13:6) is Christ's "Day" of judgment (Phil. 1:6, 10; 2:16; 1 Cor. 1:8); God's grace (Eph. 2:8, 9; Col. 1:6; Gal. 1:15) is Christ's grace (1 Thess. 5:28; Gal. 1:6; 6:18); God's salvation (Col. 1:13) is Christ's salvation (1 Thess. 1:10); and God's will (Eph. 1:11; 1 Thess. 4:3; Gal. 1:4) is Christ's will (Eph. 5:17; cf. 1 Thess. 5:18). So it is no surprise to hear Paul say that he is both God's slave (Rom. 1:9) and Christ's (Rom. 1:1; Gal. 1:10), that he lives for that glory which is both God's (Rom. 5:2; Gal. 1:24) and Christ's (2 Cor. 8:19,23; cf. 2 Cor. 4:6), that his faith is in God (1 Thess. 1:8,9; Rom. 4:1–5) and in Christ Jesus (Gal. 3:22), and that to know God, which is salvation (Gal. 4:8; 1 Thess. 4:5), is to know Christ (2 Cor. 4:6).[44]

_____ *Ask . . .* _____

- Did you know that the name Yahweh (or Jehovah) conveys the idea of *eternal self-existence?*

- Is it not clear, then, that Jesus *as* Yahweh is eternally self-existent, and never came into being at a point in time?

_____

Jesus has always existed in and of Himself. He is the self-existent one who brought the universe into being. As the Creator of *all* things (John 1:3; Colossians 1:16; Hebrews

1:2,10; cf. Psalm 102:25), Christ Himself must necessarily be *un*created. "If God exists endlessly, then He never came into existence nor was He ever caused to come into existence. He is endlessly self-existent."[45]

Colossians 1:17 tells us that Christ "is before all things, and by him all things consist." If Christ is "*before* all things," then He does not depend on anyone or anything outside Himself for His own existence. This is emphasized in John 5:26, where we are told that the Son has life in Himself (*see* John 1:4). Of course, we should not be surprised that Christ is immutable and self-existent. After all, He is God.

It is also important to note that in terms of His divine nature, Christ is immutable. That Christ as God is immutable simply means that He is unchangeable, and thus unchanging. "This does not mean that He is immobile or inactive, but rather, that He is never inconsistent or growing or developing."[46] The doctrine of Christ's immutability once again affirms that Jesus did not come into being at a point in time, procreated by the Father. Christ in His divine nature has always been God, for all eternity, and that aspect of His being never, ever changes.

A key passage about the immutability of Christ is Hebrews 1:10–12, where the Father speaks of the Son's unchanging nature: "Thou, Lord, in the beginning hast laid the foundation of the earth; and the heavens are the works of thine hands. They shall perish, but thou remainest: and they all shall wax old as doth a garment; And as a vesture shalt thou fold them up, and they shall be changed: but thou art the same, and thy years shall not fail."

Christ's immutability is also affirmed in Hebrews 13:8: "Jesus Christ the same yesterday, and today, and for ever." It is true that in the incarnation Christ added a human nature, but orthodox scholars have always held that "the divine nature of Christ remains unchanged and is, therefore, immutable."[47]

The Mormons do not set forth the Jesus of the Bible. The apostle Paul warns of those who preach "another Jesus" (2 Corinthians 11:4). Believing in a *counterfeit Jesus* who preaches a *counterfeit gospel* yields only a *counterfeit salvation*. The Jesus of Mormonism does not save; to place one's trust in him is to be doomed for all eternity.

16

The Mormon Doctrine of Man: Were Humans Premortal Spirits?

According to Mormon theology, our Heavenly Father once lived on an earthlike planet and had many wives. He proved himself worthy to *his* Father-god by living an obedient and chaste life.

Eventually he, his wives, and children died and were subsequently resurrected. He continued his "progression" until he finally reached godhood.

Then, apparently, he was given the space to create his own heaven where he, along with his wives, would sexually procreate children in spirit-form.[1] Their firstborn was Jesus, known then as Jehovah. Their second-born was Lucifer. And then, most likely, came Adam and Eve. According to Mormonism, all the people who have ever inhabited the earth were *first* born in spirit form in heaven.

In the book *Mormon Doctrine,* Bruce McConkie tells us that "pre-existence is the term commonly used to describe the premortal existence of the spirit children of God the Father."[2] All men and women are "literally the sons and daughters of Deity," the "offspring of celestial parentage."[3]

Mormon theology teaches that "these spirit beings, the off-spring of exalted parents, were men and women, appearing in all respects as mortal persons do, excepting only that their spirit-bodies were made of a more pure and refined substance than the elements from which mortal bodies are made."[4]

All this brings up an interesting point. When the Mormon tells you that all of us are children of our Heavenly Father, *they mean that literally.* And when they say, "Jesus is our elder brother," they mean it in a literal sense. Since all of us— including Jesus—are spirit offspring of God, we are literally the brother of Jesus.

According to Mormonism, in the pre-existence Jesus was chosen over Lucifer to be the Savior of the world, thereby assuring the resurrection of all humankind (Mormons are taught that salvation essentially means resurrection). As the story goes, Lucifer offered to go to earth and be the Savior. But he wanted to *force* everyone to be saved and do everything himself.

Because Jesus desired to give man "free agency" (so man could prove his worthiness for exaltation), the Father chose Jesus' plan over Lucifer's. This allegedly made Lucifer angry, and he rebelled against his Father's preferential treatment. He persuaded one-third of the existing spirits in heaven to take sides and rebel also. This, in Mormonism, is known as "the war in heaven," and is the reason that group was cast out of heaven to become the Devil and his demons.

One of the most disconcerting aspects of the Mormon doctrine of pre-existence is the racist concept that black people are dark-skinned because God is punishing them for wrong choices they supposedly made before they were born. In the 1966 edition of *Mormon Doctrine,* Bruce McConkie commented on the pre-existence as it relates to black people:

> In the pre-existent eternity various degrees of valiance and devotion to the truth were exhibited by different groups of our Father's spirit offspring. One third of the spirit hosts of heaven came out in open rebellion and were cast out without

bodies, becoming the devil and his angels (D&C 29:36–41; Rev. 12:2–9). The other two-thirds stood affirmatively for Christ; there were no neutrals. To stand neutral in the midst of war is a philosophical impossibility. The Lord said: "He that is not with me is against me; and he that gathereth not with me scattereth abroad" (Mt. 12:30). Of the two-thirds that followed Christ, however, some were more valiant than others. . . . The whole house of Israel was chosen to come to mortality as children of Jacob (Deut. 32:7–8). Those who were less valiant in the pre-existence and who thereby had certain restrictions imposed upon them during mortality are known to us as negroes. Such spirits are sent to earth through the lineage of Cain, the mark put upon him for his rebellion against God and his murder of Abel being a black skin. (Moses 5:16–41; 7:8,12,22.) Noah's son Ham married Egyptus, a descendant of Cain, thus preserving the negro lineage through the flood (Abra. 1:2–27.)[5]

What implications did the curse of dark skin have in regard to entering the Mormon priesthood? Prior to 1978, the situation was as follows:

Negroes in this life are denied the priesthood; under no circumstances can they hold this delegation of authority from the Almighty (Abra. 1:20–27). The gospel message of salvation is not carried affirmatively to them (Moses 7:8,12,22), although sometimes negroes search out the truth, join the Church, and become by righteous living heirs of the celestial kingdom of heaven. . . . The present status of the negro purely and simply rests upon the foundation of pre-existence. Along with all races and peoples he is receiving here what he merits as a result of the long pre-mortal probation in the presence of the Lord. . . . The negroes are not equal with other races where the receipt of certain spiritual blessings are concerned, particularly the priesthood and the temple blessings that flow therefrom, but this inequality is not of man's origin. It is the Lord's doing, is based on his eternal laws of justice, and grows out of the lack of spiritual valiance of those concerned in their first estate.[6]

Pre-existence, then, has a great deal to do with a person's present lot in mortal life. A person's behavior in the pre-existence determines whether he is born with advantages or disadvantages in this life. The late apostle Mark E. Petersen explained it this way:

> Is there reason then why the type of birth we receive in this life is not a reflection of our worthiness or lack of it in the pre-existent life? . . . Can we account in any other way for the birth of some of the children of God in darkest Africa, or in flood-ridden China, or among the starving hordes of India, while some of the rest of us are born here in the United States? We cannot escape the conclusion that because of performance in our pre-existence some of us are born as Chinese, some as Japanese, some as Latter-day Saints. These are rewards and punishments, fully in harmony with His established policy in dealing with sinners and saints, rewarding all according to their deeds. [7]

Similarly, in *Doctrines of Salvation,* we read, "There is a reason why one man is born black and with other disadvantages, while another is born white with great advantages. The reason is that we once had an estate before we came here, and were obedient, more or less, to the laws that were given us there. Those who where faithful in all things there received greater blessings here, and those who were not faithful received less." [8]

With such blatant racism at the heart of Mormon doctrine, it is not surprising that the Mormons came under severe criticism in the 1960s and 1970s. The LDS church was brought under tremendous pressure by people both inside and outside the church—including those involved in the civil rights movement. On June 9, 1978, the late Spencer W. Kimball—then President of the Mormon church—received a convenient "revelation" from God that said all worthy male church members were eligible for the priesthood, *regardless of race.* Therefore, in the next edition of McConkie's *Mormon Doctrine,* the above-quoted information about black people was excised.

Underlying this Mormon racism is the idea that during our preexistence, we were allegedly under probation. "The preexistent life was thus a period—undoubtedly an infinitely long one—of probation, progression, and schooling."[9] Joseph Fielding Smith, in *The Life and Teaching of Jesus and His Apostles,* said, "During the ages in which we dwelt in the premortal state we not only developed our various characteristics and showed our worthiness and ability, or lack of it, but we were also where such progress could be observed."[10]

According to Mormons, the very fact that a person has been born on earth is a proof, in itself, that he or she, as a spirit child of God, has used his or her "agency" in the preexistence wisely.[11] It is a proof that he or she did not follow Lucifer in the great rebellion. (Remember, Lucifer and the spirits who joined him were cast out *without bodies.*) *Gospel Principles* tells us, "Because we are here on earth and have mortal bodies we know that we chose to follow Jesus Christ and our Heavenly Father. . . . In our pre-earth life, we chose the right. We must continue to choose the right here on earth."[12]

When a person is born on earth, a spirit-offspring of the Heavenly Father has left heaven to dwell in a physical body. And, according to Mormons, the spirit-child loses all remembrance of his time in heaven when he "passes through the veil" and comes to receive his physical body on earth.

REASONING FROM THE SCRIPTURES

Mormonism's Racist Past

When you challenge the Mormon about his church's long history of racism, you will want to show that Scripture—from the first book of the Bible to the last—emphasizes the *absolute unity* of the human race (which entails that no one ethnic group is better or worse than another). God created *all people* in His image, and therefore all are equally valuable to Him (Genesis 1:26–28).

The unity of the human race is consistently affirmed throughout Scripture in the *creation* (Genesis 1:28; 5:1–2), *the sin problem* (Romans 3:23), *God's love for all men* (John 3:16), and the *scope of salvation* (Genesis 12:3; Matthew 28:19; Colossians 3:11).

The apostle Paul emphasized humankind's unity in his sermon to the Athenians: God "hath made of one blood all nations of men for to dwell on all the face of the earth, and hath determined the times before appointed, and the bounds of their habitation" (Acts 17:26). Revelation 5:9 tells us that God's redeemed will come from "every kindred, and tongue, and people, and nation." Because of the unity of humanity, there is no place for racial discrimination—white, black, or otherwise—for all men are equal in God's sight. The racist doctrines of Mormonism's past have no justification from the true God of the Bible.

_____ *Ask . . .* _____

- Did you know that the unity of the human race is consistently affirmed throughout Scripture in the *creation* (Genesis 1:28; 5:1–2), *the sin problem* (Romans 3:23), *God's love for all men* (John 3:16), and the *scope of salvation* (Genesis 12:3; Matthew 28:19; Colossians 3:11)? (Look up some of these verses if you need to.)

- Did you know that Acts 17:26 teaches that God "hath made of *one blood* all nations of men for to dwell on all the face of the earth, and hath determined the times before appointed, and the bounds of their habitation"?

- What do you think Acts 17:26 means when it says all nations came from "one blood"? (Emphasize the unity of the human race.)

- Did you know that Revelation 5:9 tells us that God's redeemed will come from "every kindred, and tongue, and people, and nation"?

Jeremiah 1:5—*The "Pre-existence" of Jeremiah*

The Mormon Teaching. In Jeremiah 1:5 we read God's words to the prophet: "Before I formed thee in the belly I knew thee; and before thou camest forth out of the womb I sanctified thee, and I ordained thee a prophet unto the nations."

According to James E. Talmage's book *A Study of the Articles of Faith,* Jeremiah 1:5 firmly establishes the pre-existence of Jeremiah.[13] Likewise, in *A Marvelous Work and a Wonder,* we read that Jeremiah 1:5 is proof that "we all lived in the spirit before we were born in the flesh. . . . Jeremiah could not have been so called and ordained before he was born if he did not exist."[14]

The Biblical Teaching. The Mormons are reading an idea into Jeremiah 1:5 that simply is not there. We must remember that in the Bible we are dealing with an absolutely sovereign, all-knowing, all-powerful, and everywhere-present God. God, as an *all-knowing being,* sovereignly "knew" Jeremiah before God formed him "in the belly."[15]

It is critically important to understand the meaning of the Hebrew word for "know" in this context. According to Hebrew scholars, "know" indicates God's act of making Jeremiah the special object of His sovereign choice.[16] Norman Geisler and Thomas Howe state that "the word 'know' (Hebrew: *yada*) implies a special relationship of commitment (cf. Amos 3:2). It is supported by words like 'sanctified' (set apart) and 'ordained,' which reveal that God had a special assignment for Jeremiah (and Paul, Gal. 1:15–16), even before birth. Therefore, these passages do not imply *preexistence* of a soul; rather, they affirm *preordination* of an individual to a special ministry."[17]

Jeremiah 1:5, then, speaks of God calling and setting apart Jeremiah before he was born (cf. Psalm 51:6; 139:13–16). It says nothing about Jeremiah pre-existing in any state whatsoever.

_____ *Ask . . .* _____

- Did you know that Hebrew scholars say the word for "know" in Jeremiah 1:5 indicates God's act of making Jeremiah the special object of His sovereign choice?

- If the Hebrew word for "know" indicates *preordination,* and not *pre-existence,* as Hebrew scholars unanimously maintain, then isn't the Mormon church reading an idea into Jeremiah 1:5 that isn't there?

- Did you know that because of God's foreknowledge, He knows everything and everyone before it occurs or is born (Romans 4:17)?

It is noteworthy that the book of Jeremiah itself teaches that God *created* human beings, not *procreated* them. Indeed, in Jeremiah 27:5 we find God Himself proclaiming, "I have made the earth, the man and the beast that are upon the ground, by my great power and by my outstretched arm."

_____ *Ask . . .* _____

- Would you please read aloud from Jeremiah 27:5?

- Is it not clear from this verse that God *created* man, not *procreated* him?

After making this point, you might want to open your Bible and read aloud from Genesis 2:7: "The LORD God formed man of the dust of the ground, and breathed into his nostrils the breath of life; and man became a living soul." Notice that when man was created, there was no pre-existing spirit that entered a physical tabernacle of flesh. Rather, God created man's physical being, and then "breathed into his nostrils the breath of life; and man became a living soul." It appears that *at that moment* God created both man's material *and* immaterial aspects.

_____ *Ask . . .* _____

- Doesn't a plain reading of Genesis 2:7 seem to indicate that God created both man's material *and* immaterial aspects *at the same time?*

- Where is there the slightest hint in Genesis 2:7 that a pre-existing spirit-being entered a "tabernacle" of human flesh?

Then ask the Mormon to open the Bible to 1 Corinthians 15:46, where we find Paul talking about the distinction between the earthly body and the spiritual resurrection body that we will all one day receive as Christians: "Howbeit that was not first which is spiritual, but that which is natural; and afterward that which is spiritual." In other words, the "first Adam" was the first earthly man and he and all his descendants received natural, earthly bodies. The "last Adam," Jesus Christ, received a glorified, spiritual body at His resurrection from the dead. In the future, we too will receive a glorified, spiritual resurrection body.

Now, Mormons try to argue that all human beings had some kind of spiritual body first and then took on tabernacles of human flesh (that is, physical bodies). But 1 Corinthians 15:46 tells us that we all take on physical bodies *first,* and *later* are resurrected with a glorious, spiritual resurrection body.*

---

*Please note that in the context of 1 Corinthians 15:46 the word "spiritual" does not indicate "nonphysical." Rather, the word simply means that the resurrection body will be a spirit-*dominated* physical body.

___ *Ask . . .* ___

- Does the Mormon church teach that all humans have spirit-bodies in the pre-existence, and then they take on physical bodies when born on earth?

- How do you reconcile that with 1 Corinthians 15:46, where the apostle Paul tells us about the order in which we receive our natural and spiritual bodies: "Howbeit that was not first which is spiritual, but that which is natural; and afterward that which is spiritual"?

- Doesn't 1 Corinthians 15:46 seem to say that we all take on physical bodies *first* and later are resurrected with a glorious, spiritual resurrection body?

John 17:5—*Spirit Existence Before Fleshly Existence?*

The Mormon Teaching. In John 17:5 we read a portion of Jesus' High-Priestly prayer to the Father: "And now, O Father, glorify thou me with thine own self with the glory which I had with thee before the world was."

According to James E. Talmage's book *The Articles of Faith,* John 17:5 supports the idea of a spirit existence prior to fleshly existence.[18] LeGrand Richards, the late Mormon apostle, likewise concludes from this verse that "we all lived in the spirit before we were born in the flesh."[19]

The Biblical Teaching. The fundamental flaw in Mormon thinking here is the idea that everyone—Jesus included—pre-existed as literal spirit-offspring of the Father, and that Jesus (by being firstborn in heaven) is our "elder brother." The Mormons then reason that we are "like Jesus" in this regard, when, in fact, we are not like Jesus—except, of course, that He shares in our humanity. We must stress that Jesus *is eternal God.* You and I *are not* eternal God. Christ pre-existed with the Father. You and I did not pre-exist, but rather came into being at a point in time.

Jesus is the *only* man who pre-existed (He is the *God-man*). John 3:13,31 tells us, "No man hath ascended up to heaven, but he that came down from heaven, even the Son of man which is in heaven. . . . He that cometh from above is above all: he that is of the earth is earthly, and speaketh of the earth: he that cometh from heaven is above all." John 8:23–24 likewise says, "And he said unto them, Ye are from beneath; I am from above: ye are of this world; I am not of this world. I said therefore unto you, that ye shall die in your sins: for if ye believe not that I am he, ye shall die in your sins."

There is a clear dichotomy between the *one* from heaven and the *ones* from the earth. If we *all* came from heaven, then these verses about coming from above or from the earth would have no meaning.

_____ *Ask* . . . _____

- Would you please read aloud from John 3:13,31?

- Would you please read aloud from John 8:23–24?

- Can you see that there is a clear dichotomy between the one from heaven and the ones from the earth?

- Can you see that if we all came from heaven, these verses about coming from above or from the earth would have no meaning?

You will also want to focus some attention on Jesus' preincarnate glory *as God*. Tell the Mormon that the word "glory," when used in the Bible to speak of God, refers to the brilliantly luminous manifestation of God's Person. [20] According to the apostle Paul, God dwells in a "light which no man can approach" (1 Timothy 6:16). So brilliant and glorious is this light that no human being can go anywhere near it and live (*see* Revelation 1:17).

This definition of "glory" is confirmed by the many ways the word is used in Scripture. For example, *brilliant light* consistently accompanies the divine manifestation in His glory (Matthew 17:2–3; 1 Timothy 6:16; Revelation 1:16). Moreover, the word "glory" is often linked with verbs of *seeing* (Exodus 16:7; 33:18; Isaiah 40:5) and verbs of *appearing* (Exodus 16:10; Deuteronomy 5:24). God's glory also includes the presence of *smoke* (Isaiah 6:4) and a *cloud* (Numbers 16:42).

The fact that Jesus Himself manifested the divine glory is an extremely powerful argument for His deity. Indeed, in the Old Testament God said that "I am the LORD: that is my name: and my glory will I not give to another, neither my praise to graven images" (Isaiah 42:8). Yet Jesus too manifested the divine glory (*see* Matthew 17:1–23). That Jesus did this can mean only one thing: *Jesus is God.*

Next, let's turn our attention to Isaiah 6:1–5. Here we read that Isaiah had a vision in the temple—a vision in which he suddenly found himself in the presence of God's glory:

> In the year that king Uzziah died I saw also the Lord sitting upon a throne, high and lifted up, and his train filled the temple. Above it stood the seraphim: each one had six wings; with twain he covered his face, and with twain he covered his feet, and with twain he did fly. And one cried unto another, and said, Holy, holy, holy, is the LORD of hosts: the whole earth is full of his glory. And the posts of the door moved at the voice of him that cried, and the house was filled with smoke. Then said I, Woe is me! for I am undone; because I am a man of unclean lips, and I dwell in the midst of a people of unclean lips: for mine eyes have seen the King, the LORD of hosts (Isaiah 6:1–5).

Isaiah saw the Lord God Almighty seated on a throne, "high and exalted." God's long and flowing robe portrays His kingly majesty. Isaiah also saw seraphim above God's throne. These were magnificent angels who proclaimed God's holiness and glory. The word *seraph* comes from a root word meaning "to burn," emphasizing the purity and brightness of these angelic beings.

As soon as Isaiah saw God's great glory and holiness, he recognized his own utter sinfulness (Isaiah 6:5). The prophet painfully discovered that uncleanness shows up best in the midst of brilliant light. Isaiah cried, "I am ruined" when he saw God. He no doubt recalled the Old Testament teaching that anyone who saw God was expected to die immediately (Genesis 32:30).

All this becomes extremely significant when we go to John's Gospel and read that Isaiah actually saw *Jesus'* glory. Isaiah 6:3 refers to the glory of "the LORD Almighty" (or, more literally, the "Yahweh of hosts"), but John says these words were talking about Jesus Christ. The implication of this is startling: *Jesus is the Lord Almighty.* This is a powerful proof text for the absolute deity of Christ (*see* John 1:18; 10:30; 20:28; Colossians 2:9).

In John 17:5, then, Jesus prayed to the Father about His restoration to a position of glory. The picture in Isaiah 6 helps us understand the magnitude of Christ's glory before He came to earth. Emphasize to the Mormon that while it is true that Christ pre-existed and was in a state of glory prior to the resurrection, these things are so simply because *Christ is God.* Christ pre-existed *as God.* Christ was in a position of glory *as God.*

_____ *Ask . . .* _____

- Did you know that according to Isaiah 42:8, God said He would not give His glory to another?

- Since Christ has this glory, according to Matthew 17:1–23, what does this tell us about Jesus Christ?

- Since Jesus is absolute deity, we would expect Him to be pre-existent, right?

- But you and I are not God. So we can't use John 17:5 to support the idea of a pre-existence for us, can we?

Acts 17:28–29—*The "Offspring" of God*

The Mormon Teaching. In Acts 17:28–29 the apostle Paul says, "In him we live, and move, and have our being; as certain also of your own poets have said, For we are also his offspring. Forasmuch then as we are the offspring of God, we ought not to think that the Godhead is like unto gold, or silver, or stone, graven by art and man's device."

Mormons often cite this reference to the "offspring of God" to support the idea that the Heavenly Father and Mother gave birth to spirit-children in the pre-existence. Jesus was allegedly an "offspring" of God; you and I allegedly are "offspring" of God; all people are "offspring of exalted parents."[21]

The Biblical Teaching. The Mormons have misconstrued the meaning of Acts 17:28–29 by reading into the text an idea that is not there. Here's the context: Paul was preaching to the Athenians. They weren't believers in the true God. But despite their unbelief, Paul goes on to affirm that we are all "offspring of God." Why? Simply because God is the *Creator* of us all. Whether we believe in Him or not, all of us were nevertheless created by Him, and thus are rightly called His "offspring."[22]

Paul even set the context for his "offspring" statement a few verses earlier when he referred to the "God that made the world and all things therein. . . . And hath made of one blood all nations of men for to dwell on all the face of the earth, and hath determined the times before appointed, and the bounds of their habitation" (Acts 17:24,26). All people are God's "offspring" because God "hath made of one blood all nations of men."

Malachi 2:10 confirms that truth: "Have we not all one father? hath not one God *created* us?" (emphasis added). *Fatherhood* and the *act of creating* are one and the same in this verse. God is the Father of all humanity in the sense that He created all humanity. Acts 17:28–29 says nothing at all in support of a Heavenly Father and Mother giving birth to spirit-children.

You must remember that the apostle Paul was a "Hebrew of Hebrews," and was an Old Testament scholar *par excellence*. He knew the Old Testament like the back of his hand. So, when he said, "We are his offspring," he was saying it against the broader context of the Old Testament teaching that God is the Father of us all in the sense that He is our Creator (Genesis 1; Malachi 2:10).

_____ *Ask . . .* _____

- By looking at the context of Acts 17, isn't it clear that all people are God's "offspring" (verse 29) because God "hath made of one blood all nations of men" (verse 26)?

- Isn't the emphasis in Acts 17 on God's *creation*, not *procreation*?

- Please show me a single reference in any book written by the apostle Paul that explicitly states that humans pre-exist in spirit-bodies.

- Please show me a single reference in any book written by the apostle Paul that even remotely alludes to a Heavenly Mother.

- Please show me a single reference in any book written by the apostle Paul that says the Heavenly Father had sexual relations with a Heavenly Mother to give birth to spirit-children.

- By the way, if every Heavenly Father has a Father, who himself has a Father, who then himself has a Father, and so on up the hierarchy, *who was the first Father?* What "Father" got things started in the very beginning of beginnings?

Romans 8:16–17—*"Children" of God*

The Mormon Teaching. In Romans 8:16–17 the apostle Paul says, "The Spirit itself beareth witness with our spirit, that we are the children of God: And if children, then heirs; heirs of God, and joint-heirs with Christ; if so be that we suffer with him, that we may be also glorified together."

As we saw earlier, Mormons say that we are "children of God" in the most literal sense. All of us are the spirit-offspring of our Heavenly Father and Mother. All men and women are "literally the sons and daughters of Deity," the "offspring of celestial parentage."[23]

The Biblical Teaching. If Mormons would give serious consideration to the context of Romans 8:16–17, they wouldn't interpret it to mean that we are literally the offspring of God. Instead of isolating verses 16 and 17 as proof texts, why not consult the context in verse 15?

Romans 8:15 explicitly states that people become children of God *by adoption:* "Ye have not received the spirit of bondage again to fear; but ye have received *the Spirit of adoption,* whereby we cry, Abba, Father" (emphasis added).

This is not the only place where the apostle Paul wrote about people being adopted into God's family. In Galatians 4:5–6 Paul says that God sent His Son "to redeem them that were under the law, *that we might receive the adoption of sons.* And because ye are sons, God hath sent forth the Spirit of his Son into your hearts, crying, Abba, Father" (emphasis added). Notice that these individuals are called God's "sons" *only* because they have been adopted.

In Ephesians 1:5, Paul talks about God "having predestinated us *unto the adoption of children by Jesus Christ to himself,* according to the good pleasure of his will" (emphasis added). As we can see, then, those who place their faith in Jesus Christ for salvation are adopted into God's family.

___ *Ask* . . . ___

- There's a big difference between a natural son (via conception and birth) and an adopted son, right?

- Based on Romans 8:15, Galatians 4:5–6, and Ephesians 1:5, how do each of us come into God's family—by conception and birth, or by adoption?

- Since Paul sets the context of Romans 8:16–17 by referring to adoption in verse 15, it's not accurate for the Mormon church to cite this passage to support the idea that a Heavenly Father and Mother give birth to spirit children, is it?

You might add that according to the New Testament, believers become "God's children" (or "God's sons") by the new birth. John 1:12, for example, tells us, "As many as received him, to them gave he power to become the sons of God, even to them that believe on his name."

17

Salvation in Mormonism— Part 1: Understanding Mormon Terminology

When talking about salvation with Mormons, it is critical to recognize that they use salvation words in a distinct way. Just because they use a word that *sounds* biblical doesn't mean they are using it biblically. As we will see in this chapter, Mormons talk about salvation, eternal life, and heaven—but they completely redefine these words to fit their cultic theology.

Mormons teach that there is both general salvation and individual salvation. *General* salvation, Bruce McConkie tells us, is "that which comes by grace alone without obedience to gospel law, [and] consists in the mere fact of being resurrected. In this sense salvation is synonymous with immortality; it is the inseparable connection of body and spirit so that the resurrected personage lives forever. . . . This kind of salvation eventually will come to all mankind, excepting the sons of perdition."[1] (The "sons of perdition" includes mainly apostates. Their ultimate destiny is the "outer darkness.")

Individual salvation, however, refers to "that which man merits through his own acts through life and by obedience to the laws and ordinances of the gospel."[2] We are told that "salvation in its true and full meaning is synonymous with exaltation or eternal life and consists in gaining an inheritance in the highest of the three heavens within the celestial kingdom. . . .This full salvation is obtained in and through the continuation of the family unit in eternity, and those who obtain it are gods."[3]

Notice the key concepts mentioned in the above paragraph: *exaltation, eternal life,* the *highest of the three heavens,* and the *family unit.* As we will see in this chapter and the chapters to come, these terms are at the heart of the Mormon system of salvation; they are closely related in Mormon theology. Indeed, gaining eternal life, exaltation, and having an eternal family all relate in some way to the Mormon concept of becoming a god. Let's look at the issue of godhood first.

The Mormon Goal of Godhood

A perusal of Mormon literature quickly makes clear that the ultimate goal in Mormonism is godhood. Brigham Young, for example, said that "the Lord created you and me for the purpose of becoming Gods like himself. . . . We are created . . . to become Gods like unto our Father in heaven."[4]

Doctrine and Covenants likewise tells us, "Then shall they be gods, because they have no end; therefore shall they be from everlasting to everlasting, because they continue; then shall they be above all, because all things are subject unto them. Then shall they be gods, because they have all power, and the angels are subject unto them."[5]

Now, this exaltation to godhood is known as attaining "eternal life" to Mormons. The official *Gospel Principles* manual tells us that "exaltation is eternal life, the kind of life that God lives. . . . We can become Gods like our heavenly Father. This is exaltation."[6] Joseph Fielding Smith said that "eternal life is the name of the kind of life possessed by the Father and the Son; it is exaltation in the eternal realm."[7]

Now, what does the family unit have to do with godhood? In Mormon theology, having an eternal family (the union of a celestial husband and wife) enables a person to have spirit-children for all eternity. Eventually these spirit-children will have the opportunity to gain godhood and procreate their own spirit-children. This process has supposedly been going on for all eternity and will continue for all eternity. It is an endless cycle of procreation.

When we look at the evidence around us, it seems that today's Mormons talk more about attaining eternal life and having an eternal family than they talk about actual godhood. But in Mormon theology, attaining eternal life and having an eternal family requires godhood. *Only a God* can have eternal life, and *only a God* can have an eternal family.

The Mormon Emphasis on Perfection

Regardless of the terms used—eternal life, eternal family, exaltation—it is clear that the ultimate goal in Mormonism is the attaining of godhood. This is the fundamental fact that you must keep in mind if you want to understand and refute the Mormon concept of salvation.

While godhood is the Mormon's ultimate goal, his or her more immediate goal is perfection. It is perfection that allegedly moves people closer and closer to godhood. Mormons believe there is biblical support for this idea.

Matthew 5:48—*Attaining Perfection*

The Mormon Teaching. In Matthew 5:48 we read, "Be ye therefore perfect, even as your Father which is in heaven is perfect." In *The Way to Perfection,* Joseph Fielding Smith said, "The words of the Savior in his Sermon on the Mount, 'Be ye therefore perfect, even as your Father which is in heaven is perfect,' have served as a text for many a sermon. We have been informed that his meaning is that we, in this life, should try to perform every duty and keep every law and thus endeavor to be perfect in our sphere as the Father is in his."[8]

Elsewhere Smith wrote that "it is our duty to be better today than we were yesterday, and better tomorrow than we are today. Why? Because we are on that road . . . to perfection, and that can only come through obedience and the desire in our heart to overcome the world."[9] This road ultimately leads to godhood. This is an attainable goal. As Mormons will often ask, "Would Jesus give us a command that we couldn't keep?"

The Biblical Teaching. Matthew 5:48 is *not* communicating the idea that human beings can become perfect or attain sinless perfection in this life. Such an idea is foreign not only to the immediate context of Matthew's Gospel but also to the broader context of all of Scripture. This is because of the problem of human sin. Jesus taught that, without exception, people are utterly sinful. He taught that human beings have a grave sin problem that is *beyond their means to solve.* He taught that man is evil (Matthew 12:34) and is capable of great wickedness (Mark 7:20–23). Moreover, He said that man is lost (Luke 19:10), that he is a sinner (Luke 15:10), that he is in need of repentance before a holy God (Mark 1:15), and that he needs to be born again (John 3:3,5,7).

Jesus often spoke of sin in metaphors that illustrate the havoc sin can wreak in a person's life. He described sin as blindness (Matthew 23:16–26), sickness (Matthew 9:12), being enslaved in bondage (John 8:34), and living in darkness (John 8:12; 12:35–46). Moreover, Jesus said that this is a *universal condition* and that all people are guilty before God (Luke 7:37–48).

Jesus also taught that both inner thoughts and external acts render a person guilty (Matthew 5:28). He taught that from within the human heart comes evil thoughts, sexual immorality, theft, murder, adultery, greed, malice, deceit, envy, slander, arrogance, and folly (Mark 7:21–23). Moreover, He affirmed that God is fully aware of every person's sins, both external acts and inner thoughts; nothing escapes His notice (Matthew 22:18; Luke 6:8; John 4:17–19).

We will talk about the Mormon concept of sin a bit later. For now we simply want to emphasize that in view of man's dire sin problem *as defined by Scripture,* there is no way that we can interpret Matthew 5:48 to mean that human beings can attain perfection in this life.

How can we make sense of this verse, then? If we look at the context, we see that Matthew 5:48 is found in a section of Scripture dealing with the law of love. The Jewish leaders of Jesus' day had taught that we should love those who are near and dear to us (Leviticus 19:18), but hate those who are enemies. Jesus refutes this idea and instructs us to love even our enemies (Matthew 5:44). After all, Jesus said, God's love extends to all people (Matthew 5:45). And since God is our righteous standard, we should seek to imitate His example. We are to be "perfect" *in showing love* just as He is perfect in showing love.

Bible expositor Louis A. Barbieri gives this explanation to help us understand Matthew 5:48: "Murder, lust, hate, deception, and retaliation obviously do not characterize God. He did not lower His standard to accommodate humans; instead He set forth His absolute holiness as the standard. Though this standard can never be perfectly met by man himself, *a person who by faith trusts in God enjoys His righteousness being reproduced in his life*" [10] (emphasis added).

The key, then, is this: As we walk by faith in Christ, Christ's perfection is reproduced in our lives day by day. This is the only way Christians move toward any kind of real "perfection." It's all based on what Christ accomplished for us.

Of course, Mormons know they are not perfect *now.* That's why they typically read a "future perfection" into Matthew 5:48. That is, even though they are not perfect *now,* they are progressively *moving toward* perfection and will eventually attain godhood. If the Mormon uses this argument, emphasize the *present tense* of Matthew 5:48: "*Be* ye perfect" (that is, *now!*).

Mark Cares, a pastor in Mormon country, says that "we need to repeatedly and persistently tell them that God demands perfection now. We cannot let them ignore that.

They need to sweat over it. They need to lose sleep over it. They need to despair of trying to become perfect themselves. Then, and only then, will they be ready to look to Jesus for salvation."[11] Don't let the Mormon escape the force of this: Matthew 5:48 says "*be* perfect," not "*become* perfect."

We should then take the Mormon to Hebrews 10:14, which speaks of what Christ Himself has accomplished on our behalf: "By one offering *he hath perfected for ever* them that are sanctified" (emphasis added).[12] Christ has done it all! Christ has "perfected for ever" those who have trusted in Him.

Next you'll want to cite James 2:10: "Whosoever shall keep the whole law, and yet offend in one point, he is guilty of all." With a motive of love, you'll want to "drive the stake in" as forcefully as you can: *Help the Mormon see that he or she is automatically doomed to fail in the quest to reach perfection by self-effort—both now and always.* Only then will the Mormon recognize his or her need for Christ, who was perfect on our behalf and wiped away all our sins by His death on the cross.

As Hebrews 10:17–18 says, "Their sins and iniquities will I remember no more. Now where remission of these is, there is no more offering for sin." Mormons desperately need to hear these liberating words.

_____ *Ask . . .* _____

- Are you perfect *now?*

- Have you considered what James 2:10 says about your present state of perfection? ("Whosoever shall keep the whole law, and yet offend in one point, he is guilty of all.")

- Can I share with you how I've been liberated from this bondage of perfection? It's all based on what Jesus did. Hebrews 10:14 says, "By one offering *he hath perfected for ever* them that are sanctified" (emphasis added).

Understanding Eternal Progression

Fundamental to understanding the Mormon concept of exaltation is the doctrine of *eternal progression*. According to Mormons, we do not just seek perfection in this life. This goal continues beyond the grave. Salvation does not come all at once. Mormons tell us that we are commanded to be perfect even as our Father in heaven is perfect—and it will take us *ages* to accomplish this end. For the worthy, there will be great progress beyond the grave.

Joseph Smith describes eternal progression this way:

> Here, then, is eternal life—to know the only wise and true God; and you have got to learn how to be Gods yourselves, and to be kings and priests to God, the same as all Gods have done before you, namely, *by going from one small degree to another, and from a small capacity to a great one; from grace to grace, from exaltation to exaltation* (emphasis added). [13]

In the book *Gospel Principles* Joseph Smith once compared eternal progression to climbing a ladder:

> When you climb up a ladder, you must begin at the bottom, and ascend step by step, until you arrive at the top; and so it is with the principles of the Gospel—you must begin with the first, and go on until you learn all the principles of exaltation. But it will be a great while after you have passed through the veil [died] before you will have learned them. It is not all to be comprehended in this world; it will be a great work to learn our salvation and exaltation beyond the grave. [14]

Joseph Fielding Smith urges us: "We have to pass through mortality and receive the resurrection and then go on to perfection just as our Father did before us." [15] The perfection process will go *on* and *on* and *on*.*

---

*We will examine the Mormon view of salvation and premortality, mortality, and postmortality in chapter 18.

Romans 8:16–17—*Ultimate Godhood?*

The Mormon Teaching. In Romans 8:16–17 we read, "The Spirit itself beareth witness with our spirit, that we are the children of God: And if children, then heirs; heirs of God, and joint-heirs with Christ; if so be that we suffer with him, that we may be also glorified together."

Mormons tell us that these verses point to the result of eternal progression: Godhood. In his book *Mormon Doctrine,* Bruce McConkie said, "Those who gain eternal life receive exaltation; they are sons of God, joint heirs with Christ, members of the Church of the Firstborn; they overcome all things, have all power, and receive the fullness of the Father. They are gods."[16]

The Biblical Teaching. The Mormon interpretation of Romans 8:16–17 fails to consider the immediate context of the verses. As we saw in the previous chapter, the apostle Paul explicitly states in Romans 8:15 that people become "children of God" *by adoption:* "Ye have not received the spirit of bondage again to fear; but ye have received *the Spirit of adoption,* whereby we cry, Abba, Father" (emphasis added).

We become "children of God" *not by nature,* but rather, we are *adopted into* God's family. This is extremely important: We do not have the seed of godhood in us that can become exalted and grow to godhood. We are adopted into God's family *as humans.*

In addition, Paul's statement that we can become "co-heirs" with Christ has nothing to do with becoming exalted as a God. Heirs are people who inherit something. In many families, children inherit their parents' entire estate. Every child in the family is an heir, and the children together are co-heirs.

As Christians, then, we are co-heirs with Christ. And what do we inherit? Paul tells us that we inherit all spiritual blessings *in this life* (Ephesians 1:3), and in the *life to come* we will share with the Lord Jesus in all the riches of God's glorious kingdom (1 Corinthians 3:21–23).

Now, did Paul have any illusions about being (or becoming) a god? Point the Mormon to Acts 14, where Paul clearly demonstrated that he was an uncompromising monotheist. After Paul healed a man in Lystra, "the people saw what Paul had done" and they shouted, "The gods are come down to us in the likeness of men" (verse 11). The people were prepared to worship Paul and Barnabas as gods! When Paul and Barnabas understood what was going on, "they rent their clothes, and ran in among the people, crying out, And saying, Sirs, why do ye these things? *We also are men* of like passions with you, and preach unto you that ye should turn from these vanities unto *the living God,* which made heaven, and earth, and the sea, and all things that are therein" (Acts 14:14–15, emphasis added). Paul and Barnabas not only emphatically denied that they were gods, but they also spoke of the only true God who created the universe—thereby drawing a clear distinction between the Creator and the creation.

_____ *Ask . . .* _____

- Would you please read aloud from Acts 14:8–15?

- What was Paul's reaction when he understood that the people thought he was a god?

- Doesn't Paul draw a clear distinction between the one true God and human beings?

Paul and Barnabas's attitude is in clear contrast to the folly of Herod in Acts 12:21–23. After Herod had given a public address, the people shouted, "It is the voice of a god, and not of a man." Immediately, because Herod did not give praise to God, an angel of the Lord struck him down, and he was eaten by worms and died. Clearly, God does not look kindly on human pretenders to the throne of divinity.

_____ *Ask* . . . _____

- Would you please read aloud from Acts 12:21–23?
- What did Herod do to provoke God's punishment?
- What was the true God's response?

You might offer one final biblical illustration of God's attitude toward human pretenders to the divine throne. The encounter with the Pharaoh of Egypt well illustrates God's sovereignty over man. More specifically, in Exodus 9:14 God instructed Moses to tell Pharaoh, "I will at this time send all my plagues upon thine heart, and upon thy servants, and upon thy people; *that thou mayest know that there is none like me in all the earth*" (emphasis added).

Now, it's important to tell the Mormon that these words were spoken to a man who was himself considered a god. The Pharaoh was thought to be the incarnation of the Egyptian sun god, Ra, and was therefore considered a "god" in his own right.[17] But God told the Pharaoh that no human being is a god, and that He alone was God.

_____ *Ask* . . . _____

- Would you please read from Exodus 9:13–14?

- Did you know that the Pharaoh was thought to be the incarnation of the Egyptian sun god, Ra, and was therefore considered a "god" in his own right?

- Yet how does the one true God respond to Pharaoh? Please quote God's words exactly (verse 14).

Then open your Bible and read aloud from Isaiah 44:8, where God Himself asks, "Is there a God beside me? yea, there is no God; I know not any." Next turn to Isaiah 43:10, where God declares, *"Before me* there was no God formed, neither shall there be *after me"* (emphasis added).

Since there were no gods *before* the God of the Bible, this means that God had no Father-gods or Grandfather-gods *before* Him. Since no gods will come *after* God, this means that none of His children will *become* gods. The God of the Bible says there are no other Gods than Him! (And note that these verses aren't referring to the nonexistence of *pagan* gods or idols, as some Mormons claim; God says there are *no other gods whatsoever.*) Ultimately, then, the Mormon doctrine of exaltation cannot be true. For there are no beings in the universe that we can rightly call God, according to the God of the Bible.

_____ *Ask . . .* _____

- Would you please read aloud from Isaiah 44:8?

- How do you reconcile this verse with the Mormon claim that God has a Father-god, and the Father-god has a Father-god, and so on? Did the God of Isaiah 44:8 forget His own Father?

- Would you please read aloud from Isaiah 43:10?

- Since there were no gods *before* the God of the Bible, doesn't this mean that our "Father" had no Father or Grandfather-gods *before* him?

- Since no gods will come *after* God, doesn't this mean that none of His children will *become* gods?

- Don't these verses clearly show that you and I cannot become gods ourselves?

You will also want to mention that the Book of Mormon teaches plainly that there is only one God. If the Mormon has a Book of Mormon on hand, ask him or her to look up Alma 11:22–31. In this passage, a man named Amulek opens a dialogue with Zeezrom by stating that he cannot say anything contrary to God's spirit. Hence, the words of Amulek are essentially the words of God himself. Zeezrom asks Amulek, "Is there more than one God?" Amulek answers, "No." Zeezrom then asks, "How knowest thou these things?" Amulek replies, "An angel hath made them known to me."

Obviously if there is not "more than one God," then human beings do not become exalted and attain godhood. The Mormon view of exaltation and eternal life is clearly refuted by Alma 11:22–31.

_____ *Ask* . . . _____

- The Book of Mormon has something important to say about attaining godhood. Would you please read aloud from Alma 11:22–31?

- Doesn't this passage indicate that there is only one God?

- That being the case, doesn't the Book of Mormon refute the church's later teaching of the doctrine of eternal progression?

If the attaining of eternal life is *not* exaltation to godhood, as Mormons believe, then what is it? Share with the Mormon that eternal life is a *present possession* of those who believe in Jesus Christ. It is not a goal that a person works toward and attains via perfection. In John 6:47, Jesus affirms, "Verily, verily, I say unto you, He that believeth on me hath everlasting life." Notice the key word "hath" in this verse. It is in the present tense. This means that people who believe in Jesus Christ have eternal life as a present possession—they have it *now!*

_____ *Ask . . .* _____

- Would you please read aloud from John 6:47?

- Did you know that the word "hath" in this verse is in the present tense, indicating that people who believe in Jesus Christ have eternal life *as a present possession*?

Then explain to the Mormon what the Bible has to say about eternal life. According to the Gospels of Matthew, Mark, and Luke, eternal life (Matthew 19:16; Mark 10:17; Luke 18:18) is consistently equated with *being saved* (Matthew 19:25; Mark 10:26–27; Luke 18:26–27) and *entering into the kingdom of heaven* (Matthew 19:23–24; Mark 10:24; Luke 18:24). Nowhere in the New Testament is eternal life used to mean "attain godhood."

Eternal life is always portrayed as something received by faith in Christ (John 3:16; 6:28–29), not something that is achieved or worked for. Moreover, eternal life is not just *quantitative* (meaning that it lasts forever), it is also *qualitative* (meaning that it is an infinitely high quality of life in living fellowship with God, both now and forever).

18

Salvation in Mormonism—Part 2: Premortality, Mortality, and Postmortality

E xaltation to godhood in Mormon theology ultimately involves not just what a person does in this earthly life *(mortality),* but also what he has already done in *premortality* (that is, in his "pre-existence" as a spirit-child) and in *postmortality* (that is, in his return to the spirit world following physical death). A person's progression toward godhood is an extended process.

A key concept related to this process has to do with the word *agency*—which, in Mormon thinking, describes each human being's right to choose between good and evil. From the moment of birth, people are born not only with the capacity to choose, but, according to Mormons, that capacity is itself inclined toward doing good.

Agency is very important, Mormons say, for without it humanity cannot "progress." People progress toward godhood by making "wise use" of their agency. And people must make wise use of agency in premortality, mortality, *and* postmortality. Let's look now at each of these states of existence.

Premortality

Premortality is also called pre-existence, or our "First Estate." As the book *Gospel Principles* tells us, "Man, as a spirit, was begotten and born of heavenly parents, and reared to maturity in the eternal mansion of the Father, prior to coming upon the earth in a temporal [physical] body"[1] (insert added).

Mormons believe that because we were born as spirit-children of our Heavenly Father, we have the very nature of God. As Spencer W. Kimball put it, "Man has in himself the seeds of godhood, which can germinate and grow and develop. As the acorn becomes the oak, the mortal man becomes a god."[2] But this all hinges on proper use of agency.

In Mormon theology, spirit-children begin progressing toward godhood in the premortal state. Mormons believe that their being born on earth is a sign that they used their agency wisely in the preexistence. It proves that they didn't follow Lucifer in the rebellion against God. "Because we are here on earth and have mortal bodies we know that we chose to follow Jesus Christ and our Heavenly Father. . . . In our pre-earth life, we chose the right."[3] We must continue choosing the right during our mortal existence.

Mortality

Mortality—the earthly life, or "Second Estate"—is a time of testing for the Mormon. This is because the person now has a physical body.

The logic goes this way: In order to become a god a person must face (and overcome) physical temptations and trials. Such growth *is not possible* for a spirit-child, because, without a physical body, it's not possible to encounter physical temptation. That's why spirit-children take on human bodies, and during this time of mortality they face physical temptations and make progress toward godhood.

Once a person has entered mortality and gained a physical body, he must fulfill an unbelievable list of requirements in his endeavor to make progress toward exaltation, or godhood. This includes repentance, baptism, membership in the LDS church, innumerable good works, abiding by the Mormon "Word of Wisdom" (which prohibits the use of coffee, tea, alcohol, or tobacco), marriage and other temple rituals (including those on behalf of the dead), and "keeping all the Lord's commandments until the end of [one's] life on earth"[4] (insert added). As we will see in the pages ahead, each of these requirements has a critical role in the Mormon system of salvation.

Baptism and Salvation

Baptism carries a great deal of significance for Mormons. Indeed, Mormons identify baptism with being "born again" (in Christian theology, this is known as "baptismal regeneration"). Bruce McConkie said that "the second birth begins when men are legally baptized in water by a legal administrator."[5] The phrase "legally baptized in water by a legal administrator" means that a person must be baptized by a member of the Mormon priesthood who is in good standing. Orson Pratt explains:

> But who in this generation have authority to baptize? None but those who have received authority in the Church of Jesus Christ of Latter-day Saints; all other churches are entirely destitute of all authority from God; and any person who receives baptism or the Lord's Supper from their hands will highly offend God; for He looks upon them as the most corrupt of all people, both Catholics and Protestants are nothing less than the "whore of Babylon" whom the Lord denounces by the mouth of John the Revelator as having corrupted all the earth by their fornications and wickedness.[6]

Acts 2:38—*Repent and Be Baptized*

The Mormon Teaching. In Acts 2:38 we read, "Peter said unto them, Repent, and be baptized every one of you in the name of Jesus Christ for the remission of sins, and ye shall receive the gift of the Holy Ghost."

Mormons think this verse says a person must be baptized to receive forgiveness of sins and be saved. James Talmage tells us that "biblical proofs that baptism is designed as a means of securing to man a remission of his sins are abundant."[7] One of these proofs, Talmage assures us, is Acts 2:38.

The Biblical Teaching. Admittedly, Acts 2:38 is not an easy verse to interpret. But a basic principle of Bible interpretation is to interpret difficult passages in light of the easy, clear verses. We should never build a theology on difficult passages alone.

Now, the great majority of New Testament Bible passages dealing with salvation affirm that salvation is by faith. We've already looked at some of those verses in the previous chapter (e.g., John 3:16–17). In view of those clear passages, how is Acts 2:38 to be interpreted? A single word in the verse gives us the answer: "Peter said unto them, Repent, and be baptized every one of you in the name of Jesus Christ *for* the remission of sins, and ye shall receive the gift of the Holy Ghost" (emphasis added).

Students of the Greek language have pointed out that the word "for" in the Greek text—*eis*—is a preposition that can indicate *causality* ("in order to attain") or a *result* ("because of").[8] An example of using "for" in a *resultant* sense is the sentence, "I'm taking an aspirin *for* my headache." This means I'm taking an aspirin *because of* my headache. I'm not taking an aspirin *in order to attain* a headache. An example of using "for" in a *causal* sense is the sentence, "I'm going to the office *for* my paycheck." This means I'm going to the office *in order to attain* my paycheck.

Now, in Acts 2:38 the word "for" is used in a resultant sense. The verse might be paraphrased, "Repent, and be baptized every one of you in the name of Jesus Christ *because of* [or *as a result of*] the remission of sins." The verse is not saying, "Repent, and be baptized every one of you in the name of Jesus Christ *in order to attain* the remission of sins."

Acts 2:38 is saying that the people who had already received remission of sins by believing in Jesus Christ should now be baptized in water. Water baptism *follows* being born again.

_____ *Ask* . . . _____

- Did you know that Greek scholars say the word "for" is a preposition that can indicate either *causality* ("in order to attain") or a *result* ("because of")?

- An example of using "for" in a *resultant* sense is the sentence, "I'm taking an aspirin *for [as a result of]* my headache."

- An example of using "for" in a *causal* sense is the sentence, "I'm going to the office *for [in order to attain]* my paycheck."

- What would Acts 2:38 be saying if "for" is being used in a resultant sense?

Remind the Mormon that in this same book of Acts, when the desperate Philippian jailer asked Paul what he must do to obtain salvation and have eternal life, Paul said virtually nothing about baptism. Paul merely said, "Believe on the Lord Jesus Christ, and thou shalt be saved" (Acts 16:31). Simple and to the point!

This is consistent with what we see elsewhere in Scripture. Consider the following:

- John 3:15—"Whosoever believeth in him should not perish, but have eternal life."
- John 5:24—"Verily, verily, I say unto you, He that heareth my word, and believeth on him that sent me, hath everlasting life, and shall not come into condemnation; but is passed from death unto life."

- John 11:25—"Jesus said unto her, I am the resurrection, and the life: he that believeth in me, though he were dead, yet shall he live."
- John 12:46—"I am come a light into the world, that whosoever believeth on me should not abide in darkness."
- John 20:31—"These are written, that ye might believe that Jesus is the Christ, the Son of God; and that believing ye might have life through his name."

John 3:1–5—*Born of Water*

The Mormon Teaching. In John 3:1–5 we read,

There was a man of the Pharisees, named Nicodemus, a ruler of the Jews: The same came to Jesus by night, and said unto him, Rabbi, we know that thou art a teacher come from God: for no man can do these miracles that thou doest, except God be with him. Jesus answered and said unto him, Verily, verily, I say unto thee, *Except a man be born again, he cannot see the kingdom of God.* Nicodemus saith unto him, How can a man be born when he is old? Can he enter the second time into his mother's womb, and be born? Jesus answered, Verily, verily, I say unto thee, Except a man be born of water and of the Spirit, he cannot enter into the kingdom of God (emphasis added).

James E. Talmage tells us that "the words of the Savior, spoken while He ministered in the flesh, declare baptism to be essential to salvation. . . . It is practically indisputable that the watery birth here referred to as essential to entrance into the kingdom is baptism."[9]

The Biblical Teaching. Consulting the context of John 3 clears up Jesus' intended meaning. Let us begin by emphasizing that being "born again" (literally, "born from above") simply refers to God giving eternal life to the person who believes in Christ (Titus 3:5). Being born again places a person in God's eternal family (1 Peter 1:23), and gives the believer a new capacity and desire to please the Father (2 Corinthians 5:17).

Now, critical to a proper understanding of John 3:1–5 is verse 6: "That which is born of the flesh is flesh; and that which is born of the Spirit is spirit." Flesh can *only* reproduce itself as flesh—and this is not acceptable to God (cf. Romans 8:8). "The law of reproduction is 'after its kind.' So likewise the Spirit produces spirit, a life born, nurtured, and matured by the Spirit of God." [10]

In Nicodemus's case, we find a Pharisee who would have been trusting in his physical descent from Abraham for entrance into the Messiah's kingdom. The Jews believed that because they were physically related to Abraham, they were in a specially privileged position before God. Christ, however, denied such a possibility. As Bible scholar J. Dwight Pentecost observes, "parents can transmit to their children only the nature which they themselves possess. Since each parent's nature, because of Adam's sin, is sinful, each parent transmits a sinful nature to the child. What is sinful cannot enter the kingdom of God (v. 5)." [11] The only way a person can enter God's kingdom is through *spiritual* rebirth, and this is precisely what Jesus is saying to Nicodemus.

The problem is, Nicodemus did not comprehend Jesus' meaning. Nicodemus wrongly concluded that Jesus was speaking about *physical* birth, but could not understand how a person could go through physical birth a second time (John 3:4). So, Jesus picked up on Nicodemus's line of thought and sought to move the discussion from physical birth to spiritual birth.

Notice what Jesus said to Nicodemus: First He spoke about being "born of water and the Spirit" in John 3:5; then He explained what He meant in verse 6. It would seem that "born *of water*" in verse 5 is parallel to "born *of the flesh*" in verse 6, just as "born of . . . *the Spirit*" and "born of *the Spirit*" are parallel in verses 5 and 6. Jesus' message, then, is that just as a person has had a physical birth, so also must a person have a spiritual birth if he wants to enter the kingdom of God. He must be "born from above."[12]

_____ *Ask . . .* _____

- Would you please read aloud from John 3:5? What two kinds of birth does Jesus mention?

- Would you please read aloud from John 3:6? What two kinds of birth does Jesus mention?

- In context, is it not clear that Jesus defines what He means in verse 5 by the more precise statement in verse 6?

- That being the case, isn't Jesus saying that just as a person has had a physical birth ("born of the flesh"), so also must a person have a spiritual birth if he wants to enter the kingdom of God?

Mark 16:16—*Belief and Baptism Together?*

The Mormon Teaching. In Mark 16:16 we read, "He that believeth and is baptized shall be saved; but he that believeth not shall be damned." Mere belief is clearly not enough, Mormons say; a person must also be baptized in order to be saved.[13]

The Biblical Teaching. This is another difficult passage to interpret. But again, a basic principle of Bible interpretation is to interpret the difficult passages in light of the easy, clear verses.

Now, we want to focus our attention on the latter part of the verse: "He that believeth and is baptized shall be saved; but *he that believeth not shall be damned.*" It is *unbelief* that brings damnation, not a lack of being baptized. When a person rejects the gospel and refuses to believe it, he or she is damned.

In your discussion about baptism, you might want to mention these words from the apostle Paul: "Christ sent me not to baptize, but to preach the gospel: not with wisdom of words, lest the cross of Christ should be made of none effect" (1 Corinthians 1:17). Paul here draws a clear distinction between baptism and the gospel. And since it is the gospel that saves people (1 Corinthians 15:1–2), clearly baptism is not necessary to attain salvation.

_____ *Ask* . . . _____

- Would you read aloud from Mark 16:16? According to the last half of the verse, what is the basis of damnation?

- According to 1 Corinthians 15:1–2, does baptism save or the gospel? (The Mormon may, at this point, say that the "gospel" has to do with the intricate plan of salvation in Mormonism—including baptism. Keep going . . .)

- Would you read aloud from 1 Corinthians 1:17? If the gospel saves, and if Paul draws a clear distinction between the gospel and baptism, doesn't that mean that baptism has no part in salvation?

(Next you might read aloud from 1 Corinthians 15:1–4, where the apostle Paul clearly defines what he means by "the gospel.")

Church Membership Required

Mormons teach that membership in the Mormon church has a role in salvation. Indeed, "salvation is in the church, and of the church, and is obtained only through the church."[14]

Milton R. Hunter affirms that the person on the road to godhood "must become a member and live the gospel principles and ordinances of the true church of the Master—which is the

Church of Jesus Christ of Latter-day Saints, restored to earth through divine revelations to the prophet Joseph Smith."[15]

This brings up a key difference between Mormons and evangelical Christians: While Christians believe church attendance is important (Hebrews 10:25), they do not believe that church membership is related to—or required for—salvation. The church is not the "mediator" between God and man. As 1 Timothy 2:5 tells us, "there is one God, and one mediator between God and men, the man Christ Jesus." Jesus Himself said, "I am the way, the truth, and the life: no man cometh unto the Father, but by me" (John 14:6). Thus, Christians believe it is your *relationship with Christ* that counts, not church membership.

For the Mormon, however, even attending the Mormon church is not enough, for there is also . . .

The Necessity of Good Works

Ultimate salvation in Mormonism involves a consistent life of good works. Complete salvation—eternal life—is said to result from man's endeavor to conform to God's laws and commandments. Human beings essentially save themselves with the aid of the Lord.

Mormons assert that "one common erroneous concept is that belief alone in the Lord Jesus Christ is the only requirement for salvation. . . . Salvation comes through living the Lord's commandments and doing good works."[16] Indeed, "keeping the commandments of God will cleanse away the stain of sin."[17] Among the Bible passages Mormons cite to support this view are James 2:17,26; Philippians 2:12; and 1 John 2:3–5. Let's take a closer look at the first two passages.

James 2:17,26—*Faith Without Works Is Dead*

The Mormon Teaching. In James 2:17,26 we read, "Even so faith, if it hath not works, is dead, being alone. . . . For as the body without the spirit is dead, so faith without works is dead also."

Bruce McConkie, after citing James 2, argues against such "perversions" of Scripture as the idea that a person is "justified through faith alone, without works."[18] James 2 makes it clear that good works are a necessity.

James E. Talmage likewise says that "in spite of the plain word of God, dogmas of men have been promulgated to the effect that by faith alone may salvation be attained. . . . The scriptures . . . and man's inherent sense of justice furnish a sufficient refutation of these false assertions."[19]

The Biblical Teaching. Martin Luther said it best: James 2 is not teaching that a person is saved by works. Rather a person is "justified" (declared righteous before God) by faith alone, but *not by a faith that is alone.* In other words, genuine faith will always *result* in good works in the saved person's life.*

James is writing to Jewish Christians (1:1, "to the twelve tribes") who were in danger of giving nothing but lip service to Jesus. His intent, therefore, is to distinguish true faith from false faith. He shows that true faith results in works, which then become visible evidences of faith's invisible presence. In other words, good works are the "vital signs" indicating that faith is alive.[20]

Apparently some of these Jewish Christians had made a false claim of faith. "It is the spurious boast of faith that James condemned. . . . Merely claiming to have faith is not enough. Genuine faith is evidenced by works."[21]

> Workless faith is worthless faith; it is unproductive, sterile, barren, dead! Great claims may be made about a corpse that is supposed to have come to life, but if it does not move, if there are no vital signs, no heartbeat, no perceptible pulse, it is still dead. The false claims are silenced by the evidence.[22]

---

*We will address the issue of justification further in chapter 19.

The fact is, *apart from the spirit,* the body is dead; it's a lifeless corpse. By analogy, *apart from the evidence of good works,* faith is dead. It is lifeless and nonproductive. That is what James is teaching in this passage.

When talking to a Mormon about James 2, it is probably unrealistic to expect that he or she will immediately understand what the Bible says about the relationship between faith and works. Keep in mind that many Mormons have grown up in a works-environment—some of them since childhood. That is what they're used to. They will find it difficult to break loose from this mentality.

At the very least, however, you'll want them to understand that James 2 is no threat to the "salvation by grace alone" message of Scripture. After you take the theological wind out of their works-oriented sails in James 2, focus on the glorious liberty and freedom that you've discovered in Jesus Christ. By doing so, you will draw a clear contrast between Mormonism and Christianity.

You might show the Mormon what the apostle Paul said in Romans 3:20: "By the deeds of the law there shall no flesh be justified in his sight." Combine this with Ephesians 2:8–9: "By grace are ye saved through faith; and that not of yourselves: it is the gift of God: Not of works, lest any man should boast."* Taken together, these verses spell L-I-B-E-R-T-Y from the impossible requirements of the law.

---

*Possible Mormon comeback:** Some Mormons may attempt to argue that Ephesians 2:8–9 was written to counter the idea that we can save ourselves by our works *independent of Christ* (see *A Sure Foundation: Answers to Difficult Gospel Questions* [Salt Lake City, UT: Deseret Book Company, 1988], p. 124). They say that we must *build* on Christ's atonement with works of righteousness to merit salvation. In response, you will want to emphasize that, according to Ephesians 2:8–9, salvation is a *free gift* completely apart from *any* works. *Gifts cannot be earned.*

___ *Ask* . . . ___

- James 2:26 says that *apart from the spirit,* the body is dead, right?

- By analogy, is it not clear that *apart from the evidence of good works,* faith is dead?

- Can you see, then, that good works are the "vital signs" indicating that faith is alive?

- Would you please read aloud from Romans 3:20 and tell me what you think it means?

- Can I share one of my favorite passages with you—Ephesians 2:8–9?

Philippians 2:12—*Work Out Your Own Salvation*

The Mormon Teaching. In Philippians 2:12 we read, "Wherefore, my beloved, as ye have always obeyed, not as in my presence only, but now much more in my absence, work out your own salvation with fear and trembling." Mormons say that while the death of Christ provided a salvation that redeems us from death (guaranteeing us a resurrection), we still have to "work out" our own salvation by our own efforts if we want to attain godhood and an inheritance in the celestial kingdom. [23]

The Biblical Teaching. What does Philippians 2:12 mean when it says, "Work out your own salvation with fear and trembling"? A careful study reveals that this verse has nothing to do with eternal salvation for individual believers.

As a backdrop, we must keep in mind the situation at the church in Philippi. This church was plagued by 1) rivalries and individuals with personal ambition (Philippians 2:3–4; 4:2); 2) the teaching of Judaizers (who said that circumcision was necessary for salvation—3:1–3); 3) perfectionism (the

view that one could attain sinless perfection in this life—
3:12–14); and 4) the influence of "antinomian libertines"
(people who took excessive liberty in how they lived their
lives, ignoring or going against God's law—3:18–19).[24]
Because of such problems, this church *as a unit* was in need
of "salvation" (that is, salvation in the temporal, experiential
sense, not in the eternal sense).

"Salvation," in this context, refers to the *community* of
believers in Philippi and not to *individuals.* Salvation is spoken
of in a corporate sense. The Philippians were called by the
apostle Paul to "keep on working out" (continuously) the
"deliverance of the church into a state of Christian maturity."[25]

The Greek word for "work out" *(katergazomai)* is a com-
pound verb that indicates "achievement" or "bringing to a conclusion." Paul was calling the Philippians to solve all the
church's problems and thus bring corporate "salvation" or
deliverance to a state of final achievement. Paul would not permit things to continue as they were. He wanted the problems
solved. The Philippians were to "work it out to the finish."[26]

In the phrase "work out your own salvation," the words
"your own" are emphatic in the Greek text. As Bible scholar
H.C.G. Moule notes, "the Apostle is in fact bidding them
'learn to walk alone,' instead of leaning too much on *his*
presence and personal influence. 'Do not make me your
proxy in spiritual duties which must be your own.' "[27] This
was all the more necessary because Paul was absent from the
church (Philippians 2:12a).

The Philippians were to accomplish their appointed task
with an attitude of "fear and trembling." This doesn't mean
Paul wanted the Philippians to have terror in their hearts as a
motivation. Rather, the words "fear and trembling" comprise
a Jewish idiomatic expression that speaks of great reverence
for God and a humble frame of mind. (Remember, many
people in Philippi were prideful and had little reverence for
God.) Such humility and reverence for God would help the
Philippians to overcome the problems they were experiencing

in their church (cf. 1 Corinthians 2:3; 2 Corinthians 7:15; Ephesians 6:5).

_____ *Ask . . .* _____

- Would you mind if I shared with you the context of Philippians 2:12? (Go over the above details.)

- Can you see that from the contextual and historical points of view, this verse makes great sense when we interpret it as referring to *corporate* salvation of the church in Philippi—a church that had problems Paul wanted them to solve?

- Did you know that the same apostle Paul who wrote Philippians 2:12 also wrote Ephesians 2:8–9—"By grace are ye saved through faith; and that not of yourselves: it is the gift of God: Not of works, lest any man should boast"?

When you talk to a Mormon about his or her view that good works are necessary for salvation, you will want to emphasize that in Mormonism a person must measure up to utter perfection *now.* No failure is allowed. Sin is not permissable. Repentance must be absolute. Help the Mormon to see the *impossibility* of his or her being perfect enough to merit exaltation.

Joseph Fielding Smith said that "to enter the celestial kingdom and obtain exaltation it is necessary that the whole law be kept."[28] *Gospel Principles* tells us that "we must keep all our covenants with exactness. If we do, our Heavenly Father promises us that we will receive exaltation in the celestial kingdom."[29]

President Kimball once said that "each command we obey sends us another rung up the ladder to perfected manhood and toward godhood; and every law disobeyed is a sliding toward the bottom where man merges into the brute world.

Only he who obeys law is free."[30] Kimball also said that "the forsaking of sin must be a permanent one. True repentance does not permit making the same mistake again. . . . There can be no holding back. If the sinner neglects his tithing, misses his meetings, breaks the Sabbath, or fails in his prayers and other responsibilities, he is not completely repentant."[31]

___ *Ask* . . . _____

- Have you ever made the same mistake twice?

- President Kimball said, "The forsaking of sin must be a permanent one. True repentance *does not permit making the same mistake again.*" Is your life characterized by repentance as defined by President Kimball?

- How do you interpret James 2:10? "Whosoever shall keep the whole law, and yet offend in one point, he is guilty of all."

- Can I share one of my favorite verses with you— Ephesians 2:8–9?

You might want to point out what the apostle Paul said in Romans 7:15: "That which I do I allow not: for what I would, that do I not; but what I hate, that do I." Apparently the apostle Paul would not pass President Kimball's standards! According to Paul's own testimony, against his inmost will he repeatedly did things he knew he shouldn't do, and he neglected the things he knew he should be doing.

Help the Mormon discover what the apostle Paul discovered. *It is impossible to be perfect in one's self.* Paul tried and failed. In fact, the more he tried, the more he failed. Through it all, he learned the pivotal concept of grace: "By grace are ye saved through faith; and that not of yourselves: it is the gift of God: Not of works, lest any man should boast" (Ephesians 2:8–9). (We know we're repeating this verse a lot, but you need to keep emphasizing to the Mormon that God's salvation is a free grace-gift.*)

Being Found Worthy

Closely related to good works is the Mormon concept of worthiness. Being "worthy" involves living a good, clean, moral life. It involves obedience to God's law and commandments. When you read through Mormon articles and books, you will find that a great deal of emphasis is placed on being worthy.

To give you an example, a Mormon must be found worthy before he can gain entrance to one of the church's temples (not simply a meetinghouse, but a special, sacred structure where rituals necessary for eternal life are performed). The book *Gospel Principles* tells us that "before we can go to the temple, each of us must have been an active, worthy member of the Church for at least one year."[32] Worthiness is also essential if a Mormon wants to progress within the Mormon church.

The Word of Wisdom

A key element in the Mormon works-system of salvation is their emphasis on the "Word of Wisdom," revered as "the Lord's law of health." This "revelation" (found in Doctrine and Covenants 89) is interpreted as a command to abstain from coffee, liquor, and tobacco. Obeying the Word of Wisdom is considered one of the fundamental requirements of being worthy. Spencer W. Kimball said, "For observing the Word of Wisdom the reward is life, not only prolonged mortal life but life eternal."[33]

---

*You need to proceed with caution on this matter because Mormons have *redefined* the role of grace in salvation. We'll address this problem in the next chapter.

In *Doctrines of Salvation* we read, "If you drink coffee or tea, or take tobacco, you are letting a cup of tea or a little tobacco stand in the road and bar you from the celestial kingdom of God, where you might otherwise have received a fulness of glory. . . . God is not going to save every man and woman in the celestial kingdom."[34] The penalty for not heeding the Word of Wisdom, then, is severe.

When you discuss the Word of Wisdom, you should try to draw a stark contrast between the Mormon position and the words of Jesus:

> Are ye so without understanding also? Do ye not perceive, that whatsoever thing from without entereth into the man, it cannot defile him; Because it entereth not into his heart, but into the belly, and goeth out into the draught, purging all meats? And he said, That which cometh out of the man, that defileth the man. For from within, out of the heart of men, proceed evil thoughts, adulteries, fornications, murders, thefts, covetousness, wickedness, deceit, lasciviousness, an evil eye, blasphemy, pride, foolishness: All these evil things come from within, and defile the man (Mark 7:18–23).

_____ *Ask . . .* _____

- What do you think Jesus meant when He said, "Whatsoever thing from without entereth into the man, *it cannot defile him;* Because it entereth not into his heart, but into the belly"?

- Do you agree with Jesus that it's not what goes *into* a man that defiles him, but what comes *from* his heart that defiles him?

You will also want to share the words of the apostle Paul in Colossians 2:16: "Let no man therefore judge you in meat, or in drink, or in respect of a holy day, or of the new moon, or of the sabbath days." The Jews in Paul's day had created unscriptural regulations involving food and drink. But Paul instructed believers to pay no heed to such rules. For, indeed, salvation is based not upon food or drink but upon faith in Christ, who paid our debt of sin (Colossians 2:14). [35]

Temple Work

A key to progression in Mormon theology is what is called "temple work." In fact, a Mormon cannot attain exaltation without the temple. This temple work involves Mormon rituals—such as endowments, marriages, and baptisms.

Yet there are restrictions; only worthy Mormons can enter the temple. Mormons are interviewed by a bishop to determine their worthiness. If they are found worthy in their moral life and obedience to the Word of Wisdom, they are issued a "temple recommend." When entering the temple, the Mormon must show the temple recommend at the door. It is a "key of access" into the temple.

Among the temple rituals are ceremonies that are performed on behalf of the dead. In LDS theology, even non-Mormons in postmortality—i.e., the afterlife—have an opportunity to accept Mormonism and progress spiritually. This makes temple rituals on behalf of the dead quite important. In fact, Mormon leaders say that church members who neglect to engage in such rituals jeopardize their progress toward godhood. Joseph Fielding Smith went so far as to say that "those saints who neglect it, in behalf of their deceased relatives, do it at the peril of their own salvation." [36]

Joseph Fielding Smith informs us of the kinds of circumstances that make temple work on behalf of the dead so necessary. Such temple work is

> for those who died without having had the opportunity to hear and receive the gospel; also, for those who were faithful members of the Church who lived in foreign lands or where, during their lifetime, they did not have the privilege to go to a temple, yet they were converted and were true members of the Church. The work for the dead is not intended for those who had every opportunity to receive it,

who had it taught to them, and who then refused to receive it, or had not interest enough to attend to these ordinances when they were living.[37]

Similarly, we read in the *Journal of Discourses* that "we have a certain work to do in order to liberate those who, because of their ignorance and the unfavorable circumstances in which they were placed while here, are unprepared for eternal life; we have to open the door for them, by performing ordinances which they cannot perform for themselves, and which are essential to their release from the 'prison-house.' "[38]

Of course, we cannot help but ask: If temple worship has truly been "restored" by the Mormon church, why does it differ in so many ways from the original temple worship that is described in the Bible? For example, in the Bible both grain and animal sacrifices were offered in the temple. Why aren't such sacrifices offered in the Mormon temple?

The Scriptures also show that "unworthy" people were permitted to enter the temple—people who wouldn't pass the Mormon standards for worthiness. In Luke 18:11-12, for example, Jesus describes a temple scene in which "the Pharisee stood and prayed thus with himself, God, I thank thee, that I am not as other men are, extortioners, unjust, adulterers, or even as this publican [tax-gatherer]. I fast twice in the week, I give tithes of all that I possess."

This "unworthy" publican certainly had no temple recommend. (Publicans were known for unscrupulously lining their pockets by overcharging taxes.) He was not worthy by the standard given in the Mormons' *General Handbook of Instructions,* the manual used by bishops and other church officials. But note what is said in verses 13 and 14: "The publican, standing afar off, would not lift up so much as his eyes unto heaven, but smote upon his breast, saying, God be merciful to me a sinner. I tell you, this man went down to his house justified rather than the other: for every one that exalteth himself shall be abased; and he that humbleth himself shall be exalted."

Doesn't this go against the entire tenor of the Mormon "temple recommend" mentality? An unworthy sinner was welcome in *God*'s temple in Luke 18:13–14! You will want to question the Mormon about this.

____ *Ask . . .* ____

- Would you please read aloud from Luke 18:9–14?

- In this passage, isn't an unworthy publican welcome in God's temple?

- What does this tell you about God's view of temple recommends?

Joseph Fielding Smith said that the "greatest commandment given us, and made obligatory, is the temple work in our own behalf and in behalf of our dead."[39]

By contrast, Jesus Christ said:

> The first of all the commandments is, Hear, O Israel; The Lord our God is one Lord: And thou shalt love the Lord thy God with all thy heart, and with all thy soul, and with all thy mind, and with all thy strength: this is the first commandment. And the second is like, namely this, Thou shalt love thy neighbor as thyself. There is none other commandment greater than these (Mark 12:29–31).

Who is right? Joseph Fielding Smith or Jesus Christ?

Baptism for the Dead

The premise behind the Mormon doctrine of baptism for the dead is the idea that spirits can allegedly accept Mormonism in the spirit world. But there's a problem: Spirits don't have physical bodies. And since baptism is necessary for progression—*and* since baptism requires a physical body—a living person is needed to act out the baptism on behalf of the physically dead spirit-person.

As explained in *Doctrines of Salvation,* "water is an element of this world, and how could spirits be baptized in it, or receive the laying on of hands for the gift of the Holy Ghost? The only way it can be done is vicariously, someone who is living acting as a substitute for the dead."[40]

1 Corinthians 15:29—*Baptism for the Dead?*

The Mormon Teaching. In 1 Corinthians 15:29 we read, "Else what shall they do which are baptized for the dead, if the dead rise not at all? why are they then baptized for the dead?"

James E. Talmage says, "These words are unambiguous and the fact that they are presented without explanation or comment argues that the principle of baptism for the dead was understood among the people to whom the letter was addressed."[41] Indeed, "herein is shown the necessity of vicarious work—the living ministering in behalf of the dead; the children doing for their progenitors what is beyond the power of the latter to do for themselves."[42]

The Biblical Teaching. Even though evangelical scholars offer different interpretations of what Paul is talking about in 1 Corinthians 15:29, they unanimously agree that the Mormon interpretation is wrong. Scripture clearly states that this life on earth is the *only* time we have to choose either *for* or *against* Christ. Once we die, all opportunities vanish. Hebrews 9:27 tells us, "It is appointed unto men once to die, but after this the judgment."

Now, it is critical to recognize that throughout 1 Corinthians, Paul refers to the Corinthian believers and himself using first-person pronouns ("we," "ye," "I"). But when he comes to 1 Corinthians 15:29—the verse dealing with baptism for the dead—Paul switches to the third person ("they"). With that in mind, a plain reading of the text seems to indicate that Paul is referring to people outside the Christian camp in Corinth. And Paul seems to be disassociating himself from the group practicing baptism for the dead.

Note the words of Charles R. Hield and Russell Ralston:

> A careful reading of this epistle shows that the Apostle Paul writes to the Corinthian Saints using the words "I," "we," "ye," "you," when referring to them and/or himself all the way through his message; but when he mentions baptism for the dead, he changes to "they." "What shall they do?" "Why are they then baptized for the dead?" In the verses following, he returns to the use of "we" and "you." Thus he seems to disassociate himself and the righteous Saints from the methods used by those groups who at that time were practicing baptism for the dead.
>
> The Apostle Paul did not urge his hearers to practice the principle, nor did he command it. He merely used the case as an illustration. Paul did not worship the "unknown God" of the pagans because he found an altar to the pagan unknown god (Acts 17:23). . . . There is no mention of baptism for the dead in the Bible up until Paul—and no mention afterward. Paul, as well as the other apostles, rather than endorsing baptism for the dead as then practiced, seems to have exercised a counteracting influence upon this ordinance, for it was perpetuated only among heretics.
>
> The Bible contains no specific authorization of this doctrine. Christ does not mention it, nor do any of the apostles, save Paul; who makes only an indirect reference to it.[43]

___ *Ask* . . . ___

- Why do you think the apostle Paul uses first-person pronouns ("we," "ye," "I") throughout 1 Corinthians in reference to the Corinthian believers, but then switches to the third person ("they") in 1 Corinthians 15:29?

- If God desired us to practice baptism for the dead, why is it mentioned *only here* in the Bible (in the third person)—with no other references? Why aren't there any commands dealing with this kind of baptism?

- Why don't Paul or the other apostles command the practice if it's essential for us (as the LDS church claims today), and why aren't there any guidelines for conducting this practice?

You might find it advantageous to spend some time in Luke 16:19–31 with the Mormon.[44] This passage—dealing with the fate of the rich man and Lazarus—is not a story, nor a parable, but a real event Jesus cited in order to make a point: Once the rich man had died and ended up in a place of great suffering, he had no further opportunity for redemption. Nothing could be done at that point to ease his situation (Luke 16:24). A baptism for the dead would not have had any effect on this rich man's—or anyone else's—situation.[45]

This emphasizes the importance of Paul's exhortation in 2 Corinthians 6:2: "Now is the day of salvation." There are no opportunities beyond death's door. A person must choose *for* or *against* the Christ of the Bible in this life.

It is also interesting that even though the Book of Mormon is supposed to contain the "fulness of the everlasting gospel," baptism for the dead is not mentioned a single time within its pages. How can our activities for the dead be our "greatest responsibility" if they are not mentioned in the Book of Mormon? It doesn't make sense.

_____ *Ask . . .* _____

- Please show me a single clear reference in the Book of Mormon that supports baptism for the dead.

- If baptism for the dead is not mentioned in the Book of Mormon, and if baptism for the dead is so important in the Mormon plan of salvation, then how can the Book of Mormon be said to contain the "fulness of the everlasting gospel"?

Of course, you'll want to stress that you don't believe in the Book of Mormon. Your only objective in bringing up these questions is to give yet another example of the major and irreconcilable contradictions in Mormon doctrine.

Along these same lines, there are several verses in the Book of Mormon that say salvation must be obtained *in this life*. For example:

- Alma 34:31—"Yea, I would that ye would come forth and harden not your hearts any longer; for behold, now is the time and the day of your salvation. . . . For behold, this life is the time for men to prepare to meet God. . . . I beseech of you that ye do not procrastinate the day of your repentance until the end; for after this day of life, which is given us to prepare for eternity, behold, if we do not improve our time while in this life, then cometh the night of darkness wherein there can be no labor performed."

- 2 Nephi 9:38—"In fine, wo unto all those who die in their sins; for they shall return to God, and behold his face, and remain in their sins."

- Mosiah 26:25–27—"It shall come to pass that when the second trump shall sound then shall they that never knew me come forth and shall stand before me. And then shall they know that I am the Lord their God, that I am their Redeemer; but they would not be redeemed."

_____ *Ask* . . . _____

- If baptism for the dead is the only means of salvation for countless numbers of deceased persons—and an essential means of accomplishing "the greatest responsibility we have in this world" (the redemption of the dead)— why does the Book of Mormon say that the issue of a person's salvation must be determined *in this life?*

The Endowment Ritual

Another aspect of temple work has to do with the "endowment" ritual. This ritual constitutes a formal introduction of the Mormon into the Mormon temple. The ritual is said to "endow" Mormons with power and protection.

The ceremony itself involves ceremonial washings, anointings, the receiving of a new name, and the learning of secret handshakes. As well, sacred undergarments are given to the Mormon, who is to wear them for the rest of his or her life.* Details of these rituals are not discussed by temple Mormons (because they are considered sacred), and are all but unknown to Mormons who have not received their own endowments.

The Necessity of Eternal Marriage

In Mormon theology, marriages performed in the Mormon temple last forever. They are *sealed* for time and eternity. Why is eternal marriage so important? Mormonism teaches that a person's exaltation depends on marriage: "Our Heavenly Father has given us the law of eternal marriage so that we can become like him."[46]

Keep in mind that in the Mormon system of thought, Mormon "Gods" procreate and give birth to spirit-children. That's why marriage is a critical component of Mormon exaltation: "No man can be saved and exalted in the kingdom of God without the woman, and no woman can reach the perfection and exaltation in the kingdom of God alone."[47]

Doctrines of Salvation thus instructs:

> The duty of a man in his own family is to see that he and his wife are sealed at the altar. If married out in the world before they joined the church, or if they have been in the church and have been unable to go to the temple, it is that man's duty to go to the temple, have his wife sealed to him and have their children sealed, so that the family group,

---

*This is just a brief summary of the endowment ritual. There is a lot in this ritual that Christians can refute, but a thorough treatment is beyond the scope of this chapter. We recommend that you consult *Evolution of the Mormon Temple Ceremony: 1842–1990*, by Jerald and Sandra Tanner.

that unity to which he belongs, is made intact so that it will continue throughout eternity. That is the first duty that a man owes to himself, to his wife, and to his children. He receives this blessing by virtue of the priesthood.[48]

Christians can respond to the idea of eternal marriage by pointing to the words of Jesus in Matthew 22:30: "In the resurrection they neither marry, nor are given in marriage, but are as the angels of God in heaven." It seems clear that Christ is teaching that in the resurrection, men and women will not be in a married state. Resurrected saints will be like the angels in the sense that they will not marry and will not produce offspring.*

Postmortality

Mormonism and Death

Mormons say that at the moment of death, the spirit immediately enters the spirit world. Mormons go to a place called "paradise," where they continue in their efforts to work toward godhood. Non-Mormons go to a spirit prison, where Mormon spirits "evangelize" them through missionary activities.[49]

---

*Possible Mormon comeback: Some Mormons may argue that Matthew 22 doesn't say there would be *no* people in the married state in the resurrection, but rather says there would be no marriages *made in* the resurrection. Of course, a plain reading of the text goes against this interpretation: Jesus said that in the resurrection we will be in a state *just like the angels*—that is, we are not married nor are we given in marriage.

Some Mormons may also say these words were directed at the Sadducees and are "hardly applicable to his Saints who, through the ordinances of the priesthood and their righteousness, qualify for exaltation in the celestial kingdom, which the Lord equates with eternal marriage" (see *A Sure Foundation: Answers to Difficult Gospel Questions* [Salt Lake City, UT: Deseret, 1988], p. 115). In response, you will want to show that when Jesus said, "In the resurrection *they* neither marry . . . ," there is no indication in the text that He was limiting His words about "they" to the Sadducees. The Mormons are reading an idea into the text that is not there.

What happens if a spirit in prison accepts Mormonism? Well, that spirit can leave the prison and enter into paradise *so long as* a living relative has been baptized on his or her behalf. If no relative has undergone "baptism for the dead" on his or her behalf, then the person is stuck in spirit prison until a relative undergoes the ritual. After entering paradise, the spirit is then free to work toward his or her own progression. [50]

The Gospel Preached to the Dead?

Mormons tell us it is plain that "the Gospel must be proclaimed in the spirit world; and, that such work is provided for the scriptures abundantly prove." [51] Among the key verses Mormons cite in support of this idea are 1 Peter 3:18–19 and 1 Peter 4:6.

1 Peter 3:18–19—*Preaching to Spirits in Prison?*

The Mormon Teaching. In 1 Peter 3:18–19 we read, "Christ also hath once suffered for sins, the just for the unjust, that he might bring us to God, being put to death in the flesh, but quickened by the Spirit: By which also he went and preached unto the spirits in prison."

James E. Talmage tells us that "the inauguration of this work among the dead was effected by Christ in the interval between His death and resurrection. While His body lay in the tomb, His spirit ministered to the spirits of the departed." [52] Talmage also says:

> If it was deemed proper and just that the Gospel be carried to the spirits who were disobedient in the days of Noah, it is reasonable to conclude that like opportunities shall be placed within the reach of others who have rejected the word at different times. For the same spirit of neglect, disobedience, and opposition to divine law that characterized the time of Noah has existed since. [53]

The Biblical Teaching. As we mentioned earlier, we must interpret difficult passages like this according to the clearer passages of Scripture. These passages tell us that immediately following the moment of death comes judgment (Hebrews 9:27). There is no possibility of redemption beyond death's door (Luke 16:19–31). *Now* is the day of salvation (2 Corinthians 6:2). We can say with certainty, then, that 1 Peter 3:18–19 doesn't suggest people can respond to the gospel after they die.

Many evangelical scholars believe that the "spirits in prison" mentioned in verse 19 are fallen angels who grievously sinned against God. The idea is that these spirits are the fallen angels of Genesis 6:1–6 who were disobedient to God during the days of Noah. This same group of evil angels is mentioned in 2 Peter 2:4–5 and Jude 6. According to this interpretation, these evil angels disobeyed God, left their first estate (they forsook their proper realm), and entered into sexual relations with human women.

The Greek word for "preach" *(kerusso)* is not the word used for preaching the gospel, but rather, refers to a *proclamation*—as in a proclamation of victory. Peter H. Davids says this passage "may imply that the powers of darkness thought they had destroyed Jesus, but that in raising him from the dead God turned the tables on them . . . and Jesus Himself proclaimed their doom."[54] If this is the correct interpretation, it is clear that the verse has nothing whatsoever to do with human spirits hearing and responding to the gospel in the afterlife.

Another possible interpretation is that between His death and resurrection, Jesus went to the place of the dead and "preached" to the wicked contemporaries of Noah. The "preaching," however, was not a gospel message but was rather a proclamation of victory.

Still others believe this passage speaks of Christ preaching through the person of Noah to those who, because they rejected his message, are *now* spirits in prison:

They had rebelled against the message of God during the 120 years the ark was being built. God declared He would not tolerate people's wickedness forever, but would extend His patience for only 120 more years (Gen. 6:3). Since the entire human race except Noah (Gen. 6:5–9) was evil, God determined to "wipe mankind . . . from the face of the earth." The "spirits" referred to in 1 Peter 3:20 are probably the souls of the evil human race that existed in the days of Noah. Those "spirits" are now "in prison" awaiting the final judgment of God at the end of the Age.[55]

As for the idea of Christ "preaching through Noah," we must keep in mind that 1 Peter 1:11 tells us that the "Spirit of Christ" spoke through the Old Testament prophets. And Noah *is* later described as a "preacher of righteousness" (2 Peter 2:5). So it's possible that "the Spirit of Christ preached through Noah to the ungodly humans who, at the time of Peter's writing, were 'spirits in prison' awaiting final judgment."[56]

Regardless of which of the above interpretations is correct, evangelical scholars unanimously agree that the verses *do not* teach that people will hear and respond to the gospel in the next life. Passages like Luke 16:19–31, 2 Corinthians 6:2, and Hebrews 9:27 make this emphatically clear.

1 Peter 4:6—*Preaching to the Dead?*

The Mormon Teaching. In 1 Peter 4:6 we read, "For this cause was the gospel preached also to them that are dead, that they might be judged according to men in the flesh, but live according to God in the spirit." Mormons think this verse proves that we should preach the gospel to the dead in the spirit world.[57]

The Biblical Teaching. This is another difficult verse that we must interpret in light of what clearer verses of Scripture teach. For example, Hebrews 9:27 tells us, "It is appointed unto men once to die, but after this the judgment." In view of passages like that, it seems obvious that the phrase "preached also to them that are dead" doesn't support the idea that people can receive the gospel after they die.

Though evangelical scholars have offered several interpretations of 1 Peter 4:6, perhaps the best view is that the verse refers to those who are *now* dead but who heard the Gospel *while they were yet alive*. This especially makes sense in view of the tenses used: the Gospel was preached (in the past) to those who are dead (presently). "The preaching was a past event. . . . It is necessary to make it clear that the preaching was done not after these people had died, but while they were still alive."[58]

Again, we must point to the words of Jesus in Luke 16:19–31: Once the rich man had died and gone to a place of great suffering, he had no further opportunity for redemption. Nothing could be done for him (Luke 16:24). This clearly illustrates the urgency in Paul's words in 2 Corinthians 6:2: "*Now* is the day of salvation" (emphasis added). There are no opportunities beyond death's door; we must choose for or against the Christ of the Bible in this life.[59]

19

Salvation in Mormonism—
Part 3: Sin, Atonement, and
Forgiveness

I n this chapter we will touch briefly on the Mormon understanding of Adam's fall, the concept of original sin, the
atonement, justification by faith, the role of grace, and forgiveness. We will see that the Mormon view on these doctrines is quite different than that of orthodox Christianity
because in Mormonism, these concepts are *works-permeated*
from beginning to end.

Adam's Fall: A Good Thing?

In Mormon theology, prior to the Fall, Adam and Eve were
not yet "mortal." Now, Mormons don't define this word as
Christians do. They interpret "mortal" not in the sense of
death and dying, but primarily in the sense of *having the
capability to bear children.* So, prior to the Fall, Adam and
Eve were not mortal in the sense that they could not bear
children.

When Adam and Eve sinned, we are told, they became
mortal at that point and could bear children. So, from the
Mormon perspective, the Fall was good. In fact, Mormons
actually *commend* Adam and Eve for what they did.[1] That's
because spirit-children need bodies before they can progress

toward godhood. What Adam did made it possible for these spirit-children to get those needed bodies.

Of course, the Mormon view is a gross distortion of the biblical account. God commanded Adam and Eve to be fruitful and multiply *immediately after* He created them (Genesis 1:28). They had the capacity to bear children prior to the Fall (Genesis 3). Moreover, after Adam and Eve *did* fall, God did not commend them; rather, He pronounced severe judgment against them and cast them out of the Garden of Eden (Genesis 3:16–19).

_____ *Ask* . . . _____

- According to Genesis 1:28, didn't God command Adam and Eve to be fruitful and multiply *immediately after* creating them?

- Doesn't this mean, then, that Adam and Eve could bear children prior to the Fall, which doesn't take place until Genesis 3?

- According to Genesis 3:16–19, did God think it was good for Adam and Eve to disobey Him?

No Original Sin

Mormon authorities go so far as to say that Adam and Eve really didn't "sin." After all, what they did was a part of God's plan of salvation. The book *Gospel Principles* tells us that "their part in the Father's plan was to bring mortality into the world . . . Adam and Eve were among our Father's noblest children."[2] If Adam and Eve fell, it was a "fall upward." Indeed, "Adam fell, but he fell in the right direction."[3]

Bruce McConkie argues that "it is possible to transgress a law without committing a sin as in the case of Adam and Eve in the Garden of Eden."[4] In other words, even though Adam and Eve blatantly disobeyed God's command and transgressed His holy law, they nevertheless did not sin in doing so.

Joseph Smith concludes that "the so-called 'fall' became a necessary, honorable act in carrying out the plan of the Almighty."[5] Joseph Fielding Smith likewise said that "the fall of man came as a blessing in disguise. . . . I never speak of the part Eve took in this fall as a sin, nor do I accuse Adam of a sin. . . . it is not always a sin to transgress a law."[6] Mormon apostle John Widtsoe goes so far as to say that "in the true gospel of Jesus Christ, there is no original sin."[7] The so-called "Fall" was a blessing in disguise (*see* 2 Nephi 2:22–25).

Such a view clearly goes against the Bible, for, as the apostle Paul himself said, "Wherefore, as by one man sin entered into the world, and death by sin; and so death passed upon all men, for that all have sinned" (Romans 5:12). According to this forceful passage, sin entered into the world by one man—Adam. And sin is transgression of the law (1 John 3:4—"Whosoever committeth sin transgresseth also the law: for sin is the transgression of the law"). *Adam transgressed the law!*

Original sin is also emphasized in Romans 5:19: "For as by one man's disobedience many were made sinners, so by the obedience of one shall many be made righteous." Similarly, 1 Corinthians 15:21–22 tells us, "Since by man came death, by man came also the resurrection of the dead. For as in Adam all die, even so in Christ shall all be made alive."

_____ *Ask* . . . _____

- How do you reconcile the Mormon view that there is no original sin with Romans 5:12, which explicitly states that "by one man sin entered into the world"?

- How do you reconcile the Mormon view that there is no original sin with Romans 5:19, which says that "by one man's disobedience many were made sinners"?

- Romans 6:23 tells us that the penalty for sin is *death*. If there is no original sin, why is the death rate still one per person?

Romans 3:23 notes that "all have sinned, and come short of the glory of God." This "all" certainly included Adam and Eve. The whole human race is portrayed in the book of Romans as *fallen in sin*. Moreover, "If we say that we have no sin, we deceive ourselves, and the truth is not in us" (1 John 1:8).

While we as Christians reject the Book of Mormon, it is worthwhile to show the Mormon that the doctrine of original sin is clearly taught within its pages. For example:

- 2 Nephi 2:21b tells us, "He gave commandment that all men must repent; for he showed unto all men that they were lost, because of the transgression of their parents."
- Mosiah 3:19 says, "The natural man is an enemy to God, and has been from the fall of Adam, and will be, forever and ever, unless he yields to the enticings of the Holy Spirit, and putteth off the natural man and becometh a saint through the atonement of Christ the Lord, and becometh as a child, submissive, meek, humble, patient, full of love, willing to submit to all things which the Lord seeth fit to inflict upon him, even as a child doth submit to his father."

_____ *Ask . . .* _____

- Would you please open your Book of Mormon and read aloud from 2 Nephi 2:21?

- Now, please read aloud from Mosiah 3:19.

- Since Doctrine and Covenants 20:9 claims that the Book of Mormon contains the "fulness of the everlasting gospel," and since original sin is taught in the Book of Mormon, how can you reject the concept of original sin?

Redefining Sin

Mormons have redefined sin so that it fits their peculiar theology. They say that sin basically amounts to a *wrong judgment*, a *mistake*, an *imperfection*, or an *inadequacy*. The moral sting is taken out of the word *sin* in Mormon vocabulary.

Moreover, instead of holding to the biblical doctrine of original sin, Mormons say that children are "innocent" until they reach accountability at the age of eight. Children are born innately good; they have no propensity for evil.

Christians can respond to this claim by pointing to passages like Psalm 51:5, where we read the words of David: "Behold, I was shapen in iniquity; and in sin did my mother conceive me" (cf. Genesis 8:21). According to Psalm 51:5, human beings are born into the world in a state of sin. The sin nature is passed on from conception. That is why Ephesians 2:3 says we are "*by nature* the children of wrath" (emphasis added).

Jesus Himself taught that man is *evil* (Matthew 12:34) and is capable of *great wickedness* (Mark 7:20–23). He said that man is *utterly lost* (Luke 19:10), that he is a *sinner* (Luke 15:10), that he is in need of repentance before a holy God (Mark 1:15), and that he needs to be born again (John 3:3,5,7). Jesus described sin as *blindness* (Matthew 23:16–26), *sickness* (Matthew 9:12), being *enslaved in bondage* (John 8:34), and *living in darkness* (John 8:12; 12:35–46). Moreover, Jesus taught that sin is a *universal condition* and that all people are guilty before God (Luke 7:37–48).

Jesus also taught that both inner thoughts and external acts render a person guilty (Matthew 5:28). He said that from within the human heart come evil thoughts, sexual immorality, theft, murder, adultery, greed, malice, deceit, envy, slander, arrogance, and folly (Mark 7:21–23). And He affirmed that God is fully aware of every person's sins; nothing escapes His notice (Matthew 22:18; Luke 6:8; John 4:17–19). Clearly, sin is not just a "mistake" or a "bad judgment."

The Atonement and Salvation

Theologians have long said that a weak view of sin always leads to a weak view of salvation. There are no exceptions to this. If sin is minimized, then the need for a Savior diminishes.

It is thus not surprising that in Mormonism, Jesus' role in the salvation process is much reduced. In Mormonese, Jesus' atonement simply means that He was able to *overcome physical death* for us. He "opened the door of immortality for all to walk through. He paid the price for us to rise from the grave. Through His own willful sacrifice—the infinite and eternal atonement—we all shall live again."[8] Jesus wiped out permanent physical death; because of what He accomplished, we will all be resurrected.

When talking to a Mormon, it is critical for you to keep in mind that when they talk about *salvation,* they essentially mean *resurrection.* Jesus is the "Savior" because He saved the human race from permanent physical death. Mormons say that what Jesus did on the cross was important because without a resurrected body, a person cannot become a God and give birth to spirit-children.

Despite this important feat accomplished by Jesus, Mormons still believe there is a need for good works. The official *Gospel Principles* manual tells us that Jesus "became our savior and has done his part to help us return to our heavenly home. It is now up to each of us to do our part and to prove ourselves worthy of exaltation."[9] Each individual Mormon must "work out" his own salvation (*see* chapters 17 and 18). (For more on the Mormon distortion of Jesus Christ and His role, *see* chapter 15.)

The Mormon view of salvation bears little resemblance to the "atonement" described in the Bible. Indeed, Jesus Himself defines for us the nature of the atonement. (If anyone would know, it would be Him.) The biblical Jesus taught that His mission was to provide a substitutionary atonement on the cross. By so doing, He provided a *total* salvation (eternal life) that we had absolutely no hope of procuring for ourselves.

Jesus affirmed that He came into the world to die (John 12:27). His death was a sacrificial offering *for the sins of humanity;* He said His blood "is shed for many for the remission of sins" (Matthew 26:28). Jesus took His sacrificial mission with utmost seriousness, for He knew that without Him, humanity would certainly perish (Matthew 16:25; John 3:16) and spend eternity apart from God in a place of great suffering (Matthew 10:28; 11:23; 23:33; 25:41; Luke 16:2–28).

Jesus therefore described His mission this way: "The Son of Man came not to be ministered unto, but to minister, and to give his life a ransom for many" (Matthew 20:28). And "the Son of man is come to seek and to save that which was lost" (Luke 19:10), for "God sent not his Son into the world to condemn the world; but that the world through him might be saved" (John 3:17).

In John 10, Jesus compares Himself to a good shepherd who not only gives His life to save the sheep (John 10:11) but also lays His life down of His own accord (John 10:18). This is precisely what Jesus did at the cross (Matthew 26:53): He laid His life down to atone for the sins of humanity.

Certainly this is how others perceived Jesus' mission. When He began His three-year ministry and was walking toward John the Baptist at the Jordan River, John said, "Behold the Lamb of God, which taketh away the sin of the world" (John 1:29). John's portrayal of Christ as the Lamb of God is a graphic affirmation that Jesus Himself would be the sacrifice that would atone for mankind's sins (*see* Isaiah 53:7). Jesus' atonement, then, specifically answered man's dire sin problem. It wasn't limited to merely making resurrection from the dead possible.

No Justification by Faith

Mormons feel strongly that the Christian doctrine of justification by faith is wrong. James E. Talmage goes so far as to say that "the sectarian dogma of justification by faith alone has exercised an influence for evil."[10]

Of course, with their constant emphasis on the need for good works as a prerequisite for salvation, we would expect the Mormons to reject this doctrine. In so doing, however, they must ignore many New Testament verses that teach to the contrary. Let's look at a sampling of Bible verses that affirm the doctrine of justification by faith and point out the impossibility of salvation by following the law:

- Romans 3:28—"Therefore we conclude that a man is justified by faith without the deeds of the law."
- Romans 5:1—"Therefore being justified by faith, we have peace with God through our Lord Jesus Christ."
- Galatians 3:8—"The scripture, foreseeing that God would justify the heathen through faith, preached before the gospel unto Abraham, saying, In thee shall all nations be blessed."
- Galatians 3:21—"Is the law then against the promises of God? God forbid: for if there had been a law given which could have given life, verily righteousness should have been by the law."
- Galatians 3:24—"Wherefore the law was our schoolmaster to bring us unto Christ, that we might be justified by faith."

The New Testament consistently emphasizes that salvation comes not by works but by placing personal faith in Jesus Christ. In fact, close to 200 times in the New Testament salvation is said to be *by faith alone*—with no works in sight. Consider the following:

- John 3:15 tells us that *"whosoever believeth in him should not perish, but have eternal life."*
- John 5:24 says, "Verily, verily, I say unto you, *He that heareth my word, and believeth* on him that sent me, *hath everlasting life,* and shall not come into condemnation; but is passed from death unto life."

- In John 11:25 Jesus says, "I am the resurrection, and the life: *he that believeth in me,* though he were dead, yet shall he live."
- John 12:46 says, "I am come a light into the world, that *whosoever believeth on me should not abide in darkness.*"

We must emphasize to the Mormon that if salvation were not by faith alone, then Jesus' message in the Gospel of John—as seen in the above quotations—would be deceptive, stating that there is one condition for salvation when there are allegedly two—faith *and* works.

_____ *Ask* . . . _____

- If salvation is not by faith alone, then isn't Jesus being deceptive when He states that there is one condition for salvation (faith) when there are allegedly two—faith *and* works?
- Please read John 6:27–29. How does Jesus explain the "works" of God?

Acknowledge to the Mormon that works are important in the Christian's life, but *they do not save.* Christians work *from* salvation, not *for* salvation. They do good works not to *receive* salvation, but because they have *already received* it.

We are saved *by faith* but *for works.* Works are not the *condition* of our salvation, but a *consequence* of it. As we learned in James 2, we are saved not by works but by the kind of faith that *produces* works.*

The Role of Grace

What role does grace play in the salvation process? In Mormon theology, grace is simply God's *enabling power*

---

*See chapter 18 for more on James 2.

that allows people to "lay hold on eternal life and exaltation after they have expended their own best efforts."[11] Grace *aids* people as they seek (by personal effort) to attain perfection.

It is important to recognize that in Mormon theology, God's grace alone does not save. Spencer W. Kimball said that "one of the most fallacious doctrines originated by Satan and propounded by man is that man is saved alone by the grace of God; that belief in Jesus Christ alone is all that is needed for salvation."[12] There is a great necessity, we are told, for personal striving and putting forth your "best efforts."

By contrast, the New Testament repeatedly states that salvation is by grace, and entirely apart from the law and good works:

- Ephesians 2:8–9 says, "By grace are ye saved through faith; and that not of yourselves; it is the gift of God: Not of works, lest any man should boast."
- Titus 3:5 says, "He saved us, not because of righteous things we had done, but because of his mercy" (NIV).
- Romans 3:20 tells us that "by the deeds of the law there shall no flesh be justified in his sight."
- In Galatians 2:16 Paul tells us, "Knowing that a man is not justified by the works of the law, but by the faith of Christ Jesus, even we have believed in Jesus Christ, that we might be justified by the faith of Christ, and not by the works of the law: for by the works of the law shall no flesh be justified."

You must tell the Mormon that grace (God's unmerited favor) and meritorious works are mutually exclusive. As Romans 11:6 tells us, "If by grace, then is it no more of works: otherwise grace is no more grace. But if it be of works, then is it no more grace: otherwise work is no more work." It is one or the other; which option will the Mormon take? Salvation as defined in the New Testament is *entirely* by God's grace.

Ask . . .

- Would you please read aloud from Romans 11:6?

- According to this verse, aren't grace and works mutually exclusive? Please explain.

- Can I share one of my favorite verses with you—Ephesians 2:8–9? (Share your testimony of how you received the free gift of salvation.)

You might also mention that we cannot work for _gifts_—only _wages_ can be worked for. As Romans 4:4–5 tells us, "To him that worketh is the reward not reckoned of grace, but of debt. But to him that worketh not, but believeth on him that justifieth the ungodly, his faith is counted for righteousness." Since salvation is a free gift (Ephesians 2:8–9), it cannot be earned.

Attaining Forgiveness

Forgiveness does not come easy in Mormonism. The _Gospel Principles_ manual tells us that "the Lord will not forgive us unless our hearts are fully cleansed of all hate, bitterness, and bad feelings against our fellowmen."[13] Bruce McConkie says that "complete forgiveness is reserved for those only who turn their whole hearts to the Lord and begin to keep all of his commandments."[14]

Forgiveness in Mormonism requires that the believer engage in good works: "There must be works—many works—and an all-out, total surrender, with a great humility and 'a broken heart and contrite spirit.' "[15]

What a contrast this is with the forgiveness we find in the Scriptures! You will want the Mormon to understand this dire contrast. We suggest you share some or all of the following passages:

- Hebrews 10:17–18—"Their sins and iniquities will I remember no more. Now where remission of these is, there is no more offering for sin."
- Psalm 32:1–2—"Blessed is he whose transgression is forgiven, whose sin is covered. Blessed is the man unto whom the LORD imputeth not iniquity, and in whose spirit there is no guile."
- Ephesians 1:7—"In whom we have redemption through his blood, the forgiveness of sins, according to the riches of his grace."
- Micah 7:19—"He will turn again, he will have compassion upon us; he will subdue our iniquities; and thou wilt cast all their sins into the depths of the sea."
- Psalm 103:11–12—"For as the heaven is high above the earth, so great is his mercy toward them that fear him. As far as the east is from the west, so far hath he removed our transgressions from us."

After going over these verses . . .

_____ *Ask . . .* _____

- Can you see the difference between the Mormon concept of forgiveness and the Bible's?

- Wouldn't you like to know for sure that all your sins have been forgiven? Christ has made this possible for you by His death on the cross.

- Can I share with you what it's like to know that all your sins are forgiven? (Give a brief testimony.)

20

Salvation in Mormonism— Part 4: The Three Kingdoms

Mormon apostle LeGrand Richards tells us that "one of the greatest errors in the teachings of the Christian religions is the doctrine of one heaven and one hell, so that all who go to heaven share and share alike, and all who fail to go to heaven are sent to hell where they share and share alike."[1] (By "share and share alike," Richards apparently thinks Christians believe that all who go to heaven enjoy precisely *equal* glory and *equal* rewards, regardless of how faithfully they lived on earth.)

At the end of the world, Mormons tell us, people will end up in one of *four* places: the celestial kingdom, the terrestrial kingdom, the telestial kingdom, or the "outer darkness." A person's level of worthiness determines which of these four realms he or she ends up in.

Regarding the three kingdoms, the LDS church's *Gospel Principles* manual teaches that "there are three degrees of glory in the heavens and men will be rewarded according to their actions on earth."[2] Apostle John Widtsoe, in his book *Evidences and Reconciliations,* likewise says, "A person's works, under the loving mercy of the Father, determine his final judgment, whether he shall inherit the celestial, terrestrial, or telestial glory."[3] Let's briefly examine each of these possible destinies.

The Celestial Kingdom

Mormons tell us that the celestial kingdom, the highest degree of glory, is inhabited by faithful Mormons—the "righteous, those who have been faithful in keeping the commandments of the Lord, and have been cleansed of all their sins"[4]—and children who die before the age of eight. This is the kingdom where people will live with the Heavenly Father and Jesus Christ. In this kingdom are three different levels:

1. *The Highest Level*—involves exaltation and godhood. On this level, a person has an eternal family and gives birth to spirit-children who then go on to seek progression to godhood for themselves.
2. *The Middle Level*—the purpose of which has not been revealed.
3. *The Lowest Level*—the domain of faithful Mormons whose marriages were not sealed forever in the Mormon temple while on earth. They become "ministering servants."

How does one gain entrance into this highest of kingdoms? Bruce McConkie answers:

> An inheritance in this glorious kingdom is gained by complete obedience to gospel or celestial law. By entering the gate of repentance and baptism candidates find themselves on the straight and narrow path leading to the celestial kingdom. . . . In the celestial glory there are three heavens or degrees, and in the same sense that baptism starts a person out toward an entrance into the celestial world, so celestial marriage puts a couple on the path leading to an exaltation in the highest heaven of that world.[5]

McConkie adds the following important qualification regarding the different levels in this kingdom:

Even those in the celestial kingdom, however, who do not go on to exaltation, will have immortality only and not eternal life. . . . Salvation in its true and full meaning is synonymous with exaltation or eternal life and consists in gaining an inheritance in the highest of the three heavens within the celestial kingdom. . . . This full salvation is obtained in and through the continuation of the family unit in eternity and those who obtain it are gods.[6]

The Terrestrial Kingdom

The second of the three degrees of glory is the terrestrial kingdom. According to Mormon authorities, this kingdom is reserved for non-Mormons who live moral lives (they are "morally clean"[7]) as well as for "less than valiant" Mormons. These are Mormons who did not live up to their church's expectations or requirements. No one is married in this kingdom.

There are four categories of residents for this kingdom:

1. Accountable persons who die without law (and who, of course, do not accept the gospel in the spirit world under those particular circumstances which would make them heirs of the celestial kingdom);
2. Those who reject the gospel in this life and who reverse their course and accept it in the spirit world;
3. Honorable men of the earth who are blinded by the craftiness of men and who therefore do not accept and live the gospel law; and
4. Members of the Church of Jesus Christ of Latter-day Saints who have testimonies of Christ and the divinity of the great latter-day work and who are not valiant, but who are instead lukewarm in their devotion to the Church and to righteousness.[8]

The Telestial Kingdom

The lowest of the three degrees of glory is the telestial kingdom. This lowest kingdom is where the great majority of people go. Like the terrestrial kingdom, no one is married in the telestial kingdom. While it still has significant glory, it is much lesser than the other two kingdoms.

McConkie explains that "most of the adult people who have lived from the day of Adam to the present time will go to the telestial kingdom. . . . They will be the endless hosts of people of all ages who have lived after the manner of the world; who have been carnal, sensual, and devilish; who have chosen the vain philosophies of the world rather than accept the testimony of Jesus; who have been liars, and thieves, sorcerers and adulterers, blasphemers and murderers."[9]

In Mormon theology, people must temporarily suffer through hell before entering the telestial kingdom. After people "suffer in full" for their sins, they are then permitted to enter into the telestial kingdom. "These, after they have been punished for their sins and have been turned over to the torments of Satan, shall eventually come forth after the Millennium, to receive the telestial kingdom."[10]

The "Outer Darkness"

The "outer darkness" is the afterlife punishment most closely resembling the biblical doctrine of hell. This is where the "sons of perdition" (such as apostates) go. Alma 40:13–14 (in the Book of Mormon) tells us:

And then shall it come to pass, that the spirits of the wicked, yea, who are evil—for behold, they have no part nor portion of the Spirit of the Lord; for behold, they chose evil works rather than good; therefore the spirit of the devil did enter into them, and take possession of their house—and these shall be cast out into outer darkness; there shall be weeping, and wailing, and gnashing of teeth, and this because of their own iniquity, being led captive by the will of the devil. Now this is the state of the souls of the wicked, yea, in darkness, and a state of awful, fearful looking for the fiery indignation of the wrath of God upon them; thus they remain in this state, as well as the righteous in paradise, until the time of their resurrection.

According to Mormons, hell is a temporary place of suffering for wicked spirits. Hell is "that part of the spirit world inhabited by wicked spirits who are awaiting the eventual day of their resurrection." Hell does not refer to a place of *eternal* punishment. Indeed, "Hell will have an end."[11]

Regarding the temporary nature of hell, James Talmage tells us that "no soul shall be kept in prison or continued in torment beyond the time requisite to work the needed reformation and vindicate justice for which ends alone punishment is imposed."[12] He also tells us that "after the debt has been paid the prison doors shall be opened, and the spirits once confined in suffering, then chastened and clean, shall come forth to partake of the glory provided in their class."[13]

REASONING FROM THE SCRIPTURES

There Are Only Two Possible Destinies

The Scriptures consistently categorize people into one of two classes (*saved/unsaved,* also called *believers/unbelievers*) and portray the final destiny of every person as being one of two realities (*heaven* or *hell*). In a moment we will look at how Mormons twist Scripture to support their view of three kingdoms, but for now, let's focus our attention on the scriptural evidence for *two classes of people* and *two possible destinies.*

- In Matthew 13:30, in a parable, Jesus said, "Let both [tares and wheat] grow together until the harvest: and in the time of harvest I will say to the reapers, Gather ye together first the tares, and bind them in bundles to burn them: but gather the wheat into my barn." Here, unbelievers and believers are spoken of as *tares* and *wheat.*

Two classes! (And note that the Bible doesn't mention three categories of wheat, each going to a different kingdom.) *All* the wheat is gathered into Christ's one "barn."

- In Matthew 13:49 Jesus said, "So shall it be at the end of the world: the angels shall come forth, and sever the wicked from among the just." Again, two classes are mentioned—unbelievers and believers identified as the *wicked* and the *just.*

- In Matthew 25:32 Jesus said that following His second coming, "before him shall be gathered all nations: and he shall separate them one from another, as a shepherd divideth his sheep from the goats." Here believers and unbelievers are differentiated as *sheep* and *goats.* The sheep (all of them together) will enter into God's (single) kingdom (verse 34) and inherit eternal life (verse 46). The goats go into eternal punishment (verse 46).

- In Luke 16:26 Jesus describes a scene taking place in the afterlife. He quotes Abraham talking with an unsaved rich man: "Between us and you there is a great gulf fixed: so that they which would pass from hence to you cannot; neither can they pass to us, that would come from thence." Hades apparently had two compartments: "paradise" for the saved, and "torments" for the unsaved—and these compartments were separated by a great chasm or gulf. Notice once again that all the saved went to one place (paradise) and all the unsaved went to another (torments).*

Clearly, then, Scripture speaks of *two classes of people* (the saved and the unsaved) and *two possible destinies* (heaven for the saved; hell for the unsaved). And each respective person ends up in one of these destinies based

---

*Since Christ's ascension into heaven, believers at the moment of death go *directly to heaven* into Christ's presence. Paul had the "desire to depart, and to be with Christ" (Philippians 1:23). He said he would "rather to be absent from the body, and to be present with the Lord" (2 Corinthians 5:8).

upon whether or not they placed saving faith in Christ during their time on earth (Acts 16:31).

_____ *Ask* . . . _____

- Would you please read aloud from Matthew 13:30? Matthew 13:49? Matthew 25:32? Luke 16:26?

- Don't all these verses point to *two classes of people* and *two possible destinies*?

Now, you need to emphasize that the unsaved includes *all* who have not placed their faith in Christ. This includes moral people who are committed to different religions. Scripture places *all* who do not believe in Jesus Christ—regardless of their level of morality—in the camp of the unsaved. (Anyone who thinks that good morals alone can save you should read the book of Romans.)

The Justice of God: Degrees of Punishment in Hell

At the beginning of this chapter, we noted that LeGrand Richards criticizes the view that "all who fail to go to heaven are sent to hell where they share and share alike."[14] In orthodox Christianity, all who fail to believe in Jesus Christ *are* sent to hell, but they *do not* "share and share alike." Scripture clearly shows that there are degrees of punishment in hell. Certainly an Adolf Hitler will suffer much more than a Christ-rejecting moralist.

The following passages confirm that there are various degrees of punishment in hell:

- Matthew 10:15—"Verily I say unto you, It shall be *more tolerable* for the land of Sodom and Gomorrha in the day of judgment, than for that city" (emphasis added).
- Matthew 11:21–24—"Woe unto thee, Chorazin! woe unto thee, Bethsaida! for if the mighty works, which

were done in you, had been done in Tyre and Sidon, they would have repented long ago in sackcloth and ashes. But I say unto you, It shall be more tolerable for Tyre and Sidon at the day of judgment, than for you. And thou, Capernaum, which art exalted unto heaven, shalt be brought down to hell: for if the mighty works, which have been done in thee, had been done in Sodom, it would have remained until this day. But I say unto you, That *it shall be more tolerable* for the land of Sodom in the day of judgment, *than for thee*" (emphasis added).

- Matthew 16:27—"The Son of man shall come in the glory of his Father with his angels; and then he shall reward every man *according to his works*" (emphasis added). (Be careful here—this verse is dealing not with *salvation* by works but with meting out justice according to works. Don't let the Mormon turn the tables on you by arguing for a works-salvation from this verse!)

- Luke 12:47–48—"That servant, which knew his lord's will, and prepared not himself, neither did according to his will, shall be beaten *with many stripes*. But he that knew not, and did commit things worthy of stripes, shall be beaten *with few stripes*. For unto whomsoever much is given, of him shall be *much required:* and to whom men have committed much, of him they will ask the more" (emphasis added).

- Hebrews 10:29—"Of how much *sorer punishment,* suppose ye, shall he be thought worthy, who hath trodden under foot the Son of God, and hath counted the blood of the covenant, wherewith he was sanctified, an unholy thing, and hath done despite unto the Spirit of grace?" (emphasis added).

- Revelation 20:11–15—"I saw a great white throne, and him that sat on it, from whose face the earth and the heaven fled away; and there was found no place for them. And I saw the dead, small and great, stand before God; and the books were opened: and another book was opened, which is the book of life: and the dead were judged out of those things which were written in the books, *according to their works.* And the sea gave up the dead which were in it; and death and hell delivered up the dead which were in them: and they were judged every man *according to their works.* And death and hell were cast into the lake of fire. This is the second death. And whosoever was not found written in the book of life was cast into the lake of fire" (emphasis added).

- Revelation 22:12—"Behold, I come quickly; and my reward is with me, to give every man *according as his work shall be*" (emphasis added).

Clearly, then, God will judge the wicked according to the things they have done in this life—and He will punish some people more severely than others because of the more heinous things they have done. The biblical God is a God of justice.

_____ *Ask* . . . _____

- Would you please read aloud from Matthew 10:15? Matthew 11:2–24? Luke 12:4–48? Hebrews 10:29? (Just a few of these will do.)

- Don't these verses tell us that God will judge the wicked according to the things they have done in this life—and He will punish some people more severely than others because of the more heinous things they have done?

The Justice of God: Rewards in Heaven

Not only are there degrees of punishment in hell, there are also varying degrees of reward in heaven. When the Lord returns at the Second Coming, He will judge believers in regard to their works and will reward them accordingly.

- 1 Corinthians 3:11–15—"For other foundation can no man lay than that is laid, which is Jesus Christ. Now if any man build upon this foundation gold, silver, precious stones, wood, hay, stubble; Every man's work shall be made manifest: for the day shall declare it, because it shall be revealed by fire; and the fire shall try every man's work of what sort it is. If any man's work abide which he hath built thereupon, he shall receive a reward. If any man's work shall be burned, he shall suffer loss: but he himself shall be saved; yet so as by fire."
- 2 Corinthians 5:10—"For we must all appear before the judgment seat of Christ; that every one may receive the things done in his body, according to that he hath done, whether it be good or bad."

These verses indicate that every believer in Christ will be judged and rewarded (or suffer the loss of a reward) according to his or her works. Hence, when LeGrand Richards criticizes the view that "all who go to heaven share and share alike,"[15] he is criticizing a view that Christians do not hold to. Christians believe that our just God will judge every believer according to his or her works and give different levels of rewards. But despite the fact that believers will have varying degrees of rewards . . .

All Believers Will Be with Christ in One Place

Jesus promised, "If any man serve me, let him follow me; and where I am, *there shall also my servant be:* if any man serve me, him will my Father honor" (John 12:26, emphasis added). No mention of three kingdoms here! Whoever follows Christ will be *where Christ* is (heaven). *All* who believe in Christ are heirs of the eternal kingdom (singular) (Galatians 3:29; 4:28–31; Titus 3:7; James 2:5).

In Romans 3:22 we read that the righteousness of God that leads to life in heaven is available *"unto all and upon all them that believe:* for there is no difference" (emphasis added). Furthermore, in John 10:16 Jesus affirms that all who believe in Him will be in *"one* fold" under *"one* shepherd." There will not be three separate "folds" or kingdoms." One fold, one Shepherd! One kingdom, one King.

1 Corinthians 15:40–42—*Three Kingdoms of Glory?*

The Mormon Teaching. In 1 Corinthians 15:40–42 we read, "There are also celestial bodies, and bodies terrestrial: but the glory of the celestial is one, and the glory of the terrestrial is another. There is one glory of the sun, and another glory of the moon, and another glory of the stars: for one star differeth from another star in glory. So also is the resurrection of the dead. It is sown in corruption; it is raised in incorruption."

Mormons say this passage confirms their belief in three heavenly kingdoms.[16] Citing these verses, Bruce McConkie explains that "contrary to the views found in the uninspired teachings and creeds of modern Christendom, there are in eternity kingdoms of glory to which all resurrected persons (except the sons of perdition) will eventually go."[17]

LeGrand Richards explains the Mormon view that resurrection bodies will have different degrees of glory:

> There is a glory of the sun, or celestial glory; another glory like the moon, or the terrestrial glory; and another glory like the stars, or, as we will learn, the telestial glory; and since "one star differeth from another star in glory," so also "is the resurrection of the dead." From this we learn that the great multitude in the resurrection will be likened unto the stars in heaven; and just as their works have differed in importance and faithfulness here upon the earth, so also shall their condition in the resurrection differ, even as the stars in heaven differ in glory.[18]

The Biblical Teaching. Perhaps what we should note first is that 1 Corinthians 15:40–42 does not even include "telestial."

Only the words "terrestrial" and "celestial" are mentioned. This automatically disqualifies this passage as a support for the idea that there is a telestial kingdom. Mormons are reading something into the passage that simply is not there. [19]

Now, the context of 1 Corinthians 15:40–42 is set for us in verse 35, where two questions are asked: "How are the dead raised up? and with what body do they come?" The rest of 1 Corinthians 15 seeks to answer these questions. So *yes,* Paul was talking about resurrection bodies, but *no,* there is no mention of any kingdoms.

Point out to the Mormon that the word "celestial" literally means "heavenly," and the word "terrestrial" literally means "earthly." Paul is talking about the heavenly body as opposed to the earthly body. As we read onward to verses 42–44, we see that the earthly body is fallen, temporal, imperfect, and weak. The heavenly body, by contrast, will be eternal, perfect, and powerful (cf. 2 Corinthians 5:1–4).

Notice the series of contrasts Paul makes between the earthly body and the heavenly body in verses 40–50: perishable/imperishable, weak/powerful, natural/supernatural, and mortal/immortal. Contextually, there is no way to read a theology of three kingdoms into a passage dealing with two kinds of bodies: the earthly and the heavenly.

THE EARTHLY BODY VERSUS THE HEAVENLY BODY IN 1 CORINTHIANS 15

Scripture Passage	Preresurrection (Terrestrial) Body	Postresurrection (Celestial) Body
1 Corinthians 15:40	Earthly	Heavenly
1 Corinthians 15:42	Perishable	Imperishable
1 Corinthians 15:43	Weak	Powerful
1 Corinthians 15:44	Natural	Supernatural
1 Corinthians 15:53	Mortal	Immortal [20]

___*Ask* . . . _____

- According to 1 Corinthians 15:35, what questions does Paul seek to answer throughout the rest of 1 Corinthians 15?

- Since the context clearly shows that Paul is contrasting the *earthly* (mortal) body with the *heavenly* (resurrected, glorified) body, where do you find three kingdoms of glory in this passage?

There's no doubt the Mormon will respond to your questions by mentioning the sun, moon, and stars in 1 Corinthians 15:41 and explaining how each of these have a different level of glory and splendor. You must emphasize to the Mormon that his or her church makes much too much of this verse and is reading a whole theology into it. All Paul is saying here is that the differences in splendor between *earthly* bodies (animals, birds, fish—*see* verse 39) and *heavenly* bodies (sun, moon, stars—*see* verse 41) serve as an illustration for the incredible difference in splendor between an earthly *human* body and a heavenly, resurrected *human* body (cf. Daniel 12:3; Matthew 13:43).

___*Ask* . . . _____

- Isn't it clear from the context that all Paul is talking about is that the differences in splendor between *earthly* bodies (animals, birds, fish) and *heavenly* bodies (sun, moon, stars) illustrate the difference in splendor between an earthly *human* body and a heavenly, resurrected *human* body?

(If the Mormon argues about this interpretation, go through the entire passage *verse by verse,* beginning with verse 35. Emphasize context, context, context.)

After explaining this to the Mormon, you might go on to say that the doctrine of three kingdoms of glory is not in harmony with the Book of Mormon. According to 1 Nephi 15:35 there is only a heaven and a hell: "There is a place prepared, yea, even that awful hell of which I have spoken, and the devil is the preparator of it; wherefore the final state of the souls of men is to dwell in the kingdom of God, or to be cast out because of that justice of which I have spoken" (*see also* Mormon 9:23; Ether 4:18; Helaman 14:18–19; Alma 3:26; 40:26; 41:4; Mosiah 16:11; 2 Nephi 2:28–29; 9:16; 28:21–22; 3 Nephi 27:11,17).

_____ *Ask . . .* _____

- Would you please open your Book of Mormon to 1 Nephi 15:35 and read it aloud?

- Doesn't this passage indicate that there is only a heaven and a hell?

- How do you reconcile this with the Mormon view of the three kingdoms?

2 Corinthians 12:2—*Three Degrees of Glory?*

The Mormon Teaching. In 2 Corinthians 12:2 we read, "I knew a man in Christ above fourteen years ago, (whether in the body, I cannot tell; or whether out of the body, I cannot tell: God knoweth;) such an one caught up to the third heaven." Mormons say this verse adds support to the idea that there are three degrees of glory.[21] LeGrand Richards says, "It is obvious there could not be a third heaven unless there is also a first and a second heaven. We therefore have three heavens."[22]

The Biblical Teaching. Mormons are reading into this verse an idea that simply is not there. Remind the Mormon of the interpretive principle that *Scripture interprets Scripture.* By comparing various Scripture passages dealing with heaven, it quickly becomes clear what Paul is talking about in 2 Corinthians 12:2.

There *are* three "heavens" mentioned in the Bible—the *atmospheric* heaven (Deuteronomy 11:11), the *starry* heaven (Genesis 1:14), and the *highest* heaven—God's realm where believers go upon death (Isaiah 63:15). It is this last heaven that Paul mentions in 2 Corinthians 12:2.

When Hebrews 4:14 speaks of Christ having passed "into the heavens," it is the atmospheric and starry heavens that are in mind. Indeed, Christ "ascended up far above all heavens" (Ephesians 4:10), and has been "made higher than the heavens" (Hebrews 7:26). Christ dwells in the highest heaven (the third heaven), and that is the realm to which the apostle Paul was caught up.

_____ *Ask* . . . _____

- Would you read aloud from Deuteronomy 11:11? Isn't "heaven" in this verse clearly a reference to the *atmospheric* heaven, from which rain comes?

- Would you read aloud from Genesis 1:14? Isn't "heaven" in this verse clearly a reference to the *stellar* heaven, where God has placed "lights" (stars)?

- Would you read aloud from Isaiah 63:15? Isn't "heaven" in this verse the *highest* heaven where God dwells"?

- Is it not clear from these verses that the three "heavens" are the *atmospheric* heaven, the *stellar* heaven, and the *highest* or *third* heaven where God dwells? (Emphasize that Scripture interprets Scripture.)

The Biblical Doctrine of Hell

The Bible reveals that those who go into eternity having rejected Jesus Christ will suffer forever and ever in hell. There is no second chance. Contrary to the Mormon view, a person (including the *moral* person) who dies without placing a saving faith in the true Jesus of the Bible will spend eternity apart from Christ in a place of great suffering. Let's look now at a few passages in support of this.

Matthew 25:46 tells us, "These shall go away into everlasting punishment: but the righteous into life eternal." A critical point to make about this verse is that the punishment is said to be *eternal*. The Greek adjective *aionion* in this verse means "everlasting, without end." You might want to tell the Mormon that this same adjective is predicated of God (the "eternal" God) in Romans 16:26, 1 Timothy 1:17, Hebrews 9:14, 13:8, and Revelation 4:9. The punishment of the wicked is just as eternal as our eternal God. Moreover, as Professor Alan Gomes notes,

> What is particularly determinative here is the fact that the duration of punishment for the wicked forms a parallel with the duration of life for the righteous: the adjective *aionion* is used to describe both the length of punishment for the wicked and the length of eternal life for the righteous. One cannot limit the duration of punishment for the wicked without at the same time limiting the duration of eternal life for the redeemed. It would do violence to the parallel to give it an unlimited signification in the case of eternal life, but a limited one when applied to the punishment of the wicked.[23]

In view of this, you might want to . . .

_____ *Ask* . . . _____

- The same Greek word for "eternal" in the phrase "eternal punishment" is used to describe the eternality of God (1 Timothy 1:17; Romans 16:26; Hebrews 9:14;

13:8; Revelation 4:9). Doesn't this indicate that the punishment of the wicked will be *just as eternal as God is?*

• Since the same Greek word for "eternal" in the phrase
"eternal punishment" in Matthew 25:46 is used in the
phrase "eternal life" (same verse), doesn't this indicate
that the punishment of the wicked is just as eternal as the
life of the righteous?

You'll also want to point the Mormon to Revelation
14:9–11:

> The third angel followed them, saying with a loud voice,
> If any man worship the beast and his image, and receive
> his mark in his forehead, or in his hand, The same shall
> drink of the wine of the wrath of God, which is poured out
> without mixture into the cup of his indignation; and *he
> shall be tormented with fire and brimstone* in the presence
> of the holy angels, and in the presence of the Lamb: And
> *the smoke of their torment ascendeth up for ever and ever:
> and they have no rest day nor night,* who worship the
> beast and his image, and whosoever receiveth the mark of
> his name (emphasis added).

In this passage, the Greek word for "torment" is *basanizo.*
Joseph Thayer's lexicon says the word means "to vex with
grievous pains . . . to torment."[24] Likewise, Arndt and
Gingrich's lexicon tells us the word means "to torture, torment."[25] When we examine the way this word is used
throughout Scripture, it becomes plain that it is always used
in contexts of great pain and conscious misery.

This torment is also described as never-ending: "The
smoke of their torment asendeth up *for ever and ever:* and
they have no rest day nor night . . ." (verse 11, emphasis
added). The words "for ever and ever" translate an emphatic
Greek phrase, *eis aionas aionon* ("unto the ages of the
ages"). The twofold use of the term *aionas* is used in
Scripture to emphasize the concept of eternity. And the plural

forms ("unto the *ages* of the *ages*") reinforces the idea of never-ending duration. Lutheran scholar R.C.H. Lenski comments:

> The strongest expression for our "forever" is *eis tous aionan ton aionon,* "for the eons of eons"; many eons, each of vast duration, are multiplied by many more, which we imitate by "forever and ever." Human language is able to use only temporal terms to express what is altogether beyond time and timeless. The Greek takes its greatest term for time, the eon, pluralizes this, and then multiplies it by its own plural, even using articles which make these eons the definite ones. [26]

You'll want to let the Mormon know that this same emphatic construction is used to speak of the never-ending worship of God in Revelation 1:6, 4:9, and 5:3. It is also used to describe the eternality of God in Revelation 4:10 and 10:6. We cannot emphasize too strongly that this phrase shows beyond doubt that the physical torment of the wicked is forever and ever and ever.

___ *Ask . . .* ___

- The Greek words that are used to describe God's eternality in Revelation 4:10 are the same as the Greek words used to describe the "for ever and ever" torment in Revelation 14:11. Doesn't that tell us that the torment of the wicked is just as eternal as God Himself?

The use of the words "day nor night" in Revelation 14:11 is also significant. Gomes comments, "The expression 'day and night' is indicative of ceaseless activity. This same phrase is used of the never-ending worship of God in Revelation 4:8 and

7:15. By juxtaposing the words 'day and night' with 'forever and ever' in 20:10 [another passage dealing with eternal torment], we have the most emphatic expression of unending, ceaseless activity possible in the Greek language"[27] (insert added).

It's also interesting to note that many of the most graphic descriptions we have of the eternal perdition of the lost come from the lips of Jesus Himself.[28] And the truths that Jesus taught about the lost suffering eternally were communicated very clearly. We must therefore ask: "Had Christ wished to teach that there would not be eternal suffering in hell, is it reasonable that He would have selected language guaranteed to lead His church astray?"[29]

You might also want to point out to the Mormon that Mosiah 2:39 in the Book of Mormon makes reference to "never-ending" torment (cf. Alma 34:35). This is but another example of how the Book of Mormon disagrees with current Mormon doctrine.

Where Do True Believers Go Upon Death?

The Mormon church teaches that at the moment of death, believers enter a spirit world where they eventually continue on their progression toward exaltation and godhood. But the Bible says otherwise. At the moment of death, believers are ushered immediately into the presence of Jesus Christ Himself. Let us consider a few verses that affirm this.

In Philippians 1:21–23 we read, "For to me to live is Christ, and to die is gain. But if I live in the flesh, this is the fruit of my labor: yet what I shall choose I wot not. For I am in a strait betwixt two, having a desire to depart, and to be with Christ; which is far better."

What Paul meant by "gain" is clear from the context, for he defines that gain as departing the physical body *to be with*

Christ. Being with Christ is far better, Paul says, than remaining in the physical body.

In this passage, Paul is saying that the very moment after physical death occurs he will be with Christ. How do we know this? It's clear from the Greek text. Without going into too much detail, suffice it to say that an aorist infinitive ("to depart") is linked by a single article with a present infinitive ("*to be* with Christ"). The infinitives thus belong together. "The single article ties the two infinitives together, so that the actions depicted by the two infinitives are to be considered two aspects of the same thing, or two sides of the same coin."[30] Thus, Paul is saying that the very moment after he "departs" the body or dies, he will be with Christ in heaven

We see this same truth taught in 2 Corinthians 5:6–8: "We are always confident, knowing that, whilst we are at home in the body, we are absent from the Lord: (For we walk by faith, not by sight:) We are confident, I say, and willing rather to be absent from the body, and to be present with the Lord."

The Greek text from which this passage was translated is highly informative. The phrases "at home in the body" and "absent from the Lord" are present tenses (which indicate continuing action). We could paraphrase Paul's words this way: "Being always of good courage, and knowing that while we are *continuing to be at home in the body* we are *continuing to be absent from the Lord.*"[31]

By contrast, the latter part of the passage contains two aorist infinitives. Anthony Hoekema explains: "Whereas the present tenses in verse 6 picture a continuing at-homeness in the body and a continuing away-from-homeness as to the Lord, the aorist infinitives of verse 8 point to a once-for-all momentary happening. What can this be? There is only one answer: *death,* which is an immediate transition from being at home in the body to being away from home as to the body."[32] The moment a Christian dies, he or she is immediately in the presence of Christ.

It is also noteworthy that the Greek word *pros* is used for "with" in the phrase "be at home *with* the Lord." This word suggests very close fellowship—that is, face-to-face. It is a word used to speak of intimate relationships. Paul is telling us that he expects to have intimate fellowship with Christ immediately following his physical death.

As believers, we can look forward to spending eternity with Christ in heaven. This is the destiny of the saved! In the heavenly estate, "the tabernacle of God is with men, and he will dwell with them, and they shall be his people, and God himself shall be with them, and be their God. And God shall wipe away all tears from their eyes; and there shall be no more death, neither sorrow, nor crying, neither shall there be any more pain: for the former things are passed away" (Revelation 21:3–4).

There are, then, only two possible destinies for human beings—*heaven or hell*. It is one or the other. It is our prayer that this book will help you introduce the Mormon to the true Jesus of Scripture so he or she can enjoy eternity in the true heaven of Scripture.

21

Evangelism Among Mormons

In this book, we have devoted much space to answering Mormon arguments with the help of specific passages in the Bible. In this closing chapter—which is short and to the point—our intention is to depart from our focus on Mormon theology and turn our attention to some final hints on witnessing to the Mormons.

Many of these hints were gleaned from the personal experience of Dr. Walter Martin, who witnessed to Mormons and other cultists for decades. We have adopted his methods as our own, and we acknowledge our indebtedness to him for the insights contained on the following pages.

During one of his many speaking engagements, Dr. Martin said that there are both *do's* and *don'ts* to observe when we witness to cultists like the Mormons.[1] Let's look now at his four *do's* and two *don'ts*.

Identify with the Mormons

First, DO IDENTIFY WITH THE MORMONS. Martin says you must "convince him (or her) that you consider him to be a person in his own right—worthwhile, basically honest,

391

and not trying to put something over on you. Cultists are *people* before they're *cultists.* They have families, they have children, they have needs, they have frustrations and fears, and they are brothers and sisters *in Adam,* though not *in Christ.*"[2]

Acts 17:26–28 tells us that all people on earth, by virtue of being created by God, are "offspring" of God. In Adam, then, all of us share a common heritage. In view of this, Martin suggests, let's talk to Mormons from the *"family-of-Adam* perspective,*"* prayerfully hoping to bring them to the *"family-of-God* perspective."[3]

Mormons are *people* before they're *cultists.* They have families and children and all the other things that are important to human beings. If you can keep in mind that Mormons are people before they're cultists—people with families and children; people who have the need for friendship, love, and security; people who laugh and cry; and so on—you will find it much easier to treat him or her with respect and kindness when they show up on your doorstep.

Labor Persistently with the Mormons

Second, DO LABOR PERSISTENTLY WITH THE MORMONS. Never give up unless he or she decisively refuses further contact. Martin says, "until they pull the plug, we need to hang in there—remembering that the Lord blesses His Word."[4] Remember what God said about His sovereign Word in the book of Isaiah : "It shall not return unto me void, but it shall accomplish that which I please, and it shall prosper in the thing whereto I sent it" (Isaiah 55:11).

You must keep in mind that God's Word is alive and powerful. Hebrews 4:12 says, "The word of God is *quick* [living], and *powerful,* and sharper than any twoedged sword, piercing even to the dividing asunder of soul and spirit, and of the joints and marrow, and is a discerner of the thoughts and intents of the heart" (emphasis and insert added). As you persist in sharing insights from the Word of God, you can be sure that God is at work in the Mormon's heart.

Now, we know from personal experience that it's not easy to labor persistently with the Mormons. Sometimes when a Mormon you have met pays you another visit unexpectedly, the temptation is to say, "This is not a good time; would you mind coming back later?" (This is especially true if you've already got your day planned.) The problem is, *he or she may not come back later*—and hence, this may be your last opportunity to share the truth with them. Let's face it: If you want to serve as an effective witness for Christ, you need to *expect* unexpected time interruptions.

Answer the Questions of Mormons

Third, DO EXHAUST EVERY EFFORT TO ANSWER THE QUESTIONS OF MORMONS. We must share not only *what* we believe as Christians, but *why* we believe it as well. Can you give convincing reasons for your beliefs? Dr. Martin notes that "the apostles were apologists [defenders of the faith] as well as evangelists. They not only proclaimed Christ, but when they were questioned, they had good, solid reasons for their faith."[5] This is why the apostle Peter said, "Be ready always to give an answer to every man that asketh you a reason of the hope that is in you" (1 Peter 3:15).

What happens if you don't know the answer to a question asked by the Mormon? Following Walter Martin's lead (from his *early* days of witnessing to cultists), just say, "That's a good question. I'm not sure what the answer is, but I'm going to do some research this week and find the answer. Can we talk about this the next time you stop by?" The Mormon will invariably go along with your request. Hopefully, the book you're holding in your hand will go a long way toward providing the answers you need.

Allow the Mormon to Save Face

Fourth, DO ALLOW THE MORMON TO SAVE FACE. When you share the gospel with a Mormon and defend your position from Scripture, there will come a time in your encounter when you know that you've "won the argument." When that moment arrives, you must make every effort to let love shine through and allow the Mormon to save face. Otherwise, he will resent you and fight you, even though he knows in his heart that you're right.

Dr. Martin suggests handling it this way: "When you sense that the person has lost the argument and is deflated, that's the time to be magnanimous and say to the person, lovingly: 'I realize that we can get awfully uptight in these areas if we let ourselves. Let's just forget that you're a Mormon and I'm a Baptist (or whatever you are). And let's just think of ourselves as two people who want more than anything else to know the whole truth and the whole counsel of God. *Right?*' I haven't met a cultist yet who wouldn't say 'Right' in response."[6] Disarming the situation in this way will help lower defensive barriers and will create an atmosphere in which the Mormon will actually want to hear what you have to say.

Former cultists attest to the importance of taking a loving, disarming approach. One such person points out that "empathy is so very important when reaching out to these misled individuals. Try to think of how you would want others to speak to you, if you were the one who was misled. Then remember that 'all things whatsoever ye would that men should do to you, do ye even so to them' (Matthew 7:12)."[7]

No Spiritual Chips on the Shoulder

The first *don't* to keep in mind when witnessing to the Mormons is, DON'T APPROACH A MORMON WITH A SPIRITUAL CHIP ON YOUR SHOULDER. Martin says that "a spiritual chip is the communication of the feeling that you are looking down on the cultist because you have something he or she doesn't have. Such an attitude will turn them off as fast as anything you could imagine."[8]

Christians who have thoroughly prepared themselves by learning hard-hitting scriptural answers to Mormon errors (such as those contained in this book) may find themselves tempted to *talk down* at the Mormon instead of *conversing with* him or her. Don't let this happen. Be on your guard and make every effort, with God's help, to remain humble during your witnessing encounter. Watch out for spiritual pride; *it's deadly!*

Be Patient

A second *don't* is, DON'T LOSE YOUR PATIENCE, REGARDLESS OF HOW DENSE YOU MAY THINK THE MORMON IS (2 Timothy 2:24–26). This is an extremely important point. Dr. Martin advises, "Remember how dense you and I were—until the Lord managed to break through. Because cultists are bound in the chains of slavery to sin, you need to be patient. And being patient means being willing to go over something ten times if necessary, believing that the Lord will bless your efforts."[9]

If you should lose your patience and raise your voice at the Mormon, the likelihood is that the Mormon will not come to your house again. You don't want that to happen. After all, it may take multiple exposures to the truth before the Mormon comes to see that the Mormon church has led him astray. You need to maintain a witnessing environment such that the Mormon will feel free to stop by your house without fearing a verbal assault.

We can personally attest that the above *do's* and *don'ts* will help you as you seek to share the gospel with Mormons. But as important as these are, you must not forget that the Holy Spirit's role is central to effective evangelism—with

Mormons and everyone else. After all, it is *He* who touches their souls; it is *He* who convinces them of sin and of righteousness and of judgment (John 16:8). And we become *in His hands* effective instruments for the Master's use (cf. 1 Corinthians 6:19; 12:11; Ephesians 5:18).[10]

Remember, only God can lift the veil of darkness that Mormon theology has cast over the hearts of individual Mormons. Your success in bringing a Mormon to Christ depends in a big way on the Holy Spirit's work in that person's life. For this reason, be sure to pray fervently for the Holy Spirit's involvement in all your witnessing encounters (1 Corinthians 7:5; Philippians 4:6; 1 Thessalonians 5:17).

We close with an invitation: If we can help you in your work of witnessing for Christ, please feel free to contact us at the address below.

Ron Rhodes and Marian Bodine
Christian Research Institute
P.O. Box 500
San Juan Capistrano, CA 92693 USA

Notes

Introduction: Mormonism Today

1. Theologically speaking, a cult is a religious group that claims to be Christian but in fact denies one or more of the essential doctrines of historic, orthodox Christianity (as defined in the major historic creeds of Christianity). Such groups deny or distort essential Christian doctrines such as the deity of Christ, the personality and deity of the Holy Spirit, the Trinity, and salvation by grace through faith alone.
2. *See,* for example, Ruth A. Tucker, *Another Gospel: Alternative Religions and the New Age Movement* (Grand Rapids, MI: Zondervan Publishing House, 1989), p. 90.
3. Russell Chandler, *Racing Toward 2001* (Grand Rapids, MI: Zondervan Publishing House, 1992), p. 188.
4. *Church News,* 5 October 1991; cited in *Christian Research Newsletter,* "What's New in the Headlines," November/December 1991, p. 6.
5. *The Arizona Republic;* cited in *Christian Research Newsletter,* "What's New in the Headlines," September/October 1991, p. 6. For a detailed study of the Mormon church's financial dealings, *see* John Heinerman and Anson Shupe, *The Mormon Corporate Empire* (Boston, MA: Beacon Press, 1985).
6. *The Arizona Republic;* cited in *Christian Research Newsletter,* p. 6.
7. *The Arizona Republic;* cited in *Christian Research Newsletter,* p. 6.
8. *The Arizona Republic;* cited in *Christian Research Newsletter,* p. 6.
9. *The Arizona Republic,* June 30–July 3, 1991; cited in *Christian Research Newsletter,* "What's New in the Headlines," September/October 1991, p. 6.
10. "LDS Church Gains Converts Through Media Campaign," *The Salt Lake Tribune,* 6 December 1989, p. 16A.
11. Andy Hall, Jerry Kammer, and Mark Trahant, "LDS Media Empire: A Voice for Mormon Values," *Las Vegas Review-Journal,* 18 July 1991, p. 2D.
12. *New York Times,* 21 December 1992; cited in *Christian Research Newsletter,* "What's New in the Headlines," January/February 1993, p. 4.
13. William Alnor, "Sects Increasingly Using Media to Bolster Ranks," *Christian Research Journal,* Winter 1991, p. 5.
14. Alnor, p. 5.
15. Alnor, p. 5.
16. Hall, Kammer, and Trahant, p. 2D.
17. Alnor, p. 5.
18. Alnor, p. 5.
19. "Media Messages Boost Missionary Work," p. 106.
20. Hall, Kammer, and Trahant, p. 1D.
21. Hall, Kammer, and Trahant, p. 1D.
22. "Media Messages Boost Missionary Work," p. 106.
23. "LDS Church Gains Converts Through Media Campaign," *The Salt Lake Tribune,* 6 December 1989.
24. However, Mormon scholars acknowledge that "members of the Church of Jesus Christ of Latter-day Saints are not Protestants and the Church itself is not a Protestant church." (Bruce McConkie, *Mormon Doctrine* [Salt Lake City, UT: Bookcraft, 1966], p. 610.)
25. "Mormons Forge Links With Other Faiths," Associated Press report; on file at CRI.
26. "Mormons Forge Links With Other Faiths."
27. "Mormons Forge Links With Other Faiths."
28. Stephen E. Robinson, *Are Mormons Christians?* (Salt Lake City, UT: Bookcraft, 1991), p. vii.
29. Gordon R. Lewis, "A Summary Critique," *Are Mormons Christians?* by Stephen E. Robinson, *Christian Research Journal,* Fall 1992, p. 33.
30. Lewis, p. 33.

Chapter 1—Where Did Mormonism Come From?

1. Joseph Fielding Smith, *The Life and Teachings of Jesus and His Apostles* (Salt Lake City, UT: The Church of Jesus Christ of Latter-day Saints, n.d.), p. 59.
2. For a basic but thorough presentation of Mormon beliefs, see *Gospel Principles* (Salt Lake City, UT: Church of Jesus Christ of Latter-day Saints, 1981).

3. Joseph Smith—History, 1:3–8.
4. Joseph Smith—History, 1:17,19.
5. Joseph Smith—History, 1:28.
6. For a detailed account of Joseph Smith's involvement in occultic practices, *see* Jerald and Sandra Tanner, *Mormonism, Magic and Masonry* (Salt Lake City, UT: Utah Lighthouse Ministry, 1988).
7. Ezra Taft Benson, *Church News*, 23 December 1967, p. 12.
8. David O. McKay, *Gospel Ideals* (Salt Lake City, UT: Improvement Era, 1953), p. 85.
9. Derived from Wesley P. Walters, "Another Look at the First Vision," Christian Research Institute Reprint DM-230, on file at CRI.
10. For a thorough examination of the serious conflicts among the First Vision accounts, *see* Jerald and Sandra Tanner, *Major Problems of Mormonism* (Salt Lake City, UT: Utah Lighthouse Ministry, 1989), pp. 54–58.
11. Joseph Smith, Pearl of Great Price 1:29.
12. Joseph Smith—History, 1:34,35.
13. Joseph Smith—History, 1:29–42.
14. Mormon 9:32.
15. David Whitmer, *An Address to All Believers in Christ* (Concord, CA: Pacific Publishing Co., 1887), p. 12.
16. Joseph Smith—History, 1:68–72. For a good analysis of this account and of other problems with Mormonism's "restored priesthood," *see* Hal Hougey, *Latter-day Saints: Where Do You Get Your Authority?* (Concord, CA: Pacific Publishing Co., 1990).
17. Doctrine and Covenants 37:1.
18. *History of the Church of Jesus Christ of Latter-day Saints* (Salt Lake City, UT: Deseret, 1978), 1:40–42.
19. Doctrine and Covenants 37:1.
20. Note, however, that Mormons now claim that "Zion" is a term referring to "the Saints." (*See* Bruce McConkie, *Mormon Doctrine* [Salt Lake City, UT: Bookcraft, 1966], p. 854.) Joseph Smith said that all of North and South America comprise the land of Zion. (*See* Joseph Fielding Smith, *Teachings of the Prophet Joseph Smith* [Salt Lake City, UT: Deseret, 1979], p. 362.)
21. Doctrine and Covenants 57:6.
22. For example, at this very time Smith received revelations that "Zion will not be moved from this place." *See* Jerald and Sandra Tanner, *The Changing World of Mormonism* (Chicago, IL: Moody Press, 1981), pp. 420–24.
23. For a fuller account and refutation, *see* Charles M. Larson, *By His Own Hand Upon Papyrus* (Grand Rapids, MI: Institute for Religious Research, 1985).
24. *History of the Church,* 3:175.
25. David A. Reed and John R. Farkas, *Mormons Answered Verse by Verse* (Grand Rapids, MI: Baker Book House, 1993), p. 12.

Chapter 2—Witnessing to Mormons

1. David A. Reed and John R. Farkas, *How to Rescue Your Loved One from Mormonism* (Grand Rapids, MI: Baker Book House, 1994), pp. 23–24.
2. Lorri MacGregor, *Coping with the Cults* (Eugene, OR: Harvest House Publishers, 1992), p. 45.
3. Orson Pratt, *The Seer* (Washington, D.C.: n.p., 1853–54), pp. 15–16.
4. Joseph Fielding Smith, *Doctrines of Salvation* (Salt Lake City, UT: Bookcraft, 1954), 1:188.
5. *Journal of Discourses* (London: Latter-day Saints' Book Depot, 1854–56), 16:46.
6. David A. Reed and John R. Farkas, *Mormons Answered Verse by Verse* (Grand Rapids, MI: Baker Book House, 1992), pp. 21–22.
7. Contact Utah Lighthouse Ministry, Box 1884, Salt Lake City, Utah, 84110.
8. Walter Martin, "Mormons and Biblical Terminology," *Christian Research Newsletter*, vol. 4, issue 5, p. 5.
9. David A. Reed, *Jehovah's Witnesses Answered Verse by Verse* (Grand Rapids, MI: Baker Book House, 1992), p. 114.
10. Wesley P. Walters, "Mormonism," in *Evangelizing the Cults*, ed. Ronald Enroth (Ann Arbor, MI: Servant Publications, 1990), p. 83.
11. *See* Marian Bodine, "Witnessing to Mormons—Some First Principles," *Christian Research Journal*, Fall 1987, CRI Reprint DM-501.
12. "Witnessing to Mormons," CRI Perspective, Christian Research Institute.
13. Reed, *Jehovah's Witnesses Answered Verse by Verse*, p. 115.

Chapter 3—The Mormon Church: The Restored Church?

1. Joseph Smith, *History of the Church of Jesus Christ of Latter-day Saints* (Salt Lake City, UT: Deseret Book Company, 1973), 1:17–19.
2. *Church History in the Fulness of Times*, Church Educational System (Salt Lake City, UT: The Church of Jesus Christ of Latter-day Saints, 1989).
3. *Church History in the Fulness of Times*, p. 2.

4. *Church History in the Fulness of Times*, p. 4.
5. The new church was named the "Church of Christ" in 1830 (Doctrine and Covenants 1:20). In May of 1834, it was renamed the "Church of the Latter-day Saints" (*History of the Church of Jesus Christ of Latter-day Saints*, 2:63). Finally, on April 26, 1838 it was renamed the "Church of Jesus Christ of Latter-day Saints."
6. *Encyclopedia of Mormonism*, ed. Daniel H. Ludlow (New York, NY: Macmillan, 1992), 1:56.
7. Brigham Young, *Journal of Discourses* (London: Latter-day Saints' Book Depot, 1854–56), 8:171.
8. Orson Pratt, *The Seer* (Washington, D.C.: n.p., 1853–54), p. 255.
9. Bruce McConkie, *Doctrinal New Testament Commentary*, vol. 2 (Salt Lake City, UT: Bookcraft, 1976), p. 113; cf. 366, 458–59, 506–07.
10. Bruce McConkie, *Mormon Doctrine*, 2d ed. (Salt Lake City, UT: Bookcraft, 1977), p. 626.
11. McConkie, p. 603.
12. George Q. Cannon, *Gospel Truth* (Salt Lake City, UT: Deseret Book Company, 1987), p. 324.
13. *History of the Church of Jesus Christ of Latter-day Saints*, 1:XL.
14. LeGrand Richards, *A Marvelous Work and a Wonder* (Salt Lake City, UT: Deseret Book Company, 1958), p. 35.
15. *See* Bruce R. McConkie, *Mormon Doctrine* (Salt Lake City, UT: Bookcraft, 1966), p. 635.
16. Craig S. Keener, *The IVP Bible Background Commentary* (Downers Grove, IL: InterVarsity Press, 1993), p. 332.
17. Spiros Zodhiates, *The Complete Word Study Dictionary* (Chattanooga, TN: AMG Publishers, 1992), p. 226.
18. James E. Talmage, *The Articles of Faith* (Salt Lake City, UT: The Church of Jesus Christ of Latter-day Saints, 1982), pp. 203–04.
19. *The Wycliffe Bible Commentary*, eds. Charles F. Pfeiffer and Everett F. Harrison (Chicago, IL: Moody Press, 1974), p. 1162; cf. *The Bible Knowledge Commentary*, New Testament, eds. John F. Walvoord and Roy B. Zuck (Wheaton, IL: Victor Books, 1989), p. 414.
20. F.F. Bruce, *The Book of the Acts* (Grand Rapids, MI: Eerdmans, 1986), p. 417.
21. Talmage, pp. 203–04; cf. McConkie, p. 334.
22. *New Bible Commentary*, eds. G.J. Wenham, J.A. Motyer, D.A. Carson, and R.T. France (Downers Grove, IL: InterVarsity Press, 1994), p. 1209.
23. David A. Reed and John R. Farkas, *Mormons Answered Verse by Verse* (Grand Rapids, MI: Baker Book House, 1993), p. 89.
24. G. Walter Hansen, *Galatians* (Downers Grove, IL: InterVarsity Press, 1994), p. 37.
25. James E. Talmage, *The Great Apostasy* (Salt Lake City, UT: Deseret Book Company, 1975), p. 41; cf. McConkie, p. 43.
26. Talmage, pp. 203–04.
27. *The Bible Knowledge Commentary*, p. 718.
28. *The Bible Knowledge Commentary*, p. 718.
29. Talmage, pp. 203–04; cf. McConkie, p. 205.
30. *The Bible Knowledge Commentary*, p. 739.
31. *The Bible Knowledge Commentary*, p. 739.
32. *History of the Church*, p. xl.
33. *See*, for example, the footnote for Revelation 14:6 in the LDS Bible, which refers the reader to the heading "Restoration of the Gospel" in the volume's Topical Guide.
34. *See* Talmage, pp. 203–04.
35. *The Bible Knowledge Commentary*, p. 964.
36. Reed and Farkas, p. 90.
37. Note, however, that as recently as 1966 Mormon apostle Bruce McConkie wrote that through Smith's vision "the creeds of Christendom were shattered to smithereens" (McConkie, p. 284).
38. Robert M. Bowman, Jr., "How Mormons Are Defending Mormon Doctrine," *Christian Research Journal*, Fall 1989, p. 26.
39. Bowman, p. 26.
40. Joseph Smith—History, 1:19.
41. Cited by Bowman, p. 26.
42. Daniel C. Peterson and Stephen D. Ricks, *Offenders for a Word: How Anti-Mormons Play Word Games to Attack Latter-day Saints* (Salt Lake City, UT: Aspen Books, 1992), p. 211.
43. Bowman, p. 26.

Chapter 4—Mormon Leaders: True Prophets of God?

1. Joseph Fielding Smith, *Doctrines of Salvation* (Salt Lake City, UT: Bookcraft, 1975), 1:172.
2. *Encyclopedia of Mormonism*, ed. Daniel Ludlow (New York, NY: Macmillan Publishing Company, 1992), 1:1331–33.
3. *The Ensign*, June 1994, p. 20.
4. Bruce McConkie, *This Generation Shall Have My Word Through You*, pp. 4–5; cited in *The Ensign*, June 1994, p. 20.
5. Doctrine and Covenants (Salt Lake City, UT: The Church of Jesus Christ of Latter-day Saints, 1990), 21:1,2.

6. *Encyclopedia of Mormonism,* 13:1218.
7. Bruce R. McConkie, *Mormon Doctrine* (Salt Lake City, UT: Bookcraft, 1966), p. 49.
8. Smith, *Doctrines of Salvation,* 1:188.
9. Smith, *Doctrines of Salvation,* 1:188.
10. McConkie, p. 606.
11. Although there is a sense in which various church authorities—its First Presidency, Council of the Twelve apostles, and Patriarch—are also regarded as "prophets, seers, and revelators." *See* McConkie, p. 606.
12. *The Bible Knowledge Commentary,* Old Testament, eds. John F. Walvoord and Roy B. Zuck (Wheaton, IL: Victor Books, 1985), p. 1433.
13. Doctrine and Covenants 84:3–5.
14. Joseph Smith, *History of the Church of Jesus Christ of Latter-day Saints* (Salt Lake City, UT: Deseret Book Company, 1973), 5:394.
15. Brigham Young, *Journal of Discourses* (London: Latter-day Saints' Book Depot, 1854–56), 10:250.
16. Young, *Journal of Discourses,* 13:271.
17. Mark J. Cares, *Speaking the Truth in Love to Mormons* (Milwaukee, WI: Northwestern Publishing House, 1993), p. 110.
18. McConkie, pp. 606–07.
19. *See* Norman L. Geisler and William Nix, *A General Introduction to the Bible* (Chicago, IL: Moody Press, 1968).
20. Remember that the Mormons make a distinction between a person's being an apostle in a general sense (which could apply to any of them) and being one "in an ordained sense" as are top church leaders. (*See* McConkie, pp. 46–47.)
21. Michael Green, *The Second Epistle of Peter and the Epistle of Jude* (Grand Rapids, MI: Eerdmans, 1968), p. 159.
22. Walter Bauer, *A Greek-English Lexicon of the New Testament and Other Early Christian Literature,* trans. William F. Arndt and F. Wilbur Gingrich (Chicago, IL: University of Chicago Press, 1957), p. 669.
23. McConkie, p. 140.
24. McConkie, p. 607.
25. 2 Nephi 31:21; Mosiah 15:4–5; Alma 11:26–29,44.
26. Doctrine and Covenants 76:58; 121:28,32; 132:17,20,37.
27. Book of Abraham, chapters 4–5.
28. Published in all editions of Doctrine and Covenants from 1835 to 1921.
29. Jacob 2:24.
30. Doctrine and Covenants 132:1
31. *Journal of Discourses,* 1:50,51; Brigham Young, delivered in the Tabernacle, June 8, and reported in the *Deseret News,* June 18, 1873 (#308).
32. *Journal of Discourses,* 13:95.
33. *Journal of Discourses,* 13:254.
34. *Improvement Era,* June 1945, p. 354.
35. Smith, *Doctrines of Salvation,* 1:187.
36. "Fourteen Fundamentals in Following the Prophets," *1980 Devotional Speeches of the Year* (Provo, UT: Brigham Young University Press, 1981), p. 27.
37. *The Arizona Republic,* 22 May 1994, p. C1. Steve Benson resigned from the Mormon church in late 1993.
38. *Los Angeles Times,* 22 October 1994, p. B9.
39. Joseph Smith, *The Evening and Morning Star,* July 1833, p. 1.

Chapter 5—The Book of Mormon—Part 1: Is It "Another Testament" of Jesus Christ?

1. Joseph Smith, *History of the Church of Jesus Christ of Latter-day Saints* (Salt Lake City, UT: Deseret Book Company, 1973), 4:461.
2. Doctrine and Covenants (Salt Lake City, UT: The Church of Jesus Christ of Latter-day Saints, 1990), 20:9; 42:12; 135:3.
3. 2 Nephi 5:21.
4. Book of Mormon (Salt Lake City, UT: The Church of Jesus Christ of Latter-day Saints, 1990), "Introduction."
5. 1 Nephi 10:4–7.
6. Book of Mormon, "Introduction."
7. Book of Mormon, "Introduction."
8. Book of Mormon, "Introduction."
9. 1 Nephi 1:2.
10. Bruce R. McConkie, *Mormon Doctrine* (Salt Lake City, UT: Bookcraft, 1966), pp. 98–99.
11. LeGrand Richards, *A Marvelous Work and a Wonder* (Salt Lake City, UT: Deseret Book Company, 1973), p. 56.
12. David A. Reed and John R. Farkas, *Mormons Answered Verse by Verse* (Grand Rapids, MI: Baker Book House, 1993), p. 49.
13. Reed and Farkas, p. 49

14. Orson Pratt, *Divine Authenticity of the Book of Mormon* (Utah, 1891), pp. 293–94; quoted by James E. Talmage, *A Study of the Articles of Faith* (Salt Lake City, UT: The Church of Jesus Christ of Latter-day Saints, 1977), pp. 278–79.
15. Talmage, p. 278.
16. Richards, p. 69.
17. *The Bible Knowledge Commentary*, Old Testament, eds. John F. Walvoord and Roy B. Zuck (Wheaton, IL: Victor Books, 1985), p. 1078.
18. *The Bethany Parallel Commentary*, Old Testament (Minneapolis, MN: Bethany House Publishers, 1985), p. 1406.
19. *The International Bible Commentary*, ed. F.F. Bruce (Grand Rapids, MI: Zondervan Publishing House, 1986), p. 740.
20. *The Bethany Parallel Commentary*, p. 1406.
21. Albert Barnes, *Notes on the New Testament* (Grand Rapids, MI: Baker Book House, 1975), p. 439.
22. Pratt, pp. 293–94; quoted by Talmage, pp. 278–79.
23. Talmage, p. 267.
24. Joseph Smith—History, 2:63–65.
25. Barnes, p. 442.
26. Richards, p. 50.
27. Richards, pp. 67–68.
28. Richards, pp. 67–68.
29. *The Bible Knowledge Commentary*, p. 1299.
30. Marian Bodine, "Mormon 'Proof-Texts' from the Bible," Fact Sheet # DM-197, Christian Research Institute; cf. *The International Bible Commentary*, ed. F.F. Bruce (Grand Rapids, MI: Zondervan Publishing House, 1986), pp. 838–39.
31. Richards, p. 53.
32. Charles C. Ryrie, *The Ryrie Study Bible* (Chicago, IL: Moody Press, 1986), p. 1603.
33. Mark J. Cares, *Speaking the Truth in Love to Mormons* (Milwaukee, WI: Northwestern Publishing House, 1993), p. 211.
34. Cares, p. 212.
35. Bill McKeever, *Answering Mormons' Questions* (Minneapolis, MN: Bethany House Publishers, 1991), p. 106.
36. This strategy is suggested by John R. Farkas and David A. Reed, *Mormonism: Changes, Contradictions, and Errors* (Grand Rapids, MI: Baker Book House, forthcoming), chapter 10, proofs.
37. Marian Bodine, "Witnessing to Mormons—Some First Principles," *Christian Research Journal*, Fall 1987.
38. Richards, p. 56.
39. Robert H. Mounce, *The Book of Revelation* (Grand Rapids, MI: Eerdmans, 1984), p. 395.

Chapter 6—The Book of Mormon—Part 2: Insurmountable Problems

1. For example, Jerald and Sandra Tanner, *3,913 Changes in the Book of Mormon* (Salt Lake City, UT: Utah Lighthouse Ministry, n.d.); Jerald and Sandra Tanner, *The Case Against Mormonism*, vols. 1–3 (Salt Lake City, UT: Utah Lighthouse Ministry, 1967); Jerald and Sandra Tanner, *Archaeology and the Book of Mormon* (Salt Lake City, UT: Modern Microfilm Company, 1969).
2. Scott Faulring, "Changes in New Triple: Part 1—The Book of Mormon," *Seventh East Press*, 21 October 1981, Provo, Utah.
3. *The Ensign*, October 1981, p. 19.
4. David Whitmer, *An Address to All Believers in Christ* (Concord, CA: Pacific Publishing Co., 1976, reprint).
5. Joseph Smith, *History of the Church of Jesus Christ of Latter-day Saints* (Salt Lake City, UT: Deseret Book Company, 1973), 1:54–55.
6. "Journal of Oliver B. Huntington," p. 168 of typed copy at Utah State Historical Society; in Jerald and Sandra Tanner, *Major Problems of Mormonism* (Salt Lake City, UT: Utah Lighthouse Ministry, 1989), p. 161.
7. Smith, 4:461.
8. Smith, 1:54–55.
9. Smith, 4:461.
10. *See* Jerald and Sandra Tanner, *3,913 Changes in the Book of Mormon*.
11. Steve and Mary Ann Benson resigned from the LDS Church in October, 1993.
12. *The Arizona Republic*, 22 May 1994, p. C1.
13. Note that there have also been changes in Doctrine and Covenants and The Pearl of Great Price. *See* Jerald and Sandra Tanner, *The Case Against Mormonism*, vol. 1, pp. 131–89.
14. Jerald and Sandra Tanner, *Major Problems of Mormonism*, pp. 148–54.
15. Based on Walter Martin, *The Maze of Mormonism* (Ventura, CA: Regal Books, 1978), pp. 329–32.
16. Jerald and Sandra Tanner, *Major Problems of Mormonism*, pp. 162–65.
17. Natural Museum of Natural History—Smithsonian Statement on the Book of Mormon #8.
18. Jerald and Sandra Tanner, *Major Problems of Mormonism*, p. 162.
19. Cited in John Ankerberg and John Weldon, *Cult Watch: What You Need to Know About Spiritual Deception* (Eugene, OR: Harvest House Publishers, 1991), p. 38.

20. Letter on file at Christian Research Institute.
21. Letter dated February 4, 1982, National Geographic Society; cited in Jerald and Sandra Tanner, *Major Problems in Mormonism*, p. 162.
22. Letter from Dr. Chris Moser of the Mesoamerican Archaeology Study Unit. Available at Christian Research Institute.
23. Dee F. Green, *Dialogue: A Journal of Mormon Thought*, Summer 1969, pp. 76–78.
24. Rob Bowman, "How Mormons Are Defending the Book of Mormon," Part Three, *Christian Research Journal*, Summer 1989, p. 28.

Chapter 7—What Mormons Say About the Bible

1. James E. Talmage, *A Study of the Articles of Faith* (Salt Lake City, UT: The Church of Jesus Christ of Latter-day Saints, 1982), p. 236.
2. It is ironic that the Mormons publish their own edition of the King James Version, make positive statements about the Bible in *Church News* (an official Mormon publication), and even join in promoting national Bible Week-type events. Mormons want to have it both ways; they want to say nice things about the Bible and criticize it at the same time.
3. Robert J. Matthews, "What the Book of Mormon Tells Us About the Bible," Brigham Young University, 26 October 1991.
4. Mark E. Petersen, *As Translated Correctly* (Salt Lake City, UT: Deseret, 1966), p. 4.
5. Petersen, p. 4.
6. Orson Pratt, *Divine Authenticity of the Book of Mormon*, p. 47; cited in Bill McKeever and Eric Johnson, *Questions to Ask Your Mormon Friend* (Minneapolis, MN: Bethany House Publishers, 1994), p. 47.
7. Orson Pratt, *A Series of Pamphlets* (Liverpool, England: n.p., 1851), pp. 70–71.
8. Robert J. Matthews, *A Sure Foundation* (Salt Lake City, UT: Deseret, 1988), p. 165.
9. Jerald and Sandra Tanner, *The Changing World of Mormonism* (Chicago, IL: Moody Press, 1980), p. 367.
10. Pratt, *Divine Authenticity of the Book of Mormon*; cited in McKeever and Johnson, p. 47. For a photocopy, contact Utah Lighthouse Ministry, Box 1884, Salt Lake City, UT, 84110.
11. Bruce R. McConkie, *Mormon Doctrine*, 2d ed. (Salt Lake City, UT: Bookcraft, 1966), p. 47.
12. Wesley P. Walters, "Mormonism," in *Evangelizing the Cults*, ed. Ronald Enroth (Ann Arbor, MI: Servant Publications, 1992), p. 84.
13. Bill McKeever, *Answering Mormons' Questions* (Minneapolis, MN: Bethany House Publishers, 1991), p. 50.
14. McConkie, p. 383.
15. John A. Widtsoe, *Evidences and Reconciliations* (Salt Lake City, UT: Bookcraft, 1987), p. 97f.
16. Anthony A. Hoekema, *The Four Major Cults* (Grand Rapids, MI: Eerdmans, 1978), p. 19.
17. Joseph Smith, Genesis 40:33, *Inspired Version*.
18. David A. Reed and John R. Farkas, *Mormons Answered Verse by Verse* (Grand Rapids, MI: Baker Book House, 1992), p. 29. Note also that Emma Smith kept the *Inspired Version* in her possession. Therefore the RLDS church has that original copy.
19. Note that Deseret bookstores sell the RLDS edition of the Joseph Smith Translation.
20. Reed and Farkas, p. 29.
21. Hoekema, p. 23.

Chapter 8—The Inspiration, Inerrancy, and Authority of the Bible

1. Robert P. Lightner, *Evangelical Theology: A Survey and Review* (Grand Rapids, MI: Baker Book House, 1986), p. 12.
2. Norman L. Geisler and William E. Nix, *A General Introduction to the Bible* (Chicago, IL: Moody Press, 1968), p. 29.
3. Based on Charles C. Ryrie, *What You Should Know About Inerrancy* (Chicago, IL: Moody Press, 1981), p. 40.
4. Ryrie, p. 47.
5. Geisler and Nix, p. 28.
6. Lightner, p. 13.
7. E.J. Young, *Thy Word Is Truth* (Grand Rapids, MI: Eerdmans, 1957), p. 113.
8. *Explaining Inerrancy: A Commentary* (Oakland, CA: International Council on Biblical Inerrancy, 1980), pp. 17–18.
9. One issue that may come up from time to time when talking with Mormons has to do with canonicity—that is, which books belong in the Bible.

    What is *canonicity?* Canonicity refers to the "character of a biblical book which marks it as a part of the canon of Scripture, namely, the divine inspiration and authority which designate a book as part of the rule or standard of faith and practice" (Geisler and Nix, p. 449).

It is critical to note that canonicity is determined by God. Geisler and Nix explain that "a book is not inspired because men made it canonical; it is canonical because God inspired it. . . . Canonicity is determined or established authoritatively by God; it is merely discovered by man. . . . The distinction between God's determination and man's discovery is essential to the correct view of canonicity, and should be drawn carefully....It is God who *regulated* the canon; man merely *recognized* the divine authority God gave to it" (Geisler and Nix, pp. 136–37).

THE INCORRECT VIEW	THE CORRECT VIEW
The church is determiner of canon	The church is discoverer of canon
The church is mother of canon	The church is child of canon
The church is magistrate of canon	The church is minister of canon
The church is regulator of canon	The church is recognizer of canon
The church is judge of canon	The church is witness of canon
The church is master of canon	The church is servant of canon

How did the church "discover" what books belong in the canon of Scripture? Five key principles guided the early fathers in their recognition of which books were canonical (*see* Geisler and Nix, p. 138). These were:

1. Is the book *authoritative*—does it come with God's authority?
2. Is the book *prophetic*—was it written by or approved by a prophet or apostle?
3. Is the book *authentic*—does it tell the truth about the doctrines of God, man (and so forth), agreeing with previous books already known to be Scripture?
4. Is the book *dynamic*—does it have life-transforming power?
5. Was the book *received*—was it read and widely used by God's people and churches?

By following such principles, and under the guidance of the Holy Spirit, the 66 books in our present Bible were recognized as the books that God *determined* to be canonical.

Of course, as noted in the chapter, many books were recognized as belonging in the canon even during New Testament days. Paul's writings, for example, were recognized as Scripture by the apostle Peter (2 Peter 3:16). Luke's Gospel was recognized as Scripture within just three years of its being written (1 Timothy 5:18; cf. Deuteronomy 25:4; Luke 10:7). If you are interested in doing a detailed study of canonicity, excellent materials are available. A good place to start is Geisler and Nix's *General Introduction to the Bible* (pp. 127–207).

10. Based on Norman L. Geisler, "What Jesus Affirmed About the Bible," class notes from course on Bibliology, Dallas Theological Seminary.
11. Decision of the Synod of 1961.
12. Dan Story, *Defending Your Faith: How to Answer the Tough Questions* (Nashville, TN: Thomas Nelson Publishers, 1992), p. 47.
13. Nelson Glueck, *Rivers in the Desert* (Philadelphia, PA: Jewish Publications Society of America, 1969), p. 31.
14. Donald J. Wiseman, "Archaeological Confirmation of the Old Testament"; in Norman L. Geisler, *Christian Apologetics* (Grand Rapids, MI: Baker Book House, 1976), p. 322.
15. William F. Albright; cited in Josh McDowell, *Evidence That Demands a Verdict* (San Bernardino, CA: Campus Crusade for Christ, 1972), p. 68.
16. Gary R. Habermas, *Ancient Evidence for the Life of Jesus* (Nashville, TN: Thomas Nelson Publishers, 1984), p. 65.
17. Habermas, p. 66.
18. Geisler and Nix, p. 186.
19. Geisler and Nix, p. 190.
20. Geisler and Nix, p. 190.
21. Geisler and Nix, p. 190.
22. Story, p. 45.
23. Lightner, p. 16.
24. *Explaining Hermeneutics: A Commentary*, ed. Norman L. Geisler, with Exposition by J.I. Packer (Oakland, CA: International Council on Biblical Inerrancy, 1983), p. 3.
25. Rene Pache, *The Inspiration and Authority of Scripture* (Chicago, IL: Moody Press, 1978), p. 305.

Chapter 9—Manuscript Support for the Bible's Reliability

1. Norman L. Geisler and William E. Nix, *A General Introduction to the Bible* (Chicago, IL: Moody Press, 1968).
2. *See* Geisler and Nix for a thorough discussion of this.

404

3. Rene Pache, *The Inspiration and Authority of Scripture* (Chicago, IL: Moody Press, 1978), p. 193.
4. John A. Widtsoe, *Evidences and Reconciliations* (Salt Lake City, UT: Bookcraft, 1943), pp. 97–101.
5. Geisler and Nix, p. 49.
6. Pache, p. 193.
7. *Explaining Inerrancy: A Commentary* (Oakland, CA: International Council on Biblical Inerrancy, 1980), p. 24.
8. Anthony Hoekema, *The Four Major Cults* (Grand Rapids, MI: Eerdmans, 1978), pp. 30–31.
9. F.F. Bruce, *The New Testament Documents: Are They Reliable?* (Downers Grove, IL: InterVarsity Press, 1984), p. 19.
10. Norman L. Geisler, *Christian Apologetics* (Grand Rapids, MI: Baker Book House, 1976), p. 306.
11. Pache, p. 192.
12. Pache, p. 193.
13. This chart is adapted from Geisler, *Christian Apologetics*, p. 307.
14. Geisler, *Christian Apologetics*, p. 308.
15. Geisler, *Christian Apologetics*, p. 308.
16. Dan Story, *Defending Your Faith: How to Answer the Tough Questions* (Nashville, TN: Thomas Nelson Publishers, 1992), pp. 38–39.
17. Geisler and Nix, p. 357.
18. Story, p. 35.
19. Gleason Archer, *A Survey of Old Testament Introduction* (Chicago, IL: Moody Press, 1964), p. 19.
20. Story, p. 35.
21. Bill McKeever and Eric Johnson, *Questions to Ask Your Mormon Friend* (Minneapolis, MN: Bethany House Publishers, 1994), p. 50.
22. Jerald and Sandra Tanner, *The Changing World of Mormonism* (Chicago, IL: Moody Press, 1980), p. 372.
23. Story, p. 35; cf. Josh McDowell, *Evidence That Demands a Verdict* (San Bernardino, CA: Campus Crusade for Christ, 1972), p. 22.
24. The Westminster Confession.
25. Greg L. Bahnsen, "The Inerrancy of the Autographa," in *Inerrancy*, ed. Norman L. Geisler (Grand Rapids, MI: Zondervan Publishing House, 1980), p. 161.
26. Bahnsen, p. 169.

Chapter 10—Rightly Interpreting the Bible

1. Robert A. Traina, *Methodical Bible Study* (Wilmore, KY: Asbury Theological Seminary, 1952), p. 5.
2. Charles Ryrie, *Basic Theology* (Wheaton, IL: Victor Books, 1986), p. 113.
3. Norman L. Geisler, *Explaining Hermeneutics: A Commentary*, with Exposition by J.I. Packer (Oakland, CA: International Council on Biblical Inerrancy, 1983), p. 7.
4. Paul Enns, *Approaching God* (Chicago, IL: Moody Press, 1991), March 20.
5. *See* Ron Rhodes, *The New Age Movement*, ed. Alan Gomes (Grand Rapids, MI: Zondervan Publishing House, 1995).
6. Bernard Ramm, *Protestant Bible Interpretation* (Grand Rapids, MI: Baker Book House, 1978), p. 105.
7. J.I. Packer, *"Fundamentalism" and the Word of God* (Grand Rapids, MI: Eerdmans, 1958), p. 102.
8. "The Westminster Confession" in Bruce Milne, *Know the Truth* (Downers Grove, IL: InterVarsity Press, 1982), p. 46.
9. Geisler, p. 13.
10. Geisler, p. 31.
11. Geisler, p. 11.
12. Benjamin B. Warfield, *Biblical and Theological Studies* (Phillipsburg, NJ: Presbyterian and Reformed Publishing Co., 1968), p. 30.
13. Robert P. Lightner, *Evangelical Theology* (Grand Rapids, MI: Baker Book House, 1986), p. 22.
14. This chart is based on the class notes of Norman L. Geisler, "Bibliology," Dallas Theological Seminary.
15. Enns, March 3.
16. For example, Roy B. Zuck, "The Role of the Holy Spirit in Hermeneutics," *Bibliotheca Sacra* 141 (April–June 1984):120–30.
17. James W. Sire, *Scripture Twisting: Twenty Ways the Cults Misread the Bible* (Downers Grove, IL: InterVarsity Press, 1980), p. 17.
18. Zuck, p. 126.
19. Ramm, p. 14.
20. Ramm, p. 18.
21. Robert P. Lightner, *The Saviour and the Scriptures* (Grand Rapids, MI: Baker Book House, 1966), p. 30.
22. John A. Widtsoe, *Evidences and Reconciliations* (Salt Lake City, UT: Bookcraft, 1943), pp. 18–19.
23. It is possible that some Mormons may appeal to Matthew 13 in an attempt to refute the idea that Jesus *always* taught openly and with clarity. In Matthew 13, Jesus is portrayed as being in front of a mixed multitude comprised of both believers and unbelievers. He did not attempt to separate the believers from the unbelievers and then instruct only the believers. Rather, He constructed His teaching in such a way that believers would understand what He said but unbelievers *would not*—and He did this by using parables.

After teaching one such parable, a disciple asked Jesus, "Why speakest thou unto them in parables?" (Matthew 13:10). Jesus answered, "Because it is given unto you [believers] to know the mysteries of the kingdom of heaven, but to them [unbelievers] it is not given" (verse 11, inserts added). What did Jesus mean by the word "secrets" in this verse?

The Greek word for "secret"simply means "mystery," and is even translated this way in the New American Standard Bible. A mystery, in the biblical sense, is a truth that cannot be discerned simply by human investigation, but requires special revelation from God. Generally speaking, a mystery refers to a truth that was unknown to people living in Old Testament times but is now revealed to humankind by God (see Matthew 13:17 and Colossians 1:26). In Matthew 13, Jesus provides information to believers about the kingdom of heaven—information that has never been revealed before.

Some people have wondered why Jesus presented His parabolic teaching so that believers could understand His teaching but unbelievers could not. The backdrop to this is that the disciples, having responded favorably to Jesus' teaching and placed their faith in Him, already knew much truth about the Messiah. Careful reflection on Jesus' parables would enlighten them even further.

However, hardened unbelievers who had willfully and persistently refused Jesus' previous teachings—such as those set forth in the Sermon on the Mount—were prevented from understanding the parables. Jesus was apparently following an injunction He provided earlier in the Sermon on the Mount: "Do not give dogs what is sacred; do not throw your pearls to pigs" (Matthew 7:6). Yet there is grace even here. For, as many scholars have noted, it is possible that Jesus may have prevented unbelievers from understanding the parables because He did not want to add more responsibility to them by imparting new truth for which they would be held accountable.

That Jesus wanted believers to understand His parables is evident in the fact that He carefully interpreted two of them for the disciples—the parables of the sower (Matthew 13:3–9) and the tares (13:24–30). He did this not only to clarify their meaning, but also to help believers know the proper method to use in interpreting the other parables. The fact that Christ did not interpret His subsequent parables indicates that He fully expected believers to understand what He taught by following the methodology He illustrated for them.

24. *The Bible Knowledge Commentary*, New Testament, eds. John F. Walvoord and Roy B. Zuck (Wheaton, IL: Victor Books, 1983), p. 757.

Chapter 11—The Alleged Migration to Ancient America

1. Ether 3:34.
2. Ether 1:1. Ether had inscribed the history on 24 plates, which were found by the people of Limhi and abridged by Moroni.
3. 2 Nephi 5:21.
4. James E. Talmage, *A Study of the Articles of Faith* (Salt Lake City, UT: The Church of Jesus Christ of Latter-day Saints, 1977), p. 261; cf. Bruce R. McConkie, *Mormon Doctrine* (Salt Lake City, UT: Bookcraft, 1966), p. 98.
5. Francis Brown, S.R. Driver, and Charles A. Briggs, *A Hebrew and English Lexicon of the Old Testament* (Oxford: Clarendon Press, 1980), p. 76.
6. Joseph Fielding Smith, *Doctrines of Salvation* (Salt Lake City, UT: Bookcraft, 1975), 3:214.
7. David A. Reed and John R. Farkas, *Mormons Answered Verse by Verse* (Grand Rapids, MI: Baker Book House, 1993), p. 68.
8. Craig S. Keener, *The IVP Bible Background Commentary* (Downers Grove, IL: InterVarsity Press, 1993), p. 88.
9. Smith, *Doctrines of Salvation*, 3:214; cf. 3 Nephi 15:11–24.
10. See Leon Morris, *The Gospel According to John* (Grand Rapids, MI: Eerdmans, 1987), p. 512; cf. F.F. Bruce, *The Gospel of John* (London: Pickering, 1983), pp. 227–28.
11. Cited in John Ankerberg and John Weldon, *Cult Watch: What You Need to Know About Spiritual Deception* (Eugene, OR: Harvest House Publishers, 1991), p. 38.
12. Michael Coe, *Biblical Archaeology Review*, September/October 1985; cited in Bill McKeever, *Answering Mormons' Questions* (Minneapolis, MN: Bethany House Publishers, 1991), p. 79.

Chapter 12—The "Restoration" of the Aaronic and Melchizedek Priesthoods

1. Doctrine and Covenants (Salt Lake City, UT: The Church of Jesus Christ of Latter-day Saints, 1990), 107:1, 6, 10.
2. Joseph Smith, *History of the Church of Jesus Christ of Latter-day Saints* (Salt Lake City, UT: Deseret Book Company, 1973), 1:69–70.
3. Smith, 1:69–70.
4. Bruce R. McConkie, *Mormon Doctrine* (Salt Lake City, UT: Bookcraft, 1966), pp. 393–94.
5. McConkie, p. 478.
6. Joseph Fielding Smith, ed., *Teachings of the Prophet Joseph Smith* (Salt Lake City, UT: Deseret Book Company, 1977), p. 158.

7. Doctrine and Covenants 84:19–22.
8. McConkie, p. 481.
9. McConkie, p. 480.
10. James E. Talmage, *A Study of the Articles of Faith* (Salt Lake City, UT: The Church of Jesus Christ of Latter-day Saints, 1977), p. 204.
11. McConkie, p. 478.
12. Mormons do not have to hold all these positions to go on to the Melchizedek priesthood.
13. *Gospel Principles* (Salt Lake City, UT: The Church of Jesus Christ of Latter-day Saints, 1986), pp. 81–85.
14. There is, in effect, just one priesthood. The book *Gospel Principles* tells us that "the lesser [Aaronic] priesthood is an appendage to the Melchizedek priesthood" (p. 79).
15. *See* McConkie, pp. 69–72.
16. Doctrine and Covenants 107:2–4.
17. Doctrine and Covenants 107:2–4.
18. McConkie, p. 474.
19. *Webster's New International Dictionary of the English Language*, 2d ed.; cited in John F. Walvoord, *Jesus Christ Our Lord* (Chicago, IL: Moody Press, 1980), p. 62.
20. Donald K. Campbell, "The Interpretation of Types," *Bibliotheca Sacra* (July 1955), p. 250.
21. Walvoord, p. 62; cf. Lewis Sperry Chafer, *Systematic Theology*, 8 vols. (Dallas, TX: Dallas Theological Seminary, 1948), 1:30.
22. Paul Lee Tan, *The Interpretation of Prophecy* (Rockville, MD: Assurance Publishers, 1974), p. 168.
23. A. Berkeley Mickelsen, *Interpreting the Bible* (Grand Rapids, MI: Eerdmans, 1977), p. 237.
24. F.F. Bruce, *The Epistle to the Hebrews* (Grand Rapids, MI: Eerdmans, 1979), pp. 137–38.
25. Gleason Archer, *Encyclopedia of Bible Difficulties* (Grand Rapids, MI: Zondervan Publishing House, 1982), pp. 91–92.
26. Archer, pp. 91–92.
27. Walter Martin, *The Kingdom of the Cults* (Minneapolis, MN: Bethany House Publishers, 1985), p. 198.
28. McConkie, p. 476.
29. *Teachings*, p. 157–58, 323; cited in McConkie, p. 477.
30. McConkie, p. 477.
31. Doctrine and Covenants 84:26–28.
32. *The Bible Knowledge Commentary*, Old Testament, eds. John F. Walvoord and Roy B. Zuck (Wheaton, IL: Victor Books, 1985), p. 874.
33. Ruth Tucker, *Another Gospel: Alternative Religions and the New Age Movement* (Grand Rapids, MI: Zondervan Publishing House, 1989), p. 75.
34. McConkie, 1958 edition, p. 477.
35. *See* Tucker, p. 76. Also note that a new temple had been built in Brazil—and since many Brazilians have some Negro blood, there were not many "faithful Mormons" who could go into the temple. *See* Mark L. Groves, "The Mormon Priesthood Revelation and the Sao Paulo, Brazil Temple," *Dialogue: A Journal of Mormon Thought*, vol. 23, Spring 1990, pp. 39–53.
36. Martin, p. 198.
37. Joseph Thayer; cited in Martin, p. 198. Note, however, that *Vine's Expository Dictionary of Biblical Words* says this meaning is not to be preferred. Vine prefers "unalterable, inviolable." (*Vine's Expository Dictionary of Biblical Words*, eds. W.E. Vine, Merrill F. Unger, and William White [Nashville, TN: Thomas Nelson Publishers, 1985], p. 649.)
38. *Theological Dictionary of the New Testament*, eds. Gerhard Kittel and Gerhard Friedrich (Grand Rapids, MI: Eerdmans, 1985), p. 772.
39. *The Complete Word Study Dictionary*, ed. Spiros Zodhiates (Chattanooga, TN: AMG Publishers, 1992), p. 204.
40. LeGrand Richards, *A Marvelous Work and a Wonder* (Salt Lake City, UT: Deseret Book Company, 1973), p. 82.
41. David A. Reed and John R. Farkas, *Mormons Answered Verse by Verse* (Grand Rapids, MI: Baker Book House, 1993), p. 78.
42. Bill McKeever and Eric Johnson, *Questions to Ask Your Mormon Friend* (Minneapolis, MN: Bethany House Publishers, 1994), p. 89.
43. *Duties and Blessings of the Priesthood A*, p. 1, emphasis added; cited in Mark J. Cares, *Speaking the Truth in Love to Mormons* (Milwaukee, WI: Northwestern Publishing House, 1993), p. 104.
44. *Duties and Blessings of the Priesthood B*, p. 19, emphasis added; cited in Cares, p. 104.
45. Bruce, pp. 92–93.
46. Marian Bodine, "Witnessing Tips," *Forward*, Spring-Summer 1986), p. 7.
47. *See* Jerald and Sandra Tanner, *The Case Against Mormonism*, vol. 2 (Salt Lake City, UT: Utah Lighthouse Ministry, 1967), pp. 113–44.
48. Doctrines of Salvation 3:247.
49. Alma 10:3.
50. Genesis 41:45,50–51.
51. *The International Standard Bible Encyclopedia* (Grand Rapids, MI: Eerdmans, 1976), 1:266.
52. Genesis 39:1.

Chapter 13—The Mormon Doctrine of God—Part1: Does God Have a Human Body?

1. Joseph Smith, *History of the Church*, 6:305.
2. Smith, *History of the Church*, 6:306.
3. Milton R. Hunter, *The Gospel Through the Ages* (Salt Lake City, UT: Deseret Book Co., 1958), p. 104.
4. Brigham Young, *Journal of Discourses* (London: Latter-day Saints' Book Depot, 1854–56), 1:123.
5. Bruce R. McConkie, *Mormon Doctrine* (Salt Lake City, UT: Bookcraft, 1966), p. 278.
6. Joseph Smith; cited in McConkie, p. 321.
7. James E. Talmage, *A Study of the Articles of Faith* (Salt Lake City, UT: The Church of Jesus Christ of Latter-day Saints, 1977), p. 48.
8. McConkie, p. 318.
9. Note that in Mormon theology the preincarnate Christ had no physical body, nor does the "Holy Ghost."
10. Joseph Fielding Smith, *Doctrines of Salvation* (Salt Lake City, UT: Bookcraft, 1975), 1:3.
11. Donald Grey Barnhouse, *Genesis: A Devotional Exposition* (Grand Rapids, MI: Zondervan Publishing House, 1973), p. 12.
12. *The Bible Knowledge Commentary*, Old Testament, eds. John F. Walvoord and Roy B. Zuck (Wheaton, IL: Victor Books, 1985), p. 29.
13. LeGrand Richards, *A Marvelous Work and a Wonder* (Salt Lake City, UT: Deseret, 1978), p. 16.
14. Norman Geisler and Thomas Howe, *When Critics Ask* (Wheaton, IL: Victor Books, 1992), p. 58.
15. *Vine's Expository Dictionary of Biblical Words*, eds. W.E. Vine, Merrill F. Unger, and William White (Nashville, TN: Thomas Nelson Publishers, 1985), p. 75.
16. *The Bible Knowledge Commentary*, p. 157.
17. Walter C. Kaiser, *Hard Sayings of the Old Testament* (Downers Grove, IL: InterVarsity Press, 1988), p. 83.
18. Kaiser, p. 83
19. Kaiser, p. 84.
20. Kaiser, p. 84.
21. Smith, *Doctrines of Salvation*, 1:27.
22. Doctrine and Covenants Salt Lake City, UT: The Church of Jesus Christ of Latter-day Saints, 1990), 84:21–22.
23. Talmage, p. 41.
24. Talmage, p. 41.
25. Talmage, p. 42.
26. Charles C. Ryrie, *The Ryrie Study Bible* (Chicago, IL: Moody Press, 1986), p. 1667.
27. Ray C. Stedman, *Hebrews* (Downers Grove, IL: InterVarsity Press, 1992), p. 24.
28. David A. Reed and John R. Farkas, *Mormons Answered Verse by Verse* (Grand Rapids, MI: Baker Book House, 1993), p. 97.
29. Gerald F. Hawthorne, "Hebrews," in *International Bible Commentary*, ed. F.F. Bruce (Grand Rapids, MI: Zondervan Publishing House, 1979), p. 1506.
30. William R. Newell, *Hebrews: Verse by Verse* (Chicago, IL: Moody Press, 1947), p. 11.
31. *See* Norman L. Geisler, "Colossians," in *The Bible Knowledge Commentary*, p. 672.
32. Curtis Vaughan, "Colossians," in *The Expositor's Bible Commentary*, vol. 11, ed. Frank E. Gaebelein (Grand Rapids, MI: Zondervan Publishing House, 1978), p. 182.
33. In Joseph Smith's translation, the traditional John 1:18 is labeled John 1:19.
34. Robert P. Lightner, *The God of the Bible* (Grand Rapids, MI: Baker Book House, 1978), p. 55.
35. Ron Rhodes, *Christ Before the Manger: The Life and Times of the Preincarnate Christ* (Grand Rapids, MI: Baker Book House, 1991).
36. F.F. Bruce, *The Gospel of John* (London: Pickering, 1983), p. 44.
37. Moroni 8:18.

Chapter 14—The Mormon Doctrine of God—Part 2: The Plurality of Gods

1. Bruce R. McConkie, *Mormon Doctrine* (Salt Lake City, UT: Bookcraft, 1966), p. 319.
2. McConkie, p. 319.
3. McConkie, p. 576.
4. Joseph Fielding Smith, ed., *Teachings of the Prophet Joseph Smith* (Salt Lake City, UT: Deseret Book Company, 1977), p. 370.
5. Joseph Fielding Smith, *Doctrines of Salvation* (Salt Lake City, UT: Bookcraft, 1975), 1:98.
6. Spencer W. Kimball, *The Ensign*, Salt Lake City, November 1975, p. 80.
7. Brigham Young, in *Discourses of Brigham Young*, arranged by John A. Widtsoe (Salt Lake City, UT: Deseret Book Company, 1954), pp. 22–23.
8. Orson Pratt, *Journal of Discourses* (London: Latter-day Saint's Book Depot, 1854–56), 2:345.
9. For an excellent critique of this aspect of the Mormon concept of God, *see* Francis J. Beckwith, "Philosophical Problems with the Mormon Concept of God," *Christian Research Journal*, Spring 1992, pp. 24–29.
10. Smith, ed., *Teachings of the Prophet Joseph Smith*, pp. 370, 373; cited in McConkie, p. 322.

11. Smith, *Doctrines of Salvation*, 1:12.
12. James E. Talmage, *A Study of the Articles of Faith* (Salt Lake City, UT: The Church of Jesus Christ of Latter-day Saints, 1977), p. 443.
13. Joseph Fielding Smith, *Man: His Origin and Destiny* (Salt Lake City, UT), p. 335.
14. Milton R. Hunter, *The Gospel Through the Ages* (Salt Lake City, UT: Deseret Publishing Company, 1958), p. 98.
15. Orson Pratt, *The Seer* (Washington, D.C.: n.p., 1853–54), pp. 37–38.
16. Smith, ed., *Teachings of the Prophet Joseph Smith*, p. 371.
17. Smith, ed., *Teachings of the Prophet Joseph Smith*, pp. 370, 372.
18. Joseph Smith, *Journal of Discourses*, 6:5; Smith, ed., *Teachings of the Prophet Joseph Smith*, p. 349; Joseph Smith, *History of the Church of Jesus Christ of Latter-day Saints* (Salt Lake City, UT: Deseret Book Company, 1973), 6:308.
19. Abraham 4:1–2; cf. verses 3–31.
20. Abraham 4:26,27.
21. Norman Geisler and Thomas Howe, *When Critics Ask* (Wheaton, IL: Victor Books, 1992), p. 31.
22. Geisler and Howe, p. 31.
23. Geisler and Howe, p. 31.
24. McConkie, p. 321.
25. Walter C. Kaiser, *Hard Sayings of the Old Testament* (Downers Grove, IL: InterVarsity Press, 1988), p. 167.
26. Gleason Archer, *Encyclopedia of Bible Difficulties* (Grand Rapids, MI: Zondervan Publishing House, 1982), p. 373.
27. F.F. Bruce, *The Gospel of John* (London: Pickering, 1983), p. 234.
28. See *The New Treasury of Scripture Knowledge*, ed. Jerome H. Smith (Nashville, TN: Thomas Nelson Publishers, 1992), p. 645.
29. Robert M. Bowman, Jr., "The Biblical Basis of the Doctrine of the Trinity: An Outline Study" (Irvine, CA: Christian Research Institute, n.d.), p. 3; cf. Geisler and Howe, p. 417.
30. Talmage, pp. 39–40.
31. *The New Treasury of Scripture Knowledge*, pp. 1095–96.
32. Benjamin B. Warfield, *The Person and Work of Christ* (Philadelphia, PA: Presbyterian and Reformed Publishing Co., 1950), p. 66.
33. Robert L. Reymond, *Jesus: Divine Messiah* (Phillipsburg, NJ: Presbyterian and Reformed Publishing Co., 1990), p. 84.
34. Talmage, p. 40.
35. Charles C. Ryrie, *The Ryrie Study Bible* (Chicago, IL: Moody Press, 1986), p. 1667.
36. Ray C. Stedman, *Hebrews* (Downers Grove, IL: InterVarsity Press, 1992), p. 24.
37. Joseph Fielding Smith, *Teachings of the Prophet Joseph Smith*, p. 371; cited in McConkie, p. 577.
38. Joseph Fielding Smith, *Teachings of the Prophet Joseph Smith*, pp. 370, 372.
39. McConkie, p. 579.
40. David A. Reed and John R. Farkas, *Mormons Answered Verse by Verse* (Grand Rapids, MI: Baker Book House, 1993), pp. 83–84.
41. *See* Reed and Farkas, p. 84.

Chapter 15—The Person of Jesus Christ in Mormonism

1. Gilbert W. Scharffs, *The Truth About "The God Makers"* (Salt Lake City, UT: Publishers Press, 1986), pp. 6–20.
2. Robert M. Bowman, "How Mormons Are Defending Mormon Doctrine," *Christian Research Journal*, Fall 1989, p. 24.
3. Bruce R. McConkie, *Mormon Doctrine* (Salt Lake City, UT: Bookcraft, 1966), p. 129.
4. *The Life and Teaching of Jesus & His Apostles*, p. 15; cited in Mark J. Cares, *Speaking the Truth in Love to Mormons* (Milwaukee, WI: Northwestern Publishing House, 1993), p. 78.
5. Note that the *pre-existence* is known as our "First Estate"; *mortality* is known as our "Second Estate."
6. "Bible Dictionary," in *The Holy Bible, Authorized King James Version with Explanatory Notes and Cross References to the Standard Works of the Church of Jesus Christ of Latter-day Saints* (Salt Lake City, UT: The Church of Jesus Christ of Latter-day Saints, 1990).
7. McConkie, pp. 546–47.
8. McConkie, p. 742.
9. Orson Pratt, *The Seer* (Washington, D.C.: n.p., 1853–54), pp. 158–59.
10. James E. Talmage, *A Study of the Articles of Faith* (Salt Lake City, UT: The Church of Jesus Christ of Latter-day Saints, 1977), p. 466.
11. Ezra Taft Benson, *The Teachings of Ezra Taft Benson* (Salt Lake City, UT: Bookcraft, 1988), p. 7.
12. Joseph Fielding Smith, *Doctrines of Salvation* (Salt Lake City, UT: Bookcraft, 1975), 1:18–20.
13. Brigham Young, *Deseret News*, October 10, 1866; cited in Jerald and Sandra Tanner, *The Changing World of Mormonism* (Chicago, IL: Moody Press, 1981), p. 180.
14. McConkie, p. 745.

15. Talmage, *A Study of the Articles of Faith*, pp. 472–73.
16. *Gospel Principles* (Salt Lake City, UT: The Church of Jesus Christ of Latter-day Saints, 1986), p. 9.
17. Doctrine and Covenants (Salt Lake City, UT: The Church of Jesus Christ of Latter-day Saints, 1990), 93:21–23.
18. Talmage, *A Study of the Articles of Faith*, p. 471.
19. Doctrine and Covenants, 93:21.
20. John Henry Evans, *An American Prophet* (New York, NY: Macmillan, 1933), p. 241.
21. McConkie, p. 193.
22. Orson Hyde, *Journal of Discourses*, 13:259.
23. *Doctrines of Salvation*, 2:65.
24. Bruce McConkie, devotional at Brigham Young University, March 2, 1982; cited in Bill McKeever, *Answering Mormons' Questions* (Minneapolis, MN: Bethany House Publishers, 1991), p. 61.
25. McConkie, *Mormon Doctrine*, p. 587.
26. As well, the Mormons' Holy Ghost somehow enjoys godhood status without now or ever passing through mortality or possessing a physical body.
27. John Eadie, *A Commentary on the Greek Text of the Epistle of Paul to the Colossians* (Grand Rapids, MI: Baker Book House, 1979), p. 51.
28. *See* Marvin R. Vincent, *Word Studies in the New Testament*, vol. 3 (Grand Rapids, MI: Eerdmans, 1975), pp. 469–70; Kenneth S. Wuest, *Wuest's Word Studies*, vol. 1 (Grand Rapids, MI: Eerdmans, 1973), p. 184.
29. "Bible Dictionary," p. 681.
30. Charles C. Ryrie, *Basic Theology* (Wheaton, IL: Victor Books, 1986), p. 46.
31. "Bible Dictionary," p. 681.
32. Robert L. Reymond, *Jesus, Divine Messiah: The New Testament Witness* (Phillipsburg, NJ: Presbyterian and Reformed Publishing Co., 1990), p. 287.
33. *Gospel Principles*, p. 9.
34. David A. Reed and John R. Farkas, *Mormons Answered Verse by Verse* (Grand Rapids, MI: Baker Book House, 1993), p. 53.
35. Leon Morris, *The Gospel According to John* (Grand Rapids, MI: Eerdmans, 1987), p. 73; *see also* Rob Bowman, *Jehovah's Witnesses, Jesus Christ, and the Gospel of John* (Grand Rapids, MI: Baker Book House, 1989), pp. 21–22.
36. Harold B. Kuhn, "Creation," in *Basic Christian Doctrines*, ed. Carl F. Henry (Grand Rapids, MI: Baker Book House, 1983), p. 61.
37. Louis Berkhof, *Manual of Christian Doctrine* (Grand Rapids, MI: Eerdmans, 1983), p. 996.
38. R.C.H. Lenski, *The Interpretation of St. John's Gospel* (Minneapolis, MN: Augsburg Publishing House, 1961), p. 27.
39. Morris, p. 73.
40. Morris, p. 77.
41. Pratt, *The Seer*, p. 159.
42. *Journal of Discourses*, 1:50–51.
43. Ron Rhodes, *Christ Before the Manger: The Life and Times of the Preincarnate Christ* (Grand Rapids, MI: Baker Book House, 1992), pp. 160–65.
44. David F. Wells, *The Person of Christ* (Westchester, IL: Crossway Books, 1984), pp. 64–65.
45. Ryrie, p. 37.
46. Ryrie, p. 37.
47. John F. Walvoord, *Jesus Christ Our Lord* (Chicago, IL: Moody Press, 1980), p. 30.

Chapter 16—The Mormon Doctrine of Man: Were Humans Premortal Spirits?

1. The spirits were "organized" from intelligence matter.
2. Bruce R. McConkie, *Mormon Doctrine* (Salt Lake City, UT: Bookcraft, 1966), p. 589.
3. McConkie, p. 589.
4. McConkie, p. 589.
5. McConkie, pp. 526–28, 1966 edition. *See* the CRI tract "The Mormon church and the African" for more information.
6. McConkie, pp. 526–28, 1966 edition.
7. Mark E. Petersen, "Race Problems—As They Affect the Church," Address at the Convention of Teachers of Religion on the College Level, delivered at Brigham Young University, Provo, Utah, August 27, 1954; cited in Jerald and Sandra Tanner, *The Changing World of Mormonism* (Chicago, IL: Moody Press, 1981), p. 294.
8. Joseph Fielding Smith, *Doctrines of Salvation* (Salt Lake City, UT: Bookcraft, 1975), 1:61.
9. McConkie, p. 590.
10. Joseph Fielding Smith, *The Life and Teaching of Jesus & His Apostles*, p. 350; cited in Mark J. Cares, *Speaking the Truth in Love to Mormons* (Milwaukee, WI: Northwestern Publishing House, 1993), p. 31.
11. Mormons say that some spirits were "dammed" (as opposed to "damned") because their progress was forever stopped by denying them earthly tabernacles.

410

12. *Gospel Principles* (Salt Lake City, UT: The Church of Jesus Christ of Latter-day Saints, 1986), p. 17.
13. James E. Talmage, *A Study of the Articles of Faith* (Salt Lake City, UT: The Church of Jesus Christ of Latter-day Saints, 1977), p. 197.
14. Richard LeGrand, *A Marvelous Work and a Wonder* (Salt Lake City, UT: Deseret Book Company, 1979), p. 39.
15. Norman Geisler and Thomas Howe, *When Critics Ask* (Wheaton, IL: Victor Books, 1992), p. 275.
16. *The Bible Knowledge Commentary*, Old Testament, eds. John F. Walvoord and Roy B. Zuck (Wheaton, IL: Victor Books, 1985), p. 1130.
17. Geisler and Howe, p. 275.
18. Talmage, p. 197.
19. Richards, p. 39; cf. Book of Moses 3:5.
20. *The New International Dictionary of New Testament Theology*, ed. Colin Brown, vol. 2 (Grand Rapids, MI: Zondervan Publishing House, 1979), p. 45.
21. McConkie, p. 589.
22. Stanley D. Toussaint, *The Bible Knowledge Commentary*, New Testament, eds. John F. Walvoord and Roy B. Zuck (Wheaton, IL: Victor Books, 1989), p. 404.
23. McConkie, p. 589.

Chapter 17—Salvation in Mormonism—Part 1: Understanding Mormon Terminology

1. Bruce R. McConkie, *Mormon Doctrine* (Salt Lake City, UT: Bookcraft, 1966), p. 669, insert added.
2. Joseph Fielding Smith, *Doctrines of Salvation* (Salt Lake City, UT: Bookcraft, 1975), 1:134.
3. McConkie, p. 670.
4. Brigham Young, *Journal of Discourses* (London: Latter-day Saint's Book Depot, 1854–56), 3:93.
5. Doctrine and Covenants (Salt Lake City, UT: The Church of Jesus Christ of Latter-day Saints, 1990), 132:19–20.
6. *Gospel Principles* (Salt Lake City, UT: The Church of Jesus Christ of Latter-day Saints, 1986), p. 290.
7. Joseph Fielding Smith, *The Life and Teachings of Jesus and His Apostles* (Salt Lake City, UT: The Church of Jesus Christ of Latter-day Saints, n.d.), p. 327.
8. Joseph Fielding Smith, *The Way to Perfection* (Salt Lake City, UT: Deseret, 1970), p. 7.
9. Smith, *The Life and Teachings of Jesus and His Apostles*, p. 292.
10. Louis A. Barbieri, *The Bible Knowledge Commentary*, New Testament, eds. John F. Walvoord and Roy B. Zuck (Wheaton, IL: Victor Books, 1989), p. 32.
11. Mark J. Cares, *Speaking the Truth in Love to Mormons* (Milwaukee, WI: Northwestern Publishing House, 1993), p. 180.
12. Cares, p. 180.
13. Joseph Fielding Smith, ed., *Teachings of the Prophet Joseph Smith* (Salt Lake City, UT: Deseret Book Company, 1977), pp. 356–57.
14. *Teachings of the Prophet Joseph Smith*, pp. 345–46; in *Gospel Principles*, p. 293.
15. Smith, *Doctrines of Salvation*, 1:12.
16. McConkie, p. 237.
17. John J. Davis, *Moses and the Gods of Egypt* (Grand Rapids, MI: Baker Book House, 1986), p. 81.

Chapter 18—Salvation in Mormonism—Part 2: Premortality, Mortality, and Postmortality

1. *Gospel Principles* (Salt Lake City, UT: Church of Jesus Christ of Latter-day Saints, 1985), p. 9.
2. Spencer W. Kimball, quoted in *Doctrines of the Gospel* (Salt Lake City, UT: Church of Jesus Christ of Latter-day Saints, 1986), p. 52.
3. *Gospel Principles*, p. 17.
4. *Gospel Principles*, pp. 292–93.
5. Bruce R. McConkie, *Mormon Doctrine* (Salt Lake City, UT: Bookcraft, 1966), p. 84.
6. Orson Pratt, *The Seer* (Washington, D.C.: n.p., 1853–54), p. 255.
7. James E. Talmage, *A Study of the Articles of Faith* (Salt Lake City, UT: The Church of Jesus Christ of Latter-day Saints, 1977), p. 122.
8. James Bjornstad, "At What Price Success? The Boston (Church of Christ) Movement," *Christian Research Journal*, Winter 1993, reprint, Christian Research Institute, p. 4.
9. Talmage, p. 129.
10. *The Wycliffe Bible Commentary*, eds. Charles F. Pfeiffer and Everett F. Harrison (Chicago, IL: Moody Press, 1974), p. 1078.
11. J. Dwight Pentecost, *The Words and Works of Jesus Christ* (Grand Rapids, MI: Zondervan Publishing House, 1982), p. 125.
12. Other evangelicals interpret this passage differently. Some believe the word "and" in John 3:5 should be translated "even": "Except a man be born of water [even] the Spirit, he cannot enter into the kingdom of God." This

would mean that *water* and *spirit* are two ways of saying the same thing. In support of this view, Jesus used the word "water" to mean "spirit" in John 4:10,14. This is also the case in John 7:37–39.

13. Talmage, p. 129.

14. *Deseret News*, Church Section, 14 April 1973, p. 14.

15. Milton R. Hunter, *The Gospel Through the Ages* (Salt Lake City, UT: Stevens and Wallis, Inc., 1945), p. 166.

16. *Deseret News*, Church Section, p. 11; in Jerry and Marian Bodine, *Witnessing to the Mormons* (Irvine, CA: n.p., 1978), p. 14.

17. Brigham Young, *Journal of Discourses* (London: Latter-day Saint's Book Depot, 1854–56), 2:4.

18. McConkie, p. 330.

19. Talmage, p. 108.

20. Mark J. Cares, *Speaking the Truth in Love to Mormons* (Milwaukee, WI: Northwestern Publishing House, 1993), p. 192.

21. *The Bible Knowledge Commentary*, New Testament, eds. John F. Walvoord and Roy B. Zuck (Wheaton, IL: Victor Books, 1989), p. 825.

22. *The Bible Knowledge Commentary*, p. 825.

23. McConkie, p. 329.

24. *The Ryrie Study Bible* (Chicago, IL: Moody Press, 1986), p. 1622.

25. *The Wycliffe Bible Commentary*, p. 1325.

26. *The NIV Study Bible*, ed. Kenneth Barker (Grand Rapids, MI: Zondervan Publishing House, 1985), p. 1806.

27. H.C.G. Moule, *Philippians* (Grand Rapids, MI: Kregel Publications, 1977), p. 72.

28. Joseph Fielding Smith, *The Way to Perfection* (Salt Lake City, UT: Deseret, n.d.), p. 206.

29. *Gospel Principles*, p. 92.

30. *The Teachings of Spencer W. Kimball*, ed. Edward Kimball (Salt Lake City, UT: Bookcraft, 1982), p. 153.

31. Spencer W. Kimball, *Repentance Brings Forgiveness* (Salt Lake City, UT: The Church of Jesus Christ of Latter-day Saints, 1984), pp. 7, 12.

32. *Gospel Principles*, p. 235.

33. Spencer W. Kimball; quoted in *Gospel Principles*, p. 185.

34. Joseph Fielding Smith, *Doctrines of Salvation* (Salt Lake City, UT: Bookcraft, 1975), 2:16–17.

35. In fairness, we want to mention that no one is arguing in favor of alcohol or tobacco use, or saying that caffeine should not be consumed in moderation. You may also point out, however, that caffeine is not even mentioned in the Word of Wisdom, and that there is clear evidence that Joseph Smith and the Mormons of his day violated it often. Furthermore, nowadays Mormons ignore the Word of Wisdom's broad condemnation of "hot drinks" and the eating of meat except "in times of Winter, or of cold, or famine."

36. Smith, *The Way to Perfection*, p. 153.

37. Smith, *Doctrines of Salvation*, 2:184.

38. *Journal of Discourses*, 19:264.

39. Smith, *Doctrines of Salvation*, 2:149.

40. Smith, *Doctrines of Salvation*, 2:141.

41. Talmage, p. 149.

42. Talmage, pp. 149–50.

43. Charles R. Hield and Russell F. Ralston, *Baptism for the Dead* (Independence, MO: Herald Publishing House, 1951), pp. 23–24.

44. Note that Luke 16:19–31 is not a parable, as some Mormons try to argue. Jesus cited *historical people* with *specific names*.

45. Mormons may try to argue that Luke 16 is irrelevant to this issue, since "no such ordinances were performed for the dead until after Jesus died and inaugurated the preaching of the gospel in the world of departed spirits" (*A Sure Foundation*, p. 111). You will want to emphasize that Jesus was communicating a *universal message* meant for *all* people in *all* ages in Luke 16:19–31.

46. *Gospel Principles*, p. 231.

47. *The Life and Teachings of Jesus & His Apostles* (Salt Lake City, UT: Church of Jesus Christ of Latter-day Saints, 1979), p. 291.

48. Smith, *Doctrines of Salvation*, 2:206.

49. McConkie, p. 554.

50. McConkie, p. 601.

51. Talmage, p. 147.

52. Talmage, p. 147.

53. Talmage, p. 148.

54. Peter H. Davids, *More Hard Sayings of the New Testament* (Downers Grove, IL: InterVarsity Press, 1991), p. 166.

55. *The Bible Knowledge Commentary*, p. 851.

56. *The Bible Knowledge Commentary*, p. 851.

57. Talmage, p. 147.

58. *The NIV Study Bible*, p. 1894.

59. *See* Leon Morris, *The Biblical Doctrine of Judgment* (Grand Rapids, MI: Eerdmans, 1960), p. 66.

Chapter 19—Salvation in Mormonism—Part 3: Sin Atonement, and Forgiveness

1. James E. Talmage, *A Study of the Articles of Faith* (Salt Lake City, UT: The Church of Jesus Christ of Latter-day Saints, 1977), p. 65.
2. *Gospel Principles* (Salt Lake City, UT: Church of Jesus Christ of Latter-day Saints, 1985), p. 29.
3. *Deseret News*, Church Section, 31 July 1965, p. 7.
4. Bruce R. McConkie, *Mormon Doctrine* (Salt Lake City, UT: Bookcraft, 1966), p. 804.
5. John A. Widtsoe, *Joseph Smith—Seeker After Truth* (Salt Lake City, UT: Deseret, 1951), p. 160.
6. Joseph Fielding Smith, *Doctrines of Salvation* (Salt Lake City, UT: Bookcraft, 1975), 1:114–15.
7. John Widtsoe, *Evidences and Reconciliations*, arranged by G. Homer Durham (Salt Lake City, UT: Bookcraft, 1960), p. 195.
8. *Church News*, 18 March 1989, p. 16.
9. *Gospel Principles*, p. 17.
10. Talmage, p. 480.
11. *Bible Dictionary*, in *The Holy Bible* (Salt Lake City, UT: Church of Jesus Christ of Latter-day Saints, 1990), p. 697.
12. Spencer W. Kimball; quoted in *Book of Mormon Student Manual* (Salt Lake City, UT: Church of Jesus Christ of Latter-day Saints, 1989), p. 36.
13. *Gospel Principles*, p. 84.
14. McConkie, p. 295.
15. Spencer W. Kimball, *The Miracle of Forgiveness* (Salt Lake City, UT: Bookcraft, 1969), p. 324.

Chapter 20—Salvation in Mormonism—Part 4: The Three Kingdoms

1. LeGrand Richards, *A Marvelous Work and a Wonder* (Salt Lake City, UT: Deseret, 1978), p. 253.
2. *Gospel Principles* (Salt Lake City, UT: Church of Jesus Christ of Latter-day Saints, 1985), p. 108.
3. John Widtsoe, *Evidences and Reconciliations* (Salt Lake City, UT: Bookcraft, 1943), p. 277.
4. Joseph Fielding Smith, *Answers to Gospel Questions* (Salt Lake City, UT: Deseret, 1958), 2:208.
5. Bruce R. McConkie, *Mormon Doctrine* (Salt Lake City, UT: Bookcraft, 1966), pp. 116–17.
6. McConkie, p. 670.
7. Smith, *Answers to Gospel Questions*, 2:209.
8. McConkie, p. 784.
9. McConkie, pp. 778–89.
10. Smith, *Answers to Gospel Questions*, 2:209.
11. *Doctrine and Covenants Student Manual* (Salt Lake City, UT: Church of Jesus Christ of Latter-day Saints, 1981), p. 165.
12. James E. Talmage, *A Study of the Articles of Faith* (Salt Lake City, UT: The Church of Jesus Christ of Latter-day Saints, 1977), pp. 146–47.
13. Talmage, p. 148.
14. Richards, p. 253.
15. Richards, p. 253.
16. Talmage, p. 405.
17. McConkie, p. 420.
18. Richards, p. 255.
19. Mormons may respond by arguing that the telestial kingdom was made known by modern revelation.
20. Norman Geisler and Thomas Howe, *When Critics Ask* (Wheaton, IL: Victor Books, 1992), p. 466.
21. Talmage, p. 409.
22. Richards, p. 255.
23. Alan Gomes, "Evangelicals and the Annihilation of Hell," Part One, *Christian Research Journal*, Spring 1991, p. 18.
24. Joseph Thayer, *A Greek-English Lexicon of the New Testament* (Grand Rapids, MI: Zondervan Publishing House, 1963), p. 96.
25. William F. Arndt and F. Wilbur Gingrich, *A Greek-English Lexicon of the New Testament and Other Early Christian Literature* (Chicago, IL: The University of Chicago Press, 1957), p. 134.
26. R.C.H. Lenski, *Revelation* (Minneapolis, MN: Augsburg, 1961), p. 438.
27. Gomes, Part Two, p. 18.
28. *The Bible Knowledge Commentary*, New Testament, eds. John F. Walvoord and Roy B. Zuck (Wheaton, IL: Victor Books, 1983), p. 964.
29. Gomes, Part One, p. 19.
30. Gomes, Part One, p. 19.
31. Anthony A. Hoekema, *The Four Major Cults* (Grand Rapids, MI: Eerdmans, 1978), p. 356.
32. Hoekema, p. 356.

Chapter 21—Evangelism Among Mormons

1. Walter Martin, "The Do's and Don'ts of Witnessing to Cultists," *Christian Research Newsletter*, January–February 1992, p. 4.
2. Martin, p. 4.
3. Martin, p. 4.
4. Martin, p. 4.
5. Martin, p. 4.
6. Martin, p. 4.
7. David Reed, *Jehovah's Witnesses Answered Verse by Verse* (Grand Rapids, MI: Baker Book House, 1992), pp. 115–16.
8. Martin, p. 4.
9. Martin, p. 4.
10. Martin, p. 4.

Bibliography

1. CHRISTIAN CRITIQUES ON MORMONISM

Ankerberg, John and John Weldon. *Cult Watch: What You Need to Know About Spiritual Deception*. Eugene, OR: Harvest House Publishers, 1991.

Cares, Mark J. *Speaking the Truth in Love to Mormons*. Milwaukee, WI: Northwestern Publishing House, 1993.

Farkas, John R. and David A. Reed. *Mormonism: Changes, Contradictions, and Errors*. Grand Rapids, MI: Baker Book House, forthcoming.

Hoekema, Anthony A. *The Four Major Cults*. Grand Rapids, MI: Eerdmans, 1978.

Martin, Walter. *The Kingdom of the Cults*. Minneapolis, MN: Bethany House Publishers, 1985.

_____. *The Maze of Mormonism*. Ventura, CA: Regal Books, 1978.

McKeever, Bill and Eric Johnson. *Questions to Ask Your Mormon Friend*. Minneapolis, MN: Bethany House Publishers, 1994.

McKeever, Bill. *Answering Mormons' Questions*. Minneapolis, MN: Bethany House Publishers, 1991.

Reed, David A. and John R. Farkas. *How to Rescue Your Loved One from Mormonism*. Grand Rapids, MI: Baker Book House, 1994.

_____. *Mormons Answered Verse by Verse*. Grand Rapids, MI: Baker Book House, 1993.

Tanner, Jerald and Sandra. *3,913 Changes in the Book of Mormon*. Salt Lake City, UT: Utah Lighthouse Ministry, n.d.

_____. *Archaeology and the Book of Mormon*. Salt Lake City, UT: Modern Microfilm Company, 1969.

_____. *Major Problems of Mormonism*. Salt Lake City, UT: Utah Lighthouse Ministry, 1989.

_____. *The Changing World of Mormonism*. Chicago, IL: Moody Press, 1981.

Tanner, Sandra. *Mormonism, Magic and Masonry*. Salt Lake City, UT: Utah Lighthouse Ministry, 1988.

Tucker, Ruth. *Another Gospel: Alternative Religions and the New Age Movement*. Grand Rapids, MI: Zondervan Publishing House, 1989.

2. PRIMARY MORMON PUBLICATIONS

Benson, Ezra Taft. *The Teachings of Ezra Taft Benson*. Salt Lake City, UT: Bookcraft, 1988.

Bible Dictionary, in *The Holy Bible*. Salt Lake City, UT: Church of Jesus Christ of Latter-day Saints, 1990.

Book of Mormon. Salt Lake City, UT: The Church of Jesus Christ of Latter-day Saints, 1990.

Cannon, George Q. *Gospel Truth*. Salt Lake City, UT: Deseret Book Company, 1987.

Doctrine and Covenants. Salt Lake City, UT: The Church of Jesus Christ of Latter-day Saints, 1990.

Encyclopedia of Mormonism, ed. Daniel H. Ludlow. New York: Macmillan, 1992.

Gospel Principles. Salt Lake City, UT: Church of Jesus Christ of Latter-day Saints, 1981.

Hunter, Milton R. *The Gospel Through the Ages*. Salt Lake City, UT: Deseret Book Company, 1958.

Kimball, Edward, ed. *The Teachings of Spencer W. Kimball*. Salt Lake City, UT: Bookcraft, 1982.

Kimball, Spencer W. *Repentance Brings Forgiveness*. Salt Lake City, UT: The Church of Jesus Christ of Latter-day Saints, 1984.

————. *The Miracle of Forgiveness*. Salt Lake City, UT: Bookcraft, 1969.

Matthews, Robert J. *A Sure Foundation*. Salt Lake City, UT: Deseret Book Company, 1988.

McConkie, Bruce. *Doctrinal New Testament Commentary*, vol. 2. Salt Lake City, UT: Bookcraft, 1976.

————. *Mormon Doctrine*, 2d ed. Salt Lake City, UT: Bookcraft, 1977.

McKay, David O. *Gospel Ideals*. Salt Lake City, UT: Improvement Era, 1953.

Petersen, Mark E. *As Translated Correctly*. Salt Lake City, UT: Deseret Book Company, 1966.

Pratt, Orson. *The Seer*. Washington, D.C.: n.p., 1853–54.

Richards, LeGrand. *A Marvelous Work and a Wonder*. Salt Lake City, UT: Deseret Book Company, 1958.

Smith, Joseph. *History of the Church of Jesus Christ of Latter-day Saints*. Salt Lake City, UT: Deseret Book Company, 1973.

Smith, Joseph Fielding. *Doctrines of Salvation*. Salt Lake City, UT: Bookcraft, 1975.

————. *Man: His Origin and Destiny*. Salt Lake City, UT.

————. *The Way to Perfection*. Salt Lake City, UT: Deseret Book Company, n.d.

Talmage, James E. *The Articles of Faith*. Salt Lake City, UT: The Church of Jesus Christ of Latter-day Saints, 1982.

————. *The Great Apostasy*. Salt Lake City, UT: Deseret Book Company, 1975.

Widtsoe, John A. *Evidences and Reconciliations*. Salt Lake City, UT: Bookcraft, 1987.

————. *Joseph Smith—Seeker After Truth*. Salt Lake City, UT: Deseret Book Company, 1951.

Young, Brigham. *Journal of Discourses*. London: Latter-day Saints' Book Depot, 1854–56.

3. BOOKS ON JESUS CHRIST

Ankerberg, John; John Weldon, and Walter C. Kaiser. *The Case for Jesus the Messiah.* Chattanooga, TN: The John Ankerberg Evangelistic Association, 1989.

Buell, Jon A. and O. Quentin Hyder. *Jesus: God, Ghost or Guru?* Grand Rapids, MI: Zondervan Publishing House, 1978.

Erickson, Millard J. *The Word Became Flesh: A Contemporary Incarnational Christology.* Grand Rapids, MI: Baker Book House, 1991.

Geisler, Norman. *To Understand the Bible Look for Jesus.* Grand Rapids, MI: Baker Book House, 1979.

Gromacki, Robert G. *The Virgin Birth: Doctrine of Deity.* Grand Rapids, MI: Baker Book House, 1984.

Machen, J. Gresham. *The Virgin Birth of Christ.* New York, NY: Harper, 1930.

McDowell, Josh and Bart Larson. *Jesus: A Biblical Defense of His Deity.* San Bernardino, CA: Here's Life Publishers Inc., 1983.

Pentecost, J. Dwight. *The Words and Works of Jesus Christ.* Grand Rapids, MI: Zondervan Publishing House, 1982.

Reymond, Robert L. *Jesus Divine Messiah: The New Testament Witness.* Phillipsburg, NJ: Presbyterian and Reformed Publishing Co., 1990.

_____. *Jesus Divine Messiah: The Old Testament Witness.* Scotland, Great Britain: Christian Focus Publications, 1990.

Rhodes, Ron. *Christ Before the Manger: The Life and Times of the Preincarnate Christ.* Grand Rapids, MI: Baker Book House, 1992.

Shephard, J.W. *The Christ of the Gospels.* Grand Rapids, MI: Eerdmans, 1975.

Walvoord, John F. *Jesus Christ Our Lord.* Chicago, IL: Moody Press, 1980.

Warfield, Benjamin B. *The Lord of Glory.* Grand Rapids, MI: Baker Book House, 1974.

_____. *The Person and Work of Christ.* Philadelphia, PA: Presbyterian and Reformed Publishing Co., 1950.

Wells, David F. *The Person of Christ.* Westchester, IL: Crossway Books, 1984.

4. BOOKS ON GENERAL THEOLOGY

Basic Christian Doctrines, ed. Carl F. Henry. Grand Rapids, MI: Baker Book House, 1983.

Berkhof, Louis. *Manual of Christian Doctrine.* Grand Rapids, MI: Eerdmans, 1983

_____. *Systematic Theology.* Grand Rapids, MI: Eerdmans, 1982.

Buswell, James Oliver. *A Systematic Theology of the Christian Religion.* Grand Rapids, MI: Zondervan Publishing House, 1979.

Calvin, John. *Institutes of the Christian Religion,* ed. John T. McNeill trans. Ford Lewis Battles. Philadelphia, PA: The Westminster Press, 1960.

Chafer, Lewis Sperry. *Systematic Theology.* Wheaton, IL: Victor Books, 1988.

Enns, Paul. *The Moody Handbook of Theology.* Chicago, IL: Moody Press 1989

Erickson, Millard J. *Christian Theology,* unabridged one-volume edition. Grand Rapids, MI: Baker Book House, 1987.

Hodge, Charles. *Systematic Theology,* abridged edition, ed. Edward N. Gross. Grand Rapids, MI: Baker Book House, 1988.

Lightner, Robert P. *Evangelical Theology.* Grand Rapids, MI: Baker Book House, 1986.

_____. *The God of the Bible.* Grand Rapids. MI: Baker Book House, 1978.

_____. *The Saviour and the Scriptures.* Grand Rapids, MI: Baker Book House, 1966.

Packer, J.I. *Knowing God.* Downers Grove, IL: InterVarsity Press, 1979.

Ryrie, Charles C. *Basic Theology.* Wheaton, IL: Victor Books, 1986.

_____. *The Holy Spirit.* Chicago, IL: Moody Press, 1965.

Thiessen, Henry Clarence. *Lectures in Systematic Theology.* Grand Rapids, MI: Eerdmans, 1981.

Vos, Geerhardus. *Biblical Theology: Old and New Testaments.* Grand Rapids, MI: Eerdmans, 1985.

Walvoord, John F. *The Holy Spirit.* Grand Rapids, MI: Zondervan Publishing House, 1958.

Warfield, Benjamin B. *Biblical and Theological Studies.* Phillipsburg, NJ: Presbyterian and Reformed Publishing Co., 1968.

5. COMMENTARIES

Barnes, Albert. *Barnes Notes on the Old and New Testaments.* Grand Rapids, MI: Baker Book House, 1977.

Bruce, F.F. *The Book of Acts.* Grand Rapids, MI: Eerdmans, 1986.

_____. *The Epistle to the Hebrews.* Grand Rapids, MI: Eerdmans, 1979.

_____. *The Gospel of John.* Grand Rapids, MI: Eerdmans, 1984.

Cole, R. Alan. *Exodus: An Introduction and Commentary.* Downers Grove, IL: InterVarsity Press, 1973.

Eadie, John. *A Commentary on the Greek Text of the Epistle of Paul to the Colossians.* Grand Rapids, MI: Baker Book House, 1979.

English, E. Schuyler. *Studies in the Epistle to the Hebrews.* Neptune, NJ: Loizeaux Brothers, 1976.

Evangelical Commentary on the Bible, ed. Walter A. Elwell. Grand Rapids, MI: Baker Book House, 1989.

Gaebelein, Arno C. *The Gospel of Matthew.* Neptune, NJ: Loizeaux Brothers, 1977.

Hansen, G. Walter. *Galatians.* Downers Grove, IL: InterVarsity Press, 1994.

Hendriksen, William. *Exposition of the Gospel According to John.* Grand Rapids, MI: Baker Book House, 1976.

Henry, Matthew. *Commentary on the Whole Bible.* Grand Rapids, MI: Zondervan Publishing House, 1974.

Jamieson, Robert; A.R. Fausset; and David Brown. *A Commentary—Critical Experimental and Practical—on the Old and New Testaments.* Grand Rapids, MI: Eerdmans, 1973.

Keener, Craig S. *The IVP Bible Background Commentary.* Downers Grove, IL: InterVarsity Press. 1993.

Keil, C.F. and Franz Delitzsch. *Biblical Commentary on the Old Testament.* Grand Rapids, MI: Eerdmans, 1954.

Kidner, Derek. *Genesis: An Introduction and Commentary.* Downers Grove: InterVarsity Press, 1967.

Lenski, R.C.H. *1 Corinthians.* Minneapolis, MN: Augsburg Publishing House, 1961.

_____. *First Peter.* Minneapolis, MN: Augsburg Publishing House, 1961.

_____. *Hebrews.* Minneapolis, MN: Augsburg Publishing House, 1961.

_____. *The Interpretation of St. John's Gospel.* Minneapolis, MN: Augsburg Publishing House, 1961.

Leupold, H.C. *Exposition of Genesis* vol. 1. Grand Rapids, MI: Baker Book House, 1968.

Lightfoot, J.B. *St. Paul's Epistles to the Colossians and to Philemon.* Grand Rapids, MI: Zondervan Publishing House, 1979.

MacArthur, John. *Hebrews.* Chicago, IL: Moody Press, 1983.

_____. *The Superiority of Christ.* Chicago, IL: Moody Press, 1986.

Morris, Leon. *The First Epistle of Paul to the Corinthians,* Tyndale New Testament Commentaries. Grand Rapids, MI: Eerdmans, 1976.

_____. *The Gospel According to John.* Grand Rapids, MI: Eerdmans, 1971.

_____. *The Gospel According to St. Luke.* Grand Rapids, MI: Eerdmans, 1983.

Moule, H.C.G. *Studies in Colossians & Philemon.* Grand Rapids, MI: Kregel Publications, 1977.

Newell, William R. *Hebrews: Verse by Verse.* Chicago, IL: Moody Press, 1947.

Pink, Arthur W. *Exposition of the Gospel of John.* Swengel, PA: Bible Truth Depot, 1945.

Robertson, A.T. *Word Pictures.* Nashville, TN: Broadman Press, 1930.

Shedd, William G.T. *Romans.* New York, NY: Scribner, 1879.

The Bible Knowledge Commentary, Old Testament, eds. John F. Walvoord and Roy B. Zuck. Wheaton, IL: Victor Books, 1985.

The Expositor's Bible Commentary, ed. Frank E. Gaebelein. Grand Rapids, MI: Zondervan Publishing House, 1978.

The International Bible Commentary, ed. F.F. Bruce. Grand Rapids, MI: Zondervan Publishing House, 1979.

The Wycliffe Bible Commentary, eds. Charles F. Pfeiffer and Everett F. Harrison. Chicago, IL: Moody Press, 1974.

Toussaint, Stanley D. *Behold the King: A Study of Matthew.* Portland, OR: Multnomah Press, 1980.

Vincent, Marvin R. *Word Studies in the New Testament.* Grand Rapids, MI: Eerdmans, 1975.

Walvoord, John F. *Daniel: The Key to Prophetic Revelation.* Chicago, IL: Moody Press, 1981.

_____. *Revelation.* Chicago, IL: Moody Press, 1980.

_____. *The Revelation of Jesus Christ.* Chicago, IL: Moody Press, 1980.

Westcott, Brooke Foss. *The Epistle to the Hebrews.* Grand Rapids, MI: Eerdmans, 1974.

Wuest, Kenneth S. *Wuest's Word Studies.* Grand Rapids, MI: Eerdmans, 1953.

6. REFERENCES WORKS

Archer, Gleason. *Encyclopedia of Bible Difficulties*. Grand Rapids, MI: Zondervan Publishing House, 1982.

Arndt, William and Wilbur Gingrich. *A Greek-English Lexicon of the New Testament and Other Early Christian Literature*. Chicago, IL: The University of Chicago Press, 1957.

Brown, Francis; S.R. Driver; and Charles A. Briggs. *A Hebrew and English Lexicon of the Old Testament*. Oxford: Clarendon Press, 1980.

Geisler, Norman and Thomas Howe. *When Critics Ask*. Wheaton, IL: Victor Books, 1992.

Ryrie, Charles C. *The Ryrie Study Bible*. Chicago, IL: Moody Press, 1986.

Thayer, J.H. *A Greek-English Lexicon of the New Testament*. Grand Rapids, MI: Zondervan Publishing House, 1963.

The New Bible Dictionary, ed. J.D. Douglas. Wheaton IL: Tyndale House Publishers, 1982.

The New International Dictionary of New Testament Theology, ed. Colin Brown. Grand Rapids, MI: Zondervan Publishing House, 1979.

The New Treasury of Scripture Knowledge, ed. Jerome H. Smith. Nashville, TN: Thomas Nelson Publishers, 1992.

The Zondervan Pictorial Encyclopedia of the Bible, ed. Merrill C. Tenney. Grand Rapids, MI: Zondervan Publishing House, 1978.

Theological Wordbook of the Old Testament, ed. R. Laird Harris, vol. 2. Chicago, IL: Moody Press, 1981.

Vine's Expository Dictionary of Biblical Words, eds. W.E. Vine, Merrill F. Unger, and William White. Nashville, TN: Thomas Nelson Publishers, 1985.

Zodhiates, Spiros. *The Complete Word Study Dictionary*. Chattanooga, TN: AMG Publishers, 1992.

Subject Index

421

Scripture Index

Following are the *primary* Scripture passages dealt with in this book:

Other Good
Harvest House Reading

REASONING FROM THE SCRIPTURES WITH THE JEHOVAH'S WITNESSES
by *Ron Rhodes*

Many outstanding features make this the complete hands-on guide to sharing the truth of God's Word in a loving gracious way. Includes favorite tactics used by the Witnesses and effective biblical responses.

EVERYTHING YOU EVER WANTED TO KNOW ABOUT MORMONISM
by *John Ankerberg and John Weldon*

Like no book before it, this definitive work covers every aspect of the history, beliefs, and practices of the largest, wealthiest, and most influential sect in America.

DECKER'S COMPLETE HANDBOOK ON MORMONISM
by *Ed Decker*

The ultimate A-to-Z reference guide on the beliefs, teachings, and traditions of the Church of Jesus Christ of Latter-day Saints. Presents the official Mormon position and the corresponding biblical response on more than 150 topics.

THE CULTING OF AMERICA
by *Ron Rhodes*

Traces the relentless invasion of humanism, lack of basic Bible knowledge, and the failure of America's churches to make a moral difference as contributing factors toward this country becoming a haven of darkness for the cults